POPULAR SONG INDEX

First Supplement

by
Patricia Pate Havlice

The Scarecrow Press, Inc.
Metuchen, N.J. & London
1978

ST. PHILIP'S COLLEGE LIBRARY

Library of Congress Cataloging in Publication Data

Havlice, Patricia Pate.
    Popular song index.

    1. Songs--Indexes. I. Title.
ML128.S3H4Suppl.   784   77-25219
ISBN 0-8108-1099-9

Copyright © 1978 by Patricia Pate Havlice

Manufactured in the United States of America

PREFACE

This First Supplement follows the same format and layout as Popular Song Index. In the main section (Part II), song titles appear in single quotes, with FL: and FLC: referring to the first line and first line of chorus of the song. Numbers following song title entries refer back to the Bibliography (Part I). A composer and lyricist index appears in Part III. Some song books published in years covered by the main volume are included here because they were unavailable earlier.

I am again indebted to the Du Page Library System and especially the Batavia Public Library for excellent service, moral support and 3 x 5 scratch cards.

P. P. H.

iii

Part I

BIBLIOGRAPHY

1 Agay, Denes. Best Loved Songs of the American People. New
   York: Doubleday, 1975.

2 Allen, Jules Verne. Cowboy Lore. San Antonio, Texas: Nay-
   lor, 1971.

3 American Musical Miscellany: A Collection of the Newest and
   Most Approved Songs, Set to Music. Reprint of 1798 edition. New York: Da Capo, 1972.

4 Arnett, Hazel. I Hear America Singing! New York: Praeger,
   1975.

5 Barton, William E. Old Plantation Hymns. Reprint of 1899
   edition. New York: AMS Press, 1972.

6 The Best of Broadway: 80 Great Songs of the American Musical Theatre. New York: Chappell Music Co., 197?.

7 Boette, Marie. Singa Hipsy Doodle and Other Folks Songs of
   West Virginia. Parsons, West Virginia: McClain Printing
   Co., 1971.

8 Brand, Oscar. Songs of '76: A Folksinger's History of the
   Revolution. New York: M. Evans & Co., 1972.

9 Broderick, Richard. The New York Times Great Latin Songs.
   New York: Quadrangle, 1974.

10 Broderick, Richard. The New York Times 100 Great Country
   Songs. New York: Quadrangle, 1973.

11 Bronson, Bertrand Harris. The Traditional Tunes of the Child
   Ballads: with Their Texts According to Extant Records of
   Great Britain and America. Princeton, New Jersey: Prince-
   ton University Press, 1959.

12 Brown, Irving. The New York Times Nostalgic Years in Song.
   New York: Quadrangle, 1974.

13 Bruderhof Communities. Sing Through the Seasons: 99 Songs
   for Children. Rifton, New York: Plough Publishing House,
   1972.

5

ST. PHILIP'S COLLEGE LIBRARY

14 Cyporyn, Dennis. The Bluegrass Songbook. New York: Mac-
millan, 1972.

15 Dalton, David. Janis. New York: Simon and Schuster, 1971.

16 Dalton, David. Rolling Stones. New York: Amsco Music
Publishing Co. , 1972.

17 Davison, Peter. Songs of the British Music Hall ... with a
Critical History of the Songs and Their Times. New
York: Oak, 1971.

18 Fife, Austin and Alta Fife. Heaven on Horseback: Revivalist
Songs and Verse in the Cowboy Idiom (Western Texts Society series Vol. 1 No. 1). Logan, Utah: Utah State University Press, 1970.

19 Fowke, Edith and Joe Glazer. Songs of Work and Protest.
Reprint of 1960 edition. New York: Dover, 1973.

20 Fremont, Robert A. Favorite Songs of the Nineties: Complete Original Sheet Music for 89 Songs. New York:
Dover, 1973.

21 Gershwin, George. The New York Times Gershwin Years in
Song. New York: Quadrangle, 1973.

22 Gillington, Alice E. Songs of the Open Road: Didakei Ditties
and Gypsy Dances. Reprint of 1911 edition. Norwood,
Pennsylvania: Norwood Editions, 1973.

23 Golden Encyclopedia of Folk Music. New York: Charles Hansen Educational Music and Books, n. d.

24 Hammerstein, Oscar. The Songs of Oscar Hammerstein II.
New York: Schirmer, 1974.

25 Hansen, Charles. 400 Super Song Fest: Folk Songs of Today.
New York: Folk World, Inc. , 1973.

26 Heseltine, Philip. English Ayres, for Voice and Piano.
London: Oxford University Press, n. d.

27 Hurst, Jack. Nashville's Grand Ole Opry. New York:
Abrams, 1975.

28 Jackson, Bruce. Wake Up Dead Man: Afro-American Work-
songs from Texas Prisons. Cambridge, Massachusetts:
Harvard University Press, 1972.

29 Joyner, Charles W. Folk Song in South Carolina. Columbia,
South Carolina: University of South Carolina Press, 1971.

ST. PHILIP'S COLLEGE LIBRARY

30 Karpeles, Maud. Folk Songs from Newfoundland. Hamden,
    Connecticut: Archon Books, 1970.

31 King, Sandy. World's Greatest Hits from 1900-1919. Miami
    Beach, Florida: Charles Hansen Music Corp., 1973.

32 Langstaff, John. Gather My Gold Together: Four Songs for
    Four Seasons. New York: Doubleday, 1971.

33 Langstaff, John. The Season for Singing: American Songs
    and Carols. New York: Doubleday, 1974.

34 Leisy, James. The Good Times Song Book: 160 Songs for
    Informal Singing. Nashville, Tennessee: Abingdon Press,
    1974.

35 Leisy, James F. Hootennany Tonight. Greenwich, Connecti-
    cut: Fawcett, 1964.

36 Levy, Lester S. Flashes of Merriment: A Century of Hu-
    morous Songs in America, 1805-1905. Norman, Oklahoma:
    University of Oklahoma Press, 1971.

37 McIntosh, David S. Folk Songs and Singing Games of the Illi-
    nois Ozarks. Carbondale, Illinois: Southern Illinois Uni-
    versity Press, 1974.

38 Marsh, J. B. T. The Story of the Jubilee Singers; with Their
    Songs. Rev. ed. Reprint of 1881 edition. New York:
    Negro Universities Press, 1969.

39 Martin, Claude Trimble. Dean Martin's Book of Musical
    Americana. Englewood Cliffs, New Jersey: Prentice-
    Hall, 1970.

40 Molnar, John W. Songs from the Williamsburg Theatre: A
    Selection of Fifty Songs Performed on the Stage in Williams-
    burg in the Eighteenth Century. Williamsburg, Virginia:
    Colonial Williamsburg Foundation, 1972.

41 Munch, Peter A. The Song Tradition of Tristan da Cunha.
    Bloomington, Indiana: Indiana University Research Center
    for the Language Sciences, 1970.

42 The New York Times Great Songs of Broadway. New York:
    Quadrangle, 1973.

43 Ohrlin, Glenn. The Hell-Bound Train: A Cowboy Songbook.
    Urbana, Illinois: University of Illinois Press, 1973.

44 Okun, Milton. Great Songs of Lennon and McCartney: All
    Musical Compositions by John Lennon and Paul McCartney.

New York: Quadrangle, 1973.

45 Okun, Milton. The New York Times Great Songs of the Six-
    ties Vol. 2. New York: Quadrangle, 1974.

46 100 Best Songs of the 20's and 30's. New York: Harmony,
    1973.

47 100 Top Pop Songs. 3rd ed. n.p., n.d.

48 Poston, Elizabeth. The Baby's Song Book. New York:
    Crowell, 1972.

49 Rabson, Carolyn. Songbook of the American Revolution.
    Peaks Island, Maine: NEO Press, 1974.

50 Riddle, Almeda. A Singer and Her Songs: Almeda Riddle's
    Book of Ballads. Baton Rouge, Louisiana: Louisiana
    State University Press, 1970.

51 Rockwell, Anne. El Toro Pinto and Other Songs in Spanish.
    New York: Macmillan, 1971.

52 Schiff, Ronny. World's Greatest Hits of the Fifties. Miami
    Beach, Florida: Charles Hansen, 1972.

53 Schiff, Ronny. World's Greatest Hits of the Thirties. Miami
    Beach, Florida: Charles H. Hansen Music Corp., 1972.

54 Schiff, Ronny. World's Greatest Hits of the Twenties. Miami
    Beach, Florida: Charles Hansen Music Corp., 1972.

55 Silber, Irwin. Songs of Independence. Harrisburg, Pennsyl-
    vania: Stackpole, 1973.

56 Silverman, Jerry. The Flat-Picker's Guitar Guide. New
    York: Oak, 1963.

57 Silverman, Jerry. Folk Song Encyclopedia. New York:
    Chappell, 1975.

58 Silverman, Jerry. The Liberated Woman's Songbook. New
    York: Macmillan, 1971.

59 Simon, George T. The Big Bands Songbook. New York:
    Crowell, 1975.

60 Simon, Paul. The Songs of Paul Simon as Sung by Simon and
    Garfunkel and Paul Simon Himself. New York: Knopf,
    1972.

61 Smith, Reed. South Carolina Ballads; With a Study of the

Traditional Ballad Today. Reprint of 1928 edition. Spartanburg, South Carolina: Reprint Co., 1972.

62 Thorp, N. Howard. Songs of the Cowboys. New York: Clarkson N. Potter, 1966.

63 Turner, Michael P. The Parlour Song Book. New York: Viking, 1973.

64 The University Society, Inc. The Sounds of Change. New York: Charles Hansen, 1974.

65 Vinson, Lee. The Early American Songbook. Englewood Cliffs, New Jersey: Prentice-Hall, 1974.

66 Warner, James. Songs that Made America. New York: Grossman, 1972.

67 Welk, Lawrence. Lawrence Welk's Sing-A-Long Book. New York: Crown, 1975?

68 Winn, Marie. The Fireside Book of Fun and Game Songs. New York: Simon and Schuster, 1974.

69 Winstock, Lewis. Songs and Music of the Redcoats: A History of War Music of the British Army 1642-1902. Harrisburg, Pennsylvania: Stackpole Books, 1970.

70 World's Greatest Hits of the Forties. Miami Beach, Florida: Charles H. Hansen Music Corp., 1971.

71 World's Greatest Hits of the Sixties. Miami Beach, Florida: Charles H. Hansen Music Corp., 1971.

72 Yolen, Jane. The Fireside Song Book of Birds and Beasts. New York: Simon and Schuster, 1972.

Part II

INDEX OF TITLES AND FIRST LINES

'A-hunting we will go' FL: The
dusky night rides down the sky,
and ushers in the morn. 25
'Aiken Drum' FL: There was a
man lived in the moon. 48
'Aileen Aroon' Carrol O'Daly. FL:
Duca tu non vanna tu, Aileen
Aroon. 40
Ainst a beggar came out ower the
lea see 'Jolly beggar'
Ain't gonna work in the city see
'Roll in my sweet baby's arms'
Ain't gonna work on the railroad
see 'Roll in my sweet baby's
arms'
Ain't got no money, can't buy no
grub see 'Things about com-
in' my way'
Ain't got no use for your red ap-
ple juice see 'Red apple
juice'
'Ain't it a shame?' FL: Ain't it
a shame to beat your wife on
Sunday. 34, 57
Ain't it hard to stumble when
you're got no place to fall
see 'I'm a stranger here'
'Ain't misbehavin' Andy Razaf,
Thomas Waller and Harry
Brooks. FL: Like Jack Horner in the corner FLC: No one
to talk with, all by myself.
12, 59
Ain't my brother or my sister
see 'Standing in the need of
prayer'
'Ain't no more cane on the
Brazis' FL: There ain't no
more cane on the Brazis. 57
'Ain't she sweet' Jack Yellen and
Milton Ager. FL: There she
is! There she is! FLC: Ain't
she sweet. 46
Ain't that a pity and a shame, O
Lord see 'Poor little Jesus'
'Ain't we got fun' Gus Kahn, Ray-
mond B. Egan and Richard A.
Whiting. FL: Bill collectors
gather round and rather FLC:
Every morning, every evening,
ain't we got fun. 46
'Al Bowen' FL: Twas Christmas
Eve and the night so dark. 50
'Al canto de una laguna' FL:
same. 51
'Al olivo subi' FL: Al olivo, al
olivo, y al olivo subi. 51
'Alabama bound' FL: I'm Alabama

bound. 57
'Alan Bane' FL: They're taking
me to the gallows mother. 37
Alas, my love, you do me wrong
see 'Greensleeves'
'Alberta' FL: See Alberta comin'
down that road. 28
'Alberta, let your hair hang low'
FL: same. 57
'Alfie' Hal David and Burt Bacha-
rach. FL: What's it all about
Alfie? 47, 71
Alicante ha sucedido la toree nueva
see 'La torre de Alicante'
Alive, alive, o alive alive O see
'Cockles and mussels'
'Alknomook' Anne Home Hunter.
FL: The sun sets at night and
the stars shun the day. 65
All alone I stand see 'Sweethearts
on parade'
All alone one evening I happened
to stray see 'Little Mohee'
'All around my hat' FL: All around
my hat I wear the green willow.
22
All around the cobbler's bench
see 'Pop! goes the weasel'
'All around the Maypole' Kane
O'Hara. FL: All around the
Maypole how they trot, hot, pot.
40
All around the mulberry bush see
'Pop goes the weasel'
All at once you find your dreams
are comin' true see 'The story
of love'
All day, all night, Mary Ann see
'Mary Ann'
All day de people look at de
steeple see 'Somebody bad
stole de wedding bell'
All day in the saddle on the prairie
I ride see 'The cowboy'
All day I've faced a barren waste
see 'Cool water'
All day o'er the prairies alone I
ride see 'The cowboy's solilo-
quy'
All day on the prairie in the saddle
I ride see 'The cowboy'; 'The
cowboy's soliloquy'
'All God's children got shoes' FL:
I got a shoe, you got a shoe.
34
All hail, superior sex, exalted fair
see 'The female patriots'
All hail the power of Jesus' name

see 'I want to die a-shouting'
'Amelia Earhart's last flight' David
McEnery. FL: Well, a ship out
on the ocean FLC: There's a
beautiful, beautiful field. 58
'America' Asahel Benham. FL:
Amid surrounding foes. 65
'America' Paul Simon. FL: Let
us be lovers. 60
'America' Samuel Francis Smith.
FL: My country, tis of thee.
1, 34
'America' Dr. Byles and William
Billings. FL: To thee the tune-
ful anthem soars. 55
'America, commerce and freedom'
Alexander Reinagle. FL: How
blest the life a sailor leads FLC:
Then under full sail. 65
'America, the beautiful' Katherine
Lee Bates and Samuel Augustus
Ward. FL: O beautiful for
spacious skies. 34, 57, 67
America, thou fractious nation
see 'Gage's proclamation'
'An American frigate' FL: An
American frigate called Richard
by name. 8
An American frigate and a frigate
of fame see 'Paul Jones' vic-
tory'
'American heart of oak' J. W.
Hewlings. FL: Come, rouse
up, my lads and join this great
cause FLC: For so just is our
cause and so valiant our men.
65
'The American hero' Nathaniel
Miles and Andrew Law. FL:
Why should vain mortals tremble
at the sight. 55, 65
'The American rule Britannia' FL:
When Britons first by Heaven's
command. 55
'American taxation' Peter St. John.
FL: While I relate my story,
Americans give ear. 8
'The American vicar of Bray' FL:
When royal George ruled o'er
this land. 49, 55
Amid surrounding foes see
'America'
'Among the blue flowers and the
yellow' FL: O Willie, my son,
what makes ye sae sad. 11
'Amor' Ricardo Lopez Mendez and
Gabriel Ruiz. FL: Nació de
Dios, para los dos FLC: Amor,

amor, amor. 9
'Amor' Sunny Skylar and Gabriel
Ruiz. FL: Would you deny this
heart that I FLC: Amor, amor,
amor. 9
'L'amour est bleu' Andre Popp, and
Pierre Cour. FL: Doux, doux,
l'am est doux. 71
An' a howdy, howdy, brother see
'Howdy, howdy'
An' a Lawd, dese dry bones of
mine see 'Dese dry bones of
mine'
An' if those mourners would believe
see 'I'll be there'
An' jus' lots of folks is like dis
foolish frog of mine see 'May
Irwin's frog song'
An' now to be brief, let's pass over
the rest see 'The king and the
tinker'
Anacreon they say was a jolly old
blade see 'New Anacreontic
song'
'Anacreontic song' Ralph Tomlinson.
FL: To Anacreon in heaven. 65
'Anchor in the Lord' FL: Throw it
to my dear mother's door FLC:
Anchor, believer, anchor, anchor
in the Lord. 38
An ancient story I'll tell you anon
see 'King John'; 'King John and
the Abbot of Canterbury'
And a-begging we will go, will go
will go see 'The jovial beggar'
And all of her conversation was
see 'The husband with no cour-
age in him'
And as I came home on Monday
night as drunk as I could be see
'The Seven drunken nights'
And ay wor Nanny's a mazer an'
a mazer she remains see 'Wor
Nanny's a mazer'
And be there forever at home see
'Sawyer's exit'
And did those feet in ancient time
see 'A New Jerusalem'
And didn't he ramble see 'Birming-
ham Bull'
And didn't he ramble, ramble see
'Didn't he ramble'
And drill, ye tarriers, drill see
'Drill, ye tarriers, drill'
And every little movement has a
meaning of its own see 'Every
little movement'
And every man neath his vine and

fig tree <u>see</u> 'Vine and fig tree'

And fare thee well, you sweethearts <u>see</u> 'Fare Thee well, you sweethearts'

'And her golden hair was hanging down her back' Felix McGlennon. FL: There once was a country maiden came to London for a trip FLC: But oh! Flo! such a change you know. 17

And here's to you Mrs. Robinson <u>see</u> 'Mrs. Robinson'

And here's to you, my ramblin' boy <u>see</u> 'My ramblin' boy'

And I ain't got weary yet <u>see</u> 'I ain't got weary yet'

And I couldn't hear nobody pray <u>see</u> 'I couldn't hear nobody pray'

And I feel just as happy as a big sunflower <u>see</u> 'The big sunflower'

And I have been frequently sold <u>see</u> 'Acres of clams'

And I have to hear the lonesome whistle blow <u>see</u> 'Nine hundred miles'

'And I love her' Lennon and McCartney. FL: I give her all my love. 44, 47

And I say oh, oh, oh <u>see</u> 'Ball and chain'

And I soon shall be done with the troubles of the world <u>see</u> 'These are my father's children'

And I think it's gonna be all right <u>see</u> 'Red rubber ball'

And I wake up in the morning with my hair down in my eyes <u>see</u> 'Little green apples'

And I wish that heaven was a mine <u>see</u> 'Save me, Lord, save'

And I would love you all the day <u>see</u> 'Over the hills and far away'

And if this train runs me right <u>see</u> 'Nine hundred miles'

And if those mourners would believe <u>see</u> 'Down by the river'

And I'll be true to my love <u>see</u> 'Bow and balance'

And I'm on show in the daytime, I'm off show at night <u>see</u> 'Prehistoric man'

And I'm proud to be an Okie from Muskogee <u>see</u> 'Okie from Muskogee'

And it looks like, I'm never gonna cease my wanderin' <u>see</u> 'Wanderin' '

And it's alright in the summertime <u>see</u> 'It's alright in the summertime'

And it's oh! what will become of me <u>see</u> 'Nobody coming to marry me'

And just because he's human <u>see</u> 'United front'

And just lots of folks are like that foolish frog o' mine <u>see</u> 'Nothing else to do'

And many a Redcoat here tonight <u>see</u> 'Mad Anthony Wayne'

And many a Redcoat here tonight, the Continentals scorning <u>see</u> 'Anthony Wayne'

And must I be to judgment brought <u>see</u> 'We're some of the praying people'

And now my friends you ask me what makes me sad and still <u>see</u> 'Utah Carroll'

And now our senators are gone <u>see</u> 'The recess'

And now, the end is near <u>see</u> 'My way'

And now the purple dusk of twilight time <u>see</u> 'Star dust'

And now we are aged and gray <u>see</u> 'When you and I were young, Maggie'

And she sailed upon the low and lonesome low <u>see</u> 'The golden Vanity'

And sing, blow away the morning dew <u>see</u> 'Blow away the morning dew'

And so I departed for Puget Sound <u>see</u> 'Acres of clams'

And so we took a stroll <u>see</u> 'Spiders and snakes'

And taxing we will go <u>see</u> 'A Junto song'

'And the angels sing' Johnny Mercer and Ziggie Elman. FL: We meet and the angels sing. 53, 59

And the boy spread his breast and away swimmed he <u>see</u> 'The Golden Vanity'

And the green grass grows all around, all around <u>see</u> 'The

green grass grows all around'
And the sea is a-roar, roar, roar
 see 'The mermaid'
And then he'd row, row, row see
 'Row, row, row'
'And this is my beloved' Robert
 Wright and George Forrest.
 FL: Dawn's promising skies.
 6
And this is the law, that I'll main-
 tain see 'The vicar of Bray'
And we'll all go together see
 'Will you go lassie, go?'
And we'll gang nae mair a-roving
 see 'The jolly beggar'
And what do you think he saw?
 see 'The bear went over the
 mountain'
'And when I die' Laura Nyro.
 FL: I'm not scared of dyin'
 and I really don't care FLC:
 And when I die. 45
And when I told them how beauti-
 ful you are see 'They didn't
 believe me'
And when she came to the king's
 fair court see 'The knight
 and the shepherd's daughter'
And when the saints go marching in
 see 'When the saints go marching in'
And where did Robinson Crusoe go
 with Friday on Saturday night?
 see 'Where did Robinson Crusoe go with Friday on Saturday
 night?'
And where is the landlady see
 'Lamkin'
'And would you see my mistress'
 face?' Thomas Campion and
 Philip Rosseter. FL: same.
 26
'Andrew Bardan' FL: Oh what now
 says Andrew Bardan. 11
'Andrew Bardee' FL: Three
 brothers, three brothers in
 Scotland did dwell. 11
'Andrew Bardeen' FL: There was
 three brothers in old Scotland.
 11
'Andrew Bardeen' FL: There were
 three brothers in old Scotland.
 11
'Andrew Bardeen' FL: Three loving
 brothers in Scotland did dwell.
 11
'Andrew Bartin' FL: Three bold
 brothers of merrie Scotland. 11,

61
'Andrew Batan' FL: There were
 three brothers from merry Scot-
 land. 11
'Andrew Batan' FL: There once
 were three brothers from merry
 Scotland. 11
'Andrew Battam' FL: There were
 three brothers in merry Scotland.
 11
'Andrew Battan' FL: Go back, go
 back, cries Andrew Battan. 11
'Andrew Briton' FL: There were
 three brothers in old Scotland.
 11
'Andrew Lammie' FL: At Mill o'
 Tifty lived a man. 11
'Andrew Lammie' FL: O, Annie dear,
 O Annie dear. 11
'Andrew Marteen' FL: In boney Scot-
 land three brothers did dwell.
 11
'Andy Bardean' FL: Three loving
 brothers from old Scotland. 11
'Andy Bardeen' FL: Three younger
 brothers all cast lots. 11
'Angel band' FL: My evening sun is
 sinking fast; FLC: Oh, come,
 angel band. 57
'Angel Gabriel' FL: Oh, my soul,
 my soul am a-going for to rest
 FLC: I will shout and I'll dance.
 25
'The angel rolled the stone away'
 FL: Sister Mary came a-running
 FLC: The angel rolled the stone
 away. 25
'The angels changed my name' FL:
 I went to the hillside, I went to
 pray FLC: Done changed my
 name for the coming day. 38
'Angels, from the realms of glory'
 James Montgomery and Henry
 Smart. FL: same FLC: Come
 and worship. 34
'Angels waiting at the door' FL:
 My sister's took her flight and
 gone home. 38
'Angels we have heard on high' FL:
 same. 57
'Angry' Dudley Mecum, Jules Cas-
 sard, Henry Bruneis and Merritt
 Brunies. FL: True love never
 does run smooth FLC: Angry,
 please don't be angry. 54
'Animal fair' FL: I went to the ani-
 mal fair. 57, 72
'Annabel Lee' Edgar Allan Poe.

FL: It was many and many a year ago. 23

'Annie Laurie' William Douglas. FL: Maxwellton's braes are bonnie. 25, 57

Another bride, another June see 'Makin' whoopee'

'Another man done gone' FL: same. 57

Antes de que tus labios me confirmaran see 'Un telegrama'

'Anthem of the ILGWU' FL: One battle is won, but the fight's just begun FLC: Oh, Union of the Garment Workers. 19

'Anthony Wayne' FL: His sword blade gleams and his eyelight beams FLC: And many a Redcoat here tonight, the Continentals scorning. 8

'Any time' Herbert Happy Lawson FL: Any time you're feeling lonely. 10

Any time you're Lambeth way see 'Lambeth Walk'

'Any way you want me' Aaron Schroeder and Cliff Owens. FL: I'll be as strong as a mountain or weak as a willow. 10

'Anybody here?' FL: I want to know if you love my Lord FLC: Is there anybody here. 5

Anymore it doesn't matter what's right or wrong see 'Nobody wins'

'Anything goes' Cole Porter. FL: Times have changed FLC: In the old days a glimpse of stocking. 46

'Anything to make a change' J. Bruton. FL: Existence is monotonous to me at least. 36

'An appeal to loyalists' FL: The old English cause knocks at every man's door. 49

'Applause' Lee Adams and Charles Strouse. FL: What is this that we're living for? 6

Apple trees and pear trees were aflower see 'Katiusha'

'April come she will' Paul Simon. FL: same. 60

'April in Paris' E. Y. Harburg and Vernon Duke. FL: April's in the air FLC: April in Paris. 46

Aquellos ojos verdes see 'Green

eyes'

'Arbour town' FL: In Arbour town this damsel did dwell. 30

'Archie o' Cawfield' FL: Bold Dickie, Bold Dickie, Bold Dickie, said he. 11

'Are we to part like this, Bill' Harry Castling and Charles Collins. FL: Three weeks ago, no longer. FLC: Are we to part like this, Bill. 17

Are you going to Scarborough fair? see 'Scarborough Fair'; 'Scarborough Fair/Canticles'

Are you going to Whittingham Fair see 'Whittingham Fair'

Are you listening see 'Please'

'Are you sleeping' FL: Are you sleeping, are you sleeping. 34

Are you sleeping see 'Brother John'

Are you sleeping, are you sleeping see 'Frere Jacques'

' 'arf a pint of ale' Charles Tempest. FL: I hate those chaps what talks about the things what they likes to drink FLC: Now, for breakfast I never thinks of 'aving tea. 17

'Arise and bar the door-o' FL: It happened aboot the Middlemas time. 11

Arise, arise, King Henry, he said see 'Earl Brand'

Arise, o arise, my lady fair see 'The castle by the sea'

Arise, ye sons of France, to glory see 'La Marseillaise'

Arise you up, my pretty Polly see 'Lady Isabel and the elf knight'

'The Arkansas traveller' Mose Case. FL: How long have you been living here. 36

'Arkansas traveler' FL: O, once upon a time in Arkansas. 57

'Armistice Day' Paul Simon. FL: On Armistice Day the Philharmonic will play. 60

'Arnold is as brave a man' FL: Arnold is as brave a man as ever dealt in horses FLC: Yankee Doodle, keep it up, Yankee Doodle Dandy. 8

'Around her neck she wore a yellow ribbon' FL: same FLC: Far away, far away. 4

'A-roving' FL: In Amsterdam there lives a maid, mark well what I

do say. 25
'A-roving' FL: In Plymouth town
   there lived a maid FLC: A-rov-
   ing, a-roving. 57
A-roving, a-roving see 'The
   maid of Amsterdam'
Arrows of neon and flashing
   marquees out on Main Street
   see 'Truckin' '
'Arroyo claro' FL: same. 48
'Arroz con leche' FL: same. 51
'Arthur a Bland' FL: In Notthing-
   ham there lives a jolly tanner.
   11
As a lady was riding to market
   see 'The farmer's daughter'
As all the skippers o' Scarboro'
   see 'Young Allan'
As Brangywell went forth to
   plough see 'Brangywell'
As Collinet and Phebe sat see
   'Collinet and Phebe'
As Cupid in a garden strayed
   see 'The bee'
As Dorothy Parker once said to
   her boyfriend see 'Just one
   of those things'
As down the glen one Easter
   morn to a city fair ride I
   see 'Easter rebellion song'
As Granny arose in the morning
   so soon see 'Granny Wales'
As he came in by yon town en'
   see 'The duke of Atholl's
   nurse'
As he came marching up the
   street see 'Johnny is my
   darling'
As he rode up to the old man's
   gate see 'Sweet Willie'
As I cam' by yon auld house end
   see 'The twa corbies'
As I cam in by Denniedeer see
   'The battle of Harlaw'
As I cam' in by Fiddich Side
   see 'The burning o' Auchendoun'
As I cam in by Garioch's land
   see 'Battle o' the Harlaw'
As I cam' in by Geery's lan'
   see 'The battle of Harlaw'
As I cam' in by Turra Market
   see 'The barnyards of Delgaty'
As I came down the Bowery see
   'Can't you dance the polka?'
As I came in by the Duke of
   Athole's gates see 'The Duke
   of Athole's nurse'

As I came over new London Bridge
   see 'Geordie'
As I came through Sandgate see
   'The keel row'
As I drew out one May morning
   see 'John of Hazelgreen'
As I gaed in yon greenwood side
   see 'The Duke of Athole's nurse'
As I gaed oot for to look about see
   'The gates o' Drum'
As I go down the stream of time
   see 'Prepare us'
As I lady musing all alone see
   'The maid peept out at the win-
   dow'
As I look at the letters that you
   wrote to me see 'Faded love'
As I looked over high castle wall
   see 'Lord Thomas of Winesbury'
As I looked over the castle wall
   see 'Lord Thomas of Winesbury'
As I passed by Ben Sherman's bar-
   room see 'Streets of Laredo'
As I passed by Tom Sherman's bar-
   room see 'Tom Sherman's bar-
   room'
As I rode down to Newry Town see
   'Hurroo-ri-ah'
As I rode east and as I rode west
   see 'The tropper and the maid'
As I rode on a milk white steed
   see 'Lady Isabel and the elf
   knight'
As I rode out in Nottamun town see
   'Nottamun town'
As I rode out last winter's night
   see 'Winter's night'
As I rode out one evening the moon
   it shined clearly see 'Marga-
   ret and John'
As I rode out one May morning see
   'Captain Woodstock'
As I rode over Banstead downs see
   'Georgie'
As I roded out one midsummer
   morn see 'Jock of Hazeldean'
'As I roved out' FL: As I roved
   out one fine summer's evening.
   57
As I roved out by the sea side see
   'The sea side'
As I roved out one evening all in the
   blooming spring see 'The bonny
   labouring boy'
As I roved out one evening down by
   a riverside see 'Down by a
   riverside'; 'Reilly the fisherman'
As I roved out one evening in spring

see   'The maiden's lament'
As I roved out one evening in the
lovely month of may   see   'The
new mown hay'
As I roved out one evening, it
happened in the month of May
see   'Proud Nancy'
As I roved out one fine summer's
evening   see   'As I roved out'
As I roved out one morning in
May   see   'The Bleaches so
green'; 'The false bride, or six
weeks before Easter'; 'George
Collins'; 'Giles Collins'
As I roved out one morning in
spring   see   'Floro'
As I roved out one morning in
the lovely month of May   see
'Young men, come marry me'
As I sailed out one Friday night
see   'The mermaid'
As I sat down   see   'I got the
blues'
As I sat down to muse awhile
see   'Pretty Nancy'
As I sat on a sunny bank'   see
'I saw three ships'
As I sit here tonight   see   'It
wasn't God who made honky
tonk angels'
As I stand by your flame   see
'I got the blues'
As I stand here and remember
see   'The constant rain'
As I strolled out one bright dew
morning   see   'The new mown
hay'
As I strolled out the other day
see   'The blonde that never
dyes'
As I take my morning promenade
see   'When I take my morning
promenade'
As I teach the girls to float, the
sea goes down each throat
see   'The swimming master'
'As I the silly fish deceive'
Robert Jones. FL: same. 26
As I took a walk one May morning
down by John Sander's lane
see   'Six questions'; 'Mr.
Woodburn's courtship'
As I walk along the Bois Boolong
see   'The man that broke the
bank at Monte Carlo'
As I walk along the Bois de Bou-
logne   see   'The man who
broke the bank at Monte Carlo'

As I walked in the streets of La-
redo   see   'The cowboy's lament'
As I walked into the depot, boy
see   'Poor boy'
As I walked on a pleasant green
see   'The three brothers'
As I walked out in a sandy grove
see   'The cambric shirt'
As I walked out in the streets of
Laredo   see   'The cowboy's la-
ment'; 'The streets of Laredo'
As I walked out in yonder dell   see
'The elfin knight'
As I walked out of a London bridge
see   'Geordie'
As I walked out of my father's hall
see   'The cruel mother'
As I walked out on a moonlight sum-
mer's evening   see   'Margaret
and John'
As I walked out one bright May
morn   see   'New mown hay O'
As I walked out one evening down
by the strawberry lane   see
'Bold Robbington'
As I walked out one evening fair
see   'The mermaid'
As I walked out one evening upon a
night's career   see   'The fire-
ship'
As I walked out one fair May morning   see   'John of Hazelgreen';
'John over the Hazel Green'
As I walked out one fine summer's
evening   see   'Willie of Hazel
Green'
As I walked out one holiday   see
'Sir Hugh'
As I walked out one May morning
see   'The baffled knight'; 'John
o' the Hazelgreen'; 'New mown
hay'
As I walked out one midsummer
morn all in the month of May,
sir   see   'The dew is on the
grass'
As I walked out one morning   see
'The baffled knight'; 'The carnal
and the crane'
As I walked out one morning in May
see   'Bold Dickie'
As I walked out one morning this
spring   see   'Young Hunting'
As I walked out one summer's day
see   'The husband with no courage in him'
As I walked out one sunny morn to
view the meadow round   see

'Blow ye winds in the morning'
As I walked out yonders green
  wood tree see 'John over the
  Hazel Green'
As I walked over London Bridge
  see 'Georgie'
'As I walked over London's Bridge'
  FL: same. 11
As I was acrossing London's
  bridge see 'Georgie'
As I was a-ridin' the streets of
  Laredo see 'The streets of
  Laredo'
As I was a-sailing one cold win-
  ter's night see 'Henry Martin'
As I was a walkin' round Kilgary
  Mountain see 'Whiskey in the
  jar'
As I was a-walking down by the
  seashore see 'Every rose grows
  merry in time'
As I was a-walking down Paradise
  Street see 'Blow the man down'
As I was a-walkin' one morning
  for pleasure see 'Git along
  little dogies'
As I was a-walking one morning
  in spring see 'The green
  bushes'
As I was a-walking thru Dublin
  city see 'Dublin City'
As I was a-walking up Strawberry
  Lane see 'Strawberry Lane'
As I was goin' down the road see
  'Turkey in the straw'
As I was going to Darby upon a
  market day see 'The Darby
  ram'
As I was going to my father's
  house see 'The cruel mother'
As I was lumbering down the
  street see 'Buffalo gals'
As I was out walking down by the
  seashore see 'She appeared
  to be eighteen or nineteen years
  old'
As I was pacing father's hall see
  'Down by the greenwood side-e-o'
As I was riding down past Tom
  Sheridan's barroom see
  'Streets of Laredo'
As I was setting with a jug and a
  spoon see 'The jug of punch'
As I was walkin' round the town
  see 'Stung right'
As I was walking all alane see
  'The twa corbies'
As I was walking all alone see

'The wee wee man'
As I was walking down by the seaside see 'The herring song'
As I was walking down the street
  see 'The billboard song'; 'Buffa-
  lo gals'; 'Rig a jig jig'
As I was walking my father's hall
  see 'The cruel mother'
As I was walking out one wondering
  morn see 'John of Hazelgreen'
As I was walking up on Kilgary
  Mountain see 'Kilgary Mountain'
As I went down in the valley to
  pray see 'Come, let us all go
  down'
As I went down to the huckleberry
  picnic see 'The kickin' mule'
As I went down to the mowin' field
  see 'Fod'
As I went down to the river, poor
  boy see 'Poor boy'
As I went forth to take the air see
  'Jock o Hazelgreen'
As I went linking o'er the lee see
  'The auld beggarman'
'As I went out ae May morning' FL:
  same. 11
As I went out in Dublin City see
  'Wheel of fortune'
As I went out one evening down by
  my father's lawn see 'Lord
  Robinson's only child'
As I went out one morning see
  'Blow away the morning dew'
As I went out one mornin' to take
  the pleasant air see 'Lolly-too-
  dum-day'
As I went out one morning to take
  the morning air see 'Lolly too
  dum'
As I went out to Birmingham upon
  a summer day see 'Birmingham
  Bull'
As I went out walking for pleasure
  one day see 'The pretty Mohea'
As I went out walking one evening
  of late see 'The pride of Glencoe'
As I went out walking one morning
  in May see 'A true lover of
  mine'
As I went out walking upon a fine
  day see 'Little Mohee'
As I went over Bonny Moor Hill
  see 'Every rose is bonny in
  time'
As I went over London Bridge see
  'Geordie'

As I were walking down the road
see 'John of Hazelgreen'
As in quarters we lay, which you
quickly shall hear, hear see
'Sahagun'
'As it fell on a holy day' FL:
same. 11
As it fell out on a light dully day
see 'Dives and Lazarus'
As it fell out upon one day see
'Dives and Lazarus'; 'Diverus
and Lazarus'; 'Lazarus'
As Jinny come in from jogging
his plough see 'The wife
wrapt in wether's skin'
As Jock the Leg and the merry
merchant see 'Jock the Leg
and the merry merchant'
As Johnson and the young colonel
see 'Johnson and the colonel'
As Joseph and Mary were a-walking the green see 'The cherry
tree carol'
As Lady Margaret was going to
bed see 'Young Hunting'
As Lily was walking out on the
strand see 'The cruel mother'
As Margaret was sitting in her
bower one day see 'Fair Margaret and Sweet William'
As Mars, great god of battles
lay see 'A parody on Wat'ry
god'
As Mary and Joseph was walking
through a meadow, so fair see
'The cherry tree Carol'
As Miss Margaret was sat in her
bower one day see 'William
and Margaret'
As Mysie May geed up the toon
see 'Wee toon clerk'
As Mysie she gaed up the street
see 'The wee toun clerk'
As near beauteous Boston lying
see 'The destruction of the
tea'; 'A tea party song'
As old Queen Charlotte a worth-
less old varlet see 'Perry's
victory'
As on a lonely hill I strayed see
'The cottager'
As our king lay dreaming upon
his bed see 'King Henry V
and the King of France'
As our king lay musing on his bed
see 'The battle of Agincourt';
'King Henry V's conquest of
France'

As Robin Hood and Little John see
'Robin Hood's death'
As Robin Hood in the green wood
stood see 'The rescue of Will
Stutly'
As Robin Hood ranged the woods
all around see 'Robin Hood'
As she was a-walking her father's
hall see 'The cruel mother'
As she was looking over her fa-
ther's castle wall see 'Willie
o' Winsbury'
As she was sitting in her dower
room see 'Fair Margaret and
Sweet William'
As she went to the merry green
wood see 'The merry Broom-
field'
As shepherds in Jewry were guard-
ing their sheep see 'Shepherds
in Judea'
As smart a man as ever lived was
I when in my prime see 'Young
men taken in and done for'
As the blackbird in the spring see
'Aura Lee'
'As the dew flies over the green
valley' FL: Sweet Willie cam
jogging home from the plow. 11
As the duke's fair daughter of Scot-
land was out riding one day see
'Buff the Quilt'; 'Captain Wedder-
burn's courtship'
As they flew over Pinkville the chop-
pers could see 'Pinkville heli-
copter'
As they steered east as they steered
west see 'Lord Bateman'
As t'other day in harmless chat
see 'The charming creature'
As we come marching, marching in
the beauty of the day see
'Bread and roses'
As we marched down to Fernario
see 'Peggy-o'
As we rode over London Bridge
see 'Geordie'
As we sailed on the water blue see
'Whiskey Johnny'
As we were gone sailing five cold
frosty nights see 'The lofty tall
ship'
As you go down to yonder town see
'The elfin knight'
As you go through Yandro's town
see 'The cambric shirt'
As you go through yonder town see
'Rose de Mariantime'

As you read this letter I write to
you see 'Love, come home'
'The ash grove' FL: Down yon-
der green valley, where streamlets meander. 25
Ashville Junction, Swannanoa Tunnel see 'Swannanoa Tunnel'
'Asleep in the deep' Arthur J.
Lamb and H. W. Petrie. FL:
Stormy the night and the waves
roll high FLC: Loudly the bell
in the old tower rings. 20
Assembled round the patriot's
grave see 'A funeral dirge
on the death of General George
Washington'
At a gay reception given in a
mansion grand and old see
'The moth and the flame'
'At a Georgia camp meeting'
Kerry Mills. FL: A camp
meeting took place in a wide
open space FLC: When the big
brass band began to play.
1
At a time like this see 'Be mine
tonight'
At dawn of day I saw a man see
'The drunkard's doom'
'At dawning' Nelle R. Eberhart
and Charles W. Cadman. FL:
When the dawn flames in the
sky. 1
'At Eastertime' Frederick A.
Jackson and H. v. Müller. FL:
At Eastertime the lilies fair.
13
At five in the morning as jolly as
any see 'Miner's doom'
'At her fair hands' Walter Davison
and Martin Peerson. FL: At
her fair hands how have I grace
intreated. 26
At midnight when the cattle are
sleeping see 'The cowboy's
meditation'; 'The great round-
up'
At Mill o' Tiftie lived a man
see 'Mill o'Tiftie's Annie'
At Mill o' Tifty lived a man
see 'Andrew Lammie'; 'Tifty's
Annie'
'At my time of life' T. W. Connor. FL: Now ever since I
tied the knot, and which it
ain't a day. 17
At that critical moment some
birds came in sight see

'Bang went the chance of a life-
time'
At the age of 19 I was diggin' the
land see 'The Kerry recruit'
At the close of the day when the
hamlet was still see 'The her-
mit'
'At the crèche' Seymour Barab. FL:
In a stable lies a baby FLC:
Welcome the world, the people
are singing. 33
At the door on summer evening
see 'Hiawatha'
'At the gate of heaven' FL: At the
gate of heaven little shoes they
are giving. 13
'At the foot of yonder mountain' FL:
At the foot of yonder mountain
there runs a clear stream. 57
At the old concert hall on the Bowery see 'She is more to be
pitied, than censured'
At the well below the valley-o see
'The well below the valley'
'At the zoo' Paul Simon. FL: Someone told me it's all happening at
the zoo. 60
At war with that great nation Spain
see 'Battleship of Maine'
At words poetic I'm so pathetic
see 'You're the top'
'A-tisket, a-tasket' Ella Fitzgerald
and Van Alexander. FL: same.
59
'Attend, all ye fair' Arthur Murphy
and Smith. FL: same. 40
Attention pray give, while of hobbies I sing see 'The hobbies'
'Au claire de la lune' FL: same.
34, 48, 57
'The auld beggarman' FL: As I
went linking o'er the lee FLC:
With his tooran noorna non ton
nee. 11
'The auld deil cam' FL: The auld
deil cam to the man at the
pleugh. 11
'Auld lang syne' Robert Burns. FL:
Should auld acquaintance be for-
get FLC: For auld lang syne, my
friends. 1, 23, 25, 34, 57, 68
'Aunt Dinah's quilting party' FL:
In the sky the bright stars glit-
tered. 25
'Aunt Rhody' FL: Go tell Aunt
Rhody. 25, 57
'Auntie' Fred E. Weatherly and A.
H. Behrend. FL: You're my

little true lover. 63

'Auprès de ma blonde' FL: Dans les jardins d'mon père FLC: Auprès de ma blonde. 25

'Aura Lee' W. W. Fosdick and George R. Poulton. FL: As the blackbird in the spring FLC: Aura Lee! Aura Lee! 1, 23, 25, 57

'Automation' Joe Glazer. FL: I went down down, down to the factory. 4, 19

'Autumn hiking song' FL: The blue of the sky stretches high o'er the trees. 13

'Autumn in New York' Vernon Duke. FL: It's time to end my lonely holiday FLC: Autumn in New York. 46

'Autumn leaves' Johnny Mercer, Jacques Prevert and Joseph Kosma. FL: Oh! je vousdrais tant que tu te souviennes FLC: The falling leaves drift by the window. 70

'Autumn roundelay' Max T. Krone. FL: Here I sit and wait for you. 13

'Autumn song' Phyllis McGinley and Marlys Swinger. FL: When the swallows. 13

'Avalon' Al Jolson, B. G. De Sylva and Vincent Rose. FL: Every morning memories stray FLC: I found my love in Avalon. 46

'Average rein' FL: Some cowboys once told me about the horse I drew. 43

Aw! come now I'll sing you a song see 'The silly old man'

Aw, come on, get acquainted see 'Pardon me pretty baby'

Awa, awa, ye carle's dother see 'Earl Richard'

Awake, O sol! see 'Ode for the New Year'

Away above my head I see the strangest sight see 'Fiddler on the roof'

Away and away, we're bound for the mountain see 'The Cumberland Mountain deer chase'

Away, away, we're bound for the mountain see 'Cumberland Mountain bear chase'

Away, away with rum by gum see 'Away with rum'; 'The

song of the Salvation Army'

Away, brave boys to Dublin jig see 'One and all'

Away by the river so clear see 'Little Moses'

Away down a yonder in Yankety Yank see 'May Irwin's frog song'; 'Nothing else to do'

Away from home, away from home see 'Five hundred miles away from home'

Away from the city that hurts and mocks see 'I cover the waterfront'

'Away in a manger' FL: Away in a manger, no crib for a bed. 33

Away out here they got a name for wind and rain and fire see 'They call the wind Maria'

Away over Jordan with my blessed Jesus see 'Wear a starry crown'

Away up high in the Sierry Petes see 'The Sierry Petes'

'Away up in the Mogliones' FL: Away up high in the Mogliones, upon the mountain tops FLC: Oh, glory be to me, says he, and fame's unfadin' flower. 18

'Away with rum' FL: We're coming, coming, we're coming FLC: Away, away with rum, by gum. 57

Away with the music of Broadway see 'By Strauss'

A-well my hammer keep a-hangin', 'cause it's fallin' down see 'Fallin' down'

Awful hero, Marl'ro rife! see 'Marlborough's ghost'

Ax am a walkin' see 'Looky, looky yonder'

Ay ay ay ay ay cantaba see 'Cucu-rru-cu-cu, Paloma'

Ay, ay, ay, ay, Cielito Lindo see 'Cielito Lindo'

'Ay! Linda amiga' FL: Ay! linda amiga, que no vuelvo a verte. 57

'Ay me! Can love and beauty so conspire' FL: same. 26

'Ay me, that love should Nature's works accuse' Philip Rosseter. FL: same. 26

Aya, aya, aya, aya, twist their tails and go see 'The elephant battery'

Aye, aye, aye, aye see 'The

limerick song'
Aye ban a farmer in Minnesota
  see 'One happy Swede'
'Aye the birks a-bowing' FL: O
  we were sisters, sisters seven.
  11
Ayer salió la lancha Nueva Es-
  parta see 'El Carite'
Ay-lyu-lyu see 'Vigndig a
  fremd kind'
Az men fort kind Sevastopol see
  'Hey! Zhankoye'
Azul blanca y colorada see
  'Que bonita bandera'

- B -

'Baa, baa, black sheep' FL:
  same. 48
'Babalu' S. K. Russell and Mar-
  garita Lecuona. FL: Jungle
  drums were madly beating
  FLC: Babalu, babalu. 9
'Babalu' Margarita Lecuona.
  FL: Ta empesando lo velorio
  FLC: Babalu, babalu. 9
'The Babbitt and the bromide'
  George and Ira Gershwin.
  FL: A Babbitt and a Bromide
  on the avenue one day FLC:
  Hello! How are you? 21
'The Babe of Bethlehem' FL: Ye
  nations all on ye I call. 33
Babe, we are well met see
  'Thou swell'
Babes, o babes, I wish you
  were mine see 'The cruel
  mother'
'The baboon climbs the hill' FL:
  same. 72
'Bab'ry Ellen' FL: In Scarlet
  town where I was born. 57
Baby, Baby, been a long, long
  time see 'Long, long while'
'Baby driver' Paul Simon. FL:
  My daddy was a family bassman. 60
'Baby elephant walk' Hal David
  and Henry Mancini. FL: Make
  believe you're in a jungle
  movie! 71
'Baby face' Benny Davis and
  Harry Akst. FL: Rosy cheeks
  and turned up nose and curly
  hair FLC: Baby face, you've
  got the cutest little baby face.
  46

Baby is sleeping so cozy and fair
  see 'Rock-a-bye baby'
'Baby Mine' Charles Mackey and
  Archibald Johnston. FL: I've a
  letter from thy sire, baby mine.
  1
'Baby, please don't go' Big Bill
  Broonzy. FL: same. 57
Baby, the truth is out so don't deny
  see 'Gotta get away'
'Baby, won't you please come home'
  Charles Warfield and Clarence
  Williams. FL: When you left you
  broke my heart FLC: Baby, won't
  you please come home. 12
'Baby you're a rich man' Lennon
  and McCartney. FL: How does
  it feel to be one of the beautiful
  people. 44
'Babylon's falling' FL: Poor city,
  Babylon's falling to rise FLC: Oh,
  Babylon's falling, falling, falling.
  25
Baby's good to me, you know see
  'I feel fine'
Back about eighteen hundred and
  some see 'Billy Babyou'
Back again, back again see 'Frank-
  lin D. Roosevelt's back again'
'The Back Bay polka' George and
  Ira Gershwin. FL: Give up the
  fond embrace. 21
Back in the days of knights in ar-
  mor see 'Lorelei'
'Back in the saddle again' Gene Au-
  try and Ray Whitley. FL: I'm
  back in the saddle again. 10
'Back in the USSR' Lennon and
  McCartney. FL: Flew in from
  Miami Beach B. O. A. C. 44
'Back street girl' Mick Jagger and
  Keith Richard. FL: I don't want
  you to be high. 16
Back there, behind my father's see
  'My father's apple tree'
Backslider, don't stay away see
  'My Lord says there's room
  enough in Heaven for us all'
'Backward, turn backward' FL:
  Backward, turn backward, O
  time, in your flight. 43
Backward, turn backward, oh time
  in your flight see 'Rock me to
  sleep'
'Backward, turn backward oh time
  with your wheel' see 'Make me
  a cowboy again for a day'
'Backwater blues' FL: Well, it

55
'The battle of the kegs' FL: Gallants, attend and hear a friend
trill forth harmonious ditty.   8
'The ballad of the tea party' FL:
Tea ships near to Boston lying.
57
'The ballad of Trenton' FL: On
Christmas Day in '76.   8
'Ballin' the Jack' Jim Burris
and Chris Smith. FL: Stretch
your lovin' arms straight out
in space FLC: First you put
your two knees close up tight.
12
The ballroom was filled with
fashion's throng <u>see</u> 'A bird
in a gilded cage'
'Ballynamony' Thomas Sheridan.
FL: Where ever I'm going and
all the day long.   40
'Balm in Gilead' FL: Sometimes
I feel discouraged FLC: There
is a balm in Gilead.   57
'Baltimore fire' FL: It was on a
silver falls by a narrow FLC:
Fire, fire, I heard the cry.
57
'La Bamba' FL: Bamba, bamba.
23
'La Bamba' FL: Dance La Bamba,
a cousin of the samba.   25
'Banbury ale' FL: same.   68
'The band played on' Charles B.
Ward and John F. Palmer.
FL: Matt Casey formed a social
club FLC: Casey would waltz
with a strawberry blonde.   1,
20, 36
'Bang bang bang' FL: Oh, Johnny,
Johnny, John, come along,
come along.   68
'Bang went the chance of a life-
time' Sax Rohmer. FL: Now
old Aunt Rebecca is rich FLC:
At that critical moment some
birds came in sight.   17
Bangry Rewey a-courting did ride
<u>see</u> 'Sir Lionel'
'Bangum and the boar' FL: Old
Bangum came riding across the
glen.   11
'Bangum and the boar' FL: Old
Bangum would a-wooing ride.
11
'Bangum and the boar' FL: There
is a wild boar in these woods.
11

'The banks o Airdrie' FL: There
was three young sisters went out
for a walk.   11
'The banks of Claudy' FL: Twas on
the banks of Claudy.   11
'The banks of Fordie' FL: There
were three sisters lived in a
bower.   11
'Banks of Green willow' FL: Go and
get me some of your father's
gold.   11
'Banks of green willow' FL: Go and
get your father's good will.   11
'Banks of green willow' FL: Go
home and get some of your father's gold.   11
'Banks of green willow' FL: It's of
a sea captain.   11
'Banks of green willow' FL: It's of
a sea captain lived near the seaside O.   11
'Banks of green willow' FL: Sea
captain, sea captain, down by the
banks of the willow.   11
'The banks of Italy' FL: He's given
her a pair of shoes.   11
'The banks of the Dee' John Tait.
FL: Twas summer and softly the
breezes were blowing.   3, 8, 49,
65
'The banks of the Dee (Parody)'
Oliver Arnold.   FL: Twas winter
and blue Tory noses were freez-
ing.   55
'The banks of the Don' FL: On the
banks of the Don.   57
'Banks of the Ohio' FL: I asked my
love to take a walk FLC: Then
only say that you'll be mine.   14,
57
'Banks of the Ohio' FL: I asked my
love to walk with me.   23, 25
'The Bar-Z of a Sunday night' FL:
Yield not to temptation for yield-
ing is sin.   18
'Barbara Allen' FL: All in she
merry month of May.   11
'Barbara Allen' FL: All in the
month, the month of May.   11
'Barbara Allen' FL: All thru the
month of May.   11
'Barbara Allen' FL: Dark and gloomy
is the town.   11
'Barb'ra Allen' FL: Dark and gloomy
there was a town.   11
'Barbara Allen' FL: Down in the
London where I was raised.   11
'Barbara Allen' FL: Early early in

the spring. 29

'Barbara Allen' FL: Early, early in the spring when green buds they were swelling. 7

'Barbara Allen' FL: He sent his servant down to tell. 11

'Barbara Allen' FL: In London city where I once did dwell. 2, 11

'Barbara Allen' FL: In Reading town where I was born. 11

'Barbara Allen' FL: In Scarlet town where I did dwell. 11

'Barb'ra Allen' FL: In Scarlet town where I was born. 1, 11, 25, 35, 61

'Barbara Allen' FL: In Scotland I was born and bred. 11

'Barbara Allen' FL: In the early fair days of May. 11

'Barbara Allen' FL: In yonders town where I am bound. 11

'Barbara Allen' FL: In yonders town where I was born. 11

'Barbara Allan' FL: It fell about a Martinmas time. 11

'Barbara Allen' FL: It was a pleasant morning in May. 11

'Barbara Allen' FL: It was in the fall season of the year. 11

'Barbara Allen' FL: It was in the merry month of May. 11

'Barbara Allen' FL: It was in the new year in the month of May. 11

'Barbara Allen' FL: It was one love-ly month of May. 11

'Barbara Allen' FL: It was upon a high, high hill. 11, 61

'Barbara Allan' FL: Look down, look down, by my bedside. 41

'Barbara Allen' FL: One bright day in the month of May. 11

'Barbara Allen' FL: One cold and cloudy day in the month of May. 11

'Barbra Allen' FL: One Monday morn, in the month of May. 11

'Barb'ra Allen' FL: One morning early in the May. 11

'Barbara Allen' FL: One morning in the month of May. 11

'Barbara Allen' FL: Sweet William was down to his dwell today. 11

'Barbara Allen' FL: Twas all in the merry, merry month of May. 11, 50

'Barbara Allen' FL: Twas early,

early in the spring. 11

'Barbara Allen' FL: Twas in the lovely month of May. 11

'Barbara Allen' FL: Twas in the merry month of May. 11

'Barbara Allen' FL: Twas in the merry month of June. 11

'Barbara Allen' FL: Twas in the pleasant month of May. 11

'Barbara Allen' FL: Twas once I lived in a scornful town. 11

'Barbara Ellen' FL: All in the merry month of May. 23

'Barbara Ellen' FL: In Storytown where I did live. 11

'Barbara Ellen' FL: It was all in the month of June. 11

'Barbara Ellen' FL: The lady she died on Saturday. 11

'Barbara Ellen' FL: O early in the month of May. 11

'Barbara Ellen' FL: So this young man he were taken sick. 11

'Barbara Ellen' FL: Twas early early in the spring. 11

'Barbara Ellen' FL: Way down yon-der in London town. 11

'Barbara Ellen' FL: A way low down in London town. 11

'Barbary Ellen' FL: It was the very month of May. 11

'Barbery Allan' FL: Twas early early in the spring. 11

'Barb'ra Allyn' FL: It was early early in the summer time. 11

'Barb'ry Allen' FL: Lonely lonely was a town. 11

'Barb'ry Allum' FL: In Scarlet town where I was born. 11

'Barbery Ellen' FL: A strange young man from the north coun-try. 11

'Barbry Ellen' FL: It was all in the month of May. 11

'The Barkshire tragedy' FL: A varmer he lived in the West countree. 11

Barney Carney promised he'd be true to Molly O see 'My Bar-ney lies over the ocean'

'Barney Google' Billy Rose and Con Conrad. FL: Who's the most important man this county ever knew FLC: Barney Google with his goo goo googly eyes. 46

'The barnyards of Delgaty' FL: As I cam' in by Turra Market FLC: Linten adie-too-rin-adie. 57

bear in yon hill, and he is a
brave fellow. 72
'The bear went over the mountain' FL: same FLC: And what
do you think he saw? 1, 68,
72
'Beat me, daddy, eight to the
bar' Don Raye, Hughie Prince
and Eleanor Sheehy. FL: In
a dinky honky tonky village in
Texas FLC: The people gather
around when he gets on the
stand. 59
'Beat out that rhythm on a drum'
Oscar Hammerstein and George
Bizet. FL: I'll tell you why I
wanna dance. 24
Beauing, belleing, dancing, drinking see 'Rakes of Mallow'
'Beaulampkins' FL: Beaulampkins
was as fine a mason. 11
'The beauties of friendship' FL:
Young Myra is fair as spring's
early flower. 3
'Beautiful, beautiful brown eyes'
FL: Willie, oh Willie, I love
you FLC: Beautiful, beautiful
brown eyes. 35
A beautiful damsel, from London
came she see 'Pretty Sally'
'Beautiful dreamer' Stephen Fos-
ter. FL: Beautiful dreamer,
wake unto me. 1, 25, 57, 63
'Beautiful isle of Somewhere'
Jessie Brown Pounds and J.
S. Fearis. FL: Somewhere
the sun is shining FLC: Some-
where, somewhere. 20, 25
Beautiful miracle see 'Love is
just around the corner'
'Beauty sat bathing by a spring'
Anthony Mundau, Robert Jones
and William Corkine. FL:
same. 26
'Beauty, stand further!' Robert
Jones. FL: same. 26
Les beaux messieurs font comm'
ci see 'Sur le pont d'Avi-
gnon'
'Because' Lennon and McCartney.
FL: Because the world is
round, it turns me on. 44
'Because' Edward Teschemacher
and Guy d'Hardelot. FL:
Because you come to me with
naught save love. 1, 20, 31
Because I was evil see 'Evil-
hearted man'

'Because of you' Arthur Hammer-
stein and Dudley Wilkinson. FL:
Because of you there's a song in
my heart. 47
Because the world is round, it turns
me on see 'Because'
Because they could not sing see
'In good old colony times'; 'Old
colony times'
Because you come to me with
naught save love see 'Because'
'Because you're you' Henry Blossom
and Victor Herbert. FL: Love
is a queer little elfin sprite FLC:
Not that you are fair, dear. 1
Bed! Bed! I couldn't go to bed see
'I could have danced all night'
Bed on the floor, baby see 'Make
me a bed on the floor'
'Bedelia' William Jerome and Jean
Schwartz. FL: There's a charming Irish lady with a roguish winning way FLC: Bedelia, I want to
steal ye. 20
'The bee' FL: As Cupid in a garden
strayed. 3
'Been a listening' FL: Some say
that John the B. was nothing but
a Jew FLC: Been a listening all
night long. 38
'Been down into the sea' FL: O
won't those mourners rise and
tell FLC: Hallelujah, an a halle-
lujah. 5
'Been in the pen so long' FL: same.
57
'Been in the storm so long' FL:
I've been in the storm so long. 29
'Been on the chain gang' FL: Judge,
he give me six months 'cause I
wouldn't go to work. 28
'Been on the Charlie so long' FL:
When we got within a mile of the
place. 57
Been praying for the sinner so long
see 'I ain't got weary yet'
Been to sea for a month or more
see 'Round the Bay of Mexico'
Been washed in the blood of the
Lamb see 'I've been redeemed'
'Beer' FL: Oft times you fellows
were singing of wine. 41
'Beer barrel polka' Lew Brown,
Wladimir A. Timm, Vasek Ze-
man and Jaromir Vejvoda. FL:
There's a garden, what a garden
FLC: Roll out the barrel. 59
'The beer that made Milwaukee

famous' Dan McAvoy.   FL:
When Roger McNally retired
from the force FLC: The big
Dutch band.   36

'Before I met you' FL: I thought
I had seen pretty girls in my
time FLC: I thought I was
swinging the world by the tail.
14

'Before I'd be a slave' FL: O,
what preachin' FLC: Before I'd
be a slave.   5

'Before the parade passes by'
Jerry Herman FL: same FLC:
same.   6

Before the rising of the sun   see
'Sweet William'

Before we met I never dreamed
much   see   'I'll buy that
dream'

'The beggar laddie' FL: Doon in
yon glen I spied a swain.   11

'The beggar laddie' FL: Twas in
the merry month of June.   11

'The beggar laddie' FL: Twas in
the pleasant month of June.   11

'The beggar man' FL: For a beggar, a beggar cam owre the
lea.   11

'The beggar man' FL: For there
were an auld beggar man come
owre yon lea.   11

'The beggar man' FL: On board
of a ship and away sailed he.
11

'The beggar man' FL: There was
an auld man cam owre the lea.
11

'The beggar man' FL: Tis of a
ragged beggar man, come tripping o'er the plain.   11

The beggar man and the mighty
king are only different in name
see   'Blue bird of Happiness'

A beggar man cam' ower the lea
see   'The beggar's bride'

'The beggarman' FL: O, twas of
a young couple they lived in
this place.   11

'The beggarman' FL: There was
a dirty beggarman.   11

A beggarman came owre yon lea
see   'The jolly beggar'

A beggarman laid himself down
to sleep   see   'Rumsty-o'

'The beggar's bride' FL: A beggar man cam' ower the lea.
11

'The beggar's dawtie' FL: It was in
the merry month of June.   11

'The begging weed' FL: I know an'
fair lovey, I know an' free.   11

'Begin the beguine' Cole Porter.
FL: When they begin the Beguine.
42

'Begone, pernicious tea' FL: Begone,
pernicious, baneful tea.   8

Behind a grammer school house
see   'Maggie Murphy's home'

'Behold a wonder here' John Dowland.   FL: same.   26

Behold din me a man who's lost a
fortune on the field   see   'Could
I only back the winner'

'Behold that star' FL: There was
no room found in the inn FLC:
Behold that star.   33

Behold the way our fine feathered
friend his virtue doth parade
see   'My funny Valentine'

'Bei mir bist du schön' Sammy Cahn,
Saul Chaplin and Sholom Secunda.
FL: Of all the girls I've known
FLC: Bei mir bist du Schön.   46

'Believe I'll call the rider' FL: Captain, wo Lord.   28

'Believe me if all those endearing
young charms' FL: same.   25,
57

'Bella' FL: Bella was young and
Bella was fair.   58

The bells are ringing   see   'For me
and my gal'

'The bellyan's daughter' FL: There
was a youth and a well bred
youth.   11

'Ben Bolt' Thomas Dunn and Nelson
Kneass.   FL: Oh, don't you remember sweet Alice, Ben Bolt.
57, 63

'Beneath a weeping willow's shade'
Francis Hopkinson.   FL: same
FLC: The mockingbird sat upon a
bough.   65

Beneath it the stream gently rippled
see   'The old rustic bridge by
the mill'

'Besame mucho' Consuelo Velazquez
and Sunny Skylar.   FL: Besame
mucho, hold me, my darling and
say that you'll always be mine
FLC: Besame, besame mucho.   9

'Besame mucho' Consuelo Velazquez.
FL: Besame mucho que tengo
miedo perderte, perderte otra
vez FLC: Bésame, bésame mucho.

9

Bésame tú a mi bésame igual que
mi boca te besó see 'Frenesi'
Beside a hill, there is a still
see 'Old mountain dew'
'Bess you is my woman now'
George and Ira Gershwin and
DuBose Heyward. FL: same.
21, 64
'Bessie Bell and Mary Lee' FL:
same. 11
'Bessy Bell' FL: O Bessy Bell
and Mary Gray. 11
'Bessy Bell and Mary Grey' FL:
O Bessy Bell and Mary Gray.
11
'The best is yet to come' Caro-
lyn Leigh and Cy Coleman.
FL: Out of the tree of life I
just picked a plum. 52
'The best things in life are free'
B. G. De Sylva, Lew Brown
and Ray Henderson. FL:
There are so many kinds of
riches FLC: The moon belongs
to everyone. 42
'Bethelnie' FL: Her father being
a chaplain. 11
'Bethelnie' FL: Pale an' wan was
she. 11
'Bethelnie' FL: Six hundred brave
nobles. 11
'Bethelnie' FL: There were six
and six ladies. 11
'Betsy Gordon' FL: Did you
come by Brackley, did ye
come by Dee? 11
A better mason than Lammikin
see 'Lammikin'
'Betty and Dupree' FL: Betty
told Dupree, I want a diamond
ring. 35, 57
'Between the devil and the deep
blue sea' Ted Koehler and
Harold Arlen. FL: I forgive
you 'cause I can't forget you
FLC: I don't want you, but I
hate to loose you. 12
'Beware, oh take care' FL:
Young men, they say, are
bold and free FLC: Beware,
young ladies, they're fooling
you. 57
Beware, young ladies, they're
fooling you see 'Beware,
oh take care'
'The Bewick and the Graeme'
FL: Gude Lord Graeme is to

Carlisle gane. 11
'Bewitched' Lorenz Hart and Richard
Rodgers. FL: He's a fool and
don't I know it FLC: I'm wild
again. 6, 42
'Beyond the blue horizon' Leo Robin,
Richard A. Whiting and W.
Franke Harling. FL: Blow,
whistle blow away FLC: Beyond
the blue horizon waits a beauti-
ful day. 53
'Beyond the sea' Jack Lawrence and
Charles Trenet. FL: Somewhere
beyond the sea. 67
'Bibbidi-Bobbidi-Boo' Mack David,
Al Hoffman and Jerry Livingston.
FL: Sa-la ga doo-la men-chic-ka
boola. 47
'Bible stories' FL: Young folks old
folks, everybody come. 68
'The Bible tells me so' Dale Evans.
FL: Have faith, hope and charity.
52
'A bicycle built for two' Henry
Dacre. FL: Daisy, Daisy, give
me your answer true. 34
'Biddy Biddy Burkey' FL: Biddy
Biddy Burkey's the name of my
turkey. 48
'Bidin' my time' George and Ira
Gershwin. FL: Some fellers love
to 'Tiptoe through the tulips'
FLC: I'm biding my time. 21,
46
'The big black giant' Oscar Ham-
merstein and Richard Rodgers.
FL: The water in a river is
changed every day. 24
'The big bright green pleasure ma-
chine' Paul Simon. FL: Do
people have a tendency to dump
on you? 60
'Big camp meeting in the Promised
Land' FL: You kin hinder me
here FLC: O dis union! 5
'The big corral' FL: The bonney
brute from the cattle chute FLC:
Press along, cowboy, press
along. 57
The big Dutch band see 'The beer
that made Milwaukee famous'
'The Big Rock Candy Mountain' FL:
On a summer's day in the month
of May FLC: Oh, the buzzin' of
the bees in the cigarette trees.
25, 57
'Big Rock Candy Mountain' FL: One
night just as the sun went down.

4
Big Sam left Seattle in the year
of ninety-two <u>see</u> 'North of
Alaska'
'The big sunflower' Bobby New-
comb. FL: There is a charm
I can't explain FLC: And I
feel just as happy as a big
sunflower. 1
Big wheel keep on turning <u>see</u>
'Proud Mary'
'The Bigler' FL: Come all my
boys and listen a song I'll
sing to you. 57
'Bile them cabbage down' FL:
Raccoon up in the simmon tree
FLC: Bile them cabbage down,
boys. 14
'Bile them cabbage down' FL:
Went up on the mountain FLC:
Bile them cabbage down, down.
57
'Bill' P. G. Wodehouse, Oscar
Hammerstein and Jerome Kern.
FL: But along came Bill. 67
'Bill' P. G. Wodehouse, Oscar
Hammerstein and Jerome Kern.
FL: I used to dream that I
would discover. 6
'Bill Bailey' Hughie Cannon. FL:
Won't you come home, Bill
Bailey. 34, 56, 57, 67
'Bill Bailey won't you please
come home' Hughie Cannon.
FL: On one summer day, sun
was shining fine FLC: Won't
you come home, Billy Bailey.
1, 20, 31
Bill collectors gather round and
rather <u>see</u> 'Ain't we got fun'
'Bill Groggin's goat' FL: There
was a man. 57
Bill, I love you so <u>see</u> 'Wed-
ding bell blues'
'Bill McCandless' ride' Jerry
Silverman. FL: On the 27th
day of May. 57
'The billboard song' FL: As I
was walking down the street.
35
'Billy and Johnny' FL: There was
80 weight of good Spanish iron.
11
'Billy and Johnny' FL: There
were 9 to hold the British
ranks. 11
'Billy Barlow' FL: Let's go hunting, says Risky Rob. 57

'Billy Bayou' Roger Miller. FL:
Back about eighteen hundred and
some FLC: Billy, Billy Bayou.
10
'Billy Boy' FL: Can she bake a
cherry pie. 57
'Billy Boy' FL: Did she ask you to
sit down, Billy boy, Billy boy.
11
'Billy Boy' FL: Is she fitting for
your wife, Billy Boy. 11
'Billy Boy' FL: Oh, where, have
you been, Billy boy, Billy boy.
11, 23, 25, 36
'Billy Boy' FL: Where are you going, Billy boy, Billy boy. 11
'Billy Boy' FL: Where have you
been all the day, Billy boy,
Billy boy. 11
'Billy Boy' FL: Where have you
been Billy Boy? Where have you
been, charming Billy? 7
'Billy Boy' FL: Where hev ye been
aal the day. 11
'Billy broke locks' FL: There were
nine to hold the British ranks.
57
Billy broke locks and Billy broke
bolts <u>see</u> 'The escape of Old
John Webber'
'Billy came over the main white
ocean' FL: same. 11
'Billy Grimes' FL: Tomorrow, Ma,
I'm sweet 16, and Billy Grimes
the rover. 7
'Billy Magee Magaw' FL: There
were three crows sat on a tree.
68, 72
Billy married him a wife and he
carried her home <u>see</u> 'The wife
wrapt in wether's skin'
'Billy murdered John' FL: O, Billy,
O Billy you have come home. 11
'Billy the Kid' FL: I'll sing you a
true song of Billy the Kid. 2,
57
'Billy Venero' FL: Billy Venero
heard them say in an Arizona
town one day. 43
Billy was riding at Tucson <u>see</u>
'Ballad of Billy the bull rider'
'Binnorie' FL: There were twa
sisters sat in a bower. 11
'Binnorie' FL: Twa bonny sisters
that lived in a bower. 11
'Binnorie, O Binnorie' FL: There
were two sisters lived in a bower. 11

'Binorie' FL: There were twa sis-
ters lived in a ha'. 11
'A bird in a gilded cage' Arthur
J. Lamb and Harry von Tilzer.
FL: The ballroom was filled
with fashion's throng FLC: She's
only a bird in a gilded cage. 1,
20, 31
Bird of May, leave the spray see
'The request to the nightingale'
'The bird on Nellie's hat' Arthur
J. Lamb and Alfred Solman.
FL: Every Saturday, Willie got
his pay FLC: I'll be your little
honey. 20
'The birds' FL: From out of a
wood did a cuckoo fly. 13
Birds do it, bees do it see
'Let's do it'
The birds of the forest are call-
ing for thee see 'Gypsy love
song'
'The birds' song' FL: Hey, said
the blackbird, sittin' on a
chair FLC: Hidy, didy, diddle-
dum-die. 72
'Birmingham Bull' FL: As I went
out to Birmingham upon a sum-
mer day FLC: And didn't he
ramble. 57
'The birth of Robin Hood' FL: O
there's many loves that chase the
chase. 11
'The birth of Robin Hood' FL:
Robin Hood's father was the
earl's own steward. 11
'The birth of the blues' B. G. De
Sylva, Lew Brown and Ray
Henderson. FL: Oh! They say
some people long ago FLC:
They heard the breeze in the
trees. 46
'The bishop of Canterbury' FL:
A story, a story, a story
anon. 11
'The bishop of Canterbury' FL:
Old King John was a great
noble knight. 11
'The bishop of Herefords' enter-
tainment' FL: Some they will
talk of bold Robin Hood. 11
'Bitch' Mick Jagger and Keith
Richard. FL: I'm feeling so
tired I can't understand it. 16
'Black and white' Earl Robinson.
FL: The ink is black, the page
is white. 64
Black, black, black is the color

of my true love's hair see
'Black is the color'; 'Black is
the color of my true love's hair'
'Black, brown and white blues' Big
Bill Broonzy. FL: Just listen to
this song I'm singing. 56, 57
'Black gal' FL: Did you hear 'bout
Ida gettin' drownded. 28
Black girl, black girl don't lie to
me see 'In the pines'
'Black is the color' FL: Black,
black, black is the color of my
true love's hair. 66
'Black is the color' FL: But black
is the color of my true love's
hair. 57
'Black is the color of my true
love's hair' FL: Black, black,
black is the color of my true
love's hair. 23, 25
'Black Jack Davey' FL: Old Black
Jack Davey came a-riding by.
50
'Black Jack David' FL: Now the
Black Jack David come riding
through the plains. 11
'Black Jack Davy' FL: Black Jack
Davy came a-riding o'er the
plains. 11
'Black Jack Davy' FL: Black Jack
Davy come a-riding through the
woods. 11
'Black Jack Davy' FL: How old are
you my pretty Polly. 11
'Black Jack Davy' FL: O Black Jack
Davy crossed the field. 11
Black Jack Davy came a-singing
through the woods see 'Gypsy
Davy'
Black Jack Davy went a-riding o'er
the plains see 'Gypsy Draly'
'Blackbird' Lennon and McCartney.
FL: Blackbird singing in the
dead of night. 44
Blackbird, blackbird, singing the
blues all day see 'Bye bye
blackbird'
Blackbird singing in the dead of
night see 'Blackbird'
'Black-eyed Susie' FL: All I want
in this creation. 25
'Blah-blah-blah' George and Ira
Gershwin. FL: I've written you
a song FLC: Blah, blah, blah,
blah moon. 21
'The Blantyre explosion' FL: By
Clyde's bonny banks where I sadly did wander. 19, 57

'Blow the wind southerly' FL: They
told me last night there were
ships in the offing FLC: Blow
the wind southerly, southerly,
southerly.   25
Blow, whistle blow away see
'Beyond the blue horizon'
Blow, wind, blow see 'Winter
night'
'Blow, wind, blow, and go mill,
go' FL: same.   13
'Blow ye winds' FL: Tis adver-
tised in Boston, New York,
and Buffalo FLC: Blow ye winds,
o mornin'.   25
'Blow, ye winds, blow' FL: You
must make me a fine Holland
shirt.   11
'Blow the winds, I-ho!' FL:
There was a shepherd's son.
11
'Blow ye winds in the morning'
FL: As I walked out one sunny
morn to view the meadow round.
11
'Blow ye winds in the morning'
FL: Tis advertised in Boston,
New York and Buffalo FLC:
Singing blow ye winds in the
morning.   19, 57
Blow ye winds, o mornin' see
'Blow ye winds'
'Blow, ye winds of morning' FL:
Hear the tale of Peter Gray
FLC: Blow, ye winds of morn-
ing.   23
Blow, ye winds of morning see
'Peter Gray'
'Blow, ye winds, westerly' FL:
Come all ye young sailormen,
listen to me FLC: Then blow
ye winds westerly, westerly
blow.   57
'Blow your trumpet, Gabriel' FL:
De talles' tree in Paradise.
29
'Blue' Grant Clarke, Edgar Leslie
and Lou Handman. FL: There
was a time I was jolly FLC:
Blue because we're parted. 12
'Blue bell bull' FL: I was at the
rodeo and won the first go-
round.   43
'The blue bell of Scotland' FL:
Oh where, and oh where is
your Highland laddie gone. 25,
57
'The blue bells of Scotland' FL:

Oh where, tell me where, does
your Highland laddie dwell.   23
'Blue blue blue' George and Ira
Gershwin. FL: It's off with the
old FLC: Blue, blue, blue.   21
Blue, blue, my world is blue see
'Love is blue'
'Blue cheese' Josef Marais. FL:
My mama once gave me some
blue cheese to eat.   13
'The blue flowers and the yellow'
FL: O Willie my son, what makes
you sae sad?   11
'Blue Hawaii' Leo Robin and Ralph
Rainger. FL: Perfume in the
air and rare flowers everywhere
FLC: Night and you and blue
Hawaii.   47, 53
Blue heaven and you and I see
'The desert song'
'Blue Mountain Lake' FL: Come all
you good fellers, wherever you
be.   57
Blue night and you alone with me
see 'Love in bloom'
The blue of the sky stretches high
o'er the trees see 'Autumn
hiking song'
'Blue suede shoes' Carl Lee Per-
kins. FL: Well, you can knock
me down FLC: Well, it's one for
the money.   10
'The blue tail fly' FL: When I was
young I used to wait FLC: Jimmy
crack corn and I don't care.   1,
23, 25, 57
'Blue turning grey over you' Andy
Razaf and Thomas Waller. FL:
My, how I miss your tender kiss.
54
'Blue turns to grey' Mick Jagger
and Keith Richard. FL: So now
that she is gone.   16
'Blue velvet' Bernie Wayne and
Lee Morris. FL: She wore blue
velvet.   67
'Bluebeard' FL: A maiden from the
Bosporus with eyes as bright as
phosphorus FLC: Yuazuram,
yuazuram.   68
'Blueberry Hill' Al Lewis, Larry
Stock and Vincent Rose. FL: I
found my thrill on Blueberry
Hill.   64
'Bluebird of happiness' Edward Hey-
man and Sandor Harmati. FL:
The beggar man and the mighty
king are only different in name

FLC: So be like I, hold your head up high. 67

'Blue-eyed boy' FL: Oh who oh who will be my friend FLC: Oh, bring back my blue-eyed boy. 11

'The blues ain't nothin' FL: I'm gonna build myself a raft. 57

'The blues ain't nothin' but a good man feelin' bad' FL: I'm gonna build myself a raft. 35

'The blues ain't nothing but a good man feelin' bad' FL: I'm wondering why I feel so sad. 23

Blues jumped a rabbit and he ran a solid mile see 'Rabbit-foot blues'

'A blues serenade' Mitchell Parish and Frank Signorelli. FL: If there is a Cinderella looking for a steady fella. 12

'Boab King' FL: Boab King was a mason. 11

'Boar's head carol' FL: The boar's head in hand I bear FLC: Caput apri defero. 72

'A boat, a boat' FL: A boat, a boat to cross the ferry. 68

'Boatman dance' FL: Boatman, dance, boatman sing FLC: Dance, boatman, dance. 57

'Bobby Shaftoe' FL: Bobby Shaftoe's gone to sea. 25

'Bob-ry Allen' FL: O mother, mother, look under my bed. 11

'Body and soul' Edward Heyman, Robert Sour, Frank Eyton and Johnny Green. FL: Life's dreary for me FLC: My heart is sad and lonely. 46

'Bog in the valley-o' FL: Now in that bog there was a root FLC: Yea. ho! The rattlin' bog. 57

'Bog o' Gight' FL: Will you go to the Highlands my bonnie love. 11

'Bolakins' FL: Bolakins was a very fine mason. 11

'Bold Archer' FL: It was all in the month of June. 11

Bold Arden walked forth one summer morning see 'Robin Hood'

A bold, bad man was this desperado see 'The desperado'

'Bold Dickie' FL: As I walked out one morning in May. 11

Bold Dickie, Bold Dickie, Bold Dickie, said he see 'Archie o' Cawfield'

'A bold dragoon' FL: In the dragoon's ride from out the North. 11

'The bold dragoon and the lady' FL: My father he's a lord and a lord of high renown. 11

Bold Dunkins were as fine a mason see 'Lamkin'

'The bold Fenian men' FL: See who comes over the red blossomed heather. 57

'Bold fisherman' FL: There was a bold fisherman who sailed out from Pimlico FLC: Twink-i doodle dum. 57

'The bold granadee' FL: Oh! There was a ship in the North countrie. 11

Bold Johnstone and the young cornel see 'Young Johnstone'

'Bold Lamkon' FL: It's of some noble lord, as you shall quickly hear. 11

'The bold lieutenant' FL: In Greenock town there lived a lady. 30

'The bold lieutenant' FL: Twas near St. Giles there dwelled a lady. 30

'The bold lieutenant' FL: Twas of a lady lived in St. Giles. 30

'The bold pedlar and Robin Hood' FL: A pedlar busk and a pedlar thrum. 11

'The bold pedlar and Robin Hood' FL: There chanced to be a pedlar bold. 11

'Bold pedlar and Robin Hood' FL: There was a pedlar and a pedlar bold. 11

'Bold Robbington' FL: As I walked out one evening down by the strawberry lane. 11

Bold Robin he marched the forest along see 'Robin Hood and the widow's three sons'

'Bold Robin Hood and the pedlar' FL: What have you got, you pedlar trim? 11

Bold Robin Hood marched along the highway see 'Bold Robin Hood rescuing the three squires'

Bold Robin Hood ranged the forest all around see 'Robin Hood and the three squires'

'Bold Robin Hood rescuing the three

squires' FL: Bold Robin Hood
marched along the highway. 11
'Bold Robin' FL: Bold Robing hood
one morning he stood. 11
'Bold Robing Hood' FL: Bold Robing Hood and Little John. 11
'The bold soldier' FL: Soldier,
oh soldier, a-comin' from the
plain FLC: Fa-la-la Fa-la-la.
57
'The bold soldier' FL: There was
a bold soldier, from Dover he
came. 11
'The bold volunteer' FL: Here's to
the squire that goes on parade
FLC: Let mirth appear, every
heart cheer. 8
'Bolender Martin' FL: There lived
three brothers in fair Scotland.
11
'Boll Weevil' FL: The boll weevil
is a little bug. 72
'Boll Weevil' FL: The boll weevil
is a little black bug. 4
'The boll weevil' FL: The boll
weevil is a little black bug.
FLC: Just a-lookin' for a
home. 19
'De boll weevil' FL: Oh de boll
weevil am a little black bug.
66
'The boll weevil' FL: Oh the boll
weevil is a little black bug.
57, 67
'Boll weevil blues' FL: Farmer
asked the boll weevil'. 57
The boll weevil is a little bug
see 'Boll Weevil'
'The boll weevil song' FL: Oh,
the boll weevil is a little
black bug. 1, 23, 25
'The bombardment of Bristol'
FL: In seventeen hundred
seventy-five. 55
Bon soir le maitre et la mai-
tresse, et tout le monde du
logis see 'La Gui-Annee'
'Boney' FL: Boney was a warrior.
57
Bonie see entries spelled
Bonny
'The bonnets of Bonny Dundee'
FL: To the Lords of Conven-
tion twas Claver'se who spoke
FLC: Come fill up my cup,
come fill up my can. 25
Bonnie see entries spelled
Bonny

'Bonnie Annie' FL: There was a
rich merchant who lived in
Strathdinah. 11
'Bonny Baby Livingston' FL: Bonny
Anny Livieston. 11
'The bonny banks of Virgie-o' FL:
Three young ladies went out for
a walk. 11, 30
'Bonny Barbara Allan' FL: It was in
about the Martinmas time. 11
'Bonny black Bess' FL: When For-
tune's blind goddess had fled my
abode. 43
'The bonnie blue flag' Harry McCar-
thy. FL: We are a band of
brothers and native to the soil
FLC: Hurrah, hurrah, for
Southern rights hurrah. 1, 25
'The bonny bows o' London' FL:
There were twa sisters in a
bower. 11
'The bonny brown girl' FL: I am
as brown as brown can be, my
eyes are black as a sloe. 7
The bonney brute from the cattle
chute see 'The big corral'
'The bonny bushy broom' FL: A
wager, a wager, a wager I will
lay. 11, 22
Bonnie Charlie's now awa' see
'Will ye no come back again?'
'The bonny Earl of Murray' FL:
Ye Highlands and ye Lawlands.
11, 57
'Bonnie Eloise' FL: Oh, sweet is
the vale where the Mohawk gently
glides FLC: But sweeter, dearer,
yes dearer far than these. 25
'Bonnie George Campbell' FL: Hie
upon Hielands, and laigh upon
Tay. 11
'The bonny green woods' FL: A
gentleman to a young lady said.
11
'The bonny house o' Airlie' FL: It
fell on a day, a bonny simmer
day. 11
'The bonny house o' Airlie' FL: It
was a solemn day as ever you
did see. 11
'Bonnie house of Airlie' FL: It fell
on a day, a bonny summer day.
11
'Bonny house of Airly' FL: O gley'd
Argyle has written to Montrose.
11.
'The bonny labouring boy' FL: As
I roved out one evening all in

the blooming spring. 30
'Bonny lad, Highland lad' FL: Do
you wish to know her age, bonny lad, Highland lad. 9, 11
'Bonnie lassie I'll lie near ye' FL:
A trooperlad cam' owre the lea
FLC: Bonnie lassie, I'll lie
near ye yet. 11
Bonnie lassie, I'll lie near ye yet
see 'Trooper and maid'
'Bonnie Lizzie Lindsay' FL: There
was a braw ball in Edinbro'.
11
Bonny Maisry's to the yowe buchts
gane see 'The broom of Cow-
den-Knowes'
'Bonny Mary' FL: It was on an
evening sae saft and sae clear.
11
'Bonnie Mary is to the ewebuchts
gane' FL: Bonny Mary to the
Ewe buchts did gang. 11
'Bonny Mary of Argyle' FL: I
have heard the maves singing his
lovesong to the morn. 25
Bonnie Mary to the ewebuchts has
gane see 'The broom of Cow-
dinknowes'
Bonnie Mary to the ewe-bughts is
gane see 'The ewe-bughts'
Bonny May went out one day see
'The cunning clerk'
Bonny Meg went out one day see
'The keach in the creel'
'The bonnie ship the Diamond' FL:
The Diamond is a ship my lads,
for the Davis Strait she's bound
FLC: So it's cheer up, my lads,
let your hearts never fail. 57
'Bonnie Susie Cleland' FL: Her
father dragged her to the stake.
11
'The bonniest lass' Robert Burns.
FL: The bonniest lass that ye
meet neist. 57
'Boo-hoo' Edward Heyman, Carmen
Lombardo, and John J. Loeb.
FL: Boo-hoo, You've got me
crying for you. 59
'Bookends' Paul Simon FL: Time
it was and what a time it was.
60
Booted and spurred and bridled
rode he see 'James Campbell'
'Boothbay whale' FL: It was way
up north in Boothbay harbor
FLC: Blow hi for his black
head. 57

'The border ruffian' FL: Said Lord
Douglas to his lady. 11
'The border ruffian' FL: Said the
lord to his lady. 11
'The border widow's lament' FL:
My love built me a bonnie bower.
11
Born a poor young country boy see
'Mother Nature's son'
Born from a world of tyrants, be-
neath the western sky see 'Free
America'
'Born to lose' Ted Daffan. FL:
Born to lose, I've lived my life
in vain. 10
'Borrow love and go' FL: She may
be old, ninety years FLC: She
got to borrow love and go. 57
The boss came up to me with a
five dollar bill see 'Get thee
behind me, Satan'
The boss gets on my nerves see
'The gentleman is a dope'
The bosses are taking it on the
chin, parley-vous see 'Hinky
Dinky Parlez vous'
'Boston burglar' FL: Oh I was born
in Boston, a city you all know
well. 57
'The Boston massacre' FL: Unhappy
Boston, see thy sons deplore. 8
'Boston tea tax song' T. Comer.
FL: I snum I am a Yankee lad.
55, 57
'Botany Bay' FL: Come all ye young
men of learning. 23, 57
'Botany Bay' FL: Oh, there's Glas-
gow and Berwick and Pentonville
FLC: Oh, too-ra-ly, too-ra-ly,
oo-ra-ly. 25
The boughs do shake and the bells
do ring see 'Harvest song'
'Bound down to Derry' FL: Come
all you good people, I hope you'll
draw near. 30
'Bound for the Promised Land' FL:
On Jordan's stormy banks I
stand FLC: I am bound for the
Promised Land. 57
'Bound to ride' FL: Coming down
from Tennessee FLC: Honey babe,
I'm bound to ride. 14
'Bouquet of roses' Steve Nelson and
Bob Hilliard. FL: I'm sending
you a big bouquet of roses. 10
'Bow and balance' FL: There was
an old woman lived on the sea-
shore FLC: And I'll be true to

my love. 57
Bow down, O Lord, thine ear
    see 'Southwel new'
Bow down your head, and cry,
    poor boy see 'Poor Boy'
'The Bowery' Charles H. Hoyt
    and Percy Gaunt FL: Oh, the
    night that I struck New York
    FLC: The Bowery, the Bowery.
    20, 25, 57
'Bowling Green' FL: Wish I was
    in Bowling Green. 57
'The boxer' Paul Simon. FL:
    I am just a poor boy. 60
'The boy and the coo' FL: The
    boy went away with the cow in
    his hand. 11
'The boy and the cow' FL: Come
    all nearby me the truth I'll
    declare. 11
'The boy and the cow' FL: There
    was a rich farmer in York-
    shire did dwell. 11
A boy found a dream upon a dis-
    tant shore see 'Amapola'
The boy took his augur and over-
    board he jumped see 'The
    Golden Vanity'
The boy took the cow by the horn
    with his hand see 'The York-
    shire bite'
The boy went away with the cow
    in his hand see 'The boy and
    the coo'
'The boy with the auburn hair'
    FL: It was on a summer's
    morning all in the month of
    May. 36
Boy, you're gonna carry that
    weight, carry that weight a
    long time see 'Carry that
    weight'
'Boys around here' FL: The boys
    around here, they think them-
    selves men. 7
'A boy's best friend is his
    mother' Henry Miller and
    Joseph P. Skelly. FL: While
    plodding on our way, the toil-
    some road of life FLC: Then
    cherish her with care. 63
'The boys in blue' FL: The office
    had just opened up. 50
'Boys, keep your powder dry' FL:
    Can'st tell who lost the battle
    FLC: Not they who are deter-
    mined. 25
The boys watch the girls see

'Music to watch girls by'
'Brady' FL: Down in St. Louis at
    Twelfth and Carr FLC: Brady,
    why didn't you run. 57
'The braes of Yarrow' FL: Busk ye,
    busk ye, my bonny, bonny bride.
    11
'The brake o' briars' FL: Tis of a
    brisk and country lady! 22
Brand new state see 'Oklahoma'
'Brandy and water' Julien Carle.
    FL: O here's success to Brandy
    FLC: Here's success to Brandy.
    36
'Brangywell' FL: As Brangywell
    went forth to plough. 11
'The brass mounted army' FL: O
    whisky is the monster that ruins
    great and small FLC: O how do
    you like the army? 57
'The brave Earl Brand and the King
    of England's daughter' FL: O did
    you ever hear of the brave Earl
    Brand. 11
'Brave old Anthony Marala' FL:
    The devil he came to his house
    one day. 11
'Brave Paulding and the spy' FL:
    Come all you brave Americans
    and unto me give ear. 55
'A brave soldier' FL: Oh, I'll tell
    you of a soldier who lately came
    from war. 11
'Brave Wolfe' FL: Bad news had
    come to town, bad news is car-
    ried. 57
'Brave Wolfe' FL: Come all you
    young men all. 55, 65
'Bravo, Dublin Fusiliers' G. D.
    Wheeler. FL: Some dare to say
    that Irishmen should refuse to
    fight for Britain's crown FLC:
    Bravo, Dublin Fusiliers, you're
    not craven mutineers. 69
'Brazil' Ary Barroso. FL: Brasil,
    meu Brasil Brasileiro me mulato
    inzoneiro FLC: O abre a cortina
    do passado. 9
'Brazil' Ary Barroso. FL: Brasil,
    tierra buena y hermosa FLC:
    Oh, esas palmeras murmurantes.
    9
'Brazil' Ary Barroso and S. K.
    Russell. FL: Brazil, the Brazil
    that I knew FLC: Brazil, where
    hearts were entertaining June. 9
'Bread and roses' Caroline Kohlsaat,
    James Oppenheim and Martha

Coleman. FL: As we come
marching, marching in the
beauty of the day. 19, 57, 58

'Break the news to mother'
Charles K. Harris and Joseph
Clouder. FL: While the shot
and shell were screaming FLC:
Just break the news to mother.
20

Breakin' up big rocks on uh chain
gang see 'Work song'

'The breeze and I' Al Stillman
and Ernesto Lecuona. FL:
Ours was a love song that
seemed constant as the moon
FLC: The breeze and I are saying with a sigh. 9, 12

The breezes went steadily through
the tall pines see 'Hale in
the bush'; 'Nathan Hale'

'Brennan on the Moor' FL: It's
about a brave young highwayman my story I will tell FLC:
Oh, it's Brennan on the Moor.
23, 25

'Brennan on the Moor' FL: Tis
of a brave young highwayman
this story I will tell FLC: It
was Brennan on the moor. 57

'The briary bush' FL: O hangman
hold thy hand. 11

'Bricks in my pillow' FL: I've
got bricks in my pillow and
my head can't rest no more.
57

'Bridge over troubled water' Paul
Simon. FL: When you're weary,
feelin' small. 60, 64

'Bright dawns the day' FL: Bright
dawns the day with rosy face.
3

'Bright Phoebus' FL: Bright
Phoebus has mounted the chariot of day. 3

Bright Sol at length by Thetis
wooed see 'Lovely Stella'

'Bright sparkles in the church-
yard' FL: May the Lord, He
will be glad of me. 38

Brightest and best of the sons of
the morning see 'Star in the
East'

Bring back, bring back see
'My Bonnie'; 'My bonny lies
over the ocean'

'Bring me back the one I love'
FL: Oh, bring me back the
one I love FLC: If I was a

little bird, a darling little bird
I'd be. 7

Bring the cup see 'A blessing on
brandy and beer'

Bring the good old bugle, boys,
we'll sing another song see
'Marching through Georgia'

Bring your sleds to the coasting
hill see 'Winter fun'

'Bringing in that New Jerusalem'
FL: I've got a mother who's gone
to glory FLC: It's all free grace
and never-dying love. 29

'The brisk young bachelor' FL:
Once I was a brisk young bachelor FLC: With my whack fal lor,
the diddle and the dido. 57, 58

'Brisk young farmer' FL: I'll tell
you about a brisk young farmer.
50

'The British grenadiers' FL: Some
talk of Alexander. 25

'The British light infantry' FL: For
battle prepared in their country's
just cause. 49, 55

Britons always loyally declaim about
the way we rule the waves see
'Soldiers of the Queen'

Brocher shout your country's anthem see 'Hymn for nations'

'Broke and Hungry' FL: I am broke
and hungry, ragged and dirty too.
57

'The broke-down brakeman' FL:
Twas a very cold night in December. 50

'Bronco buster' FL: One day I
thought I'd have some fun. 62

'The broom blooms bonie' FL: It's
whispered in parlor, it's whispered in ha'. 11

'Broom, green broom' FL: There
was an old man, and he lived in
a wood. 25

'The broom of Cowden-Knowes' FL:
Bonny Maisry's to the yowe
buchts gane. 11

'The broom of Cowdenknowes' FL:
Bonnie Mary to the ewebuchts has
gane. 11

'Broom of Cowdenknows' FL: How
blyth ilk morn was I to see. 11

'The broom of Cowdenknowes' FL:
Mary to the yowe-buchts has
gane. 11

'The Broomfield Hill' FL: A wage a
love a wager, and go along with
me. 11

11

'The brown girl' FL: There was a young maiden. 11

'The brown girl' FL: A young Irish lady from London she came. 11

'Brown Robin' FL: The king but and his nobles a'. 11

'Brown sugar' Mick Jagger and Keith Richard. FL: Gold Coast slave ship FLC: Brown sugar. 16

'Brown's ferry blues' FL: Hard luck poppa a countin' his toes. 35, 56, 57

'Bruton Fair' FL: When hazel boughs be yellow. 22

Buck Creek girl, don't you want to go to Cripple Creek see 'Cripple Creek'

'Buck-eye Jim' FL: Way up yonder above the moon. 66

'Bucking Broncho' FL: My love is a rider, wild bronchos he breaks. 2

'Bucking Bronco' FL: My love is a cowboy. 62

'Bucking Bronco' FL: My love is a vaquero. 62

'Buddy, won't you roll down the line' FL: Way back yonder in Tennessee they leased the convicts out FLC: Buddy, won't you roll down the line. 57

'Buff the Quilt' FL: As the duke's fair daughter of Scotland was out riding one day. 11

'Buffalo boy' FL: When are we gonna get married, married, married. 57, 68

'Buffalo gals' FL: As I was lumbering down the street FLC: Buffalo gals, can't you come out tonight. 4

'Buffalo gals' FL: As I was walking down the street FLC: Buffalo gals, won't you come out tonight. 1, 2, 34, 57

'Buffalo gals' FL: Buffalo gals, won't you come out tonight. 25

'The buffalo skinners' FL: Come all you jolly buffalo hunters and listen to my song. 62

'Buffalo skinners' FL: Come all you old time cowboys and listen to my song. 57

'The buffalo skinners' FL: Twas in the town of Jacksboro in the spring of '73. 19, 57, 66

'Buffalo skinners, or range of the buffalo' FL: Twas in the town of Jacksboro. 2

'Bugel call rag' Jack Pettis, Billy Meyers and Elmer Schoebel. FL: You're bound to fall for the bugle call FLC: Hold me, baby. 12, 54

'Build a brick house' FL: I went downtown to build a brick house FLC: Fare you well, my darling girl. 37

'Bull riders in the sky' FL: An old cowpoke went riding to a rodeo one day FLC: Yippie-i-o, yippie-i-ay, bull riders in the sky. 43

'Bulldog and the bullfrog' FL: Oh, the bulldog on the bank FLC: Singing, tra la la la la la. 57

'The bullgine run' FL: Oh the smartest clipper you can find FLC: To my hey rig-a-jig in a low-back car. 57

'The bully of the town' Charles E. Trevathan. FL: Have you heard about the bully that's just come to town FLC: When I walk that levee round. 57

A bully ship and a bully crew, dooda, dooda see 'On the banks of the Sacramento'

'The bully song' Charles E. Trevatham. FL: Have you heard about that bully that's just come to town FLC: When I a-walk that levee. 1

A bunch of foaming mustangs see 'Keep your saddle tight'

A bunch of jolly cowboys were discussing plans at ease see 'When the work's all done this fall'

Bunda, bunda, bunda, bunda see 'Saraponda'

'Bunker Hill' FL: Twas break of day the 17th, the Yankees did surprise us. 8

'Bunker Hill' Nathaniel Niles and Andrew Law. FL: Why should vain mortals tremble. 1, 49

'Burd Helen' FL: Burd Helen was her mother's dear. 11

'Burd Isbel and Sir Patrick' FL: Sir Patrick dressed in best array. 11

'The burglar' FL: I'm just like an owl that flies by night. 11

'Burgoyne's defeat' FL: Here followeth the dire fate. 8

'The burial of the linnet' J. H.
Ewing and Alfred Scott-Gatty.
FL: Found in the garden, dead
in his beauty. 63

'The burly, burly banks of Barbro-o' FL: There were three
sisters picking flowers. 11

'Burmese tune' FL: I crave your
notice for a time, pray listen
to my song FLC: Then come
along, my hearties, together
we will ride. 69

'Burning bridges' Walter Scott.
FL: Found some letters you
wrote me this morning FLC:
Burning bridges behind me.
10

'The burning o' Auchendoun' FL:
As I cam' in by Fiddich Side.
11

'La burriquita' FL: Ya viene la
burriquita. 51

'The burrowing Yankees' FL:
Ye Yankees who, mole-like,
still throw up the earth. 8,
55

'Bury me beneath the willow'
FL: My heart is sad and I am
lonely FLC: Bury me beneath
the willow. 57

'Bury me not on the lone prairie'
FL: Oh, bury me not on the
lone prairie. 57

Buscando posada see 'Aguinaldo'

'A bushel and a peck' Frank Loesser. FL: I love you a bushel
and a peck. 6

Busk ye, busk ye, my bonny
bonny bride see 'The braes
of Yarrow'

Busted flat in Baton Rouge see
'Me and Bobby McGee'

But all that seems distant and
all that seems far see
'Shootin' with Rasputin'

But along came Bill see 'Bill'

But black is the color of my
true love's hair see 'Black
is the color'

But hurrah for Lane County, the
land of the free see 'The
Lane County Bachelor'

But I can't help but wonder where
I'm bound see 'Where I'm
bound'

But I won't be a nun, no see

'I won't be a nun'

But I'll stand interference no longer
see 'I'll get rid of my mother-
in-law'

But I'm on the water wagon now
see 'I'm on the water wagon
now'

But I'm sorry to say mine wife's
gone avay see 'I love me mine
vife'

But I've got to creep down the alleyway see 'Somewhere they can't
find me'

'But not for me' George and Ira
Gershwin. FL: Old Man Sunshine, listen, you FLC: They're
writing songs of love. 21, 46

But oh! Flo! such a change you
know see 'And her golden hair
was hanging down her back'

But sweeter, dearer, yes dearer
far than these see 'Bonnie
Eloise'

But sweetheart tell me why see
'Say "sí sí"'

But the cat came back see 'The
cat came back'

But the cat came back the very next
day see 'The cat came back'

But the poor girl didn't know see
'Poor gal didn't know'

But they came rolling down the
mountain see 'The West Virginny hills'

But we have a glowing dream see
'The commonwealth of toil'

But when you're crying see 'When
you're smiling'

'The butcher boy' FL: In London
city where I did dwell. 7, 41

'The butcher boy' FL: She went upstairs to make her bed. 57

'Butt-cut ruler' FL: Don't you walk
on down. 28

'Button up your overcoat' G. B. G.
De Sylva, Lew Brown and Ray
Henderson. FL: Listen, big boy
FLC: Button up your overcoat.
42

Button up your waistcoat see
'Rollicking rams'

'Button Willow tree' FL: The puncher being cold, he went up to bed
FLC: It's home to you home,
wherever you may be. 43

'Buttons and bows' Jay Livingston
and Ray Evans. FL: A western
ranch is just a branch FLC: East

is east and west is west. 70
By and by we'll all go down see
'Come, let us all go down'
By Clyde's bonny banks where I
sadly did wander see 'The
Blantyre explosion'
By Kilarney lakes and fells see
'Killarney'
By my faith, but I think you're
all makers of bulls see 'The
Irishman's epistle'; 'The Irish-
man's epistle to the officers
and troops at Boston'; 'To the
troops in Boston'
'By Strauss' George and Ira
Gershwin. FL: Away with the
music of Broadway FLC: When
I want a melody lilting through
the house. 21
By the high Sierras I wait now,
Cielito Lindo see 'Cielito
Lindo'
By the lake with lily flowers see
'Gomper'
'By the light of moonshine' FL:
same. 48
'By the silvery Rio Grande' FL:
In the lone star state of Texas
by the silvery Rio Grande. 57
'By the time I get to Phoenix'
Jimmy Webb. FL: By the time
I get to Phoenix she'll be risin'.
71
'By the waters of Minnetonka' J.
M. Cavanass and Thurlow Lieu-
rance. FL: Moon Deer, how
near your soul divine. 1
By yon bonnie banks and by yon
bonnie braes see 'Loch Lo-
mond'
'Bye, baby bunting' FL: same. 48
'Bye bye blackbird' Mort Dixon
and Ray Henderson. FL: Blackbird, blackbird, singing the
blues all day FLC: Pack up all
my care and woe. 46
'Byker Hill' FL: Oh, if I had another penny FLC: Byker Hill
and Walker Shore. 57

- C -

'C. C. Rider' FL: C. C. Rider,
just see what you have done. 57
'C. C. Rider' FL: C. C. Rider,
Oh what am I to do? 23
'C. C. Rider' FL: C. C. Rider,

see wha you have done. 67
CON with a con see 'Constanti-
nople'
'Cabaret' Fred Ebb and John Kan-
der. FL: No use permitting
some prophet of doom FLC:
What good is sitting alone in
your room? 6, 42
'The cabin boy' FL: Thus he spoke,
the captain of the ship. 11
'The caissons go rolling along'
Edmund L. Gruber. FL: Over
hill, over dale FLC: For it's hi
hi hee. 1, 25
'Calcutta' Lee Pockriss, Paul J.
Vance and Heino Gaze. FL: I've
kissed the girls of Naples. 47,
52
'Calen o custore me' FL: same. 25
'California dreamin'' John Phillips.
FL: I'd be safe and warm, if I
were in L.A. FLC: All the
leaves are brown. 45
'California here I come' Al Jolson,
Bud de Sylva and Joseph Meyer.
FL: When the wintery winds are
blowing FLC: California here I
come. 46
The California people are determined if they find see 'Rich
banker thieves'
'The California stage' FL: There's
no respect for youth or age FLC:
They started as a thieving line.
25
Call all hands to man the capstan
see 'Rolling home'
'Call on me' S. Andrew. FL: Well,
baby, when times are bad. 15
Call Sister, brother, to my side
see 'Dear Mother, I've come
home to die'
'Caller herrin'' Lady Nairne. FL:
When ye were sleepin' on your
pillows FLC: Who'll buy my caller herrin. 25, 72
'The Calton weaver' FL: I'm a
weaver, a Calton weaver FLC:
Oh, whiskey, whiskey, Nancy
Whiskey. 57
'The cambric shirt' FL: As I walked
out in a shady grove. 11
'The cambric shirt' FL: As you go
through Yandro's town. 11
'The cambric shirt' FL: Come buy
me a cambric shirt. 11
'The cambric shirt' FL: Madam,
will you make me a cambric

I'm Captain Jinks of the Horse
Marines FLC: same. 1, 36,
57
'Captain Kidd' FL: Oh my name
is Captain Kidd. 57
'Captain Markee' FL: There was
three brothers in merry Scot-
land. 11
'Captain Ward' FL: Come all you
gallant seamen bold, all you
that marchy drum. 11
'Captain Ward and the rainbow'
FL: Come all ye jolly mariners.
11
'Captain Ward and the rainbow' FL:
Come all you jolly sailors bold.
11
'Captain Ward and the rainbow' FL:
Our king built a ship, twas a
ship of great fame. 11
'Captain Wedderburn' FL: The laird
of Roslin's daughter. 11
'Captain Wedderburn's Courtship'
FL: As the duke's fair daughter
of Scotland was riding out one
day. 11
'Captain Wedderburn's courtship'
FL: A gentleman's fair daughter
walked down yon narrow lane.
11
'Captain Wedderburn's courtship'
FL: A lady fair one May morn-
ing. 11
'Captain Wedderburn's courtship'
FL: The laird o' Roslin's daugh-
ter walked through the wood her
lane. 11
'Captain Wedderburn's Courtship'
FL: O what is greener than the
grass. 30
'Captain Wedderburn's courtship'
FL: O, what is rounder than a
ring? 11
'Captain Wedderburn's courtship'
FL: One of fair Scotland's daugh-
ters. 30
'Captain Wedderburn's courtship'
FL: Three questions I will give
to you. 11
Captain, will you just spare me
one more day see 'Go down
old Hannah'
Captain, wo Lord see 'Believe
I'll call the rider'
'Captain Woodstock' FL: As I rode
out one May morning. 11
'The captain's shanty' FL: I've
been a sailor since my birth

FLC: Lime, scurvy, ambergris
and marmalade. 68
'Capture of Burgoyne' FL: When
Discord did rear her black
standard on high. 65
'The capture of Major Andre' FL:
Come all you brave Americans
and unto me give ear. 8
Caput apri defero see 'Boar's
head carol'
'Cara Mamma Io sono malata' FL:
same FLC: O mamma, no, no,
no. 58
'Caravan' Irving Mills, Duke Ellington, and Juan Tizol. FL: Sleep
upon my shoulder as we creep
FLC: Night and stars above that
shine so bright. 12
'The card song' FL: The king will
take the queen FLC: Here's to
you, Tom Brown. 57
'Careless love' FL: Love, oh love,
oh careless love. 1, 23, 25, 57
'Careless love' FL: O who will shoe
your little feet FLC: Careless,
love, careless love. 11
'Carioca' Edward Eliscu, Gus Kahn,
and Vincent Youmans. FL: Say,
have you seen the carioca. 67
'El Carite' FL: Ayer salió la lancha
Nueva Esparta. 51
'The carnal and the crane' FL: As
I walked out one morning. 11
'Carol of the birds' FL: From out
of the wood did a cuckoo fly. 72
'The carol of the birds' John Jacob
Niles. FL: Oh, manya bird did
wake and fly. 33
Carolina, Carolina, at last they've
got you on the map see
'Charleston'
Carolina gave me Dinah see 'Dinah'
'Carolina in the morning' Gus Kahn
and Walter Donaldson. FL:
Wishing is good time wasted. 46
'Carolina moon' Benny Davis and
Joe Burke. FL: The moon was
shining bright in Carolina FLC:
Carolina moon keep shining. 54
'The carpenter's wife' FL: Well
met, well met, my own true
love. 11
'The carrion crow' FL: A carrion
crow sat on an oak. 48, 72
'Carry me back to Old Virginny'
James A. Bland. FL: same
FLC: same. 1, 25
'Carry that weight' Lennon

The charms of Florimel see 'Florimel'

'The charms of nature' FL: The cheek enrosed with crimson dye. 3

'Chattanooga choo-choo' Mack Gordon and Harry Warren. FL: Pardon me, boy, is that the Chattanooga choo-choo. 59

The cheek enrosed with crimson dye see 'The charms of nature'

'Cheer, boys, cheer!' C. Mackay and H. Russell. FL: Cheer, boys, cheer, no more of idle sorrow. 69

'Cheer up, Buller' F. V. St. Clair. FL: Informer days the British race FLC: Cheer up, Buller, my lad. 69

'Cheerful little earful' Ira Gershwin, Billy Rose and Harry Warren. FL: I'm growing tired of lovey dove theme songs FLC: There's a cheerful little earful. 46

'Chelsea morning' Joni Mitchell. FL: Woke up, it was a Chelsea morning and the first thing that I heard. 45

'Cherish' Terry Kirkman. FL: Cherish is the world I use to describe. 71

'Cherokee' Ray Noble. FL: Sweet Indian maiden. 59

'Cherry ripe' FL: Cherry ripe, cherry ripe, ripe I cry. 25

'The cherry tree' FL: When Joseph was a young man, a young man was he. 7

'The cherry tree carol' FL: As Joseph and Mary were a-walking the green. 11

'The cherry tree carol' FL: As Mary and Joseph was walking through a meadow so fair. 11

'The cherry tree carol' FL: Joseph and Mary FLC: Then sing o the holy, holy. 11

'The cherry tree carol' FL: Joseph was a young man. 11

'The cherry tree carol' FL: Joseph was an old man. 25, 35

'The cherry tree carol' FL: Mary and Joseph together did go. 11

'The cherry tree carol' FL: O,

Joseph was an old man, and an old man was he. 11

'The cherry tree carol' FL: Then Joseph took Mary upon his right knee. 11

'The cherry tree carol' FL: When Joseph was a young man. 11

'Cherry tree carol' FL: When Joseph was an old man. 11, 23, 33, 57

'The cherry tree carol' FL: When Joseph was old and righteous was he. 11

'Chester' William Billings. FL: Let tyrants shake their iron rod. 1, 8, 49, 55, 57, 65

Chestnuts roasting on an open fire see 'The Christmas song'

'Chewing gum' FL: Mama sent me to the spring FLC: Chewing, chewing gum. 57

Chickens a-crowin' on Sourwood Mountain see 'Sourwood Mountain'

'Chickery Chick' Sylvia Dee and Sidney Lippman. FL: Everytime you're sick and tired of the same old thing FLC: Chickery chick chala chala. 67

Chicks and ducks and geese better scurry see 'The surrey with the fringe on top'

'Chil' Brenton' FL: Chil' Brenton has sent o'er the fame. 11

'Child of the moon' Mick Jagger and Keith Richard. FL: The wind blows rain into my face. 16

'Child Waters' FL: I beg you bide at hame, Margaret. 11

'Childe Maurice' FL: Child Norryce was an earl's son. 11

Childhood living is easy to do see 'Wild horses'

'Children, go where I send thee' FL: same. 32, 33

Children go where I send thee see 'Little bitty baby'

'Children we shall be free' FL: We want no cowards in our band FLC: Children, we all shall be free. 38

'Children, you'll be called on' FL: same FLC: When this warfare'll be ended. 38

Chile verde me perdiste see 'Coplas'

'Chilly winds' FL: I'm goin' where the chilly winds don't blow. 57

'Cod-liver oil' FL: I'm a young
married man and I'm tired of
life. 57

'The coerin' blue' FL: I dreamed
a dream jist sin' the strean.
11

The coffee, that they give you,
they say is mighty fine see
'Gee, but I want to go home'

'The coffin to bind me down' FL:
De coffin, de coffin to bind
me down. 5

'Cold blows the wind' FL: Cold
blows the wind o'er my true
love. 11

'Cold blows the wind' FL: Cold
blows the wind on my true
love. 11

'Cold blows the wind' FL: Cold
blows the wind to my true
love. 11

'Cold blows the wind' FL: Cold
blows the wind tonight, sweetheart. 11

'Cold blows the wind' FL: I'll
do so much for my sweetheart.
11

'Cold blows the wind' FL: One
kiss from you, my own sweetheart. 11

'Cold blows the wind' FL: The
wind blows cold today, sweetheart. 11

Cold blows the wind to my true
love see 'Blow away the
morning dew'; 'The unquiet grave'

'Cold, icy hand' FL: O sinner,
sinner, you better pray FLC:
Cryin' O Lord! 5

Cold, no I can't believe your
heart is cold see 'Watch what
happens'

'Cold water' FL: Cold water, cold
water for me. 57

The cold wind swept the mountains
height see 'The snow storm'

'Cold winter's night' FL: I was
roving out one cold winter night.
11

'Cole Younger' FL: I am a noted
highwayman, Cole Younger is
my name. 57

'Cole Younger' FL: I am a reckless highwayman, Cole Younger
is my name. 57

'Collector man blues' FL: Hey,
hey, hey somebody knockin' at
my door. 57

'Collinet and Phebe' FL: As Collinet and Phebe sat. 49, 65

'Colonel Burnaby' W. Stubbs. FL:
Come, listen to my story, lads
FLC: Weep not, my boys, for
those who fell. 69

'The Colorado Trail' FL: Weep all
ye little rains. 57

Colored folks work on the Mississippi see 'Ol' Man River'

'Columbia' Timothy Dwight. FL:
Columbia, Columbia to glory
arise. 3

'Columbus stockade' FL: Way down
in Columbus, Georga FLC: Well,
you can go and leave me if you
want to. 56

'Columbus stockade blues' Jimmie
Davis and Eva Sargent. FL:
Way down in Columbus, Georgia.
14

'Columbus Stockade blues' FL: Way
down in Columbus, Georgia FLC:
Go and leave me if you wish to.
29

'Columbus Stockade blues' FL: Way
down in Columbus, Georgia FLC:
Well you can go and leave me.
57

Coma ti yi youpy, youpy, ya, youpy
ya see 'The old Chisholm trail'

Comb back your hair, Fair Annie,
he said see 'Fair Annie'

Come a fa la ling, come a ling
see 'Devilish Mary'

Come a kludie, come a lingo see
'Dandoo'

Come a landsman, a pensman, a
tinker, or a tailor see 'The
old maid's song'

Come a ti yi yippy yippy yi yippi
yea see 'The old Chisholm
trail'

Come all my boys and listen a song
I'll sing to you see 'The Bigler'

Come all nearby me the truth I'll
declare see 'The boy and the
cow'

Come all of you good workers see
'Which side are you on?'

'Come all ye bold Canadians' FL:
same. 55

Come all ye bold fishermen, listen
to me see 'The fishes'

'Come all ye bold seamen' FL:
Come all ye bold seamen that
goes round Cape Horn. 41

Come all ye brisk young fellows who

have a mind to roam <u>see</u> 'The
lovely Ohio'
Come all ye British heroes' <u>see</u>
'The noble lads of Canada'
'Come all ye fair and tender maid-
ens' FL: same. 23, 25, 57,
58
Come all ye good people, a story
I'll tell <u>see</u> 'Will sold the
cow'
Come all ye good people and listen
to me <u>see</u> 'Let me rove free'
Come all ye jolly fellows, how
would you like to go <u>see</u>
'Canaday-i-o'
Come all ye jolly lumbermen and
listen to my song <u>see</u>
'Canada-i-o'
Come all ye jolly mariners <u>see</u>
'Captain Ward and the rainbow'
Come all ye jolly sportsmen who
to hunt the fox <u>see</u> 'Tom
Reynard'
Come, all ye ladies, great and
small <u>see</u> 'Sweet William'
Come all ye lads of courage bold
and listen to my song <u>see</u>
'Ceylon Ballad'
Come all ye railroad section
men <u>see</u> 'Jerry, go and oil
that car'
Come all ye sons of freedom
throughout the state of Maine
<u>see</u> 'The logger's boast'
Come all ye sons of song <u>see</u>
'An ode for the 4th of July'
Come all ye spacemen in if you
want to hear <u>see</u> 'Spacey
Jones'
Come all ye Texas Rangers
wherever you may be <u>see</u>
'The Texas rangers'
Come all ye to the wilderness
<u>see</u> 'The seven blessings of
Mary'
Come all ye true born shanty boys
<u>see</u> 'The jam on Gerry's rock'
Come all ye valiant soldiers, a
story I will tell <u>see</u> 'The
battle on Shiloh's Hill'
'Come all ye Western cowboys'
FL: Come all ye western cow-
boys, bound on this sober land.
43
Come, all ye young and foolish
lads <u>see</u> 'Katie Morey'
Come all ye young fellows that fol-
low the sea <u>see</u> 'Blow the man

down'
Come all ye young men of learning
<u>see</u> 'Botany Bay'
Come all ye young people I pray
you draw near <u>see</u> 'Durie Down'
Come all ye young sailormen, listen
to me <u>see</u> 'Blow, ye winds,
westerly'
Come all ye youths whose hearts
bled <u>see</u> 'Castalio's complaint'
Come all you beggars of Paris
town <u>see</u> 'Song of the vagabonds'
Come all you bold Britons, wherever
you may be <u>see</u> 'An invitation
to North America'
Come all you bold sailors that follow the lakes <u>see</u> 'Red iron
ore'
Come all you booze buyers if you
want to hear <u>see</u> 'Kentucky
bootlegger'
Come all you brave American and
unto me give ear <u>see</u> 'Brave
Paulding and the spy'; 'The capture of Major Andre'
Come all you brave soldiers, both
valiant and free <u>see</u> 'Independ-
ence Day'; 'On independence'
Come all you Christian people,
wherever you may be <u>see</u>
'Charles Guiteau'
Come all you fair and tender ladies
<u>see</u> 'Katey Morey'; 'Rue'
Come all you gallant British hearts
<u>see</u> 'Paddy's resource'
Come all you gallant poachers that
ramble void of care <u>see</u> 'Van
Dieman's Land'
Come all you gallant seamen bold,
all you that marchy drum <u>see</u>
'Captain Ward'
Come all you good fellers wherever
you be <u>see</u> 'Blue Mountain
Lake'
Come all you good people, I hope
you'll draw near <u>see</u> 'Bound
down to Derry'
Come all you good People, I pray
pay attention <u>see</u> 'The nobleman's wedding'
Come all you good people, I pray
you draw near <u>see</u> 'A restless
night'
Come all you good people where'er
you be <u>see</u> 'The dying British
sergeant'
Come all you jolly buffalo hunters
and listen to my song <u>see</u> 'The

buffalo skinners'

Come all you jolly cowboys see 'The dreary life'

Come all you jolly jokers, if you want to have some fun see 'The great American bum'

Come all you jolly sailors bold see 'Captain Ward and the rainbow'

Come all you loyal unionists wherever you may be see 'Virginia's bloody soil'

Come, all you lusty northern lads see 'A lamentable ditty on the death of Geordie'

'Come, all you maids of honor' FL: same. 11

Come all you melancholy folks, wherever you may be see 'Old-time cowboy'

Come all you old time cowboys and listen to my song see 'Buffalo skinners'

Come all you people young and old see 'The rose of Britain's Isle'

Come all you roving cowboys, bound on the western plains see 'Lee's ferry'

Come all you sons of Erin, attention now I crave see 'Morrissey and the Russian sailor'

Come all you sporting bachelors see 'The sporting bachelors'

Come all you valiant seamen bold, with courage beat your drum see 'Ward, the pirate'

Come all you young and gentle ladies, be careful how you court men see 'Young Ladies'

Come all you young companions see 'Bad company'

Come all you young fellows so young and so fine see 'Dark as a dungeon'

Come all you young gallants, take delight in a gun see 'Shooting of his dear'

Come all you young men all see 'Brave Wolfe'

Come all you young rebels and listen while I sing see 'The patriot game'

Come all you young waddies, I'll sing you a song see 'Punchin' the dough'

'Come along' FL: I was but young when I begun FLC: Come along, come along. 5

Come along boys, and listen to my tale see 'The old Chisholm Trail'

Come along, come along see 'Get up, Jack'

Come along get you ready see 'A hot time in the old town'; 'There'll be a hot time'

Come along, girls, and listen to my noise see 'The Tex-i-an boys'

Come along, little children come along see 'Raise a ruckus'; 'Raise a ruckus tonight'

Come along, my brother, come along see 'Dem charming bells'

Come and bathe my forehead, Mother see 'Put my little shoes away'

'Come and go with me' FL: Come and go with me to that land. 34, 57

Come and meet those dancing feet see 'Forty-second Street'

Come and sit by my side if you love me see 'Red River Valley'

'Come and take tea in the arbour' J. Beuler. FL: What pleasure folks feel, when they live out of town. 36

Come and worship see 'Angels, from the realms of glory'

Come arise my bonnie lassie see 'Low low lands of Holland'

Come away to the skies, my beloved see 'Exultation'

Come away with me Lucile see 'In my merry Oldsmobile'

Come back Nanny to your simple Sammy see 'Nanny'

'Come back to Erin' FL: Come back to Erin, Mavoureen, Mavoureen. 25

Come bridle me up my milk white steed see 'Georgy O'

Come, Brother Green, and stay with me see 'Brother Green'

Come, brother, sisters, don't fall asleep see 'Take me in your lifeboat'

Come buy me come buy me a cambric shirt see 'The cambric shirt'

Come buy of poor Kate primroses I sell see 'The primrose girl'; 'Primroses'

Come, come, come and make eyes with me see 'Under the

Anheuser Bush'

Come, come, my children, I must see see 'The schoolmaster'

'Come down, angels' FL: I love to shout, I love to sing FLC: Come down, angels, trouble the water. 38

Come down, come down from that dreary gallows see 'The gallows tree'

Come, each death dog who dares venture his neck see 'Hot stuff'

'Come, every angel' Marlys Swinger. FL: Come, every angel, to the stall. 13

'Come, fair one, be kind' George Farquhar and Richard Leveridge. FL: same. 40

'Come, fair Rosina' Francis Hopkinson. FL: Come, fair Rosina, come away. 65

Come, Father, come Father, come riddle this riddle see 'Lord Thomas and Fair Ellender'

Come father, come father riddle to me see 'Lord Thomas and Fair Ellender'

Come father, come mother, come riddle my riddle see 'Lord Thomas'

Come fill up my cup, come fill up my can see 'The bonnets of Bonny Dundee'

'Come follow' FL: Come follow, follow, follow, follow. 34, 57

Come for a run by the silver sea see 'On silver sands'

Come, frontier men, awake now see 'The Indian's over the border'

Come gather round me boys and I'll tell you a tale see 'The Old Chisholm Trail'

Come gentlemen and ladies all see 'Kitty O Noory'

Come here, come here, ye freely freed see 'Kempion'

'Come here fellow servant' James Townley and Jonathan Battishell. FL: Come here, fellow servant and listen to me. 40

Come hither, my country squire see 'The modern beau'

'Come home, Father' Henry Clay Work. FL: Father, dear father, come home with me now FLC:

Hear the sweet voice of the child. 63

Come in, come in, Lord Henry, said she see 'Lord Henry'

Come in, come in, loving Henry, come in see 'Loving Henry'

Come in, come in, loving Henry, said she see 'Young Hunting'

Come in, come in, my old true love see 'Young Hunting'

Come in, come in, my own true love see 'The house carpenter'; 'Young Hunting'

Come in, come in, my pretty little bird see 'Pretty Polly or the Scotland man'

Come in, come in, my pretty little boy see 'Young Hunting'

'Come into the garden, Maud' Alfred Tennyson and M. W. Balfe. FL: same. 63

Come join hand in hand, brave Americans all see 'In freedom we're born'; 'The liberty song'

'Come join the huckleberry picnic' FL: When Angel Gabriel blows his horn FLC: Come join the huckleberry picnic, for it's gonna take place today. 7

Come jolly sons of liberty see 'A song to the sons of liberty'

Come, lads, your glasses fill with glee see 'Huzza for liberty'

'Come landlord fill the flowing bowl' FL: same. 25

'Come, let us all go down' FL: As I went down in the valley to pray FLC: By and by we'll all go down. 38

'Come, let us join the roundelay' William Beale. FL: same. 63

Come let us meet when daylight sets see 'The cat's grand concert'

Come list ye landsmen, all to me see 'The crocodile'

Come, listen, all you gals and boys see 'Jump Jim Crow'

Come listen and I'll tell you how first I went to sea see 'The Yankee privateer'

Come listen, come listen my good people all see 'The false-hearted knight'

Come, listen to my story, lads see 'Colonel Burnaby'

Come, listen unto me and a story I shall tell see 'The robber song'

'Come, little leaves' George Cooper. FL: Come, little leaves, said the wind one day. 13

Come live with me and be my love see 'The passionate shepherd to his love'

Come loose every sail to the breeze see 'Homeward bound'

Come, love, come, the boat lies low see 'Nancy Till'

Come lower your reef and come lay your ship too see 'Hendry Martin'

'Come, Mother' FL: Come, mother, come, mother, come make up my bed. 11

'Come, Mother, Mother, make my bed' FL: Now I pray you go fetch me my little footboy. 11

'Come, my brother' FL: Come, my brother, nearer, nearer. 41

'Come, my Celia' Ben Jonson and Alfonso Ferrabosco. FL: Come, my Celia, let us prove. 26

Come, my love, and go with me see 'Razors in the air'

Come, my sisters, come, my brother see 'Sung at harvest time'

Come near, come near me now, dear mother see 'Lord Thomas and Fair Ellanor'

Come, neighbors, I'll sing you a song see 'The silly old man'

'Come now all ye social powers' FL: same. 3

Come now all you good people see 'The dragoon and the lady'

Come now brave boys, we're on for marching see 'Love farewell'

'Come, o my love' FL: The winter has gone and the leaves turn green. 57

Come old and young and hear me tell see 'Tobacco Union'

Come on brave boys, let us be brave see 'A song made upon the foregoing occasion'

Come on, come on, come on, come on see 'Piece of my heart'

'Come on down to my boat' Wes Farrell and Jerry Goldstein. FL: Come on down to my boat, baby. 47

Come on, girls see 'Domestic workers' song'

Come on, my hearts of tempered steel and leave your girls and farms see 'Fare thee well, you sweethearts'

Come on, sister, with you ups and down see 'Listen to the lambs'

Come on, you children, gather around see 'Clap yo' hands'

'Come out! Come out!' Gladys Wolfe and Kees Kooper. FL: Come out! come out to hear the call. 13

'Come out, ye Continentalers' FL: Come out, ye Continentalers, we're going for to go. 8

Come riddle, come riddle, my old mother dear see 'The brown girl'

Come riddle, come riddle my own mother see 'Lord Thomas and Fair Eleanor'

Come riddle me, riddle me, my dear mother see 'Lord Thomas and Fair Ellinor'

Come riddle to me, dear mother see 'The brown girl'

Come riddle your rights, my mother dear see 'Lord Thomas'

Come rise you up, my pretty Polly see 'Lady Isabel and the elf knight'

Come round, you brave young, river men and list while I relate see 'The jam on Gerry's Rock'

'Come rouse brother Sportsman' FL: Come rouse brother Sportsman, the hunters all cry. 3

Come, rouse up, my lads, and join this great cause see 'American heart of oak'; 'A new liberty song'

'Come running back' Dick Glasser. FL: If you find your new love isn't what you thought it would be. 47

Come saddle the black steed see 'Glenlogie'

Come saddle to me the black steed said he see 'The fause lover'

'Come shake your dull noodles' FL: Come shade your dull noodles, ye pumpkins, and bawl FLC: In folly you're born and in folly you'll live. 8, 65

Come shake your dull noodles, ye pumpkins and bawl see 'A parody on a liberty song'; 'Parody

here and remember FLC: Chove
chuva, constant is the rain. 9
'The constant rain' Jorge Ben. FL:
Pois eu fazeruma prece FLC:
Chove chuva chove sem parar.
9
'Constantinople' FL: Kind friends,
your pity pray bestow FLC: C
O N, With a con. 36
'The Constitution and the Guerriere'
FL: It oft times has been told.
55
Coo coo roo coo coo, Paloma see
'Cu-cu-rru-cu-cu, Paloma'
'Cool, calm and collected' Mick
Jagger and Keith Richard. FL:
She's very wealthy it's true. 16
'Cool water' Bob Nolan. FL: All
day I've faced a barren waste
FLC: Keep a a-movin', Dan.
10
'Coonies' got a pretty tail' FL:
same. 72
'Cooper of Fife' FL: There was a
wee cooper who lived in Fife.
11
'Coplas' FL: Chile verde me per-
diste. 57
'Copper kettle' FL: Get you a cop-
per kettle. 35
'Copper kettle' FL: Oh, listen to
the story. 23
'Corena' FL: Corena, Corena,
where you been so long. 35
'Corinna' FL: Corinna, Corinna,
where you been so long. 25,
57
'The Cork leg' FL: I'll tell you a
tale now without any flam FLC:
Ri tu, di ni, ri tu, di nu, ri
na. 36
'Cornwallis Burgoyned' FL: When
British troops first landed
here. 49, 55, 65
'The Cornwallis country dance' FL:
Cornwallis led a country dance,
like was never seen, sir. 8,
65, 66
'Coronation' Edward Perronet and
Oliver Holden. FL: All hail the
power of Jesus' name. 1
'Corrina, Corrina' FL: Corrina,
Corrina, where'd you stay last
night? 23
'Corydon's ghost' N. Dwight. FL:
What sorrowful sounds do I hear.
3
'Cose, cose, cose' Joe Davis and

Armando Castro. FL: Every
time I look into your eyes FLC:
Cosé, cosé, cosé means I love
you. 9
'Cosher Bailey's engine' FL: Cosher
Bailey had an engine. 57
'The cottager' FL: As on a lonely
hill I strayed. 3
'Cotton mill girls' FL: I've worked
in the cotton mill all of my life
FLC: It's hard times, cotton
mill girls. 57, 58
'Cotton needs a-pickin'' FL: Cotton
needs a-pickin' so bad. 13
'Cotton-eyed Joe!' FL: Do you re-
member, a long time ago. 57
'Could I only back the winner' FL:
Behold in me a man who's lost a
fortune on the field FLC: Could
I only back the winner. 36
A councel grave our king did hold
see 'King Henry the 5th, his
victory over the French at Agin-
court'
'The councillor's daughter, or the
lawyer outwitted' FL: Tis of a
councillor I write. 30
'Counting the goats' FL: Where is
the goat. 72
'Country honk' Mick Jagger and
Keith Richard. FL: Sittin' in a
bar tipplin' a jar in Jackson
FLC: It's those honky tonk wo-
men. 16
Couple in the next room bound to
win a prize see 'Duncan'
'The court of King Carraticus' FL:
Oh, the court of King Carraticus
is just passing by. 68
'The coverin' blue' FL: There came
a maid to Colliston town. 11
'The cow chase' FL: To drive the
kine one summer's morn the
tanner took his way. 8
'The cowboy' FL: All day in the
saddle on the prairie I ride. 43
'The cowboy' FL: All day on the
prairie in the saddle I ride. 2
'The cowboy' FL: Oh, a man there
lives on the western plains. 57
'The cowboy' FL: There lives a
man on the western plains. 43
'A cowboy at church' FL: Sometime
ago two weeks or more. 18
'The cowboy dream' FL: Last night
as I lay on the prairie FLC:
Roll on, roll on, roll on little
doggies. 2

and Sigmund Romberg. FL: Me
han dicho que tus ojos FLC: El
ruiseñor no canta ya. 46
Cuando vuelva a tu lado <u>see</u>
    'What a difference a day made'
'Cuanto le gusta' Ray Gilbert and
    Gabriel Ruiz. FL: same FLC:
    We gotta git goin'. 9
'Los cuatro generales' FL: same.
    57
'La cucaracha' FL: Cuando no
    quiere una. 23
'La cucaracha' FL: Cuando uno
    quiere a una FLC: La cucaracha,
    la cucaracha. 57
'La cucaracha' FL: La cucaracha,
    la cucaracha, he's a merry
    little bug. 25
'La cucaracha' Stanley Adams.
    FL: Then one day when cook
    was baking FLC: La cucaracha,
    la cucaracha. 9
'La cucaracha' FL: Un panadero
    fue a misa FLC: La cucaracha,
    la cucaracha. 9
'The cuckold' FL: Oh my old man
    came home one night. 11
'The cuckold's song' FL: I went
    into the stable to see what I
    could see. 11
'The cuckold's song' FL: Now it's
    my old man came home one
    night. 11
'Cuckoo' FL: Cuckoo is a calling
    FLC: Cuckoo, cuckoo. 57
'The cuckoo' FL: The cuckoo is a
    fine bird. 30
'The cuckoo' FL: The cuckoo is a
    funny bird. 57
'Cuckoo' FL: Kuku lecza kuka. 57
'The cuckoo' FL: Oh, the cuckoo
    is a pretty bird. 7
'The cuckoo is a pretty bird' FL:
    Oh, the cuckoo is a pretty bird.
    72
'Cu-cu-rru-cu-cu, Paloma' Tomas
    Mendez. FL: Dicen que por las
    noches nomás se le iba en puro
    llorme FLC: Ay ay ay ay ya
    cantabe. 9
'Cu-cu-rru-cu-cu, Paloma' Pat
    Valando, Ronnie Carson and
    Tomas Mendez. FL: Please,
    pretty little dove FLC: Coo coo
    roo coo coo, Paloma. 9
'El Cumbanchero' Rafael Hernandez.
    FL: A cumba, cumba, cumba,
    cumbanchero. 9

'The Cumberland crew' FL: Oh ship-
    mates gather and join in my
    ditty. 57
'Cumberland Gap' FL: Cumberland
    Gap is a noted place. 66
'Cumberland Gap' FL: Me an' my
    wife an' my wife's pap FLC:
    Cumberland Gap, Cumberland
    Gap. 14, 57
'Cumberland Gap' FL: Me and my
    wife and my old grandpap. 4
'Cumberland Mountain bear chase'
    FL: Away, away, we're bound
    for the mountain. 72
'The Cumberland Mountain deer
    chase' FL: Away and away, we're
    bound for the mountain. 57
'The cunning clerk' FL: Bonny May
    went out one day. 11
'A cup of coffee, a sandwich and
    you' Billy Rose, Al Dubin and
    Joseph Meyer. FL: In the movie
    plays of nowadays FLC: A cup of
    coffee, a sandwich and you. 46
'Cupid, God of soft persuasion'
    Isaac Bickerstaffe, and Felice de
    Giardini. FL: same. 40
Cursed be the salt sea man <u>see</u>
    'The house carpenter'
'Curs'd be the time' Michael Caven-
    dish. FL: Curs'd be the time
    when first mine eyes behold. 26
'Cushie Butterfield' George Ridley
    and Harry Clifton. FL: Aa's a
    broken hairted keelman, aa's
    ower heed in luv. 17
'Custer's last fierce charge' FL:
    Twas just before Custer's last
    fierce charge. 50
'The cutty wren' FL: Oh, where are
    you going, said Milder to Malder.
    19, 57

- D -

'The D-Day Dogers' FL: We're the
    D-Day Dodgers, way out in Italy.
    57
'Dabbling in the dew' FL: Oh, where
    are you going to, my pretty little
    dear. 57, 58
'Daddy' Bobby Troup. FL: Hey!
    Listen to my story 'bout a gal
    named Daisy Mae FLC: Hey!
    Daddy! 59
Daddy dear, tell me please <u>see</u>
    'Little child'

'Daddy won't you please come home'
Sam Coslow. FL: When night is
creepin' and I should be sleepin'
in bed FLC: Night after night
I'm cryin'. 54

'Daddy's little boy' Billy Collins.
FL: Goodnight, my darling FLC:
You're an angel from heaven,
sent down from above. 52

'The daemon lover' FL: If you
could have married the king's
daughter dear. 11

'The daemon lover' FL: If you will
forsaken your house carpenter.
11

'The daemon lover' FL: O come
you home, my own true love.
11

'The daemon lover' FL: O I have
married a queen's daughter. 11

'The daemon lover' FL: She
dressed herself in scarlet red.
11

'The daemon lover' FL: She taken
her little babe on her knee. 11

'The daemon lover' FL: Well met,
well met my own true love. 11

'The daemon lover' FL: We've met,
we've met, my own true love.
11

'The daemon lover' FL: You once
could have married the king's
daughter dear. 11

'Daffodillies' A. W. I. Chitty.
FL: Daffodillies down in the
meadows green. 13

'Daisy Bell' Harry Dacre. FL:
There is a flower within my
heart FLC: Daisy, Daisy, give
me your answer true. 1, 20

Daisy, Daisy, give me your answer true see 'A bicycle built
for two'

'Dakota Land' FL: We've reached
the land of waving wheat FLC:
Dakota land, sweet Dakota land.
43

'Dame, get up and bake your pies'
FL: same. 48

'Dan Dhu' FL: There was an old
man and he lived out West. 11

'Dance a baby, Diddy' FL: same.
48

Dance, boatman, dance see
'Boatman dance'

Dance la Bamba, a cousin of the
samba see 'La bamba'

Dance, then wherever you may be

see 'The lord of the dance'

'Dance to your Daddy' FL: Dance to
your daddy, my little laddie. 57

'Dancing in the dark' Howard Dietz
and Arthur Schwartz. FL: same.
42

'Dancing on the ceiling' Lorenz Hart
and Richard Rodgers. FL: The
world is lyrical FLC: He dances
overhead on the ceiling. 46

'Dancing with tears in my eyes' Al
Dubin and Joe Burke. FL: Those
who dance and romance while
they dance FLC: For I'm dancing
with tears in my eyes. 46

'Dandelion' Marlys Swinger. FL:
I'm a happy little thing. 13

'Dandelion' Mick Jagger and Keith
Richard. FL: Prince or pauper
beggarman or king. 16

'Dandoo' FL: The good little man
come in at noon. 11

'Dandoo' FL: There was a little old
man that lived in the west FLC:
Come a kludie, come a lingo.
11

'Dang me!' Roger Miller. FL:
Well, here I sit high gettin'
ideas FLC: Dang me, dang me.
10

'Dangerous woman' FL: Well, I got
a sweet woman, yes, everybody
knows. 57

'The dangling conversation' Paul
Simon. FL: It's a still life
water color of a late afternoon.
60

'Danke schoen' Kurt Schwabach,
Milt Gabler and Bert Kaempfert.
FL: Danke schoen, darling. 47

'Danny boy' FL: Oh Danny boy, the
pipes, the pipes are calling. 57

Dans les jardins d'mon père see
'Auprès de ma blonde'

Danse, mon moin' danse see 'Ah!
Si mon moine voulait danser!'

'Danville girl' FL: My pocket book
was empty. 57

'Dan-you' FL: There was an old
man that lived in the West. 11

'Daphne' Thomas Campion and John
Dowland. FL: Daphne was not
so chaste as she was changing.
26

Dar was old Mr. Johnson see
'The cat came back'

'The Darby Ram' FL: As I was going to Darby upon a market day.

'Death or victory' FL: Hark, the din of distant war. 3

'Death song of an Indian chief' Hans Gram and Sarah Wentworth Morton. FL: Reared midst the war empurpled plain. 65

'Deck the halls' FL: Deck the halls with boughs of holly. 34, 57

'Dedicated to the one I love' Lowman Pauling and Ralph Bass. FL: While I'm far away from you my baby. 47

'Deep blue sea' FL: Dig his grave with a silver spade FLC: Deep blue sea, baby, deep blue sea. 57

'Deep in the heart of Texas' June Hershey and Don Swander. FL: There is a land, a western land FLC: The stars at night are big and bright. 10

'Deep purple' Mitchell Parish and Peter De Rose. FL: When the deep purple falls over sleepy garden walls. 59

'Deep river' FL: Deep river, my home is over Jordan. 23, 25

'Deep river' FL: Oh, don't you want to go to that Gospel feast FLC: Deep river. 38

'Deep-river blues' FL: Let it rain, let it pour. 56, 57

'Deep sea blues' Jerry Silverman. FL: Soldiers down below layin' cold and dead FLC: Oh, all day long I'm lookin' for trees. 57

'The deer song' FL: On a bright and summer's morning. 72

'The deil's awa wi' the exciseman' FL: The Deil came fiddling through the toun FLC: The Deil's awa, the Deil's awa. 25

'The dejected lass' FL: A lass that was loaden with care FLC: So merry as we twa have been. 25

'Delia' FL: Tony shot his Delia FLC: Delia's gone, one more round. 57

Delia, Delia, why don't you run see 'Delia Holmes'

'Delia Gone' FL: Miss Delia, she two timed her FLC: Delia, gone, one more time. 23

'Delia Holmes' FL: Delia, Delia, why don't you run FLC: All I had done gone, all I had done

gone. 29

Delia's gone, one more round see 'Delia'

Delights of love endure only for a day see 'Plaisir d'amour'

Delilah was a woman fine and fair see 'Samson'

'Delishious' George and Ira Gershwin. FL: What can I say to sing my praise of you FLC: You're so delishious. 21

'Dem charming bells' FL: Come along, my brother, come along FLC: Lord, I'm almost home. 5

Demon lover see 'The daemon lover'

'Depression blues' FL: If I could tell my troubles. 57

Der lived a king into da aist see 'King Orfeo'

'Derrière de chez mon père' FL: same. 48

Derry down, down, down, derry down see 'The coal owner and the pitman's wife'; 'What a court'

Derry down, down, hey derry down see 'The farce'; 'Song of the heads'

'The derry downs of Arrow' FL: I knew a lady of the North. 11

'Dese dry bones of mine' FL: What kind of shoes is dem you wear? FLC: An' a Lawd, dese dry bones of mine. 5

Desert shadows creep across purple sands see 'Misirlou'

'The desert song' Otto Harbach, Oscar Hammerstein and Sigmund Romberg. FL: My desert is waiting FLC: Blue heaven and you and I. 24

Desmond and his barrow in the market place see 'Ob-la-di ob-la-da'

'The despairing damsel' FL: Twas when the seas were roaring. 3

'The desperado' FL: He was a desperado from the wild and wooly West FLC: He was a brave, bold man and a desperado. 68

'The desperado' FL: There was a desperado from the wild and woolly West FLC: A bold, bad man was this desperado. 57

'The desponding Negro' FL: On Afric's wide plains where the lion now roaring. 3

The despot's heel is on thy shore

Dinner is ended see 'Hands
across the table'
'Diogenes surly and proud' FL:
same. 3
'The dipsy doodle' Larry Clinton.
FL: The Dipsy Doodle's a thing
to beware. 59
'Dirge' William Collins and
Thomas A. Arne. FL: To fair
Fidele's grassy tomb. 40
A dir-rum a doo a dum a day
see 'Rothesay-o'
'Dirty beggarman' FL: It's of a
jolly beggarman. 11
'Dirty beggarman' FL: This dear
young girl. 11
'Dirty beggarman' FL: With his
long staff and his pitch patch
coat. 11
'The discharged drummer' FL: In
Bristol lived a damsel. 30
'The discharged drummer' FL: In
Bristol lived a lady. 30
'Diverus and Lazarus' FL: As it
fell out upon one day. 11
'Dives and Lazarus' FL: As it fell
out on a light dully day. 11
'Dives and Lazarus' FL: As it fell
out upon one day. 11
'Dixie' Daniel D. Emmet. FL: I
wish I was in the land of cotton
FLC: Then I wish I was in Dixie.
1, 4, 25, 57
'Dixie's land' Daniel D. Emmett.
FL: I wish I was in de land ob
cotton FLC: Oh! in Dixie's land
I'll take my stand. 63
'Do-do-do' George and Ira Gersh-
win. FL: I remember the bliss
FLC: Do, do, do what you've
done, done, done before. 21,
46
Do I miss her kiss at nighttime
see 'Each and every day of the
year'
'Do, Lord, remember me' FL: O
Do Lord, oh do, Lord. 34
Do Ma! Please Ma! Now Ma! see
'O let me be a blonde, Mother'
Do not forsake me oh my darlin'
see 'High noon'
Do not jump on ancient uncles
see 'Rules'
'Do not, o do not prize' Thomas
Campion and Robert Jones. FL:
Do not, o do not prize thy beauty
at too high a rate. 26
Do not trust him, gentle lady see

'The gypsy's warning'
Do people have a tendency to dump
on you? see 'The big bright
green pleasure machine'
Do rain, do rain in American corn
see 'Little Sir Hugh'
Do ye ken John Peel with his coat
so gray see 'John Peel'
Do you believe in charms and
spells see 'It could happen to
you'
'Do you know the way to San Jose'
Hal David and Burt Bacharach.
FL: same. 71
Do you remember, a long time ago
see 'Cotton-eyed Joe'
Do you remember when you loved
me see 'Make the world go
away'
Do you see my little ploughboy
ploughing on the lea see 'The
simple ploughboy'
Do you see that good old sister see
'Go, chain the lion down'
Do you wish to know her age, bonny
lad, Highland lad see 'Bonny
lad, Highland lad'
Doctor, please some more of these
see 'Mother's little helper'
'The dodger' FL: Oh, the candidate's
a dodger yes a well-known dodger
FLC: Oh, we're all dodging, a-
dodging, dodging, dodging. 19
'The dodger song' FL: Oh, the cand-
idates a dodger FLC: Yes, we're
all dodging. 57
'Does your heart beat for me?'
Mitchell Parish, Russ Morgan
and Arnold Johnson. FL: I wonder if I still linger in your memory FLC: Tho' we said goodbye
when the moon is high. 12
Does your mother realize see 'You
must have been a beautiful baby'
'The dog-meat man' FL: Near an
old fly market, not a long time
ago FLC: Oh Yankee Doodle,
Doodle Dandy. 7
The dogs began to bark see 'Nobody coming to marry me'
'Doin' the Suzi-Q' Benny Davis and
J. Fred Coots. FL: It's spread-
ing like a flame FLC: A new
dance hit the town. 12
'Doing my time' FL: On this old
rock pile with a ball and chain.
14
'Dolly Varden' G. W. Moore and

G. W. Hunt and Alfred Lee.
FL: Oh! have you seen my little girl FLC: Dolly, Dolly, Dolly, Dolly Varden. 36

'Dolores' Frank Loesser and Louis Alter. FL: How I love the kisses of Dolores. 47

'Domestic workers' song' FL: We're coming from the nursery FLC: Come on, girls. 58

'Dona nobis pacem' FL: same. 57

'Donald Macdonald' FL: Up spoke Lady Dysie's old mother. 11

'Don'cha bother me' Mick Jagger and Keith Richard. FL: I said 'Oh no, a-don't-cha follow me no more. 16

¿Donde está la Má Teodora? see 'Ma Teodora'

'¿Donde estan las llaves?' FL: Yo tengo un castillo. 48

'Done been sanctified' FL: One day I'se a-walking along. 5

Done changed my name for the coming day see 'The angels changed my name'

'Doney gal' FL: We're alone, Doney gal, in the rain and hail. 57

'Don't bring Lulu' Billy Rose, Lew Brown and Ray Henderson. FL: Your presence is requested wrote little Johnny White FLC: Now you can bring Pearl. 46

Don't call my name out your window see 'Understand your man'

'Don't cry, lady' FL: Hooray, hooray, my father's gonna get shot FLC: Don't cry, lady. 57

Don't even go to a movie show see 'Keepin' out of mischief now'

'Don't ever leave me' Oscar Hammerstein and Jerome Kern. FL: I was created for one man alone FLC: Don't ever leave me, now that you're here. 24

Don't go away stay at home if you can see 'The dreary Black Hills'

'Don't go out into the rain' Kenny Young. FL: Please take your shoes off and make yourself comfortable FLC: Don't go out into the rain. 47

'Don't go out tonight, dear Father' M. E. Golding and W. L. Thompson. FL: same. 17

'Don't go out tonight, my darling' FL: Now your friends may be

jolly. 50

'Don't I wish I was a single girl again' FL: When I was single FLC: Lord, don't I wish I was a single girl again. 57

'Don't I wish I was a single girl again' FL: When I was single, I went dressed fine. 58

Don't keep the sunshine out of your eyes see 'Brown eyes why are you blue?'

Don't know why there's no sun up in the sky see 'Stormy weather'

'Don't let me down' Lennon and McCartney. FL: same. 44

'Don't let your deal go down' FL: same. 57

'Don't lie, Buddy' FL: Mammy Logan, she had a daughter FLC: Don't lie, buddy, don't lie. 57

'Don't look so sad, I know it's over see 'For the good times'

'Don't marry me' Oscar Hammerstein and Richard Rodgers. FL: You are young and beautiful FLC: If you want to have a rosy future. 24

'Don't rain on my parade' Bob Merrill and Jule Styne. FL: If you live your life FLC: Don't tell me not to fly. 6

Don't she rock 'em, die dio see 'Sail away, ladies'

'Don't sing love songs' FL: Don't sing love songs, you'll wake my mother. 57

Don't sing love songs, you'll wake my mother see 'Silver dagger'

'Don't sit under the apple tree' Lew Brown, Charlie Tobias and Sam H. Stept. FL: Don't sit under the apple tree with anyone else but me. 59

'Don't swat your mother' FL: Don't swat your mother, boys, just 'cause she's old. 68

'Don't take your guns to town' Johnny Cash. FL: A young cowboy named Filly Joe grew restless on the farm. 10

'Don't take your love from me' Henry Nemo. FL: You could take my castle. 10

'Don't tell me it's raining' Paul Tannen. FL: Don't tell me it's raining when the sky is blue. 47

Don't tell me not to fly see 'Don't rain on my parade'

Don't the moon look lonesome,
shinin' through the trees? see
'Sent for you yesterday'

Don't think I'll be hanging around
while you're havin' fun see
I'll go stepping too'

'Don't think twice, it's all right'
Bob Dylan. FL: It ain't no use
to sit and wonder why, Babe.
45

Don't throw bouquets at me see
'People will say we're in love'

Don't you be a good for nothin'
see 'A shine on your shoes'

'Don't you go a-rushing' FL: Don't
you go a-rushing maids, I say.
11

'Don't you go a-rushing' FL: Don't
you go a-rushing, maids in May.
11

'Don't you go a-rushing' FL: I'll
get my love a home, wherein
she may be. 11

'Don't you grieve after me' FL:
Oh, who is that a coming? 38

Don't you hear the Savior callin'
see 'In that great day'

'Don't you remember sweet Alice?'
N. Kneass. FL: Oh! don't you
remember sweet Alice, Ben
Bolt. 69

Don't you walk on down see 'Butt-
cut ruler'

Don't you want to be a soldier,
soldier, soldier see 'Rise and
shine'

'Don't you want to go?' FL: O
brother, don't you want to go?
FLC: Less go down to Jordan.
5

'Don't you weep after me' FL:
When I'm dead and buried. 57

Don't you worry 'bout what's on
your mind see 'Let's spend the
night together'

Doon Deeside cam Inverery see
'The baron of Brackley'

Doon in yon glen I spied a swain'
see 'The beggar laddie'

'Dost thou withdraw thy grace?'
John Danyel. FL: same. 26

'The Douglas tragedy' FL: Rise up,
rise up, Lord Douglas, she
says. 11

Doux, doux, l'am est doux see
'L'amour est bleu'

'The dove' FL: The dove she is a
pretty bird. 72

'The dowie dens' FL: There lives a
lady in this place. 11

'The dowie dens o' Yarrow' FL:
Late at e'en, drinking the wine.
11

'The dowie dens o' Yarrow' FL: O
sister dear, I've dreamed a
dream. 11

'The dowie dens o' Yarrow' FL:
There lived a lady in the South
(West). 11

'The dowie dens of Yarrow' FL:
There was a lady in the North.
11, 57

'The dowie dens of Yarrow' FL:
There was a squire lived in the
town. 30

Down and down she goes see
'Miss Amanda Jones'

'Down around the coast of La Barbaree' FL: Oh, it's two gallant
ships from England they did sail.
11

'Down by a riverside' FL: As I
roved out one evening down by a
riverside. 30

'Down by the greenwood side' FL:
She leaned her back ag'in the
wall. 11

'Down by the greenwood side' FL:
There was a lady lived in York.
11

'Down by the greenwood side-e-o'
FL: As I was pacing father's
hall. 11

'Down by the old millstream' FL:
same. 68

Down by the pen there the old shear-
er stands see 'Click go the
shears, boy'

'Down by the river' FL: And if those
mourners would believe FLC:
Yes, we'll gain this world. 5

'Down by the river' FL: Oh, hallelujah to the Lamb FLC: Oh,
we'll wait till Jesus comes. 38

'Down by the riverside' FL: Gonna
lay down my sword and shield
FLC: I ain't gonna study war no
more. 34, 57

'Down by the riverside' FL: Gonna
walk with my baby. 25

'Down by the riverside' FL: I'm
gonna lay down my burden down
by the riverside. 67

'Down by the Sally Gardens' William
Butler Yeats FL: It was down by
the Sally Gardens my love and I

did meet. 57

Down by the Southern sea <u>see</u> 'Drifting and dreaming'

'Down by the waters rolling' FL: There was two sisters living in the East. 11

Down came a lady <u>see</u> 'Lord Daniel's wife'

Down came the old man <u>see</u> 'Hobble and bobble'

Down come a Jewess <u>see</u> 'Sir Hugh'

'Down, down, derry down' FL: Oh! Ladies and gentleman, please to draw near. 11, 57

'Down in a coal mine' J. B. Geoghegan. FL: I am a jovial collier lad, as blithe as blithe can be FLC: Down in a coal mine, underneath the ground. 4, 19

Down in a low green valley, the fairest, flowers grow <u>see</u> 'Pearl Bryan'

'Down in a valley' Michael Cavendish. FL: Down in a valley, down in a valley. 26

Down in Carlisle there lived a lady <u>see</u> 'Lady of Carlisle'

Down in de cornfield <u>see</u> 'Massa's in de cold ground'

Down in front of Casey's <u>see</u> 'The sidewalks of New York'

Down in London where I was raised <u>see</u> 'Barbara Allen'

'Down in my heart' FL: I've got that joy, joy, joy. 57

'Down in old England there lived three brothers <u>see</u> 'The pirates'

Down in St. Louis at Twelfth and Carr <u>see</u> 'Brady'

Down in some lone valley <u>see</u> 'Pretty Saro'

Down in the canebrake, close by the mill <u>see</u> 'Nancy Till'

Down in the jungle lived a maid <u>see</u> 'Under the bamboo tree'

Down in the poolroom some of the gang <u>see</u> 'True blue Lou'

'Down in the Tules' Jim McElroy. FL: Oh, down in the tules, a wranglin' around. 43

'Down in the valley' FL: Down in the valley, valley so low. 1, 14, 23, 25, 34, 57, 67

'Down in the valley to pray' FL: O brother less go down FLC:

As I went down in the valley to pray. 5

Down in the wildwood sitting on a log <u>see</u> 'Salty dog'

'Down in the Willow Garden' FL: same. 23, 57

'Down on me' Janis Joplin. FL: Down on me, down on me. 15

'Down on Penny's farm' FL: Come you ladies and you gentlemen and listen to my song FLC: It's hard times in the country. 19

Down stepped her old father dear <u>see</u> 'Lady Maisry'

'Down the line' FL: Oh well, I believe I'll roll on down the line. 28

'Down the line' FL: Oh, won't you hear me when I call you. 28

'Down the road' FL: Now down the road just a mile or two. 14

Down the road hear from me there's an old hollow tree <u>see</u> 'Mountain dew'

Down the way where the nights are gay <u>see</u> 'Jamaica farewell'

'Down went McGinty' Joseph Flynn. FL: Sunday morning just at nine FLC: Down went McGinty to the bottom of the wall. 20, 36

Down went the gunner, a bullet was his fate <u>see</u> 'Praise the Lord and pass the ammunition!'

'Down where the Wurzburger flows' P. Vincent, P. Bryan and Harry von Tilzer. FL: Now poets may sing of the dear Fatherland FLC: Take me down, down, down. 36

'Down with darkness' Levi-Tanai and E. Amiran. FL: Down with darkness, up with light. 13

'Down with the old canoe' FL: It was twenty-five years ago when the wings of death came low FLC: Sailing out to win her fame the Titanic was her name. 29

Down yonder green valley, where streamlets meander <u>see</u> 'The ash grove'

'The Doxology' William Kethe and Louis Bourgeois. FL: All people that on earth do dwell. 34

'The Doxology' Thomas Ken and Louis Bourgeois. FL: Praise God, from whom all blessings flow. 34

Dozens of girls would storm up <u>see</u> 'Embraceable you'

when I come home. 11
'The drunken fool' FL: Well I came home the other night. 11
'Dry bones' FL: Ezekiel connected them dry bones. 23, 25
'Dry weather houses' FL: One Monday morning a landlord went FLC: Dry weather houses are not worth a cent. 57
'Du, du liegst mir im herzen' FL: same. 57, 67
'Dublin City' FL: As I was awalkin' thru Dublin City. 57
Duca tu non vanna tu, Aileen Aroon see 'Aileen Aroon'
'Ducks on a pond' FL: One duck on a pond. 68
'Duermete niño lindo' FL: Duermete niño lindo en los brazos del amor. 57
Duérmete niño lindo see 'A la ru'
'The duke o' Gordon's daughter' FL: The duke o' Gordon has three daughters. 11
'The duke of Athole's nurse' FL: As he cam in by yon toon en'. 11
'The duke of Athole's nurse' FL: As I cam in by the Duke of Athole's gates. 11
'The duke of Athole's nurse' FL: As I gaed in yon greenwood side. 11
'The duke of Athole's nurse' FL: Oh, I am the Duke o' Athole's nurse. 11
'The duke of Athole's nurse' FL: Oh, wisna she a wily wily wife. 11
'The Duke of Gordon has three daughters' FL: same. 11
The duke of Merchant's daughter walked out one summer day see 'Six questions'
'The Duke of Perth's three daughters' FL: The Duke o' Perth had three daughters. 11
'Dumbarton's drums' FL: Across the fields of bounding heather FLC: Dumbarton's drums they sound so bonny. 57
'Dumbarton's drums' FL: Dumbarton's drums beat bonnie O. 25
'Duncan' Paul Simon. FL: Couple in the next room bound to win a prize. 60
'Dunderbeck' FL: One day a little fat boy came walking in the store

FLC: Oh, Dunderbeck Dunderbeck. 57
'Dunderbeck' FL: There was a man named Dunderbeck invented a machine FLC: Oh, Dunderbeck oh, Dunderbeck, how could you be so mean? 68
'Durango' FL: What had you for supper, Durango, my son? 11
'Durie Down' FL: Come all ye young people I pray you draw near. 37
'The dusky night' FL: The dusky night rides down the sky. 3
The dusky night rides down the sky, and ushers in the morn see 'A-hunting we will go'
'Dyevooshkoo chakoi zovoot' M. Lisianskii and A. Doplukhanian. FL: Vdal' hylch prostorakh doroga rulayet. 58
'The dying British sergeant' FL: Come all you good people where'er you be. 55
'The dying cowboy' FL: Oh bury me not on the lone prairie. 2, 18
'The dying hobo' FL: Twas at some western watertank. 11
'The dying ranger' FL: The sun was sinking in the West. 2, 43, 50, 57
'The dying soldier' FL: O, Willie, take my Highland shirt. 11

- E -

'E arrivato l'Ambasciatore' FL: same. 48
'Each and every day of the year' Mick Jagger and Keith Richard. FL: Do I miss her kiss at nighttime. 16
Each night while I'm sleeping, oh, so lonely see 'Send me the pillow you dream on'
Each time I look at you is like the first time see 'The more I see you'
'The eagles they fly high' FL: Oh, the eagles they fly high over Mobile. 57
'Earl Brand' FL: Arise, arise, King Henry, he said. 11, 30
'Earl Brand' FL: He rode up to her father's gate. 11
'Earl Brand' FL: He rode up to the old man's gate. 11
'Earl Brand' FL: Lady Margaret she

mounted her milk white steed.
11
'Earl Brand' FL: Light off, light
off, Lady Margaret, he said.   11
'Earl Brand' FL: O rise you up, ye
seven brothers.   11
'Earl Brand' FL: Wake up, wake
up, you seven sleepers.   11
'Earl Brand' FL: Wake you up,
wake you up, you seven sleepers.   11
'Earl Crawford' FL: O we were
sisters, sisters seven.   11
'Earl Lithgow' FL: The lady to the
queen's court gaed.   11
'Earl Marshall' FL: Queene Eleanor was a sick woman.   11
'The earl o' Aboyne' FL: The earl
of Aboyne to London's gane.   11
'The Earl o' Roslyn's dochter' FL:
The earl o' Rosalyn's dochter
gaed out to tak the air.   11
'The Earl of Aboyne' FL: My maid-
en's fair, yousels prepare.   11
'The Earl of Douglas and Dame Oliphant' FL: Young Willie was an
earl's ae son.   11
'The Earl of Mar's daughter' FL:
It was until a pleasant time.   11
'The Earl of Moray' FL: Ye High-
lands and ye Lowlands, it's where
have ye been?   11
'Earl Richard' FL: Awa, awa, ye
carle's dother.   11
'Earl Richard' FL: He took her
round the middle so small.   11
'Earl Richard' FL: It's of a fair
pretty shepherdess.   11
'Earl Richard' FL: It's of a farm-
er's daughter dear.   11
'Earl Richard' FL: A shepherd's
daughter dear.   11
'Earl Richard' FL: Some do call
me Jim and some do call me
John.   11
'Earl Richard' FL: There was a
little shepherd maid.   11
'Earl Richard's daughter' FL:
Earl Richard had but ae daugh-
ter.   11
'Earlistoun' FL: O billy, billy,
bonnie billy.   11
'Early, early in the spring' FL:
Twas early, early all in the
spring.   30
Early early in the spring see
'Barbara Allen'
Early, early in the spring when

green buds they were swelling
see 'Barbara Allen'
'The early horn' Edward Phillips
and John Ernest Galliard.   FL:
With early horn, salute the morn.
40
'Early in the morning' FL: Well,
it's early in the morning, when
the dingdong ring.   28
Early on a Monday morning see
'Kevin Barry'
'Early one morning' FL: Early one
morning just ast the sun was ris-
ing.   25, 35
Early one morning he called for his
man see 'The Yorkshire farm-
er'
'An earthly noures (nourice) sits
and sings see 'The Great Silk-
ie'; 'The great Silkie of Sule
Skerry'
'East Colorado Blues' FL: It's a
long ways from East Colorado.
57
East is east and west is west see
'Buttons and bows'
East side, west side see 'The
sidewalks of New York'
'East Virginia' FL: I was born and
raised in East Virginia.   35, 57
'East Virginia' FL: I was born in
East Virginia.   57
'East Virginia blues' A. P. Carter.
FL: I was born in East Virginia.
14
'East West' Graham Gouldman.   FL:
East, west, over the ocean, per-
petual motion.   47
Easter Day was a holiday see
'Little Sir William'
'Easter Eggs' Percy Dearmer.   FL:
Easter eggs! Easter eggs!   13
'Easter rebellion song' FL: As down
the glen one Easter morn to a
city fair rode I.   57
'Eastmuir King' FL: Eastmuir king
and Westmuir king.   11
'Easy loving' Freddie Hart.   FL:
Easy loving, so sexy looking.
10
'Easy rider' FL: Easy Rider, just
see what you have done.   57
'Easy Street' Alan Rankin Jones.
FL: Easy Street, I'd love to live
on Easy Street.   47
'Eating goober peas' FL: Sittin' by
the roadside on a summer's day
FLC: Peas, peas, peas, peas,

F. F. V. 57
An English lord came home one
night see 'Gypsy laddie'
'Enjoy yourself' Herb Magidson and
Carl Sigman. FL: You work and
work for years and years FLC:
Enjoy yourself, it's later than
you think. 70
The enlisted men ride in a motor
launch see 'Toorali'
'Enraptured I gaze' Francis Hopkinson. FL: Enraptured I gaze
when my Delia is by. 1
'The entertainer' John Brimhall and
Scott Joplin' FL: Now the curtain
is going up. 64
'The epilogue' FL: Our farce is now
finish'd, your sport's at an end.
49
'Epilogue song' David Garrick and
Joseph Vernon. FL: A widow,
bewitched with her passion. 40
'Eppie Morrie' FL: Four and twenty
hielan' men FLC: She wadna' be
a bride. 11
'Equinoxial and Phoebe' FL: Equinoxial swore by the green leaves
on the tree, tree. 57, 58
Equinoxial swore by the green
leaves on the trees see 'Little
Phoebe'
'Era una vez' FL: Era una vez un
barco chiquitito. 51
'The Erie Canal' FL: I've got a
mule, her name is Sal FLC: Low
bridge, everybody down. 1, 23,
25, 57, 72
'E-ri-e Canal' FL: We were forty
miles from Albany FLC: Oh, the
E-ri-e was a-risin'. 4, 57, 66,
68
Es mi caballo blanco see 'Mi caballo blanco'
Es regnat auf der Brücke, und es
werd nass see 'Ringeltanz'
'The escape of Old John Webber'
FL: There were nine to guard
the British ranks FLC: Billy
broke locks and Billy broke bolts.
55
Escucha el rumor, escucha el so-
nar see 'La comparsa'
Esta tarde vi llovar see 'Yesterday I heard the rain'
Estabe el señor don Gato see 'El
Señor Don Gato'
Este es un lerum la maruxiña see
'En el portal de Belén'

'The etiquette' FL: What though
America doth pour. 55
'Even at the dead time of the night
see 'Oh ono chrio'
Even though you're only make be-
lieving see 'Laugh! Clown!
Laugh!'
The evening breeze caressed the
trees tenderly see 'Tenderly'
Evening shadows make me blue
see 'My happiness'
Evenings are crowded with memo-
ries see 'In a little Spanish
town'
Ever since that time began love has
ruled the world see 'Just a
little lovin''
Every bell in the steeple is ready
to ring see 'Mary Lou'
Every day seems like a year see
'Sometimes I'm happy'
Every evening near my home see
'Who knows why'
Every evening, rain or shine see
'Little Annie Rooney'
Every kiss, every hug see 'You're
getting to be a habit with me'
Every lassie has her laddie see
'Comin' through the rye'
'Every little breeze seems to whis-
per Louise see 'Louise'
Every little Lambeth gal see
'Lambeth Walk'
'Every little movement' K. Hoschna
and O. A. Haverbach. FL: Up
to the West End, right in the
best end FLC: And every little
movement has a meaning of its
own. 17
Every little soul, gonna shine, shine
see 'Mister Rabbit'
Every morning at half past four
see 'Hard times in the mill'
Every morning at seven o'clock see
'Drill, ye tarriers, drill'
Every morning at six o'clock I go
to my work see 'Everybody
works but father'
Every morning, every evening, ain't
we got fun see 'Ain't we got
fun'
Every morning memories stray see
'Avalon'
Every nicht I used to hing my
troosers up see 'That's the
reason noo I wear a kilt'
Every night I dream of two dear
dark eyes see 'Dark eyes'

see 'Little Musgrave and Lady
Barnard'
The first came up was the carpenter of the ship see 'The mer-
maid'
The first come down was a raven
white see 'Little Musgrave and
Lady Barnard'
First come down was a raving white
see 'Little Matty Groves'
The first good joy that Mary had
see 'The seven joys of Mary'
The first grasshopper jumped over
the second grasshopper's back
see 'Grasshopper'
First he bought her was a beaver
hat see 'The miller's daughters'
First I was Lady o' Black Riggs
see 'The lady o' Gight'
The first joy of Mary was the joy
of one see 'The seven joys of
Mary'
The first landlord was dressed in
white see 'The cruel brother'
The first night I was married, a
happy happy bride see 'The
lowland of Holland'
The first night that I came home
see 'Three nights experience'
The first night that I came home
so drunk I couldn't see see
'Three night spree'
The first night that Johnny come
home see 'Johnny come home
the other night'
First night when I came home as
drunk as I could be see 'Our
goodman'
First night when I come home
see 'Drunkard's special'; 'Five
nights experience'
'The first Nowell' FL: The first
Nowell, the angel did say FLC:
Nowell, Nowell, Nowell, Nowell.
34
The first on deck was the captain
of the ship see 'The mermaid'
The first one come down was Lord
Diner's wife see 'Little Mus-
grave and Lady Barnard'
The first that came in was scarlet
red see 'Lord Vanover'
First when I cam to Kellboggie's
toon see 'Kilboogie'
First you put your two knees close
up tight see 'Ballin' the jack'
First you say you do and then you
don't see 'Undecided'

The first you wrote me was the
sweetest see 'Old love letters'
'Fish and tea' FL: What a court
hath old England, of folly and
sin. 55
Fish got to swim and birds got to
fly see 'Can't help lovin' dat
man'
'The fishes' FL: Come all ye bold
fishermen, listen to me FLC: So
blow ye winds westerly, westerly
blow. 72
'Five foot two eyes of blue' Sam M.
Lewis, Joe Young and Ray Henderson. FL: I just saw a maniac, maniac, maniac FLC: Five
foot two eyes of blue. 54
'Five hundred miles' Hedy West.
FL: If you miss the train I'm on.
47
'Five hundred miles away from
home' Bobbie Bare, Charlie
Williams and Hedy West. FL:
I'm five hundred miles away from
home FLC: Away from home,
away from home. 45
Five jolly rogues of a feather
walked o'er the hill together
see 'Johnson's ale'
'Five nights experience' FL: First
night when I come home. 11
Five of them were wise when the
bridegroom came see 'The ten
virgins'
Five thousand dollar, friend, I lost
see 'Matilda'
'Five times five' FL: Five times
five is twenty-five. 57
'Flamingo' Ed Anderson and Ted
Grouya. FL: Flamingo, like a
flame in the sky. 47
'Flanagan' FL: Flanagan, Flanagan,
take me to the Isle of Man again.
25
Flew in from Miami Beach BOAC
see 'Back in the USSR'
'Flight 505' Mick Jagger and Keith
Richard. FL: Well I was happy
here at home. 16
'Flood of Shawneetown' G. B. Fields.
FL: In the town of Shawneetown.
37
'Flora' Thomas Greaves. FL:
Flora, sweet wanton, be not over
coy. 26
'Florimel' FL: The charms of Flori-
mel. 25
'Floro' FL: As I roved out one

morning in spring. 30
'Flow gently, Sweet Afton' Alex-
ander Hume and Robert Burns.
FL: Flow gently, Sweet Afton,
among thy green braes. 57
Flow gently, sweet Afton, among
they green braes see 'Afton
Water'
Flow, my tears, fall from your
springs see 'Lachrimae'
'The flower o' Northumberland' FL:
A maid passed by the prison door.
11
'The flower of Northumberland' FL:
There was a young lady was
walking alone. 11
'The flower of serving men' FL:
My father he built me a shady
bower. 11
'Flowers never bend with the rain-
fall' Paul Simon. FL: Through
the corridors of sleep FLC: So
I'll continue to continue to pre-
tend. 60
'Flowers of the valley' FL: There
was a knight all clothed in red.
11
'Flowers of the valley' FL: There
was a widow all forlorn. 11
'Flowers of the valley' FL: There
was a woman and she was a
widow. 11
'The flowers that bloom in the
spring' William S. Gilbert and
Arthur S. Sullivan. FL: same.
1
'The flowing can' FL: A sailor's
life is a life of woe. 3
'Fly around, my pretty little miss'
FL: The higher up the cherry
tree FLC: Fly around, my pretty little miss. 57
Fly away, fly away, Kentucky
babe see 'Kentucky babe'
Fly! Fly! Fly, swift-winged fame
see 'Ode for American independence'; 'An ode for the 4th of
July'
Fly in the buttermilk, shoo, fly,
shoo see 'Skip to my Lou
polka'
'Flying trapeze' FL: Oh once I was
happy but now I'm forlorn FLC:
Oh he flew through the air with
the greatest of ease. 36
'Fod' FL: As I went down to the
mowin' field. 57
'A foggy day' George and Ira Gersh-

win. FL: I was a stranger in
the city FLC: A foggy day in
London town. 21
'The foggy dew' FL: Over the hills
I went one day. 57
'Foggy, foggy dew' FL: Once I was
a bachelor I lived by myself. 4
'The foggy, foggy dew' FL: When I
was a bach'lor I lived all alone.
25
'The foggy, foggy dew' FL: When I
was a bachelor I lived by myself.
57
'The foggy mountain top' A. P.
Carter. FL: If I had listened to
what Mama said FLC: If I was
on some foggy mountain top. 14
'Foggy mountain top' FL: Now if
you see that girl of mine FLC:
If I was on some foggy mountain
top. 57
Fol di rum, fol di rum, di ru-di
see 'The gypsy laddie'
Folderal deray, folderal deray see
'The tea party'
'The folks on t'other side the wave
see 'To the Commons'
'The folks who live on the hill'
Oscar Hammerstein and Jerome
Kern. FL: Many men with lofty
aims FLC: Some day we'll build
a home on a hill top high. 24
'Follow me' John Denver. FL: It's
by far the hardest thing I've ever
done. 45
'Follow the drinkin' gourd' FL:
When the sun comes back and the
first quail calls FLC: Follow the
drinkin' gourd. 4
'Follow thy fair sun' Thomas Camp-
ion. FL: Follow thy fair sun,
unhappy shadow. 26
'Follow Washington' FL: The day is
broke, my boys, march on. 8
'Following in father's footsteps'
E. W. Rogers. FL: To follow in
your father's footsteps is a motto
for each boy FLC: I'm following
in father's footsteps, I'm following the dear old dad. 17
'Folsom Prison blues' Johnny Cash.
FL: I hear the train a-comin'.
10
'The fool on the hill' Lennon and
McCartney. FL: Day after day,
alone on a hill. 44
'Foolish questions' FL: Now if an
elevator boy forgets to close the

door FLC: Foolish questions,
what is there to say. 35, 57
'The foolish song' FL: Way down
south in the yankety yank. 35
'Fools rush in' Johnny Mercer and
Rube Bloom. FL: Romance is a
game for fools FLC: Fools rush
in where angels fear to tread.
70
'Footprints in the snow' FL: Now
some folks like the summer
time FLC: I traced her little
footprints in the snow. 14
For a beggar, a beggar cam owre
the lea see 'The beggar man'
For ages and ages see 'When
your lover has gone'
For an old man he is old and an old
man he is gray see 'Get away
old man'
For auld lang syne, my friends
see 'Auld lang syne'
For battle prepared in their country's just cause see 'The
British light infantry'
For Champagne Charlie is my
name see 'Champagne Charlie'
'For Emily, wherever I may find
her' Paul Simon. FL: What a
dream I had. 60
For England when with favoring
gale see 'The heaving of the
lead'
'For every man there's a woman'
Leo Robin and Harold Arlen.
FL: same. 70
For her you drownded six king's
daughters see 'My pretty
Colinn'
'For he's a jolly good fellow' FL:
same. 1, 23, 25
For I'll be there see 'I'll be
there'
For I'm a soldier, a Territorial
see 'One of the deathless army'
For I'm dancing with tears in my
eyes see 'Dancing with tears
in my eyes'
For it was Mary, Mary see
'Mary's a grand old name'
For it's did ye come by Braikley
see 'Baron o' Braikley'
For it's hi hi hee see 'The cais-
sons go rolling along'
For I've worked eight hours this
day see 'I've worked eight
hourse this day'
'For Kansas' FL: O the girls they

do grow tall in Kansas FLC: All
who want to roam in Kansas. 57
For many years I've been a rolling
stone, my darling see 'If I
should wander back tonight'
'For me and my gal' Edgar Leslie,
E. Ray Goetz and George W.
Meyer. FL: What a beautiful
day FLC: The bells are ringing.
1, 12
For my Lord says there's room
enough see 'Room enough'
For my mouth it is full of mould
Maggie see 'Sweet William's
ghost'
For next Monday morning is my
wedding see 'Half-past nine, or
My wedding day'
'For no one' Lennon and McCartney.
FL: Your day breaks, your mind
aches. 44
For oh, it is such a horrible tale
see 'A horrible tale'
'For once in your life' Walter
Marks. FL: Lady forget rhyme
or reason for once in your life.
42
For so just is our cause and so
valiant our men see 'American
heart of oak'
For some must push and some must
pull see 'The handcart song'
For the barrin' o' oor door, weel,
weel see 'Barrin' o' the door'
'For the beauty of the earth' Folliot
Sandford Pierpoint and Conrad
Kocher. FL: same. 34
'For the good times' Kris Kristoffer-
son. FL: Don't look so sad, I
know it's over. 45
For the Guardian competition is
nothing but real discrimination
see 'Guardian beauty contest'
For the raging sea goes, roar, roar,
roar see 'The mermaid'
For the raging seas do roar see
'The stormy winds do blow'
For the rifle see 'The rifle';
'Riflemen of Bennington'
For the stormy winds they do blow
see 'The mermaid'
For the sunshine that kisses your
beautiful lips see 'My rival'
For there was a lady lived in York
see 'Trooper and maid'
For there were an auld beggar man
come owre yon lea see 'The
beggar man'

For there's a change in the weather
see 'There'll be some changes
made'

For they've got no fal-loo-rum see
'Maids, when you're young never
wed an old man'

For we are the lads of honor, boys,
belonging to the crown see
'Barrosa'

For we soldiers have seen something rougher see 'Short rations'

'For what it's worth' Stephen Stills.
FL: There's battle lines bein'
drawn FLC: There's something
happening here. 45

For when men settle down see
'Just a girl that men forget'

For when my baby smiles at me
see 'When my baby smiles at
me'

For Willie's gane o'er yon high,
high hill see 'Willie's fate'

'For you, for me, for evermore'
George and Ira Gershwin. FL:
Paradise cannot refuse us FLC:
For you, for me, for evermore.
21

Forbear my friends, forbear and
ask no more see 'Sophronia'

'Forever fortune' FL: Forever,
Fortune wilt thou prove. 3

The fortune queen of New Orleans
see 'Dark lady'

'Forty-five minutes from Broadway'
George M. Cohan. FL: The
West so they say FLC: Only 45
minutes from Broadway. 20

'Forty-second Street' Al Dubin and
Harry Warren. FL: I the heart
of little old New York FLC:
Come and meet those dancing
feet. 46

Found in the garden, dead in his
beauty see 'The burial of the
linnet'

Found some letters you wrote me
this morning see 'Burning
bridges'

'The fountain in the park' Ed Haley.
FL: While strolling in the park
one day. 20

Four and twenty fair maids see
'Lord Banner'

Four and twenty gay ladies see
'Lord Banner'

Four and twenty hielan' men see
'Eppie Morrie'

Four and twenty ladies see 'Lord
Banner'

Four and twenty ladies all being at
a ball see 'Lord Banner's wife'

Four and twenty ladies being at the
ball see 'Lord Benner'

Four and twenty ladies fair all being at a ball see 'Lord Banner'

Four and twenty noblemen see
'The heir of Linne'

'Four and twenty sailor lads' FL:
same. 11

'The four brothers' FL: I had four
brothers over the sea. 48

'The four Maries' FL: Last night
there were four Maries. 35

'The four Marys' FL: Last night
there were four Marys. 34, 50,
57

'The four Marys' FL: Oh, little did
my mother think FLC: Last night
there were four Marys. 11

'Four nights' FL: First night when
I came home. 11

'Four nights drunk' FL: I came
home the other night as drunk as
I could be. 35, 57, 58

'Four pence a day' FL: The ore is
waiting in the tubes, the snow's
upon the fell. 19, 57

'The four winds' Ernesto Lecuona.
FL: Si tu supieras lo que he
pecnado. 9

'The four winds' Jacqueline Sharpe
and Ernesto Lecuona FL: Warm
as the west wind. 9

'The fox' FL: The fox went out on
a chilly night. 25, 34, 35, 57,
72

'A fox may steal your hens, sir'
John Gay and John Eccles. FL:
same. 40

The foxes have holes in the ground
see 'Hard trials'

Frae Dunidier as I cam through
see 'The battle of Harlaw'

'Frankie and Johnny' FL: Frankie
and Johnny were lovers. 1, 4,
23, 25

'Frankie and Johnny' FL: Frankie
and Johnnie were sweethearts.
57, 58, 67

Frankie, dear, your birthday gift
reveals to me see 'Funny face'

'Franklin D. Roosevelt's back again'
FL: Just hand me my old Martin
FLC: Back again, back again.
57

'Franklin Slaughter ranch' FL: A
jolly bunch of cowboys on Frank-
lin Slaughter ranch. 43
'Fray Felipe' FL: Fray Felipe,
Fray Felipe. 34
'Free America' Joseph Warren.
FL: Born from a world of ty-
rants, beneath the western sky.
57
'Free America' Joseph Warren.
FL: Lift up your hands, ye
heroes. 65
'Free America' Joseph Warren.
FL: That seat of science,
Athens. 4, 55
'Free Amerikay' Joseph Warren.
FL: Torn from a world to ty-
rants, beneath this western sky.
8
'Free at last' FL: Way down yon-
der in the graveyard walk FLC:
Free at last, free at last. 57
Free grace, free grace see 'New
born again'
Free grace, unadying love see
'Mary and Martha'
'Free little bird' FL: I'm as free
a little bird as I can be. 57
'Freedom is a constant struggle'
FL: They say that freedom is a
constant struggle. 57
'Freedom rider' Marilyn Eisenberg.
FL: Went to Mississippi on a
Greyhound busline. 4
Freedom's just another word for
nothin' left to lose see 'Me
and Bobby McGee'
'Freight train' FL: Freight train,
freight train run so fast. 57
'Freiheit' FL: Spaniens Himmel
breitet seine FLC: Die Heimat
ist weit. 57
The Frenchmen came upon the
coat see 'The Savannah song'
'Frendraught' FL: On the 23rd of
October. 11
'Frenesi' Alberto Dominguez. FL:
Bésame tú a mí bésame igual
que mi boca to te besó FLC:
Quiero que vival sólo. 9
'Frenesi' Ray Charles, S. K. Rus-
sell and Alberto Dominguez.
FL: Sometime ago I wandered
into old Mexico FLC: It was
fiesta down in Mexico. 9
'Frennett Hall' FL: When Frennett
castle's ivied wa's. 11
'Frere Jacques' FL: Are you sleep-

ing, are you sleeping. 25
'Frère Jacques' FL: Frère Jacques,
frère Jacques. 34, 48, 57
'Fresh and strong' FL: Fresh and
strong the breeze is blowing. 3
'The friar in the well' FL: It's of
an old friar as I have been told.
11
'Friendship' Bidwell. FL: Friend-
ship to every willing mind. 3
'Friendship' Cole Porter. FL: If
you're ever in a jam. 42
'A frog a-courting' FL: Oh, a frog
a-courting he did ride. 7
'Frog and crow' FL: A funny fat
frog lived in the river swim, oh.
7
'The frog and the crow' FL: A jolly
fat frog lived in the river swim
O. 48
'The frog he would a-wooing go.
FL: same. 25, 48
'The frog in the spring' FL: There
was a frog lived in the spring.
72
'Froggie went a-courtin'' FL: Oh,
Froggie went a-courtin' and he
did ride, un huh, un huh. 1, 34,
37, 50, 57, 72
'Froggie's in the meadow' FL:
Froggie's in the meadow, can't
get out. 37
'From a Jack to a king' Ned Miller.
FL: same. 10
From Buffalo my labor done see
'Niagara Falls'
'From every graveyard' FL: Going
to meet the brothers there FLC:
Just behold that number. 38
From heaven high, bright angels,
come see 'Susani'
From heaven O praise the Lord
see '148th [one hundred forty-
eighth] Psalm'
From Lewis, Monsieur Gerard came
see 'Yankee Doodle's expedition
to Rhode Island'
From Louis, Monsieur Gérard came
to Congress in this town, sir
see 'The affair at Newport'
From out of a wood did a cuckoo
fly see 'The birds'; 'Carol of
the birds'
From place to place forlorn I go
see 'Indian's song'
From place to place I traversed
long see 'Dear little cottage
maiden'

From the great Atlantic ocean to
the wide Pacific's shore see
'The Wabash cannon ball'
From the Halls of Montezuma see
'The Marines' hymn'
From the Island of Manhattan to the
coast of gold see 'Of thee I
sing'
'From the North lands there came
a Northering knight see 'The
outlandish knight'
From these prairies of life I'll be
leaving see 'Red River Valley'
From this valley they say you are
goin' see 'The cowboy love
song'; 'Red River Valley'
Fueron tus ojos los que me dieron
see 'Green eyes'
'Fugitive breakdown' Myron L.
Morey. FL: I hurried through
the darkness FLC: She had the
sun in her hair. 14
'Full moon' Bob Russell, Gonzalo
Curiel, and Marcelene Odette.
FL: Full moon filled with your
own importance FLC: Full moon
when love is in flower. 9
'Full moon' Gonzalo Curiel and
Marcelene Odette. FL: Soñar
en noche de luna. 9
'Fuller and Warren' FL: Ye sons of
Columbia your attention I do
crave. 57
'A funeral dirge on the death of
General George Washington'
Peter A. von Hagen. FL: As-
sembled round the patriot's
grave. 65
'Funiculi funicula' FL: Some think
the world is made for fun and
frolic FLC: Hearken, hearken,
music sounds afar. 57
'Funny face' George and Ira Gershwin. FL: Frankie, dear your
birthday gift reveals to me FLC:
I love your funny face. 21
A funny fat frog lived in the river
swim, oh see 'Frog and crow'
'The future Mrs. 'awkins' Albert
Chevalier. FL: I knows a
little doner, I'm about to own
'er FLC: Oh! Lizer! Sweet
Lizer! 17

- G -

'The gaberlunzie laddie' FL: Twas

in the pleasant month of June.
11
'The gaberlunzie man' FL: Oh lassie, oh lassie, ye're far owre
young FLC: Lassie wi' your tow
row ree. 11
'The gaberlunzie-man' FL: The
pawky auld carle came o'er the
lee. 11
'The gaberlunzie man' FL: There
wis an auld carle cam our the
lea. 11
'Gabriel's trumpet's going to blow'
FL: same. 38
'Gage's proclamation' FL: America,
thou fractious nation. 8
'Gaily the troubadour' Thomas H.
Bayly. FL: Gaily the troubadour
touched his guitar. 1
'The gairdner and the plooman' FL:
When I was in my sixteenth year.
11
'The gairdner child' FL: Proud
Maisrie stands at her bower
door. 11
'The gal I left behind me' FL: I
struck the trail in '79 FLC: That
sweet little gal. 2, 57
'The gal that got stuck on everything she saw' FL: Now I'd a
young lady lived up the street.
57, 58
A gallant ship was lab'ring see 'The
ship I love'
Gallants, attend and hear a friend
see 'Battle of the kegs'
'Gallants, attend, and hear a friend
trill for the harmonious ditty
see 'The battle of the kegs'
'The gallent tree' FL: Oh, slacken
the rope, oh slacken the rope.
11
'The galley slave' FL: Oh think on
my fate once I freedom enjoyed.
3
'The gallows pole' FL: Hangman,
hangman, slack your rope. 57
'The gallows tree' FL: Come down,
come down from that dreary gallows. 11
'The gallows tree' FL: My love he
was as fine a fellow. 11
'Galveston' Jimmy Webb. FL:
Galveston, oh Galveston. 10
'Gambling on the Sabbath day' FL:
A poor unworthy son who dared.
18
Gamboling on the gumbo with the

gambits all in gear see 'Truly
true'
The game of just supposing is the
sweetest game I know see
'Make believe'
'Games people play' Joe South. FL:
Oh, the games people play FLC:
Talkin' 'bout you an me. 71
'Garbage!' Bill Steele. FL: Mister
Thompson calls the waiter. 4
'The gardener' FL: Lady Margret
stands in her bower door. 11
'The gardener' FL: The gardener
stands in his bower door. 11
'The gardener and the ploughman'
FL: A gardener lad that lives
nearby. 11
'The gardener lad' FL: There was
a lass near by to this. 11
'The gardener lad' FL: Lady Mar-
gret stood in her bower door.
11
A gardener lad that lives nearby
see 'The gardener and the
ploughman'
'The gardner' FL: When I was in
my sixteenth year. 11
'Garryowen' FL: Let Bacchus' sons
be not dismayed FLC: Instead of
Spa we'll drink down ale. 57,
69
'The gates o'Drum' FL: As I gaed
oot for to look about. 11
Gather round me everybody see
'Ac-cent-tchu-ate the positive'
Gather round me people, there's a
story I would tell see 'The
ballad of Ira Hayes'
'Gathering flowers for the master's
bouquet' FL: Death is an angel
sent down from above FLC:
Gathering flowers for the Master's bouquet. 14
'Gathering flowers from the hill-
side' A. P. Carter. FL: I've
been gathering flow'rs from the
hillside. 14
'Gaudeamus Igitur' FL: Gaudeamus
igitur, juvenes dum sumus. 25
'The gay goss-hawk' FL: O well's
me o' my gay goss-hawk. 11
'A gay ranchero' Abe Tuvim,
Francia Luban and J. J. Espinosa.
FL: A gay ranchero, a caba-
llero. 9
'A gay ranchero' J. J. Espinosa.
FL: Vamos a tepa tierra soñada.
9

'Gay young clerk in a dry goods
store' Will S. Hays. FL: Oh
listen now and I'll sing a song
FLC: How are you ladies, howdy.
36
Gayo, wayo wajine heyahe see
'Paddling my canoe'
Gazing down on the Jungfrau see
'Wunderbar'
'Die Gedanken sind frei' Arthur
Kevess. FL: Die Gedanken sind
frei, my thoughts freely flower.
19
'Gee, but I want to go home' FL:
The coffee that they give you,
they say is mighty fine FLC: I
don't want no more of army life.
57
Gee but it's great to be back home
see 'Keep the customer satisfied'
Gee, but it's tough to be broke,
kid see 'I can't give you any-
thing but love'
Gee, it's all fine and dandy see
'Fine and dandy'
'Gee-up, gee-up little horse' FL:
same. 48
'The general roll' FL: O hallelujah
to the Lamb FLC: I'll be there.
38
'Gentle fair Jenny' FL: I married
me a wife and took her home.
11
'Gentle on my mind' John Hartford.
FL: It's knowing that your door
is always open. 10
'A gentle young lady' FL: Oh, a
gentle young lady way down in
yonders lane. 11
The gentleman bow this way see
'On the bridge of Avignon'
A gentleman from the courts of Eng-
land see 'Lord Beechman';
'Young Beichan'
'The gentleman is a dope' Oscar
Hammerstein and Richard Rod-
gers. FL: The boss gets on my
nerves FLC: The gentleman is a
dope. 24
'A gentleman of the courts of Eng-
land' FL: same. 11
A gentleman to a young lady said
see 'The bonny green woods'
A gentleman was passing by see
'The well below the valley'
Gentleman's fair daughter walked
down yon narrow lane see

'Captain Wedderburn's Courtship'
'Gently, Jinny, fair Rosemary' FL:
I married a wife, I took her
home. 11
'Geordie' FL: As I came over new
London Bridge. 11
'Geordie' FL: As I walked out of a
London bridge. 57
'Geordie' FL: As I went over Lon-
don bridge. 11
'Geordie' FL: As we rode over
London Bridge. 11
'Geordie' FL: Georgie never stole
no cows nor calves. 11
'Geordie' FL: O Georgie shall be
hanged in a golden chain. 11
'Geordie' FL: Saddle up, saddle
up, my milk white steed. 11
'Geordie' FL: As she rode up in
the court house yard. 11
'Geordie' FL: There was a battle
in the north. 11
George Allen rode home one dark
stormy night see 'Lady Alice'
'The George Aloe and the sweep-
stake' FL: Once there were
two ships and two ships they were
of fame. 11
'George Collins' FL: As I roved out
one morning in May. 30
'George Collins' FL: George Collins came home last Saturday
night. 11
'George Collins' FL: George Collins came home last Wednesday
night. 11
'George Collins' FL: George Collins drove home one cold winter
night. 11, 57
'George Collins' FL: George Collins rode home last Wednesday
night. 29
'George Collins' FL: George Collins walked out one May morning.
11
'George Collins' FL: She says the
coffin to be opened. 11
George Collins come home last
Friday night see 'Giles Collins'
George Collins on one winter night
see 'Giles Collins'
'George Collum' FL: George Collum rode home one cold winter
night. 11
'George Colon' FL: George Colon
rode home one cold winter night.
11

'Georgia on my mind' Stuart Gorrell and Hoagy Carmichael. FL:
Georgia, Georgia, the whole day
through. 47
'Georgie' FL: As I rode over Ban-
stead Downs. 11
'Georgie' FL: As I walked over London Bridge. 11
'Georgie' FL: As I was acrossing
London's bridge. 11
'Georgie' FL: Go bridle me my
milk-white steed. 11
'Georgie Jeems' FL: Oh who will
shoe my narrow, narrow foot.
11
Georgie never stold no cows nor
calves see 'Geordie'
'Georgie Porgie' FL: Georgie Por-
gie pudding and pie. 48
'Georgy O' FL: Come bridle me up
my milk-white steed. 11
Get along home, Cindy, Cindy see
'Cindy'
'Get away old man' FL: Now listen
all you maidens about to choose
a man FLC: For an old man he
is old and an old man he is gray.
7
'Get back' Lennon and McCartney.
FL: Jo Jo was a man who thought
he was a loner. 44
Get down, boys, go back home see
'How mountain girls can love'
Get down, get down, get down, says
he see 'Lady Isabel and the elf
knight'
Get down, get down, love Henry,
she cried see 'Love Henry'
Get down, get down, Loving Henry,
she cried see 'Loving Henry'
Get down, get down, my Heneree
see 'Young Hunting'
Get goin', Louisiana hayride see
'Louisiana hayride'
'Get off my cloud' Mick Jagger and
Keith Richard. FL: I live in an
apartment on the 99th floor of my
block. 16
Get on board, little children see
'The gospel train'
Get out the way, Old Dan Tucker
see 'Old Dan Tucker'
Get out your gun and whistle up
your dog see 'Ground hog'
'Get thee behind me, Satan' Alma-
nac Singers. FL: The boss came
up to me with a five dollar bill
FLC: Get thee behind me, Satan.

19
'Get up and bar the door' FL: It came about the Michaelmas time. 11

'Get up and bar the door' FL: It fell aboot the Martinmas time FLC: O, the barrin' o' oor door, weel. 11

'Get up and bar the door' FL: The wind blew high, the wind blew cold. 7

'Get up and shut the door' FL: Twas in the merry month of May. 11

Get up get up, darlin' Corrie see 'Darlin' Corrie'

Get up, get up, pretty Polly, he says see 'Six king's daughters'

'Get up, Jack' FL: Ships may come and ships may go FLC: Come along, come along. 57

Get way back and snap your fingers see 'Walkin' the dog'

Get ye up, get ye up, ye seven sleepers see 'The seven brothers'

Get you a copper kettle see 'Copper Kettle'

Get you ready, there's a meeting here tonight see 'There's a meeting here tonight'

'Getting ready to die' FL: When I set out I was but young FLC: Getting ready to die. 38

'Getting to know you' Rodgers and Hammerstein. FL: It's a very ancient saying FLC: Getting to know you. 6, 24

'Gideon's band' FL: I hail my sister, my sister she bow low FLC: Oh, the band of Gideon. 38

'Gideon's band' FL: Oh, keep your hat upon your head FLC: If you belong to Gideon's band. 68

'Gifts from over the sea' FL: I had four brothers over the sea. 11

'Gight's ladye' FL: Will ye gant to the Hielands, my bonnie love? 11

'Giles Collins' FL: As I roved out one morning in May. 11

'Giles Collins' FL: George Collins come home last Friday night. 11

'Giles Collins' FL: George Collins on one winter night. 11

'Giles Collins' FL: Giles Collins said to his mother one day. 11

'Giles Collins' FL: Go hand me down my looking glass. 11

'Giles Collins' FL: Lay him down, lay him down fine. 11

'Gill Morice' FL: Gill Morice was an earle's son. 11

Gimme that old time religion see 'Old time religion'

'Gimme shelter' Mick Jagger and Keith Richard. FL: Oh, a storm is threatening my very life today. 16

Gin a body meet a body see 'Comin' through the rye'

'Gin I were' FL: I never had but two richt loves FLC: Gin I were where the Gaudy runs. 57

Gipsy see entries spelled Gypsy

'Gira, gira tondo' FL: same. 48

'Girl' Lennon and McCartney. FL: Is there anybody going to listen to my story about the girl who came to stay. 44

'The girl I left behind me' FL: I'm lonesome since I crossed the hill. 1, 25

'The girl I left behind me' FL: Oh that girl, that pretty little girl. 37

'The girl I left in Missouri' FL: My parents treated me kindly, having no one but me. 43

'Girl of my dreams' Sunny Clapp. FL: If I could just hold your charms FLC: Girl of my dreams, I love you. 12

'The girl that keeps the peanut stand' Blasee and Albert Harry. FL: I wandered down the other day. 36

Girl you funny thing see 'I wanna be loved'

'Girls and boys come out to play' FL: same. 48

'Girls from the south' FL: Master bought some yellow girls. 41

The girls in the city, they are happy see 'Coaxing Polly'

'Git along home, Sally Gal' FL: Squirrel he's got a bushy tail FLC: Git along home, Sally gal. 39

'Git along little Dogies' FL: As I was a-walkin' one morning for pleasure FLC: Whoopee ti yi yo. 2, 4, 23, 25, 57, 67, 72

'Git back blues' William Broonzy.

FL: Just listen to this song I'm singin' brother FLC: Now, if you're white, you're right. 4

'Git on board little children' FL: The Gospel train's a-comin' FLC: Git on board little children. 25

'Git on the evening train' FL: Gwine to git on de evening train, train. 5

Git out of the way for Old Joe Clark see 'Old Joe Clark'

Give ear to my song, I'll not tell you a story see 'The halcyon days of Old England'

'Give ear unto a maid that lately was betrayed see 'The trap-paned maid'

Give me a ticket for an airplane see 'The letter'

'Give me Jesus' FL: O when I come to die. 38

Give me my ranch and my cattle see 'Alla en el rancho grande'; 'El rancho grande'

Give me some men who are stout-hearted men see 'Stouthearted men'

Give me some of your dada's gold see 'The outlandish knight'

'Give me that old time religion' FL: It was good for the Hebrew children FLC: Give me that old time religion. 23, 25

Give my love to Nelly, Jack and kiss her once for me see 'Jack and Joe'

'Give my regards to Broadway' George M. Cohan. FL: Did you ever see two Yankees part upon a foreign shore FLC: Give my regards to Broadway. 1, 12, 20, 31, 42, 67

'Give peace a chance' Lennon and Paul McCartney. FL: Every-body's talking about bagism, shagism. 44, 45

Give up the fond embrace see 'The Back Bay polka'

'Glasgow Peggie' FL: Hielan' lads are young and braw. 11

'Glasgow Peggy' FL: The Hielan' lads sae brisk and braw. 11

'Glasgow Peggy' FL: It was on a day and a fine summer's day. 11

'Glenkindie' FL: Glenkindie was a harper guid. 11

'Glenlogie' FL: Come saddle the black, steed. 11

'Glenlogie' FL: There was nine and nine horsemen. 11

'Glenlogie' FL: There were four and twenty nobles stood at the king's ha'. 11

'Glenlogie' FL: There were six and six nobles. 11

'Glenogie' FL: Threescore o' nobles rade up the king's ha'. 11

'Globe trotting Nellie Bly' Joe Hart. FL: I hold here in my hand a lengthy cablegram FLC: She cheered up all the crew. 36

The gloomy night before us flies see 'Jefferson and liberty'

'Gloria!' Debra Swinger. FL: Gloria, gloria. 13

Glory glory, hallelujah see 'Battle hymn of the Republic'; 'John Brown's body'

'The glow worm' Johnny Mercer and Paul Lincke. FL: Glow, little glow worm, fly of fire. 12

'Glow worm' Lila C. Robinson, and Paul Lincke. FL: When the night falls silently FLC: Shine little glow worm, glimmer. 1

Go and get me some of your father's gold see 'Banks of Green Willow'

Go and leave me if you wish to see 'Columbus stockade blues'

'Go and make me a cambric shirt' FL: same. 11

Go away from me you vulgar youth and let me quiet be see 'Many questions'

'Go away from my window' FL: same. 23

Go back from these window, and likewise this hall see 'Lord Gregory'

Go back, go back, cried Andrew Battan see 'Andrew Battan'

Go bridle me my milk white steed see 'Georgie'

Go bring me some of your father's gold see 'The king's seven daughters'; 'Pretty Polly'

Go bury my Bible at my head see 'Sir Hugh'

Go catch up my old gray horse see 'Gypsy laddie'

'Go, chain the lion down' FL: Do you see that good old sister FLC: Go, chain the lion down. 38

'Go down Moses' FL: Go down
    Moses, way down in Egypt land. 25
'Go down, Moses' FL: When Israel
    was in Egypt's land FL: Go down,
    Moses. 19, 34, 38, 57
'Go down old Hannah' FL: Captain,
    will you just spare me one more
    day. 28
'Go down old Hannah' FL: Who told
    you you could make it. 28
Go fetch out my little black horse
    see 'The gypsy lover'
Go fetch to me my little nephew
    see 'Lord George'
'Go from my window' FL: One
    night as I lay on my bed asleep. 30
Go get me some of your father's
    gold see 'Pretty Polly'
Go hand me down my looking glass
    see 'Giles Collins'
Go harness up my milk-white steed
    see 'Harrison Brady'
Go home and get some of your fa-
    ther's gold see 'Banks of Green
    Willow'
Go home with me, little Mathy
    Groves see 'Little Musgrave
    and Lady Barnard'
'Go no more a-rushing' FL: Go no
    more a-rushing, maids, in May.
    11
Go patter to lubbers and swabs, do
    ye see see 'Poor Jack'
Go saddle me my black, said she
    see 'The life of Georgie'
Go saddle me my milk white steed
    see 'Wealthy squire of Islington'
'Go tell Aunt Nancy' FL: Go tell
    Aunt Nancy, go tell Aunt Nancy.
    50
'Go tell Aunt Rhody' FL: same. 4,
    34, 72
Go tell Aunt Rhody see 'Aunt
    Rhody'; 'The old grey goose'
Go tell her to make me a cambric
    shirt see 'Save rosemary and
    rhyme'
Go tell him to clear me one acre
    of ground see 'The elfin knight'
'Go, tell it on the mountain' FL:
    Oh, when I was a sinner FLC:
    Go, tell it on the mountain. 34
'Go, tell it on the mountain' FL:
    The shepherds kept their watching
    FLC: Go tell it on the mountain.
    23
'Go tell it on the mountain' FL:
    When I was a learner FLC: Go

tell it on the mountain. 57
'Go tell it on the mountain' FL:
    When I was a seeker FLC: Go
    tell it on the mountain. 25
'Go, tell it on the mountain' FL:
    While shepherds kept their watch-
    ing o'er silent flocks by night
    FLC: Go, tell it on the mountain.
    33
'Go to bed, sweet muse' Robert
    Jones. FL: Go to bed, sweet
    muse, take thy rest. 26
'Go way from my window' FL: same.
    57
'Go, weep, sad soul' George Hand-
    ford. FL: Go, weep, sad soul,
    and to thy love complain thee.
    26
'Go where you wanna go' John
    Phillips. FL: You gotta go where
    you wanna go. 47
Godamighty look-a yonder see
    'Long hot summer days'
'God bless America' Irving Berlin.
    FL: When the storm clouds ga-
    ther FLC: God bless America. 1
God of my justice when I call see
    'Oxford'
God prosper long our noble king
    see 'The battle of Chevy Chase'
'God rest you merry, gentlemen'
    FL: same FLC: O tidings of com-
    fort and joy. 34, 57
'God save America' FL: same. 55
'God save our states' FL: God save
    the thirteen states. 8
'God save the thirteen states' FL:
    same. 65
'God the master of all pagans'
    Johann C. Beissel. FL: same.
    65
God told Hezekiah see 'Little black
    train is a-comin' '
'Goin' across the mountain' FL:
    same. 57
'Goin' down the road' FL: I'm goin'
    down the road feelin' bad. 25, 34,
    57
'Goin' down to Cairo' FL: same. 37
'Goin' down to town' FL: I used to
    have an old gray horse FLC: I'm
    a-goin' down to town. 57
'Goin' home' Mick Jagger and Keith
    Richard. FL: Spendin' too much
    time away FLC: I'm going home,
    I'm going home. 16
'Goin' out of my head' Teddy Ran-
    dazzo and Bobby Weinstein. FL:

Well, I think I'm going out of my
head. 67
'Goin' over on de uddah side of Jordan' FL: I'm gwine away to see
my Jesus FLC: O, I'm jes' a-
goin' over on de other side of
Jordan. 5
'Goin' to Germany' FL: I'm goin' to
Germany. 57
Goin' to lay down my sword and
shield see 'Going to study war
no more'
Goin' to run all night see 'Camptown races'
Goin' up Cripple Creek see
'Cripple Creek'
Goin' up on a mountain see 'Pig
in a pen'
'Goin' up the mountain' FL: Goin'
up the mountain to raise a crop
of cane FLC: It's a bye, bye,
my darling girl. 37
'Going down the road' FL: I'm
goin' down the road feelin' bad.
19
Going to meet the brothers there
see 'From every graveyard'
Going to meet those happy Chris-
tians sooner in the morning see
'I ain't going to die no more'
'Going to pull my war clothes' FL:
same FLC: Yes I'm going to
study war no more. 29
'Going to study war no more' FL:
Goin' to lay down my sword and
shield FLC: I ain't goin' to study
war no more. 19
Going to the wedding Sally Ann
see 'Sally Ann'
Gold Coast slave ship see 'Brown
sugar'
'The gold diggers' song' Al Dubin
and Harry Warren. FL: Gone
are my blues FLC: We're in the
money. 46
'Gold watch and chain' A. P. Carter. FL: Darling, how can I
stay here without you? FLC: Oh,
I'll pawn you my gold watch and
chain, love. 14
'The gol-darned wheel' FL: I can
ride the wildest bronco in the
wild and woolly West. 43
'The golden ball' FL: O hangman,
hangman, hold your ropes. 11
'Golden days of good Queen Bess'
FL: To my muse give attention
and deem it not a mystery. 3

'The golden days we no possess'
FL: In the praise of Queen Bess
lofty strains have been sung fair.
3
'Golden earring' Jay Livingston, Ray
Evans and Victor Young. FL:
One day a gypsy showed me gold-
en earrings FLC: There's a story
the gypsys know is true. 70
'The Golden Fenadier' FL: There
once sailed a ship from the
North Amerikee. 11
'The Golden Furnity' FL: Oh, once
there was a ship sailin' the
northern counteree. 11
'Golden slippers' FL: Oh, my gold-
en slippers are laid away FLC:
Oh, dem golden slippers. 25
'Golden slumbers' FL: Golden slumbers kiss your eyes. 25
'Golden slumbers' Lennon and
McCartney. FL: Once there was
a way to get back homeward. 44
'Golden Valladay' FL: I had a ship
in the northern counteree. 11
'The Golden Vanitee' FL: There
once was a man who was boasting
the quay FLC: Lowlands, lowlands. 11
'The Golden Vanity' FL: And the
boy spread his breast and away
swimmed he. 11
'The Golden Vanity' FL: The boy
took his augur and overboard he
jumped. 11
'The Golden Vanity' FL: He bore a
hole once, he bore a hole twice.
11
'The Golden Vanity' FL: I had a
little ship and I sailed on the sea.
11
'The Golden Vanity' FL: I had a
little ship in the North Counteree.
11
'The Golden Vanity' FL: I have a
ship in the North Country. 11
'The Golden Vanity' FL: It's I have
got a ship in the north country.
11
'Golden Vanity' FL: I've got a ship
in the North Count-r-ee. 11
'The Golden Vanity' FL: Jacky had
an auger that bored two holes at
once. 11
'The Golden Vanity' FL: My father
had a ship in the North Countree.
11
'The Golden Vanity' FL: My father

owned a ship in the North Country. 11
'The Golden Vanity' FL: O once I had
a ship in some foreign country.
11
'Golden Vanity' FL: O there was a
British barque in the North Amer-
icay. 11
'The Golden Vanity' FL: Once there
was a ship in the Northern counteree. 11
'The Golden Vanity' FL: Our ship
she was a-sailing to some foreign
counteree. 11
'The Golden Vanity' FL: A ship I
have got in the North countree.
11
'The Golden Vanity' FL: Some were
playing cards and others were
playing dice. 11
'The Golden Vanity' FL: There was
a little ship and she sailed upon
the sea. 11
'The Golden Vanity' FL: There was
a little ship in South Amerikee.
11
'The Golden Vanity' FL: There was
a lofty ship FLC: And she sailed
upon the low and lonesome low.
57
'The Golden Vanity' FL: There was
a man he had a ship. 11
'Golden Vanity' FL: There was a
rich merchant ship from the
northern counteree. 11
'The Golden Vanity' FL: There was
a ship a-sailing on the North
Amerikee. 11
'The Golden Vanity' FL: There was
a ship came from the north country. 11
'The Golden Vanity' FL: Twas of a
lofty ship, boys, and she put out
to sea. 11
'The Golden Vanity' FL: Wrap me
up in my black bearskin. 11
'The Golden Victory' FL: There
lies a ship in the North Countree.
11
'The Golden Victory' FL: There was
the gallant ship on yon western
counteree. 11
'The Golden Willow Tree' FL: I had
a little ship and I sailed her on
the sea. 11
'The Golden Willow Tree' FL: I
suppose you all know that in the
Northern Sea. 11

'The Golden Willow Tree' FL:
There once was a ship she was
a-sailing on the sea. 11
'The Golden Willow Tree' FL:
There was a little ship and she
sailed upon the sea. 11
'The Golden Willow Tree' FL:
There was a ship in the south
countree. 11
'Gomper' Mick Jagger and Keith
Richard. FL: By the lake with
lily flowers. 16
'Gone along' FL: My good old
auntie's gone along FLC: Thank
God, she's got religion. 5
Gone are my blues see 'The gold
diggers' song'
'Gonna get along without ya now'
Milton Kellem. FL: Got along
without you before I met you.
67
Gonna jump down, turn around see
'Pick a bale of cotton'
Gonna lay down my sword and
shield see 'Down by the river-
side'
Gonna take a sentimental journey
see 'Sentimental journey'
Gonna tell Aunt Mary 'bout Uncle
John see 'Long Tall Sally'
Gonna walk with my baby see
'Down by the riverside'
'Goober peas' FL: Just before the
battle the general hears a row
FLC: Peas, peas, peas, peas.
25
'Goober peas' FL: Sitting by the
roadside on a summer's day FLC:
Peas! Peas! Peas! Peas! 4, 66
'The good boy' FL: I have led a
good life, full of peace and quiet.
57
'Good Bye, my lady love' Joseph E.
Howard. FL: So you're going
away FLC: Goody bye, my lady
love. 20
'Good bye to America' FL: Now,
farewell, my Massa, my Missy,
adieu. 8
'Good day sunshine' Lennon and
McCartney. FL: same. 44
Good evening one and all see 'On
with the show'
Good God, don't jump see 'Save
the life of my child'
'Good King Arthur' FL: When good
King Arthur ruled this land. 48
'Good King Wenceslas' John M.

Neale. FL: Good King Wenceslas
looked out. 34, 57
The good little man come in at
noon see 'Dandoo'
The good lord he came traveling
home see 'The gypsy laddie'
'A good man is hard to find' Eddie
Green. FL: My heart's sad and
I am all forlorn FLC: A good
man is hard to find. 31
Good mornin', captain see 'I can
buckle a wheeler'
'Good morning, Mister Railroad-
man' FL: same. 57
'Good news' FL: Good news! Char-
iots acomin'. 34
'Good news' FL: There'll be peace
and freedom in this world, I
know FLC: Good news, chariot's
comin'. 57
'Good news' FL: There's a long
white robe in heaven I know
FLC: Good news! 35
Good night, good night until we
meet again see 'Adios, au
revoir, auf wiedersehn'
'Good night, ladies' FL: same
FLC: Merrily we roll along. 23,
25, 68
'Good night sweetheart' Ray Noble,
Jimmy Campbell and Reg Con-
nelly. FL: same. 59
'Good old chariot' FL: Good old
chariot, swing so low FLC:
Swing low, sweet chariot. 38
'The good old rebel' FL: O I'm a
good old Rebel. 57
'The good old Rebel Soldier' FL:
I'm a good old Rebel soldier. 57
Good people attend and soon you shall
hear see 'Lincolnshire farmer'
Good tidings to you see 'We wish
you a merry Christmas'
The good time comin, is almost
here see 'Wake Nicodemus'
'Good times, bad times' Mick Jag-
ger and Keith Richard. FL:
There've been good times. 16
'Goodbye!' G. J. Whyte-Melville,
and F. Paolo Tosti. FL: Falling
leaf and fading tree. 63
Goodbye and adieu to you, Spanish
ladies see 'Spanish ladies'
'Goodbye, brothers' FL: Goodbye,
brothers, goodbye, sisters. 38
'Goodbye, my lover, goodbye' FL:
See that train comin' round the
bend FLC: Well, it's bye, baby,

bye. 28
'Goodbye, my lover, goodbye' FL:
The ship is sailing down the bay
FLC: Singing a bye low, my
baby. 68
'Good-bye old Paint' FL: My feet
are in the stirrups, my bridle's
in my hand FLC: My foot in the
stirrup, my pony won't stand. 2
Goodbye, Old Paint, I'm a-leavin'
Cheyenne see 'Old Paint'
Goodbye Ruby Tuesday see 'Ruby
Tuesday'
Goodbye to the pals of the prairie
see 'Goodbye to the plains'
'Good-bye to the plains' FL: Good-
bye to the pals of the prairie. 18
'Goodnight, goodnight, beloved'
Henry Wadsworth Longfellow and
Ciro Pinsuti. FL: same. 63
Goodnight, my darling see 'Daddy's
little boy'
Goodnight, you moonlight ladies see
'Sweet Baby James'
'Goody Bull' FL: Goody Bull and
her daughter together fell out. 8
Goody Bull and her daughter toge-
ther fell out see 'The world
turned upside down'
'Goody goody' Johnny Mercer and
Matt Malneck. FL: So you met
someone who set you back on
your heels. 59
'The Gospel train' FL: The Gospel
train is comin' FLC: Get on
board, little children. 1, 34, 38
The Gospel train's a-comin' see
'Git on board little children'
'Got a date with an angel' Clifford
Grey, Sonnie Miller, Jack Wal-
ler and Joseph Tunbridge. FL:
same. 59
Got a good reason for taking the
easy way out see 'Day tripper'
Got a letter jis dis mawnin' see
'What! Marry dat gal?'
Got a little rhythm see 'Fascinating rhythm'
Got along, without you before I met
you see 'Gonna get along with-
out ya now'
Got de St. Louis Blues jes as blue
as I can be see 'St. Louis
blues'
Got more trouble than I can stand
see 'I'm certainly living a ragtime life'
Got myself a Cadillac see 'A

worried man'
'Got them blues' FL: Got them
  blues, but I'm too mean Lordy.
  57
'Got to get you back into my life'
  Lennon and McCartney. FL: I
  was alone, I took a ride. 44
Got to pull this timber 'fore the
  sun goes down see 'Jerry'
'Gotta get away' Mick Jagger and
  Keith Richard. FL: Baby, the
  truth is out so don't deny. 16
'The Goulden Vanitee' FL: There
  was a gallant ship, and a gallant
  ship was she. 11
Grab a cab and go down see
  'Sweet and low-down'
Grab your coat and get your hat
  see 'On the sunny side of the
  street'
'Grace' FL: Thou art great and
  Thou art good. 38
'Grace darling' FL: It was on a
  storm stone lighthouse. 41
'The graceful move' FL: When first
  I saw thee graceful move. 3
'Granada' Dorothy Dodd and Augus-
  tin Lara. FL: Granada, I'm
  falling under your spell. 9
'The grand roundup' FL: Last night
  as I lay on the prairie FLC:
  They say there's to be a grand
  roundup. 18
'Grandfather's clock' Henry C.
  Work. FL: My grandfather's
  clock was too large for the shelf
  FLC: Ninety years without slum-
  bering. 1, 25, 57, 63
'Granny Wales' FL: As Granny
  arose in the morning so soon. 8
'Grasshopper' FL: The first grass-
  hopper jumped over the second
  grasshopper's back. 72
'The grasshopper' FL: Little insect
  that on high. 3
'Grasshoppers three' FL: Grasshop-
  pers three afiddling went. 72
'Gray goose' FL: It was one Sunday
  mornin'. 72
'Gray goose' FL: Last Sunday
  mornin', Lord, Lord, Lord. 66
'The gray goose' FL: Well, last
  Monday morning, Lord, Lord,
  Lord. 57
'Gray goose' FL: Well, my papa
  Went a-hunting, well, well, well.
  28
'The grey cock' FL: All on one

summer's evening when the fever
  were a-dawning. 11
'The grey selchie of Sule Skerry'
  FL: In Norway land there lived a
  maid. 11
Gray skies are gonna clear up see
  'Put on a happy face'
'Grazing in the grass' Harry Elston
  and Philemon Hou. FL: It sho'
  is mellow grazing in the grass.
  45
'The great American bum' FL:
  Come all you jolly jokers if you
  want to have some fun FLC: I
  am a bum, a jolly old bum. 57
'Great day' FL: One of these mornings, bright and fair FLC: Great
  day. 19
'Great gettin' up mornin'' FL: Stop
  and lemme tell you 'bout the
  coming of the Savior FLC: In
  that great gettin' up mornin'. 57
'Great Grandad or Grandma' FL:
  Great Grandad when the west was
  young. 2
'The great meat pie' FL: The great
  meat pie was a tidy size. 34
'The great roundup' FL: At midnight
  when the cattle are sleeping. 18
'The great Silkie' FL: An earthly
  noures sits and sings. 57
'The Great Silkie of Sule Skerry'
  FL: An earthly nourice sits and
  sings. 72
'The great speckled bird' FL: What
  a beautiful thought I am thinking.
  27, 57
'The greatest performance of my
  life' Sandro Anderle and Oscar
  Anderle. FL: Mas hoy que estoy tan solo. 9
'The greatest performance of my
  life' R. I. Allen, Sandro Anderle,
  and Oscar Anderle. FL: Tonight
  I gave the greatest performance
  of my life. 9
'Green bottles' FL: There are ten
  green bottles a-standing on the
  wall. 68
'Green broom' FL: There was an
  old man and he lived in the
  North. 30
'The green bushes' FL: As I was
  a-walking one morning in spring.
  22
'Green bushes' FL: I'll buy you fine
  silks. 30
'Green corn' FL: All I need in this

'Gypsy Davy' FL: It was late late when the boss came home. 57, 58

'The Gypsy Davy' FL: My lord came home quiet late one night. 11

'Gypsy Davy' FL: There was a gypsy come over the hill. 11

'The Gypsy Davy' FL: There was a young lady come a-trippin along. 11

'The Gypsy Davy' FL: There was a young man, a very young man. 11

'Gypsy Davy' FL: Would you leave your house and home FLC: Rally cum a ringum ringum ray. 11

'Gipsy Draly' FL: Black Jack Davy went a-riding o'er the plains. 11

'Gypsy laddie' FL: An English lord came home one night. 11

'Gypsy laddie' FL: Go catch up my old grey horse. 11

'The gypsy laddie' FL: The good lord he come traveling home. 11

'The gypsy laddie' FL: The Gipsum Davy came a-tripping on the plain FLC: Fol di rum, fol di rum, di ru-di. 11

'The gipsy laddie' FL: he saddled up his old black horse. 11

'Gipsey laddie' FL: I once had houses, riches and lands. 11

'The gipsy laddie' FL: I'll saddle up my white milk horse. 11

'The gypsy laddie' FL: Is there any gypsies in the North. 11

'The gypsy laddie' FL: It was late in the night when the captain came home. 11

'The gypsy laddie' FL: It was late last night when the squire came home. 11

'The gypsy laddie' FL: It was late one night, landlord rode out FLC: Tu ma yaddle daddle. 11

'The gypsy laddie' FL: It'll never get too dark for me. 11

'The gypsy laddie' FL: The landlord came home so late in the night. 11

'The gypsy laddie' FL: O Davy I'm so glad to meet you. 11

'The gypsy laddie' FL: Oh, when Lord Thomas he came home. 11

'Gypsy laddie' FL: O, why did you leave your house and home? 11

'The gypsy laddie' FL: Seven dark-eyed gypsies sitting in a row. 11, 30

'The gypsy laddie' FL: The squire came home quite late in the night. 11

'The gypsy laddie' FL: The squire he came home at night. 11

'The gypsy laddie' FL: There are seven sweet gypsies in the north. 11

'The gipsy laddie' FL: There came a gang o' gipsies by. 11

'The gypsy laddie' FL: There came three gypsies to my door. 11

'The gypsie laddie' FL: There came two gypsies from the north. 11

'The gypsie laddie' FL: There were three gypsies all in a row. 11

'The gypsie laddie' FL: Three gypsies came to oor hall door. 11

'The gipsy laddie' FL: Three gipsy laddies, all in a row. 11

'Gypsy laddie' FL: Twas late in the night when the captain came home. 11

'The gipsy laddie' FL: Two little gipsies live at the East. 11, 30

'The gipsy laddie' FL: What made me leave my hooses and lan'. 11

'The gypsy laddie' FL: Would you forsake your house and home FLC: To iddle inktum the iddle ay. 11

'The gypsy laddie' FL: Young Davie he came whistling by FLC: Oh, rum diddle du, diddle dum, diddle dum. 11

'Gypsy laddie' FL: Young Gipsy laddie came merrily by. 11

'Gypsy love song' Harry B. Smith and Victor Herbert. FL: The birds of the forest are calling for thee FLC: Slumber on my little gypsy sweetheart. 20, 31

'The gypsy lover' FL: Go fetch out my little black horse. 11

'The gypsy rover' FL: The gypsy rover came over the hill. 34, 35

The gypsy rover came over the hill see 'The whistling gypsy rover'

'Gypsys, tramps and thieves' Bob Stone. FL: I was born in the wagon of a travelin' show. 64

'The gypsy's warning' FL: Do not

Hang down your head, Tom Dooley
see 'Tom Dooley'
Hang your head, Tom Dooley see
'Tom Dooley'
Hang-a-man, hang-a-man, stop
your rope see 'The hangman's
song'
'The hangerman's tree' FL: O
hangerman, o hangerman, slack
on your rope. 11
'Hangman' FL: Hangman, hangman,
hold your rope. 11
Hangman, dear hangman, do up
your rope see 'The hangman's
tree'
'Hangman, hangman' FL: Hangman,
hangman, slack your rope. 35
Hangman, hangman, hold your rope
see 'Hangman'; 'The maid saved'
Hangman, hangman, howd yo hand
see 'The hangman's tree'; 'The
maid freed from the gallows'
Hangman, hangman, slack your
rope see 'The gallows pole';
'Slack your rope'
Hangman, hangman, spare my life
see 'The maid freed from the
gallows'
Hangman, hangman swing yer rope
see 'The maid freed from the
gallows'
'Hangman, hold your rope' FL:
Hangman, hangman, hold your
rope. 11
'Hangman on the gallows tree' FL:
Oh, hangman, hangman, loosen
up the line. 50
'Hangman, slack on the line' FL:
Hangman, hangman, slack on the
line. 11
'Hangman, slack up your rope' FL:
Hangman, hangman, slack up
your rope. 11
'The hangman's rope' FL: Oh, hangman, hangman, slack your rope.
11
'The hangman's song' FL: Hang-a-
man, hang-a-man, stop your
rope. 11
'The hangman's song' FL: Hangman,
hangman, slack up your rope. 11
'The hangman's tree' FL: Hangman,
dear hangman, do up your rope.
11
'The hangman's tree' FL: Hangman,
hangman, howd yo hand. 11
'The hangman's tree' FL: Slack your
rope, hangs-a-man. 11

'Hangsman' FL: Hangsman, hangs-
man, hold your rope. 11
'Hangtown gals' FL: Hangtown gals
are plump and rosy FLC: Hang-
town gals are lovely creatures.
4, 25
'Hans Beimler' FL: Vor Madrid, im
Schützengraben. 57
'The happy clown' FL: How happy
is the rural clown. 25
'Happy darky' FL: My name it is
Joe Seaven Orange Blossom. 41
Happy day, happy day see 'Oh
happy day'
'Happy days are here again' Jack
Yellen and Milton Ager. FL:
So long, sad times FLC: 'Cause
happy days are here again. 46
'A happy goodmorning' Ivy O. East-
wick and Marlys Swinger. FL:
It is a happy morning. 13
A happy little chappie at the club
one day see 'Ziggy, ze zum
zum!'
'The happy miller' FL: There was a
jolly miller once lived by the
river Dee. 25
'A happy new year' FL: I'm running
thro' grace FLC: What a happy
new year. 38
'Happy talk' Oscar Hammerstein
and Richard Rodgers. FL: Talk
about a moon FLC: Happy talk,
keep talkin' happy talk. 24
'The happy wanderer' Antonia Ridge
and Frederick W. Moller. FL:
I love to go a wandering. 52
'Harbor lights' Jimmy Kennedy and
Hugh Williams. FL: I saw the
harbor lights. 64
'Hard, ain't it hard' FL: There is a
place in this old town FLC: It's
hard, and it's hard, ain't it hard.
56, 57
'A hard day's night' Lennon and
McCartney. FL: It's been a hard
day's night. 44, 47
'Hard hearted Hannah' Jack Yellen,
Milton Ager, Bob Bigelow and
Charles Bates. FL: In old Sa-
vannah, I said Savannah FLC:
They call her hard hearted Han-
nah. 46
'Hard is the fortune of all woman-
kind' FL: Oh, hard is the fortune of all womankind. 57, 58
'Hard luck' FL: Oh, rattle your
bones, you skinny old cayute. 57

Have you paid the rent?
17
'Have you seen but a white lily
grow' FL: Same. 57
'Have you seen Sam' Frank Spencer.
FL: I floated down the river
FLC: I don't know Sam. 36
Have you seen Stella by starlight
see 'Stella by starlight'
'Have you seen your mother, baby,
standing in the shadow?' Mick
Jagger and Keith Richard. FL:
same. 16
Have you talked to the Man upstairs
see 'The Man upstairs'
Hawaii, isles of beauty see 'Song
of the islands'
'Hawaiian love song' E. Ray Goetz,
Joe Young and Pete Wendling.
FL: I'm coming back to you. 12
'Hay aquí, madre, un jardín' FL:
same. 51
'Hayseed' FL: A hayseed one day to
himself did say. 57
'A hazy shade of winter' Paul Simon.
FL: Time, time, time, see
what's become of me. 60
'He ain't heavy ... he's my brother'
Bob Russell and Bobby Scott.
FL: The road is long, with many
a winding turn FLC: He ain't
heavy, he's my brother. 45, 64
'He ain't no relation of mine' Ned
Wayburn. FL: I beat mah wife
and I beat her good FLC: He
ain't no relation of mine. 36
'He arose' FL: The Jews killed
poor Jesus FLC: He arose, He
arose. 38
He bore a hold once, he bore a
hold twice see 'The Golden
Vanity'
He called his servants one by one
see 'The red rover'
He dances overhead on the ceiling
see 'Dancing on the ceiling'
He delivered Daniel from the lion's
den see 'Didn't my Lord deliver Daniel?'
He dressed himself in the finest of
clothes see 'Lord Thomas and
Fair Ellen'
He flies through the air with the
greatest of ease see 'The man
on the flying trapeze'
He follered me up, he follered me
down see 'Pretty Polly Ann';
'The six king's daughters'

He followed her up and he followed
her down see 'The false Sir
John'; 'Lady Isabel and the elfin
knight'
He followed her up, he followed her
down see 'Pretty Polly'
He followed me up and he followed
me down see 'The outlandish
knight'
He gave to her a beaver hat see
'The two sisters'
He is pleased with me see 'My
lord and my master'
He jumped upon the milk white
steed see 'The six fair maids'
He looked east, he looked west see
'Hughie Grame'
He knew the earth was round, ho!
see 'Christofo Columbo'
'He loves and she loves' George
and Ira Gershwin. FL: Now that
I have found you FLC: He loves
and she loves and they love. 21
He made the night a little brighter
see 'The old lamplighter'
He min't him up, and he min't him
doon see 'The heir of Linne'
He mounted her on her milk-white
steed see 'Lord William'
He mounted on his milk white steed
see 'Pretty Polly'
He played his little tune see 'The
little tune'
He promised he'd buy me a beauti-
ful fairing see 'Oh, dear what
can the matter be'
He promised to meet me at Lind-
stead Market see 'Linstead
Market'
He pulled rings off his fingers see
'Broomfield Wager'
He rode and he rode on his milk
white steed see 'Lord Lovel'
He rode up to her father's gate see
'Earl Brand'
He rode up to the old man's gate
see 'Earl Brand'; 'Sweet Willie'
'He rose from the dead' FL: The
Jews crucified Him and nailed
Him to the tree FLC: He rose,
He rose. 38
He saddled up his old black horse
see 'The gypsy laddie'
He said, 'An' if I had'n my way'
see 'Samson'
He sailed east and he sailed west
see 'Lord Bateman'
He sent his servant down to tell

see   'Barbara Allen'
'He stole my tender heart away'
    FL: The fields were green, the
    hills were gay. 3
He took her round the middle so
    small see 'Earl Richard'
He took her up on his old back
    see 'The farmer's curst wife'
He took his lady by the hand see
    'Little Matha Grove'
He took to his breast and he swim
    and he swum see 'Lonesome
    low'
'He touched me' William J. Gaither.
    FL: Shackled by a heavy burden
    FLC: He touched me. 64
He was a desperado from the wild
    and woolly West see 'The des-
    perado'
He was a high born gentleman see
    'Gypsy Davy'
He was a man and a friend always
    see 'My ramblin' boy'
He was a most peculiar man see
    'A most peculiar man'
He was just a lonely cowboy see
    'Cowboy Jack'
He was mounted on a milk white
    steed see 'The king's daughter'
'He was such a nice man' R. W.
    Alldridge and M. T. a'Beckett.
    FL: If pity dwell within your
    breast. 36
He was wild and woolly and full of
    fleas see 'The Barsted king of
    England'
He went to his gate to see what
    could be seen see 'Our goodman'
He will be our dearest friend see
    'Run to Jesus'
He will round up in glory by and
    by see 'Rounded up in glory'
He would nae lie in the kitchen, or
    neither in the byre see 'Nae
    mair I'll gang a-rovin''
He yoked up his pigs one day for to
    plow see 'The scolding wife'
De heabenlye lan' see 'Jes' gwine
    ober in de heabenlye lan''
Headed down life's crooked road
    see 'Detour'
Hear the bell and whistle calling
    see 'The Wabash Cannon Ball'
Hear the bells, joyous bells see
    'Temperance bells'
Hear the sweet voice of the child
    see 'Come home, Father'
Hear the tale of Peter Gray see

'Blow, ye winds of morning'
Hear ye e'er of the silly blind harp-
    er see 'The blind harper of
    Lochmaben'
Hear ye ever of a bluidy knight see
    'May Colvine and Fause Sir John'
Hearken, hearken, music sounds
    afar see 'Funiculi funicula'
'Heart and soul' Frank Loesser and
    Hoagy Carmichael. FL: I've let
    a pair of arms enslave me FLC:
    Heart and soul I fell in love with
    you. 47, 53, 58
Heart of gold was Mary see 'Oh!
    what a pal was Mary'
Heart of my heart I love you see
    'The story of the rose'
'Heart of stone' Mick Jagger and
    Keith Richard. FL: There've
    been so many girls that I've
    known. 16
Heart to heart, dear, how I need
    you see 'Think of what you've
    done'
'The heart to rue the pleasure of
    the eye' Michael Cavendish. FL:
    same. 26
Heartache number one was when
    you left me see 'Heartaches by
    the number'
'Heartaches' John Klenner and Al
    Hoffman. FL: Heartaches, heart-
    aches. 12, 59
'Heartaches by the number' Harlan
    Howard. FL: Heartache number
    one was when you left me FLC:
    Now I've got heartaches by the
    number. 10
'Heartbreak Hotel' Mae B. Axton,
    Tommy Durden, and Elvis Pres-
    ley. FL: Since my baby left me
    found a new place to dwell. 10,
    52
'Hearts and flowers' Mary D. Brine
    and Theo Moses-Tobani. FL:
    Out amongst the flowers sweet.
    20
Hearts may flower for an hour see
    'The vagabond king waltz'
Heave away, my bully bully boys
    see 'Cape Cod girls'
'Heaven bells ringin' and I'm a-
    going home' FL: O de heaven
    bells a-ringin' and I'm a-going
    home. 5
'Heaven bells ringin' in my soul'
    FL: Nobody knows who I am FLC:
    O de heaven bells a-ringin' in

my soul. 5

'Heaven can wait' Eddie de Lange
and Jimmy van Heusen. FL:
There are a million places FLC:
Heaven can wait. 46

'Heaven, heaven' FL: I got a robe,
you got a robe. 23

'Heaven is so high' FL: You might
as well just make up your mind
FLC: Heaven is so high, so you
can't get over it. 34, 35

'Heaven will protect an honest girl'
R. P. Weston, Bert Lee and
Harris Weston. FL: On the day
I left the village my dear mother
whispered FLC: Heaven will pro-
tect an honest girl. 17

'The heaving of the lead' FL: For
England when with favoring gale.
3

'The heavy hours' FL: The heavy
hours are almost past. 3

He-cha-lutz le' man avodah see
'Zum gali, gali'

'Heckey-hi si-bernio' FL: There
were three maids lived in a
barn. 11

Heigh, Nelly, ho! Nelly see
'Nelly Bly!'

Heigh, Sir Donkey oh heigh see
'Sir Donkey'

Die Heimat ist weit see 'Freiheit'

'The heir o' Lynne' FL: Lane he
stands and lane he gangs. 11

The heir of linne' FL: Four and
twenty nobleman. 11

'The heir of Linne' FL: He min't
him up and he min't him doon.
11

'The heiress of Northumberland'
FL: Why, fair maid, have pity
on me. 11

'He'll have to go' Joe Allison and
Audrey Allison. FL: Put your
sweet lips a little closer to the
phone. 10

'The hell-bound train' FL: A Texas
cowboy lay down on a barroom
floor. 18

'The hell-bound train.' FL: A
Texas cowboy on a barroom
floor. 43, 57

Hello darkness, my old friend see
'The sound of silence'

'Hello, Dolly!' Jerry Herman. FL:
I went away from the lights of
14th Street FLC: Hello, Dolly,
well, hello, Dolly. 6, 42, 71

'Hello girls' FL: Hello, girls, listen to my voice. 57

'Hello goodbye' Lennon and McCartney. FL: You say yes, I say
no. 44

Hello! How are you? see 'The
Babbitt and the Bromide'

'Hello, ma baby' Joseph E. Howard
and Ida Emerson. FL: I've got
a little baby, but she's out of
sight FLC: Hello, ma baby,
hello, ma honey. 1, 20

'Hello walls' Willie Nelson. FL:
Hello, walls how'd things go for
you today? 10

'Hello, young lovers' Rodgers and
Hammerstein. FL: When I think
of Tom I think about a night
FLC: Hello, young lovers. 6,
24, 42

'Help!' Lennon and McCartney. FL:
Help! I need somebody. 44

'Help me make it through the night'
Kris Kristofferson. FL: Take
the ribbon from your hair. 10

'Hen and duck' FL: The hen to herself said one beautiful day. 7

'Hendry Martin' FL: Come lower
your reef and come lay your
ship too. 11

'Henry Dear' FL: It was early all
in the spring. 41

'Henry Martin' FL: As I was a sailing one cold winter's night. 11

'Henry Martyn' FL: In merry Scotland, in merry Scotland. 11

'Henry Martin' FL: In Scotland, in
Scotland, there lived brothers
three. 11

'Henry Martin' FL: In Scotland
there dwelt three brothers of
late. 11

'Henry Martin' FL: In Scotland
there lived three brothers of
late. 11

'Henry Martin' FL: It's of three
brothers in merry Scotland. 11

'Henry Martin' FL: Oh there were
three brothers in merry Scotland.
11

'Henry Martin' FL: There lived
three brothers in merry Scotland.
11

'Henry Martin' FL: There were
three brothers in merry Scotland.
11, 25, 30, 35, 57

'Henry Martin' FL: There were
three brothers, three brothers in

London. 11, 30

'Henry Martin' FL: Three brothers in Scotland, the story is told. 23

'Henry Martyn' FL: There were three brothers in fair London town. 11

'Henry my son' FL: Where have you been all day Henry my son? 11, 57

'Henry, my son' FL: Where have you been, Henry, my son. 11

'Her absence will not alter me' FL: Though distant far from Jeffy charms. 3

Her eye so mildly beaming see 'Ho ro my nut-brown maiden'

'Her eyes don't shine like diamonds' Dave Marion. FL: Three little lads were seated one day FLC: Her eyes don't shine like diamonds. 20

Her father being a chaplain see 'Bethelnie'

Her father dragged her to the stake see 'Bonnie Susie Cleland'

Her hair it was five quarters long see 'Willie was drowned in Yarrow'

'Her rosy cheeks' Thomas Campion. FL: Her rosy cheeks, her ever-smiling eyes. 26

'Her sailor boy' FL: A fair young maid in the garden walking. 41

Her sheep had in clusters crept close by the grove see 'Sheep in the clusters'

Here, a sheer hulk lies poor Tom Bowling see 'Poor Tom or the sailor's epitaph'; 'Tom Bowling'

Here come old flattop see 'Come together'

Here comes a ship a sailing see 'Ward the pirate'

Here comes that good for nothin' brat of a boy see 'Small fry'

Here comes the farmer's son, within his budget on his back see 'The tinker'

'Here comes the sun' George Harrison. FL: Little darling, it's been a long cold lonely winter FLC: Here comes the sun. 45

Here followeth the dire fate see 'Burgoyne's defeat'

Here I lie in my hospital bed see 'Sister Morphine'

Here I sit and wait for you see

'Autumn roundelay'

Here I sit on Buttermilk Hill see 'Johnny has gone for a soldier'

Here I stand with head in hand see 'You've got to hide your love away'

Here in my twilight dreams, I dream of you, deer see 'None but the lonely heart'

Here is my song for the asking see 'Song for the asking'

Here Rattler, help, help see 'Old Rattler'

Here she comes so fresh and fair see 'Sailing at high tide'

'Here, there and everywhere' Lennon and McCartney. FL: To lead a better life I need my love to be here. 44

Here we are, out of cigarettes see 'Two sleepy people'

'Here we come a-wassailing' FL: same FLC: Love and joy come to you. 34

Here we come gathering nuts in May see 'Nuts in May'

Here we come looby look see 'Looby loo'

'Here we go again' Russell Steagall and Don Lanier. FL: same. 47

'Here we go, baby' Marvin Moore. FL: Wish I had a needle FLC: Here we go, baby, down the road. 35

'Here we go round the mulberry bush' FL: This is the way we clap our hands FLC: Here we go round the mulberry bush. 48

Here's a bumper, brave boys, to the health of our king see 'A refugee song'

'Here's a health to all good lasses' FL: same. 25

'Here's a health to all true lovers' FL: same. 11

Here's a health to Lord Ronald Macdonald see 'Lord Ronald Macdonald'

Here's a letter to you madam see 'Richie story'

Here's a little knowledge quite good see 'Say si si'

Here's adieu to you judges and juries see 'Adieu to you judges and juries'

Here's cake and ale for you, young man see 'Trooper and the maid'

Here's success to Brandy see

'Brandy and water'
Here's success to port see 'Drink it down'
Here's tae the blue and the bonny bonny blue see 'Love will find a way'
'Here's the ambassador, he's arriving' FL: same. 48
Here's to good old Yale! see 'Yale Boola!'
Here's to my best romance see 'Hooray love'
'Here's to the last to die' Captain Darling. FL: We meet neath the sounding rafters. 69
Here's to the squire that goes on parade see 'The bold volunteer'
Here's to you, Tom Brown see 'The card song'
'The hermit' FL: At the close of the day when the hamlet was still. 3
'Hernando's hideaway' Richard Adler and Jerry Ross. FL: I know a dark secluded place. 6
'Herr Doktor, die periode' Bertolt Brecht and Hans Eisler. FL: same. 58
'The herring song' FL: As I was walking down by the seaside. 72
He's a fool and don't I know it see 'Bewitched'
He's a real nowhere man see 'Nowhere man'
He's a travelin' man see 'Travelin' man'
He's big around the middle and broad across the rump see 'Old Slew Foot'
He's bought a bed and a table too see 'He's going to marry Mary Ann'
He's given her a pair of shoes see 'The banks of Italy'
'He's going to marry Mary Ann' Joseph Tabrar. FL: Oh, shout hooray for Mary Ann! FLC: He's bought a bed and a table too. 17
'He's gone away' FL: I'm goin' away for to stay a little while. 57
'He's gone, he's gone up the trail' FL: There's gloom around the ranch house tonight. 18
'He's got the whole world in his hands' FL: same. 1, 23, 25, 34, 35, 67
He's just a sentimental gentleman

from Georgia see 'Sentimental gentleman from Georgia'
He's long gone, wasn't he lucky see 'Long gone'
'He's the lily of the valley' FL: King Jesus in the chariot rides FLC: He's the lily of the valley. 38
'He's the lord of lords' FL: I will not let you go my Lord FLC: Why, He's the Lord of Lords. 38
'Hesitation blues' FL: Well, standing on the corner, with a dollar in my hand FLC: Tell me how long do I have to wait? 57
Hey babe, what's in your eyes? see 'You got the silver'
Hey bonnie May went out one day see 'The keach in the creel'
Hey! Daddy! see 'Daddy'
Hey, did you happen to see the most beautiful girl in the world? see 'The most beautiful girl'
'Hey for the life of a soldier' T. S. Cooke. FL: When I was a youngster gossips would say. 69
Hey, hey, hey, somebody knockin' at my door see 'Collector man blues'
Hey, hey, Jane, Jane see 'Jane, Jane'
Hey, ho and away we go see 'Hieland laddie'
'Hey, ho, nobody home' FL: same. 19, 34, 57
'Hey ho, to the greenwood' FL: Hey ho, to the greenwood now let us go. 72
Hey joining up with his force see 'On a raven-black horse'
'Hey Jude' Lennon and McCartney. FL: Hey Jude, don't make it bad. 44
'Hey Lidee' FL: This is a crazy kind of song FLC: Hey Lidee, Lidee, Lidee. 35
Hey! Listen to my story 'bout a gal named Daisy Mae see 'Daddy'
Hey little black sheep where's your lamb see 'All the pretty little horses'
'Hey, little boy' FL: Did you see my muley? FLC: Hey, little boy. 72
'Hey little girl' FL: Hey little girl. Satisfied! 37
'Hey Lollee' FL: This is a crazy

The hills are alive with the sound
of music see 'The sound of
music'

'Hills of Roan County' FL: In the
beautiful hills, way back in Roan
county. 14

'Hind Etin' FL: My mother's eyes
are always wet. 11

'Hind Horn' FL: Ha ho I am bound
for love. 11

'Hind Horn' FL: I'll beg from Peter
and I'll beg from Paul. 11

'Hind Horn' FL: The maid came
tripping down the stairs. 11

'Hind Horn' FL: O it's where was
you bred or where was you
born? 11

'Hind Horn' FL: She asked him if
he got it by sea or by land. 11

'Hind Horn' FL: She gave him a
gay gold ring. 11

'Hind Horn, or the beggar man' FL:
On board of the ship and away
sailed he. 30

'Hindustan' Oliver G. Wallace and
Harold Weeks. FL: Camel trap-
pings jingle FLC: Hindustan where
we stopped. 31

'Hinky dinky parlez vous' FL: The
bosses are taking it on the chin,
parley-vous. 19

'Hinky, dinky, parlee-voo' FL:
German officers crossed the
Rhine. 57

'Hinky dinky parlay-voo' FL: Mad'-
moiselle from Armentières par-
lay voo. 4

'Hinneh Mah Tov' FL: same. 57

Hip your partner, Sally tipple see
'I'ze the Bye'

Hi-ro-ji-rum see 'The rich man
and the poor man'

Hiroshima, Nagasaki, Alamogordo
see 'Old man atom'

'His lordship winked at the counsel'
George Dance and Peter Conroy.
FL: The judge took his seat in
the courthouse one day FLC: His
lordship winked at the counsel.
17

His name was old Tipperary see
'Tipperary'

His sword blade gleams and his
eyelight beams see 'Anthony
Wayne'; 'Mad Anthony Wayne'

Hit's a mighty rocky road see
'Mighty rocky road'

Ho, all to the borders, Vermonters

come down see 'The green
Mountaineer'

Ho de ho de ho see 'Minnie the
Moocher'

'Ho ro my nut-brown maiden' FL:
Her eye so mildly beaming FLC:
Ho ro my nut-brown maiden. 25

Ho, see the fleet foot hosts of men
see 'Roddy McCorby'

Ho Sergeant kick that nasty purp
see 'Shoo purp don't bodder me'

Ho! so we sing as we are riding
see 'The riff song'

'Ho! Westward ho' Ossian E. Dodge.
FL: The star of empire poets
say FLC: Ho, Westward. 1

'The hobbies' FL: Attention pray
give, while of hobbies I sing
FLC: All on hobbies. 3, 4, 55

'Hobble and Bobble' FL: Down came
the old man. 11

'Hobble and Bobble' FL: I walked
into my stable. 11

'Hobblety bobblety how now' FL:
When she churns she churns in a
boot. 11

Hoe de corn see 'Razors in the
air'

'Hojita de Guarumal' FL: same. 51

'The hokey pokey' FL: You put your
right foot in. 34

Hol' it steady, right there while I
hit it see 'Work song'

Hold me, baby see 'Bugle call
rag'

Hold my horse, little Marget, she
said see 'Lord Loving'

'Hold on' FL: Mary wore three
links of chain FLC: Hold on,
hold on. 57

'Hold the fort' Philip P. Bliss. FL:
We meet today in freedom's
couse FLC: Hold the fort for we
are coming. 19, 57

'Hold tight, hold tight' Ken Brandow,
Joseph Miller and Robinson W.
Spotswood. FL: Want some sea
food mama FLC: Hold tight, hold
tight. 12

'Hold up your hand' FL: Hold up
your hand, Old Joshuway she
said. 11

Hold up your hands and Joshua, she
cries see 'The maid freed from
the gallows'

'Hold your hands, old man' FL:
same. 11

'Hold your light' FL: Hold your light

Brudder Robert. 29
Holding hands at midnight neath a
starry sky see 'Nice work if
you can get it'
'A hole in the bucket' FL: There's
a hole in the bucket, dear Liza,
dear Liza. 68
Holi, holi, holiday see 'Lord
Donald'
Holiday, a holiday see 'Little
Musgrave and Lady Barnard'
A holiday and a holiday see
'Little Mattie Groves'
Holiday, holiday, on the very first
day of the year, year see
'Little Mathie Grove'
'Holland' Daniel Read and Isaac
Watts. FL: Stay, mighty love,
and teach my song. 65
'The Holland handkerchief' FL:
There was a lord lived in this
town. 11
'Hollin green Hollin' FL: She wadna
bake, an she wadna brew. 11
'The holly bears a berry' FL: Oh
the holly bears a berry as white
as the milk. 57
Holly, holly, holliday see 'Lord
Daniel's wife'
'Holly holy' Neil Diamond. FL:
Holy holy eyes. 45
'Holy, holy, holy' Reginald Heber
and John Bacchus Dykes. FL:
Holy, holy, holy, Lord God al-
mighty. 34
'Home' Peter Van Steeden, Harry
Clarkson and Jeff Clarkson. FL:
When crickets call, my heart is
forever yearning FLC: When sha-
dows fall and trees whisper. 12
'Home came a goodman' FL: Home
came a goodman, home came he.
11
Home came the old man, home
came he see 'Our Goodman'
'Home comes the good old man'
FL: same. 11
Home, home on the range see
'Home on the range'
Home! Home! sweet, sweet home!
see 'Home, sweet home'
'Home in that rock' FL: I've got a
home in-a that rock, don't you
see? 57
'Home on the range' FL: Oh, give
me a home where the buffalo
roam FLC: Home, home on the
range. 1, 2, 23, 25, 57, 67

'Home, sweet home' John Howard
Payne and Henry R. Bishop. FL:
Mid pleasures and palaces though
we may roam FLC: Home! Home!
sweet, sweet home! 1, 2, 14,
25, 57, 63
Homesick, heartsick, nothing seems
real see 'A little street where
old friends meet'
'The homespun dress' FL: Oh, yes
I am a Southern girl FLC: Hur-
rah! Hurrah! 4, 25
'The homestead on the farm' A. P.
Carter. FL: Well, I wonder how
the old folks are at home FLC:
You could hear the cattle lowing
in the lane. 14
'Homeward bound' FL: Come loose
every sail to the breeze. 3
'Homeward bound' Paul Simon. FL:
I'm sittin' in the railway station
got a ticket for my reservation
FLC: Homeward bound, I wish I
was homeward bound. 60
'The honest working girl' FL: One
day an honest working girl was
thirsty as could be. 39
'Honey' Seymour Simons, Haven Gil-
lespie, and Richard A. Whiting.
FL: I'm in love with you honey.
47
'Honey' Bobby Russell. FL: See
the tree, how big it's grown.
45, 67, 71
Honey baby, I'm bound to ride see
'Bound to ride'
'Honey bun' Oscar Hammerstein and
Richard Rodgers. FL: My doll
is as dainty as a sparrow FLC:
A hundred and one pounds of fun.
24
Honey, I'm in love with you see
'The honey song'
'Honey pie' Lennon and McCartney.
FL: She was a working girl north
of England way FLC: Honey Pie,
you are making me crazy. 44
'The honey song' Curt Massey and
Arbie Gibson. FL: Honey, I'm
in love with you. 70
'Honeycomb' Bob Merrill. FL: It's
a darn good life and it's kind of
funny FLC: Honeycomb, won't
cha be my baby? 10
'Honky tonk woman' Mick Jagger
and Keith Richard. FL: I met a
gin soaked barroom queen in
Memphis. 16

'The house carpenter's wife' FL: Well met, well met, my own true love. 7, 50

'The house of the rising sun' Alan Price. FL: There is a house in New Orleans they call the Rising Sun. 23, 25, 47, 57, 71

'The housewife's lament' FL: One day I was walking I heard a complaining FLC: Oh, life is a toil and love is a trouble. 57, 58

'How are things in Glocca Mora' E. Y. Harburg and Burton Lane. FL: I hear a bird, Londonderry bird FL: How are things in Glocca Morra? 6, 42

How are you ladies, howdy see 'Gay young clerk in a dry goods store'

How birent is your brow, my lady Elspat see 'Lady Elspat'

'How blest has my time been' FL: same. 3

How blest the life a sailor leads see 'America, commerce and freedom'

How Blych'ilk morn was I to see see 'The Broom of Cowdenknows'

How bright is the day when the Christian see 'Sawyer's exit'

How brimful of nothing's the life of a beau see 'The life of a beau'

How came this blood on your shirt sleeve see 'Edward'

How can a young man know where his heart will go? see 'My best love'

'How can I keep from singing' FL: My life flows on in endless song above earth's lamentation. 57

'How can I leave thee?' FL: same. 23

'How cold it is?' FL: See now the blustering Boreas blows. 3

'How cold the wind do blow' FL: How cold the wind do blow, dear love. 11

'How cold the winds do blow' FL: My time be long, my time be short. 11

How come that blood on the point of your knife? see 'Edward'

'How come that blood on your shirt sleeve?' FL: same. 11

How could you leave your house and home see 'Gypsy Davy'

How dear to my heart are the scenes of my childhood see 'The old oaken bucket'

How delightful to see see 'Sheep shearing'

How do you think I began in this world? see 'The sow took the measles'

How do you think I started in life see 'The sow got the measles'

How does it feel to be one of the beautiful people see 'Baby, you're a rich man'

How does my lady's garden grow? see 'My lady's garden'

How far away are you? see 'No other love'

How funny the various sights that appear see 'Oh, what a difference in the morning'

How glad many millions see 'I've got a crush on you'

'How happy a state does the miller possess see 'The king and the miller'

How happy is the rural clown see 'The happy clown'

'How happy the soldier' FL: How happy the soldier who lives on his pay. 3, 55, 65

How I love the kisses of Dolores see 'Dolores'

How in the world can I pick a bale a cotton? see 'Pick a bale a cotton'

'How little we know' Carolyn Leigh and Philip Springer. FL: How little we know how much to discover. 52

How long did it rain see 'How long, watchman?'

How long have you been living here see 'The Arkansas traveler'

'How long, watchman?' FL: How long did it rain FLC: O how long, watchman. 5

How long you be gone, Lord Lovel, says she see 'Lord Lovel'

How many arms have held you see 'I really don't want to know'

How many days did the water fall? see 'The old ark's a-moverin''

How many oxen and donkeys now see 'The winter season of the year'

How many times have you heard someone say see 'A satisfied mind'

'How mountain girls can love' FL:

Riding the night on the high cold wind FLC: Get down boys, go back home. 14

How much is that doggie in the window see 'That doggie in the window'

'How old are you, my pretty little miss?' FL: same FLC: Rink to my dink to my diddle diddle dum. 57

How old are you my pretty Polly see 'Black Jack Davy'

How pleasant is the wind tonight see 'The unquiet grave'

'How should I your true love know' William Shakespeare. FL: same. 57

'How stands the glass around' FL: same. 55, 65

How stands the glass around? see 'Why, soldiers, why'

'How tedious and tasteless the hours' FL: same. 50

'How ya gonna keep 'em down on the farm' Sam M. Lewis, Joe Young and Walter Donaldson. FL: Reuben, Reuben, I've been thinking FLC: How ya gonna keep 'em down on the farm? 31

'How 'ya gonna keep 'em down on the farm?' Sam M. Lewis, Joe Young and Walter Donaldson. FL: They'll never want to see a rake or plow FLC: How you gonna keep 'em down on the farm? 12

'Howdy, howdy' FL: An' a howdy, howdy, brother. 5

'Hudson River steamboat' FL: Hudson River steamboat, streaming up and down FLC: Choo, choo, to go ahead. 57

'Hugh of Lincoln' FL: It rained a mist, it rained a mist. 11

'Hughie Graham' FL: Our lords are to the mountains gane. 11

'Hughie Grame' FL: He looked east, he looked west. 11

'Humoresque' Anton Dvorak. FL: Passengers will please refrain. 57

'Humpty dumpty' FL: Humpty Dumpty sat on a wall. 48

A hundred and one pounds of fun see 'Honey Bun'

A hundred of thy friends dear child see 'Lord Thomas and brown maid'

Hunt up your mattock, whistle up

your dog see 'Groundhog'

'The hunters of Kentucky' Samuel Woodworth. FL: Ye gentlemen and ladies fair who grace this famous city FLC: Oh, Kentucky, the hunters of Kentucky. 1, 4, 57

'Hunting the hare' FL: O the yelping of hounds the skelping. 25

'Hunting the wren' FL: Let us go to the woods, says Richard to Robin. 61

'The huntsman' George A. Stevens, Albert Perry, and Fred Eplett. FL: I'm not a fireman or a 'tec, as some folks may suppose. 17

'The Huron Indian carol' FL: Twas in the moon of wintertime FLC: Jesus, your king is born. 33

Hurrah for the choice of the nation see 'Lincoln and Liberty'

Hurrah! Hurrah! see 'The homespun dress'

Hurrah, hurrah, for Southern rights hurrah see 'The bonnie blue flag'

Hurrah, hurrah, we bring the jubilee see 'Marching through Georgia'

Hurray for Greer Country! the land of the free see 'Starving to death on a government claim'

'Hurree Hurroo' FL: Smiling the land, smiling the sea FLC: Hurree, hurroo, my bonny wee lass. 57

'Hurroo-ri-ah' FL: As I rode down to Newry Town. 11

Hurry, honey, come with me see 'Stop it!'

'Hurry, hurry, hurry' Margaret Potts and Marlys Swinger. FL: Rabbit twitched his twichety ears. 13

'The husband with no courage in him' FL: As I walked out one summer's day FLC: And all of her conversation was. 57, 58

Hush, be still as any mouse see 'Lullaby'

Hush, hush, my pretty Polly dear see 'Pretty Polly'

Hush, lie still, slumber see 'Hush, my babe'

'Hush little baby' FL: Hush, little baby, don't say a word. 1, 4, 23, 25, 57, 67, 68

Hush little baby don't say a word see 'The mocking bird song'

Hush, little baby, don't you cry
    see 'All my trials'
'Hush, my babe' FL: Hush, lie still,
    slumber. 33
'Hush, my Babe' Isaac Watts. FL:
    Hush, my babe, lie still and
    slumber. 33
'Hush-a-bye baby' FL: Hush-a-bye
    baby, on the tree top. 48
Hush-you-bye see 'All the pretty
    little horses'; 'Pretty little
    horses'
'Huzza for liberty' George K. Jack-
    son. FL: Come, lads, your
    glasses fill with glee. 65
Huzza, huzza, huzza see 'Hail!
    America Hail!'
'Hymn for nations' L. Beethoven
    and Josephine Bacon. FL: Broth-
    er shout your country's anthem.
    57
'Hynd Horn' FL: Hynd Horn fair and
    Hynd Horn free. 11
'Hynd Horn' FL: Near Edinburgh
    was a young child born. 11

- I -

'I ain't going to die no more' FL:
    Going to meet those happy Chris-
    tians sooner in the morning.
    FLC: Oh! ain't I glad. 38
I ain't gonna grieve my Lord no
    more see 'Oh, you can't get
    to heaven'
I ain't gonna study war no more
    see 'Down by the riverside';
    'Going to study war no more'
I ain't gonna work on the railroad
    see 'Roll in my sweet baby's
    arms'
I ain't got no father see 'Lone-
    some cowboy'
I ain't got no use for your red
    apple juice see 'Red apple
    juice'
'I ain't got weary yet' FL: Been
    praying for the sinner so long
    FLC: And I ain't got weary yet.
    38
'I ain't marchin' any more' Phil
    Ochs. FL: Oh, I marched to
    the Battle of New Orleans. 4
'I almost lost my mind' Ivory Joe
    Hunter. FL: When I lost my
    baby. 10
I am a bolger sold,--I mean I'm a

soldier bold see 'One of the
    deathless army'
I am a brisk and sprightly lad see
    'Yeo, yeo, yeo, sir'
I am a bum, a jolly old bum see
    'The great American bum'
'I am a girl of constant sorrow'
    Sarah Ogan. FL: same. 58
I am a girl of constant sorrow see
    'I'm a girl of constant sorrow'
I am a girl what's doing very well
    in the wegetable line see
    'Wotcher 'Ria'
I am a jovial collier, lad, as blithe
    as blithe can be see 'Down in
    a coal mine'
I am a lineman for the county see
    'Wichita lineman'
'I am a lover, yet was never loved'
    Alfonso Ferrabosco. FL: same.
    26
'I am a man of constant sorrow'
    FL: same. 56
I am a man of constant sorrow see
    'Man of constant sorrow'
I am a noted highwayman, Cole
    Younger is my name see 'Cole
    Younger'
'I am a pilgrim' FL: I am a pilgrim
    and a stranger. 34, 35, 57
'I am a pilgrim' FL: I am a pil-
    grim and a stranger while
    wand'ring through this world of
    woe FLC: I'm going there to see
    my mother, she said she'd meet
    me when I come. 7
I am a poor unlucky chap see 'I
    walk the road again'
'I am a poor wayfaring stranger'
    FL: same. 25
I am a poor wayfaring stranger see
    'Wayfaring stranger'
I am a reckless highwayman, Cole
    Younger is my name see 'Cole
    Younger'
'I am a rock' Paul Simon. FL: A
    winter's day in a deep and dark
    December FLC: I am a rock. 45,
    60
'I am a union woman' Aunt Molly
    Jackson. FL: same FLC: Join
    the CIO. 4, 58
I am as brown as brown can be
    see 'The brown girl'
I am as brown as brown can be,
    my eyes are black as a sloe see
    'The bonnie brown girl'
I am bold John just returned on

shore see 'The saucy sailor'
'I am bound for the promised land'
FL: On Jordan's stormy banks I
stand FLC: I am bound for the
Promised Land. 4
I am bound for the Promised Land
see 'Bound for the Promised
Land'
I am broke and hungry, ragged and
dirty too see 'Broke and hungry'
I am he as you are he as you are
me and we are all together see
'I am the walrus'
I am his sweet Patootie and he is
my lovin' man see 'Everybody
loves my baby'
I am just a little girl who's looking
for a little boy see 'Looking
for a boy'
I am just a lonely traveler see
'When the saints go marching in'
I am just a poor boy see 'The
boxer'
I am just a weary pilgrim see
'When the saints come marching
in'
I am looking rather seedy now while
holding down my claim see 'The
little old sod shanty'
I am no profess'n Christian the sort
the cities hold see 'A Christian
cowboy's creed'
'I am so far from pitying thee'
Robert Jones. FL: same. 26
I am so lonely, I am so blue see
'Somebody's sweetheart I want to
be'
'I am the forester' FL: I am the
forester o this place FLC: Wimy
rowe rum derrity. 11
'I am the forester o' this land' FL:
same. 11
'I am the walrus' Lennon and
McCartney. FL: I am he as you
are he as you are me and we
are all together. 44
I am thinking tonight of my old cot-
tage home see 'My old cottage
home'
I am tired and weary but I must
toil on see 'There'll be peace
in the valley for me'
I am weak but Thou are strong see
'Just a closer walk with Thee'
'I am waiting' Mick Jagger and
Keith Richard. FL: I am waiting, I am waiting oh yeah, oh
yeah. 16

I 'as to play this whistle in the
gutter see 'Penny whistler'
I asked my love to take a walk see
'Banks of the Ohio'
I asked my love to walk with me
see 'Banks of the Ohio'
I beat mah wife and I beat her good
see 'He ain't no relation of
mine'
I been havin' some hard travelin'
see 'Hard traveling'
I been Norman Mailered, Maxwell
Taylored see 'A simple desultory philippic'
I beg you bide at hame, Margaret
see 'Child Waters'
I behold her and was conquered at
the start see 'I guess I'll have
to change my plan'
I brought my love a cherry without
any stone see 'The riddle song'
I buyed me a little dog, it's color
it was brown see 'Little brown
dog'
'I cain't say no' Oscar Hammerstein
and Richard Rodgers. FL: It
ain't so much a question of not
knowing what to do FLC: I'm just
a girl who cain't say no. 24
I called to my father, my father
harkened to me see 'Save me,
Lord, save'
'I called to my loving wife' FL:
same. 11
I came from old Virginny, from the
county Acomac see 'Maple leaf
rag'
I came home from town last night
was drier than I could see
'Our Goodman'
I came home the first night drunk
as I could be see 'The three
nights experience'
I came home the other night see
'Our Goodman'
I came home the other night as
drunk as I could be see 'Four
nights drunk'
I came to the place where the lone
pilgrim lay see 'The lone pil-
grim'
I came to the place where the White
Pilgrim lay see 'The White
Pilgrim'
'I can buckle a wheeler' FL: Good
mornin', Captain. 28
I can hear the soft breathing of the
girl that I love see 'Somewhere

they can't find me'; 'Wednesday
morning, 3 A. M. '
I can ride the wildest bronco in the
wild and woolly West see 'The
gol-darned wheel'
I can see the cattle grazing o'er the
hills at early morn see 'I'd
like to be in Texas'
I can see the cattle grazing on the
hills at early morn see 'Round-
up in the spring'
I can see the mustang band grazing
by the river Grand see 'My
Harding Country home'
'I can't believe that you're in love
with me' Clarence Gaskill and
Jimmy McHugh. FL: You're
telling everyone I know FLC:
Your eyes of blue, your kisses
too. 12
'I can't feel at home in this world
anymore' FL: This world is not
my home. 57
I can't forget the glamour see
'Stars fell on Alabama'
I can't forget the night I met you
see 'You call it madness'
I can't get no satisfaction see
'Satisfaction'
'I can't get started' Ira Gershwin
and Vernon Duke. FL: I'm a
glum one, it's explainable FLC:
I've flown around the world in a
plane. 42, 59
'I can't give you anything but love'
Dorothy Fields and Jimmy Mc-
Hugh. FL: Dream awhile,
scheme awhile FLC: I can't give
you anything but love. 12
'I can't give you anything but love'
Dorothy Fields and Jimmy
McHugh. FL: Gee, but it's
tough to be broke, kid FLC: I
can't give you anything but love.
1
'I can't see the wind' Ivy O. Eastwick and Marlys Swinger. FL:
same. 13
'I can't tell why I love you, but I
do' Will D. Cobb and Gus Edwards. FL: same. 31
'I care not for these ladies' Thomas
Campion. FL: I care not for
these ladies that must be wooed
and prayed. 26
I caught her dancing with another
one see 'Jealousy'
I caught you, sir, having a look at

her see 'Once in love with
Amy
I choose my bonnie love in the
woods o' Gight see 'The lady
o' Gight'
I come from Alabama with my banjo
on my knee see 'Oh! Susanna'
I come this night for to sing and
pray see 'Oh yes! Oh yes!'
I come to town the other night see
'Old Dan Tucker'
'I could have danced all night' Alan
Jay Lerner and Frederick Loewe.
FL: Bed! Bed! I couldn't go to
bed FLC: I could have danced all
night. 6, 42, 64
'I couldn't hear nobody pray' FL:
And I couldn't hear nobody pray.
25, 34
I courted pretty Polly the livelong
night see 'Pretty Polly'
'I cover the waterfront' Edward
Heyman and Johnny Green. FL:
Away from the city that hurts
and mocks FLC: I cover the
waterfront. 46
I crave your notice for a time,
pray listen to my song see
'Burmese tune'
I danced in the morning see 'The
lord of the dance'
'I didn't know what time it was'
Lorenz Hart and Richard Rodgers.
FL: Once I was young, yesterday
perhaps FLC: I didn't know what
time it was. 42
'I die whenas I do not see her' John
Danyel. FL: same. 26
I dink me vone day dot dere bisness
would pay see 'I lose me mine
vife'
I do believe in you, and I know you
believe in me see 'Feelin'
stronger every day'
I do not growl as others do or wish
that I was younger see 'Fame'
'I don't believe she'd know me' FL:
I don't believe my baby'd know
me. 57
'I don't care' Jean Lenox and Harry
O. Sutton. FL: They say I'm
crazy, got no sense FLC: I don't
care, I don't care. 20
I don't care if it rains or freezes
see 'Plastic Jesus'
I don't care if there's powder on my
nose see 'It never entered my
mind'

I don't care what the weatherman
    says see 'Jeepers creepers'
I don't care where you bury my
    body see 'Shine, shine'
'I don't hurt anymore' Jack Rollins
    and Don Robertson. FL: same.
    10
I don't know exactly how it started
    see 'You're getting to be a habit
    with me'
'I don't know how to love him' Tim
    Rice and Andrew Lloyd Webber.
    FL: same. 42, 45
I don't know Sam see 'Have you
    seen Sam'
'I don't stand a ghost of a chance
    with you' Bing Crosby, Ned
    Washington and Victor Young.
    FL: I thought at last I'd found
    you FLC: I need your love so
    badly. 12
I don't want no more of army life
    see 'Gee, but I want to go home'
'I don't want to get adjusted' FL:
    In this world of toil and trouble.
    57
'I don't want to play in your yard'
    Philip Wingate and H. W. Petrie.
    FL: Once there lived side by
    side FLC: I don't want to play in
    your yard. 20
'I don't want to see you again' Len-
    non and McCartney. FL: same.
    44
'I don't want to set the world on
    fire' Eddie Seiler, Sol Marcus,
    Bennie Benjamin and Eddie Dur-
    ham. FL: same. 59
'I don't want to spoil the party'
    John Lennon and Paul McCartney.
    FL: I don't want to spoil the
    party so I'll go. 47
I don't want to steal or rob see
    'Mandy'
'I don't want to walk without you'
    Frank Loesser and Jule Styne.
    FL: All our friends keep knock-
    ing at the door FLC: I don't want
    to walk without you, baby. 47,
    59
I don't want you, but I hate to
    loose you see 'Between the
    devil and the deep blue sea'
'I don't want you go on and leave
    me' FL: I'm traveling thro' the
    wilderness FLC: I'm a-comin'
    yes, Lord! 5
I don't want you to be high see

'Back street girl'
I don't want your greenback dollar
    see 'Greenback dollar'
'I don't want your millions, mister'
    Jim Garland. FL: same. 19
I dreaded every morning see
    'What a difference a day made'
'I dream of Jeannie with the light
    brown hair' FL: same. 25
I dream of Jeanie with the light
    brown hair see 'Jeanie with the
    light brown hair'
I dreamed a dream jist sin' the
    streen see 'The coerin' blue'
I dreamed I saw Joe Hill last night
    alive as you and me see 'Joe
    Hill'
I dreamed that I had died see
    'The mill was made of marble'
I dreamt that I dwelt in marble
    halls see 'The dream'
I dunno what my brother wants to
    stay here for see 'Soon in de
    morning'
'I fall to pieces' Harlan Howard and
    Hank Cochran. FL: I fall to
    pieces each time I see you again.
    10
I feel a sudden urge to sing see
    'It's d'lovely'
'I feel fine' Lennon and McCartney.
    FL: Baby's good to me, you
    know. 44, 47
I feel so awful blue see 'Teasing'
I feel tears wellin' up cold and deep
    inside see 'The race is on'
I floated down the river see 'Have
    you seen Sam'
I follered her up and I follered her
    down see 'Lady Isabel and the
    elf knight'
I forgive you 'cause I can't forget
    you see 'Between the devil and
    the deep blue sea'
'I found a million dollar baby' Billy
    Rose, Mort Dixon and Harry
    Warner. FL: Love comes along
    like a popular song FLC: It was
    a lucky April shower. 46
I found my love in Avalon see
    'Avalon'
I found my thrill on Blueberry Hill
    see 'Blueberry Hill'
I gave my heart to you in Old Lis-
    bon that night see 'Lisbon An-
    tigua'
'I gave my love a cherry' FL: I
    gave my love a cherry that had

no stone. 11, 23, 25, 66
I gave my love a cherry that had no
    stone see 'The riddle song'
I gave my love a cherry without a
    stone see 'The riddle song'
'I get a kick out of you' Cole Port-
    er. FL: My story is much too
    sad to be told FLC: I get no kick
    from champagne. 46
'I get along without you very well'
    Hoagy Carmichael. FL: same.
    53
I give her all my love see 'And
    I love her'
'I gonna leave old Texas now!' FL:
    same. 66
I gonna marry you, Sal, Sal see
    'Sally Ann'
I gonna tell you a story of a gal I
    know see 'The liberated wo-
    man's husband's talking blues'
I got a barrel of flour see 'Never
    no more hard times blues'
I got a cousin in Milwaukee see
    'My cousin in Milwaukee'
I got a gal at the head of the
    creek see 'Cripple Creek'
I got a girl and she loves me see
    'Cripple Creek'
I got a letter from my home see
    'Sportin' life blues'
I got a lifetime to drop 'em down
    see 'Drop 'em down'
I got a long tall yellow gal in
    Georgia see 'Tampa'
I got a pig at home in a pen see
    'Pig in a pen'
I got a ragtime dog and a ragtime
    cat see 'I'm certainly living
    a ragtime life'
'I got a record' FL: Told my mama,
    wo, Lordy. 28
'I got a robe' FL: I got a robe,
    you got a robe. 25
I got a robe, you got a robe see
    'Heaven, heaven'
I got a shoe, you got a shoe see
    'All God's children got shoes'
I got an old tom cat see 'Tom
    cat blues'
I got no change for to be turned
    loose see 'Mister Johnson,
    turn me loose'
'I got plenty o' nuttin' George and
    Ira Gershwin, DuBose Heyward.
    FL: Oh, I got plenty o' nuttin.
    6, 21, 64
'I got rhythm' George and Ira Gersh-

win. FL: Days can be sunny
    FLC: I got rhythm. 21, 46
I got spurs that jingle, jangle,
    jingle see 'Jingle jangle jingle'
'I got the blues' Mick Jagger and
    Keith Richard. FL: As I sat
    down FLC: As I stand by your
    flame. 16
I got the blues see 'The Winns-
    boro cotton mill blues'
I got the blues, I got the blues
    see 'Weave room blues'
'I got the crane wing' FL: Well, I
    got the crane wing, oh, my
    Lordy. 28
I got too much time, buddy, oh
    Lord, for the crime I done see
    'Too much time for the crime I
    done'
'I guess I'll have to change my
    plan' Howard Dietz and Arthur
    Schwartz. FL: I beheld her and
    was conquered at the start FLC:
    I guess I'll have to change my
    plan. 42, 46
I guess we haven't got a sense of
    responsibility see 'Two sleepy
    people'
I had a cat and the cat pleased me
    see 'Fiddle-i-fee'
I had a dog and his name was Blue
    see 'Old Blue'
I had a dream last night, all about
    my gal see 'Lonesome house
    blues'
I had a horse, his name Napoleon
    see 'Napoleon'
I had a horse his name was Bill
    see 'A horse named Bill'
'I had a little cat' FL: I had a
    little cat and the cat pleased me.
    32
'I had a little nut tree' FL: same.
    48
'I had a little rooster' FL: I had a
    little rooster by the barnyard
    gate. 72
I had a little ship and I sailed her
    on the sea see 'The golden
    willow tree'
I had a little ship and I sailed on
    the sea see 'The Golden Vanity'
I had a little ship in the North
    Counteree see 'The Golden
    Vanity'
'I had a rooster' FL: I had a roost-
    er and the rooster pleased me.
    57

I had a ship in the northern coun-
teree see 'Golden Valladay'
I had an old dog and his name was
Blue see 'Old Blue'
I had four brothers over the sea
see 'Gifts from over the sea';
'The four brothers'
I had to step it up and go see
'Step it up and go'
I hail my mother in the morning
see 'Zion's children'
I hail my sister, my sister she
bow low see 'Gideon's band'
I hate those chaps what talks about
the things what they likes to
drink see ''Arf a pint of ale'
I hate to see de evenin' sun go
down see 'St. Louis blues'
I have a dear old daddy see
'Father's whiskers'
I have a horse I call Napoleon see
'Napoleon'
I have a loving brother see 'When
the saints come marchin' in'
I have a neighbor, one of those
see 'Keep woman in her sphere'
I have a ship in the North country
see 'The Golden Vanity'
I have been a rover see 'Love's
been good to me'
I have bought a home and ring and
everything see 'Margie'
I have courted a waxen girl see
'Maria Martini'
I have four brothers over the sea
see 'A Paradox'; 'Perry Merry
Dictum Dominee'
I have good news to bring and that
is why I sing see 'Old Gospel
ship'
I have heard people say that they'd
startle, the world see 'Cawn't
do it ye know!'
I have heard the maves singing his
lovesong to the morn see 'Bonny Mary of Argyle'
I have just come from the salt,
salt sea see 'The house carpenter'
I have just returned from the salt,
salt sea see 'The house carpenter'
I have led a good life, full of peace
and quiet see 'The good boy'
I have often walked down this street
before see 'On the street where
you live'
I have seen the morning burning

golden on the mountain, in the
skies see 'Loving her was
easier than anything I'll ever do
again'
I have something on my mind see
'Mary Lou'
I hear a bird, Londonderry bird
see 'How are things in Glocca
Morra'
I hear de bell a-ringin', I see de
captain stand see 'Roll out,
heave dat cotton'
I hear footsteps slowly walking see
'There goes my everything'
I hear music when I look at you
see 'The song is you'
I hear the click clack of your feet
on the stairs see 'Stray cat'
I hear the drizzle of the rain see
'Kathy's song'
I hear the train a-comin' see
'Folsom Prison blues'
I heard a cow low, a bonnie cow
low see 'The Queen of Elfan's
Nourice'
I heard from heaven today see
'Peter, go ring them bells'
'I heard the bells on Christmas Day'
Henry Wadsworth Longfellow and
J. Baptiste Calkin. FL: same.
34
'I heard the reports of a pistol' FL:
Well, I heard the reports of a
pistol, whoa man, down the
right-a-way. 28
I hold here in my hand a lengthy
cablegram see 'Globe trotting
Nellie Bly'
I hurried through the darkness see
'Fugitive breakdown'
I imagine with me head on your
shoulder see 'I'll buy that
dream'
I joined Finnigan's musketeers see
'Finnigan's Musketeers'
I joined the Navy to see the world
see 'Cindy, oh Cindy'
I just arrived in town for to pass de
time away see 'Jordan is a hard
road to trabel'
I just kissed the one I love for the
last time see 'Think I'll go
somewhere'
I just saw a maniac, maniac, maniac see 'Five foot two eyes of
blue'
I keep a close watch on this heart
of mine see 'I walk the line'

I keep dreaming of a night and a
love see 'La Comparsa'
I knew a lady of the North see
'The derry downs of Arrow'
I knew a man Bojangles and he
danced for you see 'Mr. Bo-
jangles'
I knew a soldier by his horse see
'The trooper and the maid'
I knew a widow, she lived abroad
see 'The wife of Usher's Well'
I knew the little young soldier see
'The lady and the dragoon'
I know a bundle of humanity see
'Young and healthy'
I know a dark secluded place see
'Hernando's hideaway'
I know a gal that I adore, L'il Liza
Jane see 'L'll Liza Jane'
I know an' fair lovey, I know an'
free see 'The begging weed'
'I know an old lady who swallowed
a fly' FL: same. 72
I know, I know, I know it see
'Signs of spring'
I know I'm called a gay brunette
see 'O let me be a blonde,
Mother'
I know I'm right when I say it's fine
see 'The Rock Island Line'
I know it, yes, I know it see
'These bones goin' to rise agin'
I know King Edward was a noble
and great see 'Love alone'
I know moonrise, I know starrise
see 'Lay dis body down'
'I know my love' FL: I know my
love by his way o' walkin' FL:
Still she cried, "I love him the
best." 57
I know not the why and wherefore
see 'The Lorelei'
I know something but I can't express
it see 'S'posin''
'I know that my Redeemer lives'
FL: Oh, I know, I know my
Lord. 38
I know that someday you'll want me
to want you see 'Someday'
'I know where I'm going' FL: same.
34, 35, 57
'I know you, rider' FL: I know you,
rider, you're gonna miss me
when I'm gone. 57
'I know you're married but I love
you still' FL: The day I met you
my heart spoke to me FLC: You
know I love you and I always will.

14
I know you're tired of following see
'My elusive dreams'
I knows a gal that you don't know
see 'Li'l Liza Jane'
I knows a little doner, I'm about to
own 'er see 'The future Mrs.
'Awkins'
I laughed at sweethearts I met at
school see 'My heart stood
still'
I leapt before I looked see 'The
next time it happens'
'I learned about roses from Him'
FL: Twas on the Horse Shoe in
old Arizona. 43
'I left my heart in San Francisco'
FL: Douglass Cross and George
Cory. FL: The loveliness of
Paris FLC: I left my heart in
San Francisco. 71
'I left my sugar standing in the
rain' Irving Kahal and Sammy
Fain. FL: Cause I left my sugar
standing in the rain. 54
'I let a song go out of my heart'
Irving Mills, Henry Nemo, John
Redmond and Duke Ellington.
FL: Since you and I have drifted
apart FLC: I let a song go out
of my heart. 12, 59
I like icicles long and straight see
'Icicles'
I like pickled onion see 'A little
bit of cucumber'
I like to see a thunderstorm see
'The thunderstorm'
'I like winter' Lois Lenski and
Clyde R. Bulla. FL: same. 13
I live for the good of my nation
see 'Old Rosin the Beau'
I live in an apartment on the 99th
floor of my block see 'Get off
my cloud'
'I live in Trafalgar Square' C. W.
Murphy. FL: Today I'm busy
removing FLC: I live in Trafal-
gar Square. 17
I live in Vermont and one morning
last summer see 'The charming
young widow I met on the train'
I lived in Hampshire, a mason by
trade see 'The New Hampshire
bite'
'I loathe that I did love' Lord Vaux.
FL: same. 26
I looked over Jordan and what did I
see see 'Swing, low, sweet

chariot'

'I lose me mine vife' Charles A. Reade. FL: I dink me vone day dot dere bisness would pay FLC: But I'm sorry to say mine wife's gone avay. 36

I lost my eyes in the Harlan pits in the year of '56 see 'The blind fiddler'

'I love life' Irwin M. Casse and Manazucca. FL: I love life so I want to live. 1

'I love Paris' Cole Porter. FL: Every time I look down on the timeless town FLC: I love Paris in the springtime. 6, 42

'I love sixpence' FL: I love sixpence, jolly little sixpence. 48

I love the country air see 'Mother pin a rose on me'

I love the looks of you see 'All of you'

'I love the mountains' FL: same. 34

I love those dear hearts and gentle people see 'Dear hearts and gentle people'

I love to go a wandering see 'The happy wanderer'

I love to roam out yonder see 'Alla en el rancho grande'; 'El rancho grande'

I love to see the sepoy and to hear this martial tread see 'The elephant battery'

I love to shout, I love to sing see 'Come down, angels'

I love you a bushel and a peck see 'A bushel and a peck'

I love you as I never loved before see 'When you were sweet 16'

I love you, baby see 'When things go wrong with you'

I love you, there's nothing more to hide see 'There! I've said it again'

'I love you truly' Carrie Jacobs Bond. FL: O I love you truly, truly dear. 1, 20, 25, 31

I love your funny face see 'Funny face'

I love your lovin' arms see 'My honey's lovin' arms'

'I loved you once in silence' Lerner and Loewe. FL: same. 42

'I loves you Porgy' DuBose Heyward and George Gershwin. FL: I wants to stay here. 21

I made up my mind in a early see 'The trail to Mexico'

I made up my mind to change my way see 'The trail to Mexico'

I make up things to say on my way to you see 'I've told every little star'

'I married a wife' FL: Once I was single, oh then. 25

I married a wife, I brought her home see 'The wife wrapt in wether's skin'

I married a wife, I took her home see 'Gently, Jinny fair Rosemary'

I married a wife in the month of June see 'Old wetherskin''

I married me a wife and I sent her to milk see 'John Dobber'

I married me a wife and I took her home see 'The green valley'; 'Jennifer, Jenny'; 'While the dew flies over the green valley'

I married me a wife and took her home see 'Gentle fair Jenny'

I married me a wife I got her home see 'The wife wrapt in wether's skin'

I married me a wife in the month of June see 'Ti risslety rosslety'

I married me a wife, took her home see 'The wife wrapped in the wether's skin'

I may be right and I may be wrong see 'The Rock Island Line'

'I may be wrong' Harry Ruskin and Henry Sullivan. FL: When I play roulette FLC: I may be wrong. 46

I may seem proud see 'I surrender, dear'

I met a gin soaked barroom queen in Memphis see 'Honky tonk woman'

I met a little girl in Knoxville see 'Knoxville girl'

I met her on the mountain see 'Tom Dooley'

I might have married a king's daughter fair see 'The house carpenter'

I miss you darling, more and more every day see 'Faded love'

I miss you so much the 'taters need diggin' see 'Phfft! you were gone!'

I must be going no longer staying

see 'The lover's ghost'
'I need another witness' FL: Oh
well I need another witness. 28
I need your love so badly see 'I
don't stand a ghost of a chance
with you'
I never could get on with strangers
somehow see 'The man was a
stranger to me'
I never did like Old Joe Clark see
'Old Joe Clark'
'I never drink behind the bar' Ed
Harrigan and Dave Braham.
FL: I used to have a fine saloon
with mirrors on the wall FLC:
I never drink behind the bar. 36
I never feel a thing is real see
'It's only a paper moon'
I never had a barrel of money see
'Empty pocket blues'; 'Poor
man's blues'
I never had but two richt loves see
'Gin I were'
'I never will marry' FL: Oh, I
never will marry. 23, 25
'I never will marry' FL: One day
as I rambled, down by the sea
shore FLC: I never will marry,
nor be no man's wife. 56, 57
I offer to you a paper of pins see
'Paper of pins'
I once could have married a king's
daughter see 'House carpenter'
I once did courted a Waxford girl
see 'Maria Martini'
I once did know two little boys see
'The two brothers'
I once got up and went to town see
'Devilish Mary'
I once had a girl or should I say
she once had me see 'Norwegian
wood'
I once had houses, riches and lands
see 'Gypsy laddie'
I once knew a little girl and I loved
her as my life and freely see
'The two lovers'
I once knew a man by the name of
Pike see 'Old Pike'
'I once was a carman in the big
mountain con' FL: Twas once in
the saddle I used to go dashing.
62
'I pick up my hoe' FL: I pick up
my hoe and I go. 13
I picked up my gun and I whistled
for my dog see 'Ground Hog'
'I planted my wheat' FL: I planted

my wheat on the mountainside,
mountainside. 13
I pop my whip and I bring the blood
see 'The ox-driving song'
I promised I'm meet you out at
Adam's spring see 'Little
Lonie'
I raised a dog and his name was
Blue see 'Old Blue'
I read the news today oh boy see
'A day in the life'
I realize the way your eyes de-
ceived me see 'Paper roses'
'I really don't want to know' Howard
Barnes and Don Robertson. FL:
How many arms have held you.
10
I really have to tell you, Evelyn
see 'Guardian beauty contest'
I remember one September see
'Mighty day'
I remember Sunday morning see
'Sunday will never be the same'
I remember the bliss see 'Do-do-
do'
I remember when a bit of a boy
see 'I'll never get drunk any-
more'
'I remember you' Johnny Mercer
and Victor Schertzinger. FL:
Was it in Tahiti? FLC: I remem-
ber you. 70
'I ride an old paint' FL: I ride an
old paint, I lead an old Dan FLC:
Ride around, little dogies, ride
around them slow. 57, 72
'I ride an old paint' FL: I ride an
old paint, I lead an old Dan FLC:
Won't you ride around easy, ride
around slow. 25
I rode by a house with the windows
up see 'Everybody's got a home
but me'
I rode up in the Rocky Mountains
see 'Circuit rider's home'
I said I will look to my ways see
'Martyrs tune'
I said 'Oh, no a-doin't cha follow
me no more' see 'Don'cha both-
er me'
I said, silicosis you made a mighty
bad break of me see 'Silicosis
blues'
I sailed east, I sailed west see
'The jailer's daughter'; 'Young
Beichan'
I saw a blind man see 'When
you're smiling'

I saw a man at early dawn in a
grog saloon see 'The drunk-
ard's doom'
I saw a young lady a-walking all
out see 'The elfin knight'
I saw a youth and a maiden on a
lonely city street see 'Take
back your gold'
I saw her today at the reception
see 'You can't always get what
you want'
'I saw my lady wee' John Dowland.
FL: same. 26
I saw the harbor lights see
'Harbor lights'
I saw the old homestead and faces
I love see 'The miner's dream
of home'
I saw them, I saw them see
'Where they were'
'I saw three ships' FL: As I sat on
a sunny bank. 33, 34
I saw three ships come sailing by
see 'New Year's Day in the
morning'
I saw you strolling by your solitary
see 'Would you like to take a
walk'
I say the Rock Island Line is a
mighty good road see 'The
Rock Island Line'
I says to my dear sister, are ye
comin' for to walk see 'The
two sisters'
I search for phrases see 'Too
marvelous words'
I see a red door and I want it
painted black see 'Paint it
black'
I see a wren, said Roberty Boberty
see 'Roberty Boberty'
I sell the morning papers, sir see
'Jimmie Brown, the newsboy'
'I shall be released' Bob Dylan.
FL: They say everything can be
replaced. 45
'I shall not be moved' FL: I shall
not, I shall not be moved. 28
I should have known you'd bid me
farewell see 'Red rubber ball'
'I should like to marry' FL: Oh, I
should like to marry FLC: Oh, I
should like her witty. 57
'I sigh for the girl I adore' FL:
When fairies trip round the gay
green. 3
I sing you one o see 'Green grow
the rushes'

I sit alone in the golden day light
see 'All through the day'
I sit in my chair see 'Solitude'
I snum I am a Yankee lad see
'Boston tea tax song'
I snum I am a Yankee man and I'll
sing to you a ditty see 'The
tea party'; 'The tea tax'
'I sold a guiltless Negro boy' FL:
When thirst of gold enslaves the
mind. 3
I stand at your gate see 'Moon-
light serenade'
I started out to go to Haiti see
'Miami Beach rumba'
I still hear you saying see 'Moon-
glow'
I stood on the Atlantic Ocean, on
the wide Pacific shore see
'Wabash Cannonball'
I struck the trail in '79 see 'The
gal I left behind me'
I suppose you all know that in the
Northern sea see 'The Golden
Willow tree'
'I surrender, dear' Gordon Clifford
and Harry Barris. FL: I may
seem proud FLC: We've played
the game of stay away. 12
'I talk to the trees' Lerner and
Loewe FL: I talk to the trees
but they don't listen to me FLC:
same. 6
I tell you what I mean to do see
'Keep me from sinking down'
I that once was a ploughman, a sail-
or am now see 'The lucky es-
cape'
I think I'm gonna be sad see 'Ticket
to ride'
I think I sing this little song see
'Union man'
I thought at last I'd found you see
'I don't stand a ghost of a chance
with you'
I thought I had seen pretty girls in
my time see 'Before I met
you'
I thought I heard the old man say
see 'Leave her, Johnny'
I thought I was happy see 'I'm
gettin' sentimental over you'
I thought I was swinging the world
by the tail see 'Before I met
you'
I thought I'd found the man of my
dreams see 'Can't we be
friends?'

I thought one day just for fun see
'Cowboy's life'

I thought one day that just for fun
see 'The tenderfoot'

I tink I hear my brudder say see
'Stars begin to fall'

I told Mary about us see 'Devil
woman'

I took each word he said as gospel
truth see 'Can't we be friends?'

I took her by the lily-white hand
see 'Maddy Gross'

I took my girl to a fancy ball see
'Fifty cents'

I took my girl to the fancy ball, it
was a social hop see 'Took my
girl to a fancy ball'

I took my granny to a hootenanny
see 'Hootenanny Granny'

I took one look at you see 'My
heart stood still'

I touch your hand and my arms
grow strong see 'Younger than
springtime'

I traced her little footprints in the
snow see 'Footprints in the
snow'

I traveled East and I traveled west
see 'Young Beichan'

I used to be single, oh then, oh
then see 'I wish I was single
again'

I used to dream that I would discover see 'Bill'

I used to fall see 'My heart belongs to Daddy'

I used to have a fine saloon with
mirrors on the wall see 'I
never drink behind the bar'

I used to have an old gray horse
see 'Goin' down to town'

I used to walk with you along the
avenue see 'Somewhere along
the way'

I wake up each morning with a feeling in my heart see 'A very
special day'

'I walk the line' Johnny Cash. FL:
I keep a close watch on this
heart of mine. 10

'I walk the road again' FL: I am a
poor unlucky chap. 57

I walked into my stable see
'Hobble and Bobble'

I walked out one hallow day see
'Lord Darnell'

I walk-ied out one holiday see
'Little Massy Groves'

I wandered down the other day see
'The girl that keeps the peanut
stand'

I wandered today to the hill, Maggie
see 'When you and I were young
Maggie'

'I wanna be loved' Billy Rose, Edward Heyman and Johnny Green.
FL: Girl you funny thing FLC:
I wanna be loved with inspiration.
53

'I wanna be loved by you' Bert
Kalmar, Herbert Stothart and
Harry Ruby. FL: I'm not one of
the greedy kind FLC: I wanna be
loved by you. 46

I wanna go home and I ain't got suf-
ficient clothes see 'Bad luck
blues'

'I want a girl' William Dillon and
Harry von Tilzer. FL: I want a
girl just like the girl that married dear old Dad. 67

'I want to be happy' Irving Caesar
and Vincent Youmans. FL: I'm
a very ordinary man FLC: I
want to be happy. 42

I awant to be like that gal on the
river see 'Lorelei'

I want to be ready see 'Walk in
Jerusalem'

'I want to die a-shouting' FL: Jesus,
my all to heaven is gone FLC:
Amazing grace, how sweet the
sound. 5

I want to go to heaven when I die
see 'Way over Jordan'

'I want to go where Jesus is' FL:
Jesus, my all to heaven is gone
FLC: I want to go where Jesus
is. 5

'I want to hold your hand' Lennon
and McCartney. FL: Oh yeah,
I'll tell you something I think
you'll understand. 44

I want to know if you love my Lord
see 'Anybody here?'

I want to wish you a merry Christmas see 'Feliz Navidad'

'I want you to make me a cambric
shirt' FL: same. 11

I want you to make me a cambric
shirt see 'The elfin knight';
'Redio-tedio'; 'The six questions'

I wants to stay here see 'I loves
you Porgy'

I was a high-born gentleman see
'Gypsy Davy'

I was a jolly sailor and I fell into
the sea see 'Swim out O'Grady'
I was a stranger in the city see
'A foggy day'
I was alone, I took a ride see
'Got to get you back into my life'
I was at the rodeo and won the first
go-round see 'Blue bell bull'
'I was born about 10,000 years ago'
FL: same. 23, 25, 57
I was born and raised in East Vir-
ginia see 'East Virginia'
I was born and raised in Texas, a
state that you all know see
'Sam's waitin' for a train'
I was born in a cross fire hurri-
cane see 'Jumpin' Jack Flash'
I was born in East Virginia see
'East Virginia'; 'East Virginia
blues'
I was born in the wagon of a travel-
in' show see 'Gypsys, tramps
and thieves'
I was born long ago in 1894 see
'Beans, bacon and gravy'
I was born one morning when the
sun didn't shine see 'Sixteen
tons'
I was but young when I begun see
'Come along'; 'Ride on, King
Jesus'
I was by birth a lady fair see
'The famous flower of serving-
men'
I was created for one man alone
see 'Don't ever leave me'
I was down on the river, on a live
oak log see 'Haming on a live
oak log'
I was five years old in Bucktown,
Maryland see 'Ballad of Har-
riet Tubman'
I was hangin' round town just a-
spending my time see 'The
strawberry roan'
I was mighty blue see 'You do
something to me'
I was only a tiny sleepy head see
'Raisin and almonds'
I was resting comfortably face down
in the gutter see 'Just in time'
I was roving out one cold winter
night see 'Cold winter's night'
I was scarce 18 when I started
roving see 'The Spanish Main'
I was seeing Nellie home see See-
ing Nellie home'
I was sittin' down here thinkin' see

'After hours'
I was sittin' in Miami pourin'
blended whiskey down see 'Old
dogs, children, and watermelon
wine'
I was standing by the window see
'Can the circle be unbroken'
I was standing round a defense town
one day see 'U.A.W. -C.I.O. '
I was 21 years when I wrote this
song see 'Leaves that are
green'
I was weaned on cucumber see 'A
little bit of cucumber'
I washed my head in the midnight
dew see 'Pray on'
I went away from the lights of 14th
Street see 'Hello, Dolly!'
I went down, down, down, to the
factory see 'Automation'
I went down south to see my Sal
see 'Polly Wolly Doodle'
I went down to St. James Infirmary
see 'St. James Infirmary'
I went downtown to build a brick
house see 'Build a brick house'
'I went home one night' FL: The
old man come home one night.
11
I went into my stable to see what I
might see see 'Old Wicket'
I went into the stable to see what I
could see 'The cuckold's song'
I went out a-hunting one day see
'Sir Lionel'
I went out West to have some fun
see 'The horse wranglers or the
tenderfoot'
I went to Blaydon Races, twas on
the ninth of June see 'Blaydon
races'
I went to her father's house see
'Katie Morie'
I went to the alehouse as an honest
woman should see 'Knaves will
be knaves'
I went to the animal fair see
'Animal fair'
I went to the hillside, I went to
pray see 'The angels changed
my name'
'I went to the movies tomorrow'
FL: same. 68
'I went to your wedding' Jessie Mae
Robinson. FL: same. 10
I went up to old Joe's house see
'Old Joe Clark'
'I whistle a happy tune' Oscar

Hammerstein and Richard Rodgers. FL: Whenever I feel afraid. 24

I will buy ma a fol-di-rol-di till-di-toll-di see 'Jenny Jenkins'

I will never more deceive you see 'You naughty, naughty men'

I will not let you go my Lord see 'He's the Lord of Lords'

I will shout and I'll dance see 'Angel Gabriel'

I will sing you a one-o see 'The twelve Apostles'

I will sing you a song see 'Streets of Cairo'

I will sing you a song of the Merrimac at sea see 'Merrimac at sea'

I will tell you of a soldier who lately came from war see 'The soldier's wooing'

I will twine and will mingle my raven black hair see 'Wildwood flower'

I will twine and will mingle my waving black hair see 'Wildwood flower'

I will twine thru my tresses of raven black hair see 'Wildwood flower'

I will wager wi' you the morn see 'Young Allan'

'I will wait for you' Norman Gimbel and Michel Legrand. FL: If it takes forever, I will wait for you. 67

I wish I had a king, brave Wallace he said see 'Gude Wallace'

I wish I had never been born see 'My last gold dollar'

'I wish I had the shepherd's lamb' FL: same FLC: Os ó! goirim, goirim thú. 72

I wish I was in London see 'Handsome Molly'

I wish I was in the land of cotton see 'Dixie'; 'Dixie's land'

'I wish I was single again' FL: I used to be single, oh then, oh then. 7

'I wish I was single again' FL: When I was single, oh then, oh then. 23

I wish I were a single girl again see 'Single girl'

I wish I were an apple see 'Cindy'

'I wish I were single again' FL: I wish I were single, then, o then.

36

'I wish you knew' FL: If only half the things were true you say about my heart FLC: I wish you knew how hard I've tried to tell you. 14

I woke one morning, it was cloudy and cool see 'The teacher's lament'

I woke up this mornin', feelin' sad and blue see 'Lonesome blues'

I woke up this morning and my mind fell away see 'Touch the wind'

I woke up this morning between one and two see 'Farmland blues'

I woke up this morning with an awful aching head see 'Empty bed blues'

'I wonder as I wander' John Jacob Niles. FL: I wonder as I wander out under the sky. 33

I wonder if I still linger in your memory see 'Does your heart beat for me?'

'I wonder what's become of Sally?' Jack Kellen and Milton Ager. FL: Old time pals and old time gals FLC: I wonder what's become of Sally. 46

'I wonder when I'll get to be called a man' Big Bill Broonzy. FL: When I was born into the world. 57

'I wonder where you are tonight' FL: Tonight I'm sad, my heart is weary FLC: The rain is cold and slowly falling. 14

'I won't be a nun' FL: Now is it not a pity such a pretty girl as I FLC: But I won't be a nun, no. 57

I won't come back or I shall not come back see 'Little Sir Hugh'

I work at the Palace Ballroom see 'Ten cents a dance'

'I worked Old Moll' FL: I worked Old Moll and I worked old Belle. 28

Ich weiss nicht was soll es bedeuten see 'The Lorelei'

'Icicles' FL: I like icicles long and straight. 13

I'd be safe and warm, if I were in L.A. see 'California dreamin''

'I'd like to be in Texas' FL: In a lobby of a big hotel in New York town FLC: I can see the cattle

grazing o'er the hills at early
morn. 57
I'd like to get away, Junior see
'There's a small hotel'
I'd like to have you all to know
that I see 'Uncle Sam's menag-
erie'
I'd rather be a sparrow than a
snail see "El condor pasa'
I'd work for you slave for you see
'Until the real thing comes along'
'Ida, sweet as apple cider' Eddie
Leonard and Eddie Munson. FL:
In the region where the roses
always bloom FLC: Ida! sweet as
apple cider. 1, 20, 31, 67
If a body meet a body, comin'
thro the rye see 'Comin' thro'
the rye'
If a man was in trouble Fisk helped
him along see 'Jim Fisk'
If all those young men were as
rushes a-growing see 'Hares
on the mountains'
If anybody askes you who I am see
'The little cradle rock tonight'
If buttercups buzzed after the bee
see 'The world turned upside
down'
If each little kid could have fresh
milk every day see 'It could be
a wonderful world'
If ever a tailor was fond of good
sport see 'Polly Ply'
If ever I get me new house done
see 'Sail away, ladies'
'If ever I would leave you' Lerner
and Loewe. FL: same. 6, 42
'If ever I'm catched' Isaac Bicker-
staffe and William Boyce. FL:
If ever I'm catched in the regions
of smoak. 40
'If fair maids was hares' FL: If fair
maids was hares, they'd run o'er
the mountains. 11
If he is dead, I'll sell my steed
see 'Maid of Islington'
'If he walked into my life' Jerry
Herman. FL: Where's that boy
with the bugle? FLC: Did he need
a stronger hand? 6, 71
'If he'd be a buckaroo' FL: If he'd
be a buckaroo by his trade FLC:
With his ring ting tinny. 57
'If I could be with you, Henry
Creamer and Jimmy Johnson.
FL: I'm so blue I don't know
what to do FLC: If I could be

with you I'd love you strong. 46
If I could I surely would see 'Oh,
Mary, don't you weep'
If I could just hold your charms
see 'Girl of my dreams'
'If I could shut the gate against my
thoughts' John Danyel. FL:
same. 26
If I could tell my troubles see
'Depression blues'
'If I fell' Lennon and McCartney.
FL: If I fell in love with you
would you promise to be true.
44
'If I had a hammer' Lee Hayes and
Pete Seeger. FL: same. 4
If I had a nickel I know what I
would do see 'That's how much
I love you'
If I had listened to what Mama said
see 'The foggy mountain top'
'If I had the wings of a turtledove'
FL: same. 68
If I had wings like Noah's dove see
'Dink's song'
'If I hope, I pine' Thomas Campion
and Philip Rosseter. FL: If I
hope, I pine if I fear, I faint and
die. 26
'If I knock the 'L' out of Kelly'
Sam M. Lewis, Joe Young and
Bert Grant. FL: Timothy Kelly
who owned a big store FLC: If I
knock the 'L' out of Kelly. 31
'If I loved you' Rodgers and Ham-
merstein. FL: When I worked
in the mill FLC: If I loved you.
6, 24, 42, 67
If I see you tomorrow on some
street in town see 'Walk on by'
If I should take a notion see 'Tain't
nobody's biz-ness if I do'
'If I should wander back tonight'
Lester Flatt and Earl Scruggs.
FL: For many years I've been a
rolling stone, my darling FLC:
Now, if I should wander back
tonight. 14
'If I take off my silken stay' FL:
same. 11
If I was a little bird, a darling little
bird I'd be see 'Bring me back
the one I love'
If I was on some foggy mountain
top see 'The foggy mountain
top'
'If I were a carpenter' Tim Hardin.
FL: If I were a carpenter and

you were my lady. 64

'If I were a rich man' Sheldon Harnick and Jerry Bock. FL: same. 6, 42, 64

'If I were on the stage' Henry Blossom and Victor Herbert. FL: If I were asked to play the part. 20

If I'd a known my captain was blind, darlin', darlin' see 'Darlin''

If it takes forever, I will wait for you see 'I will wait for you'

If it was na' for the weavers what would they do see 'The work of the weavers'

'If it wasn't for the 'ouses in between' Edgar Bateman and George Le Brunn. FL: If you saw little backyard, 'Wot a pretty spot!' you'd cry FLC: Oh it really is a wery pretty garden. 17

If it's true that love affairs are all arranged in heaven see 'Looking for a boy'

If life's a rough path as the sages have said see 'Strew the sweet roses of pleasure between'

If Mary goes far out to sea see 'A stately song'

If my love loves me, she lets me not know see 'Willie's lykewake'

If only half the things were true you say about my heart see 'I wish you knew'

If pity dwell within your breast see 'He was such a nice man'

If religion was a thing that money could buy see 'All my trials'

'If she forsakes me' Thomas Campion and Philip Rosseter. FL: If she forsakes me I must die. 26

If the boss is in the way, we're gonna roll it over him see 'Roll the union on'

If the rain comes they run and hide their heads see 'Rain'

'If the swain we sigh for' Kane O'Hara. FL: If the swain we sigh for press us. 40

If there is a Cinderella looking for a steady fella see 'A blues serenade'

If this be a lie you are telling me see 'Lord Benner's wife'

If to force me to sing it be your intention see 'Nobody'

If we could consider each other see 'It could be a wonderful world'

If we go in a farmer's yard see 'Blow away the morning dew'

If ye will wed my daughter Janet see 'Thomas O'Winsbury'

If you belong to Gideon's band see 'Gideon's band'

If you could have married the king's daughter dear see 'The daemon lover'

'If you could read my mind' Gordon Lightfoot. FL: same. 45

If you don't answer me questions nine see 'The devil's nine questions'

If you don't take her out tonight see 'You're goin' to lose that girl'

If you find your new love isn't what you thought it would be see 'Come running back'

If you haven't got bananas, don't be blue see 'The peanut vendor'

If you lak-a-me, lak I lak-a-you see 'Under the bamboo tree'

If you listen, I'll sing you a sweet little song see 'My wild Irish rose'

If you live your life see 'Don't rain on my parade'

If you miss the train I'm on see 'Five hundred miles'

If you please, some time since I was married see 'I'll get rid of my mother-in-law'

If you saw little backyard, 'wot a pretty spot' you'd cry see 'If it wasn't for the 'ouses in between'

'If you see my mother' FL: If you see my mother, partner, tell her pray for me. 28

If you see your brother standing by the road see 'Try a little kindness'

If you want higher wages, let me tell you what to do see 'Talking union'

'If you want to go a-courtin'' FL: If you want to go a-courtin' boys. 37

If you want to have a rosy future see 'Don't marry me'

If you want to know where the privates are see 'Where they were'

If you will forsaken your house carpenter see 'The Daemon lover'

'If you will leave your house car-
penter' FL: same. 11
If you will listen well I'll sing you
a song see 'The young man
who wouldn't hoe corn'
If you'll forsake your house carpen-
ter see 'The house carpenter'
If you'll listen a while, I'll sing
you a song see 'Jim Fisk'
If you'll wait till you come to my
father's yard see 'Blow away
the morning dew'
If you're ever in a jam see
'Friendship'
If you're going to San Francisco
see 'San Francisco'
'If you're thinkin' what I'm thinkin''
Tommy Boyce and Bobby Hart.
FL: same. 47
'Il est né, Le divin enfant' FL:
same. 25
Il y'a longtemps que je t'aime see
'A la claire fontaine'
'Ilkley Moor' FL: Where has thou
been since I saw thee? FLC: On
Ilkley Moor baht 'at. 57
I'll be as strong as a mountain or
weak as a willow see 'Any way
you want me'
I'll be glad when you're dead you,
rascal, you see 'You rascal
you'
'I'll be there' FL: An' if those
mourners would believe FLC:
For I'll be there. 5
I'll be there see 'The general roll'
I'll be there in the morning see
'When that general roll is called'
I'll be your little honey see 'The
bird on Nellie's hat'
I'll beg from Peter and I'll beg
from Paul see 'Hind Horn'
I'll bet you twenty pounds, master
see 'The Broomfield wager'
'I'll build a stairway to Paradise'
B. G. De Sylva, Arthur Francis
and George Gershwin. FL: All
you preachers FLC: I'll build a
stairway to Paradise. 21
'I'll buy that dream' Herb Magidson
and Allie Wrubel. FL: Before
we met I never dreamed much
FLC: I imagine with me head on
your shoulder. 70
I'll buy you a diamong ring my
friend see 'Can't buy me love'
I'll buy you fine silks see 'Green
bushes'

I'll cut off my long yellow hair see
'Famous flower of serving men'
I'll do so much for my sweetheart
see 'Cold blows the wind'
I'll entwine and I'll mingle my raven
black hair see 'Wildwood flower'
'I'll fly away' FL: Some bright
morning when this life is over
FLC: I'll fly away, oh Lordy.
27, 57
'I'll follow my secret heart' Noel
Coward. FL: You ask me to
have a discreet heart FLC: I'll
follow my secret heart my whole
life through. 42
'I'll follow the sun' Lennon and
McCartney. FL: One day you'll
look to see I've gone. 44
'I'll get by' Fred E. Ahlert and Roy
Turk. FL: I've neither wealth
nor power FLC: I'll get by as
long as I have you. 54
I'll get my love a home, wherein
she may be see 'Don't you go
a-rushing'
'I'll get rid of my mother-in-law'
FL: If you please, some time
since I was married FLC: But
I'll stand interference no longer.
36
'I'll give my love an apple' FL: I'll
give my love an apple without
e'er a core. 11, 57
I'll give to you a paper of pins see
'Paper of pins'
I'll give you the gold and I'll give
you fee see 'The Turkey-
rogherlee'
'I'll go stepping too' Tom James and
Jerry Organ. FL: Don't think
I'll be hanging around while you're
havin' fun FLC: Yes, I'll go step-
ping too, my honey. 14
I'll go up on the mountain top see
'Liza Jane'
'I'll hang my harp' FL: Oh, who's
going to shoe my pretty little
foot? FLC: Though storms may
roll the ocean. 11
'I'll hear the trumpet sound' FL:
You may bury me in the east
FLC: In that morning. 38
'I'll never fall in love again' Hal
David and Burt Bacharach. FL:
What do you get when you fall in
love. 6, 42, 71
'I'll never get drunk anymore' Ned

Harrigan and Dave Braham. FL:
I remember when a bit of a boy
FLC: I'll never get drunk any
more. 36

'I'll never smile again' Ruth Lowe.
FL: I'll never love again FLC:
I'll never smile again. 12, 59

'I'll remember you love in my
prayers' FL: When the curtains
of night are pinned back by the
stars. 18

I'll saddle up my milk white horse
see 'The gypsy laddie'

I'll sing of a great musician see
'Um-skit-a-rat-trap-si si do!'

'I'll sing thee songs of Araby' W.
G. Wils and Frederick Clay.
FL: same. 63

I'll sing to you a good old song see
'The fine old English gentleman'

I'll sing to you about a man whose
name you'll find in history see
'Cristofo Columbo'

I'll sing to you about Lord Bateman
see 'Lord Bateman'

I'll sing you a fine old song see
'The fine old Irish gentleman'

I'll sing you a song, a good song of
the sea see 'Blow the man
down'

I'll sing you a song and it's not
very long see 'The young man
who wouldn't hoe corn'

I'll sing you a song, though it may
be a sad one see 'The Sioux
Indians'

I'll sing you a true song of Billy
the Kid see 'Billy the Kid'

I'll sing you one-oh see 'Green
grow the rushes ho'

I'll stick to the ship, lads see
'The ship I love'

'I'll string along with you' Al Dubin
and Harry Warren. FL: All my
life I waited for an angel FLC:
You may not be an angel. 46

'I'll take you home again, Kathleen'
Thomas P. Westendorf. FL:
same FLC: Oh, I will take you
back, Kathleen. 25, 57, 63

I'll tell you a story, a story anon
see 'King John and the Abbot of
Canterbury'

I'll tell you a tale now without any
flam see 'The cork leg'

I'll tell you about a brisk young
farmer see 'Brisk young farmer'

I'll tell you all a story see 'Bad
company'

I'll tell you all a story about poor
Omie Wise see 'Omie Wise'

I'll tell you how I found the Lord
see 'I'm so glad'

I'll tell you of a false hearted
knight see 'The false-hearted
knight'

I'll tell you of a Irish young sailor
see 'Lady Isabel and the elf
knight'

I'll tell you of a soldier who lately
come from sea see 'The lady
and the Dragoon'; 'The poor
soldier'

I'll tell you something ain't no joke
see 'High-price blues'

I'll tell you the story of Jonathan
Tweed see 'Song of the guaranteed wage'

I'll tell you why I want dance see
'Beat out that rhythm on a drum'

I'll twine 'mid the ringlets of my
raven black hair see 'Wildwood
flower'

I'll wager, I'll wager, says Lord
John see 'Lord John'

'I'll walk alone' Sammy Cahn and
Jule Styne. FL: They call, no
date FLC: I'll walk alone. 70

I'm a bowlegged chicken see 'The
Tennessee wig-walk'

I'm a decent boy just landed from
the town of Ballyfad see 'No
Irish need apply'

I'm a flea bit peanut monkey see
'Monkey man'

I'm a gay young sailor stout and
strong see 'Sir William Gower'

'I'm a girl of constant sorrow' FL:
I am a girl of constant sorrow.
57

I'm a glum one, it's explainable
see 'I can't get started'

I'm a goin' down to town see
'Going down to town'

I'm a goin' in Zion see 'Sabbath
has no end'

I'm a good old rebel soldier see
'The good old rebel soldier'

I'm a happy little thing see
'Dandelion'

I'm a lonely bullwhacker see 'Root,
hog or die'

I'm a lonely soldier sitting here in
Korea see 'Rotation, blues'

'I'm a loser' Lennon and McCartney.

FL: I'm a loser, I'm a loser.
44

'I'm a man of constant sorrow' FL:
same. 23, 25

I'm a modest little maiden from the
country see 'I've never lost my
last train yet'

I'm a poor broken hearted milkman
see 'Sweet Pretty Polly Perkins
from Paddington Green'

I'm a poor lonesome cowboy see
'Lonesome cowboy'

'I'm a poor wayfarin' stranger' FL:
Oh, I'm a poor wayfarin' stranger.
23

'I'm a rambler' FL: I'm a rambler,
I'm a gambler. 35

'I'm a rambler, I'm a gambler see
'The rambling gambler'

I'm a rambling gambler see 'The
rambling gambler'

I'm a rambling wretch of poverty
from Tip'ry town I came see
'The son of a gambolier'

'I'm a rolling' FL: O brothers,
won't you help me FLC: I'm a
rolling. 38

I'm a roving gambler see 'The
roving gambler'

I'm a sentimental sap, that's all
see 'You took advantage of me'

I'm a soldier for Jesus see
'Soldier for Jesus'

'I'm a stranger here' FL: Ain't it
hard to stumble when you've got
no place to fall. 57

I'm a stranger here see 'New
stranger's blues'

I'm a stranger to your city see
'The Portland Country Jail'

'I'm a traveling to the grave' FL:
My Massa died a shouting FLC:
I'm a traveling to the grave. 38

I'm a very ordinary man see 'I
want to be happy'

I'm a weaver, a Calton weaver see
'The Calton weaver'

I'm a Yankee Doodle Dandy see
'The Yankee Doodle Dandy'

I'm a young married man and I'm
tired of life see 'Cod liver oil'

I'm a-comin', yes, Lord see 'I
don't want you go on and leave
me'

I'm a-going away see 'Little
Betty Anne'

I'm a-going to tell you about the
coming of the Savior see 'In

that great getting-up morning'

I'm Alabama bound see 'Alabama
bound'

'I'm all alone' FL: I'm all alone,
all alone in this world. 7

I'm all at sea see 'Can this be
love?'

'I'm alone because I love you' Joe
Young. FL: same. 47

I'm as free a little bird as I can be
see 'Free little bird'

I'm as mild and as meek as a
mouse see 'In my own little
corner'

I'm as mild mannered man as can
be see 'The popular Wobbly'

I'm as restless as a willow in a
windstorm see 'It might as well
be spring'

I'm a-trampin', trampin' see
'Trampin''

I'm back in the saddle again see
'Back in the saddle again'

I'm beside him, mercy see 'Ma,
he's making eyes at me'

I'm bidin' my time see 'Bidin'
my time'

I'm Captain Jinks of the Horse Marines see 'Captain Jinks'

'I'm certainly living a ragtime life'
Robert S. Roberts and Gene Jefferson. FL: Got more trouble
than I can stand FLC: I got a
ragtime dog and a ragtime cat.
57

I'm come to exhort you so free see
'The Tee-to-tal Society'

I'm comin' home, I've done my
time see 'Tie a yellow ribbon
round the old oak tree'

I'm discontented with homes that
are rented see 'Tea for two'

I'm dreaming now of Hallie see
'Listen to the mocking bird'

'I'm drifting back to dreamland'
Florence Charlesworth, Charles
Harrison and Jack Sadler. FL:
I'm sitting alone by the fireside
FLC: I'm drifting back to dream-
land. 54

I'm far, far away from my Sarie
Marais see 'Sarie Marais'

I'm feeling so tired I can't understand it see 'Bitch'

I'm five hundred miles away from
home see 'Five hundred miles
away from home'

I'm following in father's footsteps,

I'm following the dear old dad
see 'Following in father's footsteps'

'I'm free' Mick Jagger and Keith
Richard. FL: I'm free to do what
I want any old time. 16

I'm gaun to sing a song see 'The
farmer and the robber'

I'm gaun to sing ye a song see
'The crafty farmer'

'I'm gettin' sentimental over you'
Ned Washington and George Bassman. FL: I thought I was happy
FLC: Never thought I'd fall. 12,
59

I'm giving you a piece of my mind
see 'Think'

'I'm glad there is you' Paul Madeira and Jimmy Dorsey. FL:
In this world of ordinary people.
59

'I'm glad there is you' Paul Madeira and Jimmy Dorsey' FL:
Said I many times. 70

I'm goin' away for to stay a little
while see 'He's gone away'

I'm goin' down the road feelin' bad
see 'Goin' down the road';
'Going down the road'

I'm goin' down town gonna get me
a sack of flour see 'Skillet
good and greasy'

I'm goin' to buy a paper doll see
'Paper doll'

I'm goin' to Kansas City see
'Kansas City'

'I'm goin' to sing' FL: We want no
cowards in our band FLC: O I'm
goin' to sing. 5

'I'm goin' to walk with Jesus by
myself' FL: same. 5

I'm goin' up home soon in de
mornin' see 'Soon in de morning'

I'm goin' where the chilly winds
don't blow see 'Chilly winds'

I'm going away for to leave you
see 'The storms are on the
ocean'

I'm going away from you, Mary
Anne see 'House Carpenter'

I'm going away to see the good Old
Daniel see 'My ship is on the
ocean'

'I'm going back to old Kentucky'
FL: When I left old Kentucky
FLC: I'm going back to old
Kentucky. 14

'I'm going home' FL: I'm going
home to stop awhile FLC: Although I like the diggings. 25

I'm going, home, I'm going home
see 'Goin' home'

I'm going there to see my mother,
she said she'd meet me when I
come see 'I am a pilgrim'

I'm going to Germany see 'Going
to Germany'

'I'm going to get married' FL; I'm
going to get married, ha, ha,
Ma, Ma. 7

I'm going to leave old Texas now
see 'The cowman's lament'

I'm going to marry just who I please
see 'Lala la chick a la le-o'

I'm going to sit at the welcome
table see 'Shine, shine'

I'm gonna be standin' on the corner
see 'Kansas City'

I'm gonna build my self a raft see
'The blues ain't nothin'

I'm gonna lay down my burden down
by the riverside see 'Down by
the riverside'

I'm gonna leave ol' Texas now see
'Ol' Texas'

I'm gonna preach you all a sermon
'bout Old Man Atom see 'Old
Man Atom'

I'm gonna ring my hammer, oh let
your hammer ring see 'Hammer
ring'

'I'm gonna sing when the spirit says
sing' FL: same. 34

'I'm gonna sit right down and write
myself a letter' Fred E. Ahlert
and Joe Young. FL: same. 59

I'm gonna take a trip on that old
Gospel ship see 'Old Gospel
ship'

I'm gonna tell you a story 'bout
grizzly bear see 'Grizzly bear'

I'm gonna walk the streets of glory
see 'The streets of glory'

'I'm going to live with Jesus' FL:
same. 38

I'm growing tired of lovey dove
theme songs see 'Cheerful little
earful'

I'm gwine away to see my Jesus
see 'Goin' over on de uddah side
of Jordan'

I'm happy now at last you are smiling see 'Take my ring from
your finger'

I'm headin' once more for the

prairie see 'My old Pinto pal'
I'm in a nice bit of trouble, I con-
    fess see 'Waiting at the church'
I'm in love with a man see 'The
    party's over'
I'm in love with you honey see
    'Honey'
I'm in New York City, gonna lay my
    line see 'New York City'
'I'm in the bottom' FL: In the bot-
    tom, oh Lordy now, wo. 28
I'm jealous of a stranger who seems
    to admire you see 'My rival'
I'm jealous of the moon that shines
    above see 'Jealous'
I'm jealous of the pretty flowers,
    too see 'Jealous'
I'm jist a girl who cain't say no
    see 'I cain't say no'
I'm just a little Jack Horner see
    'When I take my sugar to tea'
I'm just a poor wayfaring stranger
    see 'Poor Wayfaring stranger';
    'Wayfaring stranger'
I'm just a woman, a lonely woman
    see 'Am I blue?'
I'm just like an owl that flies by
    night see 'The burglar'
I'm just Paddy on the turnpike, I'll
    just be on my way see 'Paddy
    on the turnpike'
I'm just returned from sailing over
    sea see 'House carpenter'
'I'm just wild about Harry' Noble
    Sissle and Eubie Blake. FL:
    There's just one fellow for me in
    this world FLC: I'm just wild
    about Harry. 46
I'm Lady Jinks of the Foot Dragoons
    see 'Lady Jinks'
I'm lonesome and sorry see 'Lone-
    some and sorry'
I'm lonesome and the blues is in
    my way see 'Lonesome blues'
I'm lonesome since I crossed the
    hill see 'The girl I left behind
    me'
I'm longing for next Monday 'cos
    I'm going to tie the knot see
    'Half-past nine, or My wedding
    day'
I'm lookin' kind-a seedy now while
    headin' down my claim see
    'Little old sod shanty'
'I'm looking over a four leaf clover'
    Mort Dixon and Harry Woods.
    FL: Farewell every old familiar
    face FLC: I'm looking over a

four leaf clover. 46
I'm looking rather seedy now while
    holding down my claim see
    'Little old sod shanty on the
    plain'
I'm making up for all the years
    that I waited see 'Soon'
'I'm movin' on' Hank Snow. FL:
    That big eight wheeler rollin'
    down the track. 10
I'm no ways weary see 'The old
    ship of Zion'
I'm not a fireman or a 'tec, as
    some folks may suppose see
    'The huntsman'
I'm not one of the greedy kind see
    'I wanna be loved by you'
I'm not scared of dyin' and I really
    don't care see 'And when I die'
I'm not talkin' about the kind of
    clothes she wears see 'Stupid
    girl'
'I'm old fashioned' Johnny Mercer
    and Jerome Kern. FL: I'm old
    fashioned, I love the moonlight.
    67
I'm old Tom Moore from the bum-
    mer's shore see 'Days of
    Forty-nine'
'I'm on my way' FL: I'm on my
    way and I won't turn back. 34,
    57
I'm on the king's land see 'The
    king's land'
'I'm on the water wagon now' Paul
    West and John W. Bratton. FL:
    Of all the sporty, sporty boys
    who sport around the town FLC:
    But I'm on the water wagon now.
    36
I'm really very harmless, no one
    need have any fears see 'Pre-
    historic man'
I'm recallin' times when I was
    small see 'Hallelujah'
I'm riding on that New River train
    see 'New River train'
I'm riding on this train see 'Nine
    hundred miles'
I'm running thro' grace see 'A
    happy new year'
'I'm sad and I'm lonely' FL: same.
    57
I'm sending you a big bouquet of
    roses see 'Bouquet of roses'
'I'm seventeen come Sunday' FL:
    Will you court me, my pretty
    little miss? 11

In a villa in a little old Italian town
   see 'Mona Lisa'
In a village there lived an old maid
   see 'Miss Wrinkle'
In Amsterdam there lives a girl
   see 'The maid of Amsterdam'
In Amsterdam there lives a maid,
   mark well what I do say see
   'A-roving'
'In another land' Bill Wyman. FL:
   In another land where the breeze
   and the trees. 16
In Arbour town this damsel did
   dwell see 'Arbour town'
In bonney Scotland three brothers
   did dwell see 'Andrew Marteen'
'In bright mansions above' FL: My
   father's gone to glory FLC: In
   bright mansions above. 38
In Bristol lived a damsel see 'The
   discharged drummer'
In Bristol lived a lady see 'The
   discharged drummer'
'In cellar cool' FL: In cellar cool I
   sit and hold myself from cares
   and warriors. 25
In Cuba each merry maid wakes up
   with this serenade see 'The peanut vendor'
'In darkness let me dwell' John Dowland. FL: same. 26
In dear old New York, it's remark-
   able--very see 'The streets of
   New York'
In Deeside cam Inverey, whistlin'
   and playing see 'Baron of
   Brackley'
In dem beys hamikdash in a vinkl
   cheyder see 'Rozinkes mit
   mandlen'
In Devonshire lived a rich farmer
   see 'The Devonshire farmer's
   daughter'
In Dublin's fair city see 'Sweet
   Molly Malone'
In Dublin's fair city, where the
   girls are so pretty see 'Cockles
   and Mussels'
In eighteen hundred and twenty-four
   see 'The Greenland fisheries'
In eighteen hundred and forty-one
   see 'Filimiooriooriay'; 'Pat
   works on the railway'
In England lived a noble lord see
   'Lord Bateman'
In folly, you're born and in folly
   you'll live see 'Come shake
   your dull noodles'

In former days the British race
   see 'Cheer up, Buller'
'In freedom we're born' John Dickinson. FL: Come join hand in
   hand, brave Americans all FLC:
   In freedom we're born and in
   freedom we'll live. 8
In freedom, we're born and in freedom we'll live see 'The liberty
   song'
In freedom, we're born, and like
   sons of the brave see 'Massachusetts liberty song'
In freedom, you're born and like
   sons of the brave see 'Come
   swallow your bumpers'
In good King Charles's golden time
   see 'The vicar of Bray'
In good old colony days, when we
   all lived under a king see
   'Three rouguish chaps'
'In good old colony times' FL: same
   FLC: Because they could not
   sing. 57
In good old colony times see 'Old
   Colony times'
In Greenock town there lived a lady
   see 'The bold lieutenant'
In India lived a noble lord see
   'Lord Bakeman'; 'Lord Bateman'
In India there lived a noble lord
   see 'Lord Bakeman'
In London city where I did dwell
   see 'The butcher boy'
In London city where I once did
   dwell see 'Barbara Allen'
In London city you'll see me here
   see 'Whiskey Johnny'
In London lived a worthy man see
   'Young Beichan'
In London there dwelt a fair damsel
   see 'On board the Gallee'
In London there lived a mason by
   trade see 'The Yorkshire bite';
   'The Yorkshire boy'
In London there lived a rich mer-
   chant see 'The rich merchant'
In Manchester a maid dwelt whose
   name was Phoebe Brown see
   'Reuben Wright and Phoebe Brown'
In merry Scotland, in merry Scot-
   land see 'Henry Martyn'
In my adobe hacienda see 'My
   adobe hacienda'
'In my life' Lennon and McCartney.
   FL: There are places I'll remem-
   ber all my life. 44
'In my merry Oldsmobile' Vincent

Virginia see 'White dove'
In the dragoon's ride from out the
North see 'A bold dragoon'
In the early fair days of May see
'Barbara Allen'
'In the evening by the moonlight'
FL: same. 66
In the evening when I set alone a
dreaming see 'You're the
flower of my heart, sweet Ade-
line'
In the far away heavens in distant
blue skies see 'Drift along
lonely cowboy'
'In the gloaming' Mete Orred and
Annie F. Harrison. FL: In the
gloaming, o my darling. 1, 57
In the gloom of mighty cities see
'The commonwealth of toil'
'In the good old summertime' Ren
Shields and George Evans. FL:
There's a time in each year that
we always hold dear FLC: In the
good old summertime. 1, 20, 25
In the good old town of Short Creek,
in the year of '53 see 'Short
Creek Raid'
In the heart of little old New York
see 'Forty-second street'
'In the heart of the dark' Oscar
Hammerstein and Jerome Kern.
FL: Silent evening falls in a mist
FLC: In the heart of the dark.
24
In the hills of West Virginny lived
a girl named Nancy Brown see
'The West Virginny hills'
In the lobby of a big hotel in New
York town one day see 'Round-
up in the spring'
In the lone star state of Texas by
the silvery Rio Grande see
'By the silvery Rio Grande'
'In the meadow stood' Jerry Silver-
man. FL: In the meadow stood
a little birch tree. 57
In the merry green woods a-hunting
see 'Johnie Scot'
'In the middle of an island' Nick
Acquaviva and Ted Varnick. FL:
In the middle of an island in the
middle of an ocean. 52
In the middle of the night if you
hear a scream see 'Trading-
out blues'
'In the misty moonlight' Cindy Walker. FL: In the misty moonlight
by the flickering firelight. 10

In the morning I am troubled see
'Troubled in mind'
In the movie plays of nowadays see
'A cup of coffee, a sandwich
and you'
In the night while you lay sleeping
see 'Little darling pal of mine'
In the old days a glimpse of stock-
ing see 'Anything goes'
'In the pines' FL: Black girl, black
girl don't lie to me. 56
'In the pines' FL: The longest train
I ever saw FLC: In the pines, in
the pines. 14
'In the pines' FL: True love, true
love, don't lie to me FLC: To
the pines, to the pines. 34, 35,
57
In the praise of Queen Bess lofty
strains have been sung fair see
'The golden days we no possess'
'In the rain' Harvey W. Loomis.
FL: Water in the gutter. 13
In the region where the roses al-
ways bloom see 'Ida, sweet as
apple cider'
'In the river of Jordan' FL: In the
river of Jordan, John baptized
FLC: Pray on, pray on, pray on.
38
'In the shade of the old apple tree'
Harry H. Williams and Egbert
Van Alstyne. FL: The oriole
with joy was sweetly singing
FLC: In the shade of the old
apple tree. 20, 31
In the shadows see 'Shadow waltz'
In the sky the bright stars glittered
see 'Aunt Dinah's quilting party';
'Seeing Nellie home'
In the spring when the feeling was
chronic see 'You took advantage
of me'
In the town of Shawneetown see
'Flood of Shawneetown'
In the town where I was born lived
a man who sailed to sea see
'Yellow submarine'
'In the valley' FL: It was in Juda's
land FLC: In the valley. 33
In the year of 1802 see 'The
Greenland fishery'
In the years of eighteen and one,
peg and awl see 'Peg and awl'
In this world of ordinary people
see 'I'm glad there is you'
In this world of toil and trouble
see 'I don't want to get adjusted'

In Verona my late cousin Romeo
see 'This can't be love'
In Wakefield there lived a jolly
pinder see 'The jolly pinder of
Wakefield'; 'Wakefield on a green'
In yonders town where I am bound
see 'Barbara Allen'
In yonders town where I was born
see 'Barbara Allen'
In Yorkshire lived a noble knight
see 'Love Henry'
'Inching along' FL: Twas a inch by
inch I sought the Lord FLC:
Keep a inching along. 38
'Inconstant Laura' Thomas Greaves.
FL: Inconstant Laura makes me
death to crave. 26
'Independence Day' FL: Come all
you brave soldiers, both valiant
and free. 8
'The Indian chief' FL: The sun sets
at night and the stars shun the
day. 3
'Indian love call' Otto Harbach,
Oscar Hammerstein and Rudolf
Friml. FL: Ooh! so echoes of
sweet love notes gently fall FLC:
When I'm calling you. 24, 46
'The Indian philosopher' FL: Why
should our joys transform to
pain? 3
'Indian war song' FL: Wave the
spear and raise the rifle. 8
'The Indian's over the border' FL:
Come, frontier men, awake now
FLC: The Indian's over the
border. 8
'Indian's song' Sir Richard Steele
and John Ernest Galliard. FL:
From place to place forlorn I go.
40
The ink is black, the page is white
see 'Black and white'
Instead of Spa we'll drink down ale
see 'Garryowen'
An intimate friend of the Czar was
I see 'Shootin' with Raputiin'
Into my life on waves of electrical
sound see 'Janis'
'The intoxicated rat' FL: Well, the
other night when I came home.
57
Inverey cam down Deeside whistling
and playing see 'The Baron of
Brackley'
'An invitation of North America'
FL: Come all you bold Britons,
wherever you may be. 55

Ira Hayes, Ira Hayes see 'The
ballad of Ira Hayes'
'The Irish emigrant' Lady Dufferin
and George Barker. FL: I'm
sitting on the Stile, Mary, where
we sat side by side. 25, 63
'An Irish lady from Dublin she
came' FL: same. 11
'An Irish young lady' FL: An Irish
young lady to old England came.
11
'The Irishman's epistle' FL: By my
faith, but I think you're all mak-
ers of bulls. 55
'The Irishman's epistle to the officers and troops at Boston' FL:
By my faith but I think ye're all
makers of bulls. 49
The Iron Horse draws nigh with its
smoke nostrils high see 'The
Utah iron horse'
Is any of you going to Scarborough
Fair see 'Scarborough Fair'
Is it true I've lost you? see
'Think of what you've done'
Is it true that the women are worse
than the men see 'The women
are worse than the men'
Is she fitting for your wife, Billy
Boy see 'Billy Boy'
'Is that Mr. Reilly?' FL: I'm Ter-
rence O'Reilly, I'm a man of re-
nown FLC: Is that Mr. Reilly can
any one tell. 36
Is there any gypsies in the North
see 'The gypsy laddie'
Is there anybody going to listen to
my story about the girl who came
to stay see 'Girl'
Is there anybody here see 'Any-
body here?'
Is there, for honest poverty see
'A man's a man for a' that'
Is this the little girl I carried?
see 'Sunrise, sunset'
Isaac a ransom, while he lay see
'Didn't old pharaoh get lost?'
'Isaac-a-Bell and Hugh the Graeme'
FL: A knight had two sons a'
sma' fame. 11
Ise a gwinter jine de band see
'Gwine ter jine de band'
'Island in the sun' Harry Belafonte
and Lord Burgess. FL: When
morning breaks the heaven high
FLC: This is my island in the
sun. 52
'Isle of Capri' Jimmy Kennedy and

Will Grosz. FL: Twas on the Isle of Capri that I found her. 67
'Isn't it a pity?' George and Ira Gershwin. FL: Why did I wander? FLC: It's a funny thing. 21
'Isn't it romantic' Lorenz Hart and Richard Rodgers. FL: I've never met you FLC: Isn't it romantic? 53
'It ain't necessarily so' George and Ira Gershwin. FL: same. 21
It ain't no use to sit and wonder why, Babe see 'Don't think twice, it's all right'
It ain't so much a question of not knowing what to do see 'I cain't say no'
It befell at Martinmas see 'Sick, sick and very sick'
It bein' the Martinmas time see 'The barrin' o' the door'
It being of a day and a noble day see 'Little Musgrave'; 'Matthy Groves'
It came about the Michaelmas time see 'Get up and bar the door'
'It came upon a midnight clear' Richard Storrs and Willis and Edmond H. Sears. FL: same. 33, 34
'It could be a wonderful world' Lou Singer and Hy Zaret. FL: If each little kid could have fresh milk every day FLC: If we could consider each other. 19
'It could happen to you' Johnny Burke and Jimmy Van Heusen. FL: Do you believe in charms and spells FLC: Hide your heart from sight. 47, 70
'It doesn't matter' José Feliciano. FL: It's been so long since my baby has been here. 9
'It don't mean a thing' Irving Mills and Duke Ellington. FL: It makes no difference if it's sweet or hot FLC: It don't mean a thing if it ain't got that swing. 12
It fell aboot the Martinmas time see 'Get up and bar the door'
It fell about a Martinmas time see 'Barbara Allan'
It fell about Martinmas see 'Edom o' Gordon'
It fell about the Lammas tide see 'The battle of Otterbourne'
It fell about the Martinmas time see 'The barrin' o' our door'

It fell ance upon a time see 'Lord Thomas'
It fell on a day, a bonny simmer day see 'The bonny house o' Airlie'; 'Bonnie house of Airlie'
It fell once upon a day see 'Lord Thomas of Winchbury'
It fell upon a time, when the proud king of France see 'Lord Thomas of Winesberrie'
It fell upon the Martinmas time see 'The barrin' o' the door'
It had ice cream, cold cream, benzine, gasoline see 'Mrs. Murphy's chowder'
It hails, it rains in merry Scotland see 'The Jew's garden'
It happened aboot the Middlemas time see 'Arise and bar the door-o'
It happened I felt it happen see 'Have you met Miss Jones?'
It happened on a day and a fine summer's day see 'The bailie's daughter'
It happened on one holiday see 'Little Mose Groves'
It is a happy morning see 'A happy goodmorning'
It is good for the mourner see 'This old time religion'
It is of a rich merchant I am going for to tell see 'Villikins and his Dinah'
It is ten weary years since I left England's shore see 'The miner's dream of home'
It is true that the women are worse than the men? see 'Killybarn braes'
It is useful no more, yet I fondly adore see 'My mother's old red shawl'
'It isn't fair' Richard Himber, Frank Warshauer and Sylvester Sprigato. FL: It isn't fair for you to taunt me. 59
It just took a little while for me to get my head together see 'Little girl gone'
'It looks like rain in cherry blossom lane' Edgar Leslie and Joe Burke. FL: same. 53
'It makes a long-time man feel bad' FL: same. 57
It makes no difference if it's sweet or hot see 'It don't mean a thing'

'It might as well be spring' Oscar Hammerstein and Richard Rodgers. FL: The things I used to like I don't like any more FLC: I'm as restless as a willow in a windstorm. 24

It must have been moonglow see 'Moonglow'

'It never entered my mind' Lorenz Hart and Richard Rodgers. FL: I don't care if there's powder on my nose FLC: Once I laughed when I heard you saying. 42

It now lies on the shelf, it is faded and torn see 'My mother's old red shawl'

It oft times has been told see 'Yankee Doodle Dandy-o'

It oft was told me by my dad see 'Our old tom cat'

It ofttimes has been told see 'The Constitution and the Guerrière'

It rained a mess, it rained a mess see 'Sir Hugh'

'It rained a mist' FL: It rained a mist, it rained a mist. 11

'It rained a mist' FL: It rained a mist, it rained all day. 11

It rained a mist, it rained a mist see 'Hugh of Lincoln'; 'Jewish Lady'; 'The Jew's daughter'; 'The Jew's garden'; 'Little Sir Hugh'; 'Sir Hugh'

It rained, alas! it rained, alas! see 'Sir Hugh'; 'The two playmates'

It rained forty days and it rained forty nights see 'Other side of Jordan'

It rained, it hailed, it snowed, it blowed see 'The Jew's daughter'

It rained, it mist, it rained, it mist see 'Little Sir Hugh'

It rained, it poured, it rained so hard see 'Falat flower garden'

It rained one day in old Scotland see 'The Jew's garden'

It rains, it pours, it rains, it pours see 'The jeweler's daughter'

It rains, it rains in merry Scotland see 'Little Sir Hugh'; 'Sir Hugh'

It seems to me I've heard that song before see 'I've heard that song before'

It sho' is mellow grazing in the grass see 'Grazing in the grass'

It takes a long handled shovel to dig a nine foot hole see 'Long-handled shovel'

It takes a worried man see 'A worried man'

It takes a worried man to sing a worried song see 'Worried man blues'

It was a day and a high old day see 'Little Matha Grove'

It was a fine day, and a holy day see 'Little Moth Grone'

'It was a lover and his lass' FL: same FLC: In springtime, the only pretty ring time. 57

It was a lucky April shower see 'I found a million dollar baby'

It was a one-eyed, one-horned, flyin', purple, people eater see 'The purple people eater'

It was a pleasant morning in May see 'Barbara Allen'

It was a sad and a rainy nicht see 'Clerk Saunders'

It was a solemn day as ever you did see see 'The bonny house o' Airlie'

It was about the Lammes time see 'The battle of Otterburn'

It was all in the month of May see 'Barbry Ellen'

It was all in the month of June see 'Barbara Ellen'; 'Bold Archer'

It was all on a cold winter's night see 'Mary of the wild moor'

It was Brennan on the Moor see 'Brennan on the Moor'

It was brilliant autumn time when the army of the north see 'The ballad of Jane McCrea'

It was down by the Sally Gardens my love and I did meet see 'Down by the Sally Gardens'

It was down in Old Joe's barroom see 'St. James Infirmary'

It was early all in the spring see 'Henry Dear'

It was early early in the summer time see 'Barb'ra Allyn'

It was early, early one morning see 'Stag O'Lee'

It was early one mornin' see 'Prison bound'

It was early one morning as I passed St. James Hospital see 'St. James Hospital'

It was early one morning I strolled into town see 'The red light saloon'

It was fiesta down in Mexico see
'Frenesi'

It was good for the Hebrew children
see 'Give me that old time religion'

It was in and about the Martinmas
time see 'Bonny Barbara Allen'

It was in Juda's land see 'In the
valley'

It was in nineteen hundred and
twenty-nine see 'Run come see
Jerusalem'

It was in the fall season of the year
see 'Barbara Allen'

It was in the merry month of May
see 'Barbara Allen'; 'Trail to
Mexico'

It was in the merry month of June
see 'The beggar's dawtie'

It was in the Midlothian country
see 'Edward Ballad'

It was in the new year in the
month of May see 'Barbara
Allen'

It was just one of those things see
'Just one of those things'

'It was late in the night when Johnny
came home' FL: same FLC: Raddle up a dinklum, a dinktum, a
dinktum. 11

It was late in the night when the
captain came home see 'The
gypsy laddie'

It was late last night when the
squire came home see 'Gyp-
sum Davy'; 'The gypsy laddie'

It was late late when the boss came
home see 'Gypsy Davy'

It was late one night, landlord rode
out see 'The gypsy laddie'

It was Little Joe the wrangler see
'Little Joe, the wrangler'

It was long, long ago in the moonlight see 'Your love is like a
flower'

It was many and many a year ago
see 'Annabel Lee'

It was Martyr John who died of
late see 'Martyr John'

It was of a blind beggar, long time
he's been blind see 'The blind
beggar's daughter of Bethnal
Green'

It was of a comely maiden fair see
'The dark-eyed sailor'

It was of a farmer in Cheshire did
dwell see 'The farmer's curst

wife'

It was of a sea captain that followed
the sea see 'The sea captain'

It was on a day and a fine summer's day see 'Glasgow Peggy'

It was on a May, on a midsummer's
day see 'Little Harry Hughes
and the duke's daughter'

It was on a moonlight night when
the stars were shining bright
see 'The light of the moon'

It was on a morning early see
'Jock o Hazelgreen'

It was on a silver falls by a narrow
see 'Baltimore fire'

It was on a storm stone lighthouse
see 'Grace Darling'

It was on a summer's morning all
in the month of May see 'The
boy with the auburn hair'

It was on an evening sae saft and
sae clear see 'Bonny'

It was on Friday night when we set
sail see 'The mermaid'

It was on one fine, one finey holiday see 'Lord Arnold'

It was on one summer's evening
see 'Sailor on the deep blue
sea'; 'Travelin' man'

It was one lovely month of May see
'Barbara Allen'

It was one Sunday mornin' see
'Gray goose'

'It was poor little Jesus' FL: same
FLC: Wasn't that a pity and a
shame? 57

It was sad, it was sad see 'The
Titanic'

It was springtime in the Rockies
see 'Springtime in the Rockies'

It was the jolly beggar at the beggin' he had been see 'The jolly
beggar'

It was the very month of May see
'Barbary Ellen'

It was twenty years ago today see
'Sgt. Pepper's Lonely Hearts
Club Band'

It was twenty-five years ago when
the wings of death came low see
'Down with the old canoe'

It was until a pleasant time see
'The Earl of Mar's daughter'

It was upon a high, high hill see
'Barbara Allen'

It was way back in '73 see 'Trail
to Mexico'

It was way up north in Boothbay

Harbor see 'Boothbay whale'

'It wasn't God who made honky tonk angels' J. D. Miller. FL: As I sit here tonight FLC: It wasn't God who made honky tonk angels. 10

It'll never get too dark for me see 'The gypsy laddie'

It's a bye, bye, my darling girl see 'Goin' up the mountain'

It's a darn good life and it's kind of funny see 'Honeycomb'

It's a funny thing see 'Isn't it a pity?'

'It's a grand night for singing' Oscar Hammerstein and Richard Rodgers. FL: same. 24

It's a little bit funny this feeling inside see 'Your song'

It's a long and dusty road, it's a hot and heavy load see 'Where I'm bound'

It's a long ways from East Colorado see 'East Colorado blues'

It's a riddle, it's a riddle, oh my dear mother see 'The brown girl'

'It's a sin to tell a lie' Billy Mayhew. FL: You know it's a sin to tell a lie FLC: Be sure it's true. 53

It's a still life water color of a late afternoon see 'The dangling conversation'

It's a very ancient saying see 'Getting to know you'

'It's a wonderful world' Harold Adamson, Jan Savitt and Johnny Watson. FL: same. 59

It's about a brave young highwayman my story I will tell see 'Brennan on the Moor'

It's all free grace and never-dying love see 'Bringing in that New Jerusalem'

It's all out on the old railroad see 'Jubilee'

It's all those Scottish lords and chiefs see 'Sir James the Ross'

'It's alright in the summertime' Fred Murray and George Everard. FL: My old man is a very funny chap FLC: And it's alright in the summertime. 17

It's been a hard day's night see 'A hard day's night'

'It's been a long long time' Sammy Cahn and Jule Styne. FL: Never

thought that you would be FLC: Just kiss me once. 59, 70

It's been so long since my baby has been here see 'It doesn't matter'

It's by far the hardest thing I've ever done see 'Follow me'

It's carbon monoxide, the old Detroit perfume see 'Papa Hobo'

It's dark as a dungeon and damp as the dew see 'Dark as a dungeon'

It's de same old tale of a palpitating nigger, every time, every time see 'Lily of Laguna'

'It's delightful to be married' Anna Held and V. Scotto. FL: When we older grew and bolder FLC: It's delightful to be married. 12

'It's d'lovely' Cole Porter. FL: I feel a sudden urge to sing FLC: The night is young. 6, 42

It's early, early all in the spring see 'Sweet William'

'It's easy to remember' Lorenz Hart and Richard Rodgers. FL: With you I owned the earth FLC: Your sweet expression. 53

It's false Sir John's a-courting gone see 'Mary Goldan'

It's four long years since I reached the land see 'Lousy miner'

It's good mornin' you young ladies see 'Stewball'

It's good mornin' you young men see 'Stewball'

'It's hard ain't it hard' FL: It's hard, ain't it hard, ain't it hard? 23

It's hard, and it's hard, ain't it hard see 'Hard, ain't it hard'

It'a hard in the country see 'Down on Penny's farm'

It's hard times, cotton mill girls see 'Cotton mill girls'

It's hard times in the country down on Penny's farm see 'Penny's farm'

It's hard times in the Cryderville Jail see 'Cryderville Jail'

It's hard times in the mill my love see 'Hard times in the mill'

It's holi, holi holiday see 'Little Musgrave and Lady Barnard'

It's home to your home, wherever you may be see 'Button willow tree'

It's I have got a ship in the north country see 'The Golden Vanity'

It's I have got a ship in the north
  of countery see 'Lowlands low'
It's if ye tak' my mantle see 'The
  knight and the shepherd's daughter'
'It's impossible' Sid Wayne and A.
  Manzanero. FL: It's impossible,
  tell the sun to leave the sky. 9
It's June in January because I'm in
  love see 'June in January'
It's just a little street where old
  friends meet see 'A little street
  where old friends meet'
'It's just a matter of time' Clyde
  Otis, Brook Benton and Belford
  Hendricks. FL: Someday, some
  way, you'll realize you've been
  blind. 10
It's knowing that your door is always
  open see 'Gentle on my mind'
It's Lamkin was a mason good see
  'Lamkin'
It's Little Joe the wrangler he'll
  wrangle nevermore see 'Little
  Joe the wrangler'
It's love and love alone see 'Love
  alone'
It's me, it's me, it's me, oh Lord
  see 'Standing in the need of
  prayer'
'It's nine times around, said the
  captain of the ship see 'The
  raging sea, how it roars'
'It's not easy' Mick Jagger and
  Keith Richard. FL: It's not easy,
  it's not easy living on your own.
  16
It's not the pale moon that excites
  me see 'The nearness of you'
'It's not unusual' Gordon Mills and
  Les Read. FL: It's not unusual
  to be loved by anyone. 45
It's of a fair maiden that lived on
  the shore see 'The sea captain'
It's of a fair pretty shepherdess
  see 'Earl Richard'
It's of a farmer lived in the east
  see 'Katherine Joffray'
It's of a farmer's daughter dear
  see 'Earl Richard'
It's of a gallant lady all in her
  tender youth see 'Wearing of
  the blue'
It's of a jolly beggarman see
  'Dirty beggarman'
It's of a jolly farmer see 'The
  baffled knight'
It's of a jolly light dragoon so quickly you shall hear see 'The

dragoon and the lady'
It's of a little galley bark by the
  North America see 'The low-
  lands low'
It's of a little paggy-lad came trip-
  pin' over the lea see 'The
  little paggy-lad'
It's of a lord in the north countrie
  see 'The merry Broomfield'
It's of a ragged beggar man came
  tripping o'er the plain see
  'The ragged beggarman'
It's of a rich farmer in Cheshire
  see 'The highwayman outwitted'
It's of a rich squire in the North
  country see 'The squire tin the
  North countree'
It's of a sea captain see 'Banks
  of green willow'
It's of a sea captain lived near the
  seaside O see 'Banks of green
  willow'
It's of a sea captain that ploughs
  the salt seas see 'The sea
  captain'; 'The sea captain or the
  Maid on the shore'
It's of a shepherd's daughter see
  'Shepherd's daughter'
It's of a shepherd's laddie see
  'The baffled knight'
It's of a young youth and a kind
  young youth see 'Bailiff's
  daughter of Islington'
It's of a youth and a well bred
  youth see 'Bailiff's daughter'
It's of a youth and a well-beloved
  youth see 'The bailiff's daughter';
  'The bailiff's daughter of Isling-
  ton'
It's of an old farmer lived in the
  West country see 'Farmer and
  tinker'
It's of an old friar as I have been
  told see 'The friar in the well'
It's of an old man and he lived
  poor see 'Old Jokey song'
It's of and a silly old man see
  'The silly old man'
It's of seven gypsies all of a row
  see 'Wraggle taggle gypsies'
It's of some noble lord, as you shall
  quickly hear see 'Bold Lankan'
It's of three brothers in merry
  Scotland see 'Henry Martin'
It's off the hook see 'Off the hook'
It's off with the old see 'Blue
  blue blue'
It's on one Sunday morning all in

tailed blue'
I've flown around the world in a
plane see II can't get started'
I've got a belly full of whisky and a
head full of gin see 'Long-line
skinner'
'I've got a crush on you' George and
Ira Gershwin. FL: How glad
many millions FLC: I've got a
crush on you. 21, 46
I've got a gal and you've got none
see 'Li'l Liza Jane'
I've got a girl in the Sourwood Mountain see 'Sourwood Mountain'
I've got a heavy date see 'Tico-
tico'
I've got a home in'a that rock,
don't you see see 'Home in that
rock'
I've got a little baby, but she's out
of sight see 'Hello my baby'
I've got a mother who's gone to
glory see 'Bringing in that
New Jerusalem'
I've got a mule and her name is
Sal see 'Low bridge, everybody
down'
I've got a mule, her name is Sal
see 'The Erie canal'
I've got a pie all baked complete
see 'Welcome here!'
I've got a ship in the North Coun-
tree see 'Golden Vanity'
I've got a song that I sing see
'I've got the world on a string'
'I've got a tiger by the tail' Buck
Owens and Harlan Howard. FL:
Well, I thought the day I met
you FLC: I've got a tiger by the
tail. 10
I've got a wife and a five little
children see 'Rock about my
Saro Jane'
I've got bricks in my pillow and my
head can't rest, no more see
'Bricks in my pillow'
'I've got five dollars' Lorenz Hart
and Richard Rodgers. FL:
Mister Shylock as was stingy
FLC: I've got five dollars. 46
I've got my breastplate sword, and
shield see 'Stay in the field'
'I've got nasty habits see 'Live
with me'
I've got no use for a red rockin'
chair see 'Red rocking chair'
'I've got no use for the women' FL:
Now, I've got no use for the wo-

men. 25, 57
'I've got rings on my fingers' R. P.
Weston and F. J. Barnes. FL:
Now Jim O'Shea was cast away
FLC: Sure, I've got rings on my
fingers, bells on my toes. 17
I've got some so-called friends see
'Paranoia blues'
I've got that joy, joy, joy see
'Down in my heart'
I've got the Vicksburg blues and
I'm singin' it every where I go
see 'Vicksburg blues'
'I've got the world on a string' Ted
Koehler and Harold Arlen. FL:
I've got a song that I sing FLC:
I've got the world on a string.
12
'I've got the world on a string' Ted
Koehler and Harold Arlen. FL:
Merry month of May FLC: I've
got the world on a string. 1
I've got the worried blues, Lord
see 'Worried blues'
'I've got to have a reason' Lenny
Davidson and Dave Clark. FL:
There's something on your mind
but you won't tell me. 47
I've got your picture and I'm gonna
put in a frame see 'Shuckin'
sugar blues'
'I've gotta crow' Carolyn Leigh and
Mark Charlap. FL: same. 6,
52
'I've grown accustomed to her face'
Lerner and Loewe. FL: same
FLC: same. 6, 64
'I've heard that song before' Sammy
Cahn and Jule Styne. FL: Music
helps me to remember FLC: It
seems to me I've heard that song
before. 59, 70
'I've just come from the fountain'
FL: same FLC: O brothers, I
love Jesus. 38
I've just come here this nicht to ask
you for you sympathy see 'Nanny'
I've just dropped in to make a call
see 'Paul Pry'
I've just found joy see 'Sweet
Lorraine'
I've just got here through Paris
see 'The man that broke the
bank at Monte Carlo'
I've just got here through Paris
from the sunny southern shore
see 'The man who broke the
bank at Monte Carlo'

I've just returned from the salt, salt sea *see* 'The ship's carpenter'

'I've just seen a face' Lennon and McCartney. FL: I've just seen a face I can't forget. 44

I've kissed the girls of Naples *see* 'Calcutta'

I've let a pair of arms enslave me *see* 'Heart and soul'

I've 'listed and I mean to fight *see* 'We'll overtake the army'

I've neither wealth nor power *see* 'I'll get by'

I've never been to heaven but I've been told *see* 'Trampin''

'I've never lost my last train yet' George Rollit and George Le Brunn. FL: I'm a modest little maiden from the country FLC: Yey, there's nothing half so sweet. 17

I've never met you *see* 'Isn't it romantic'

'I've only been down to the club' FL: Last night I was out rather late FLC: The club had a meeting tonight, love. 36

I've reached the land of waving wheat *see* 'Saskatchewan'

I've seen a deal of gaiety *see* 'Champagne Charlie'

I've seen fire and I've seen rain *see* 'Fire and rain'

I've sung this song, but I'll sing it again *see* 'So long, it's been good to know you'

I've thrown away my toys *see* 'On the good ship Lollipop'

'I've told every little star' Oscar Hammerstein and Jerome Kern. FL: I make up things to say on my way to you FLC: I've told every little star. 24, 67

I've told you once *see* 'The last time'

I've traveled about a bit in my time *see* 'Paddle your own canoe'

I've traveled all over this country *see* 'Acres of Clams'; 'Old settler's song'

I've wandered all over this country *see* 'Acres of clams'

'I've worked eight hours this day' Felix McGlennon. FL: Have ye heard the rule, my boys FLC: For I've worked eight hours this day. 36

I've worked in the cotton mill all of my life *see* 'Cotton mill girls'

I've written you a song *see* 'Blah-blah-blah'

'I'ze the bye' FL: I'ze the bye that builds the boat FLC: Hip your partner, Sally Tipple. 57

Izza ostrova na strezhen' *see* 'Stenka Razin'

- J -

'Jack and Jill' FL: Jack and Jill went up the hill. 48

'Jack and Joan' Thomas Campion. FL: Jack and Joan they think no ill. 26

'Jack and Joe' FL: Three years ago when Jack and Joe set sail across the foam FLC: Give my love to Nelly, Jack and kiss her once for me. 7

Jack arrived in London city *see* 'Jack in London city'

Jack Davy came riding through the woods *see* 'David'

'Jack Frost' Cecily Pike and Ivor R. Davies. FL: Look out! Look out! 13

'Jack in London city' FL: Jack arrived in London city. 30

Jack is the king of the dark blue sea *see* 'Strike up the band'

'Jack o' Diamonds' FL: O Mollie, O Mollie, it's for your sake alone. 2

Jack O Diamonds ain't nothin' but a grizzly bear *see* 'Grizzly bear'

'Jack o' lantern' Lois Holt. FL: Jack o Lantern, Jack o Lantern. 13

'Jack the little Scot' FL: Johnny was as brave a knight. 11

'Jack was every inch a sailor' FL: Now twas twenty or thirty years since Jack first saw the light FLC: Jack was every inch a sailor. 25

Jack went out to plow his corn *see* 'Jack's wife'

Jackie boy *see* 'The keeper would a-hunting go'

Jackie boy, Master! *see* 'The keeper'

'Jack's wife' FL: Jack went out to plow his corn. 11

'Jackson' FL: Jackson is on sea. 57

'Jackson' Billy Edd Wheeler and
Gabby Rogers. FL: We got mar-
ried in a fever. 47
Jacky had an auger that bored two
holes at once see 'The Golden
Vanity'
'Jacky Robinson' FL: Jacky, Jacky
Robinson. 22
'Jacob's ladder' FL: We are climb-
ing Jacob's ladder. 34, 57
'The jailer's daughter' FL: I sailed
east, I sailed west. 11
'Jailhouse rock' Jerry Leiber and
Mike Stoller. FL: The warden
threw a party in the country jail.
10
'Jake and Roanie' FL: Jake and
Roanie was a-ridin' along. 43
'Jakey jump der baby' FL: Oh!
wonce ven I vas single FLC: Oh!
Jaky shump der baby. 36
'The jam on Gerry's rock' FL:
Come all ye true born shanty
boys. 57
'The jam on Gerry's rock' FL:
Come round, you brave young
river men and list' while I re-
late. 4
'Jamaica farewell' Lord Burgess.
FL: Down the way where the
nights are gay FLC: Sad to say,
I'm on my way. 52
'James Bird' Charles Miner. FL:
Sons of freedom, listen to me.
55
'James Campbell' FL: Booted and
spurred and bridled rode he. 11
'Jane, Jane' FL: Hey, hey, Jane,
Jane. 57
'Jane was a neighbor' FL: Oh, Jane
was a neighbor for six months or
more. 11
'Janis' Joe McDonald. FL: Into my
life on waves of electrical sound.
15
'January and February' Jane B. Wal-
ters. FL: When January days
are here. 13
'Jarama Valley' FL: There's a valley in Spain called Jarama. 57
'Jargon' William Billings. FL: Let
horrid jargon split the air. 65
'Jay Gould's daughter' FL: On a
Monday morning it began to rain.
4, 57
'Jealous' Tommie Malie, Dick Finch
and Jack Little. FL: I'm jealous
of the pretty flowers, too FLC:

I'm jealous of the moon that
shines above. 12, 47, 54
'The jealous lover' FL: What do you
want for your breakfast, O Willie,
my dear? 11
'Jealousy' FL: I caught her dancing
with another one. 41
'Jean' Rod McKuen. FL: Jean,
Jean, roses are red. 45, 71
'Jean o' Bethelnie' FL: There were
six and six ladies. 11
'Jeanie with the light brown hair'
Stephen Foster. FL: I dream of
Jeanie with the light brown hair
FLC: Oh, I dream of Jeanie with
the light brown hair. 1, 57, 63
'Jeepers creepers' Johnny Mercer
and Harry Warren. FL: I don't
care what the weatherman says
FLC: Jeepers creepers. 46
'Jeerusalem's dead!' Brian Daly and
John Crook. FL: I've 'ah four
'arf-pints at the Magpie and
Stump FLC: Yer won't see 'im
pullin' the barrer no more. 17
'Jefferson and liberty' FL: The
gloomy night before us flies FLC:
Rejoice, Columbia's sons, re-
joice. 4, 19, 57
'Jellon Graeme' FL: O, Jellon
Graeme sat in good greenwood.
11
'Jelly roll blues' FL: Well, it's
jelly, jelly, jelly cause jam don't
shake like that. 57
'Jennifer, Jenny' FL: I married me
a wife and I took her home. 11
'Jenny fair gentle Rosemarie' FL:
Now sweet William's to get him
a wife. 11
'Jenny, flow gentle rosemary' FL:
Sweet William went on a hoeing
ride. 11
'Jenny Jenkins' FL: Will you wear
white, my dear, O my dear?
FLC: I will buy me a fol-di-rol-
di till-di-toll-di. 4, 57, 58
'Jerry' FL: Got to pull this timber
'fore the sun goes down FLC:
Haulin' timber. 57
'Jerry, go and oil that car' FL:
Come all ye railroad section
men. 19
Jerusalem, my happy home see
'Comfort in heaven'
'Jes' gwine ober in de Heabenlye
lan'' FL: You can hinder me here
FLC: De heabenlye lan'. 5

'Jesse James' FL: Jesse James was
a lad that killed many a man
FLC: Poor Jesse had a wife to
mourn for his life.   2, 23, 25,
50, 56, 57

'Jesse James' FL: Went down to the
station not many days ago FLC:
O, Jesse leaves a wife, she's a
mourner all her life.   14

'Jessica's song' Joseph Baildon.
FL: Haste, Lorenzo, haste away.
40

'Jesus born in Bethlea' FL: same.
33

'Jesus, Jesus, rest your head' John
Jacob Niles.   FL: Have you
heard about our Jesus FLC:
Jesus, Jesus, rest your head.
33

Jesus loves the little children see
'Everything is beautiful'

Jesus, my all to heaven is gone
 see 'Hard to rise again'; 'I want
to die a-shouting'; 'I want to go
where Jesus is'

Jesus walked this lonesome valley
 see 'Lonesome valley'

Jesus, your king is born see 'The
Huron Indian carol'

'Jet' Paul McCartney and Linda
McCartney.   FL: Jet! I can almost remember their funny faces.
64

'Jeu, jeu!' FL: Por aquí pasó uno
pava.   51

'The jeweler's daughter' FL: It
rains, it pours, it rains, it
pours.   11

'Jewish lady' FL: It rained a mist,
it rained a mist.   11

The Jews crucified Him and nailed
Him to the tree see 'He rose
from the dead'

'The Jew's daughter' FL: It rained
a mist, it rained a mist.   11

'The Jew's daughter' FL: It rained,
it hailed, it snowed, it blowed.
11

'The Jew's daughter' FL: There was
a little boy.   11

'The Jew's garden' FL: It 'ails, it
rains in merry Scotland.   11

'The Jew's garden' FL: It rained, a
mist, it rained a mist.   11

'The Jew's garden' FL: It rained one
day in old Scotland.   11

The Jews killed poor Jesus see
'He arose'

'Jigsaw puzzle' Mick Jagger and
Keith Richard.   FL: There's a
tramp sitting on my doorstep.
16

'Jim crack corn' FL: When I was
young I used to wait.   4

'Jim Crow blues' FL: I'm tired of
bein' Jim Crowed.   57

'Jim Fisk' FL: If you'll listen a
while, I'll sing you a song FLC:
If a man was in trouble, Fisk
helped him along.   57

Jim Riley, Jim Riley, Jim Riley
my son see 'Lord Rendal'

'Jimmie Brown, the newsboy' A. P.
Carter.   FL: You will hear me
yelling 'Morning Star' FLC: I
sell the morning papers, sir.   14

Jimmie set sailing leave Nancy a-
weeping see 'Farewell Nancy'

'Jimmy and Nancy' FL: O Jimmy,
lovely Jimmy, what you are saying is true.   30

Jimmy crack corn and I don't care
 see 'The blue tail fly'

Jimmy Ray was a preacher's son
 see 'Son of a preacher man'

'Jingle bells' John Pierpont.   FL:
Dashing thru the snow in a one-
horse open sleigh FLC: Oh!
Jingle bells, jingle bells, jingle
all the way.   1, 57, 67

'Jingle bells' James S. Pierpont.
FL: Oh what fun it is to ride in
a one horse open sleigh FLC:
Jingle bells, jingle bells, jingle
all the way.   34

'Jingle jangle jingle' Frank Loesser
and Joseph J. Lilley.   FL: I
got spurs that jingle jangle jingle.
70

Joe Joe was a man who thought he
was a loner see 'Get back'

Joan was quizzical, studied pataphysical science in the home see
'Maxwell's silver hammer'

'Jock o' 'Hazeldean' FL: Why weep
ye by the tide, fair maid.   11

'Jock o' Hazeldean' FL: Why weep
ye by the tide ladye?   11

'Jock o' Hazelgreen' FL: As I went
forth to take the air.   11

'Jock o' Hazelgreen' FL: It was on
a morning early.   11

'Jock o' the side' FL: Now Liddesdale has ridden a raid.   11

'Jock o' the Syde' FL: The laird's
Jock ane, the laird's wat twa.   11

'Jock of Hazeldean' FL: As I roded
out one midsummer morn. 11
'Jock sheep' FL: There was a shep-
herd's son. 11
'Jock the leg' FL: Jock the Leg and
the merry merchant. 11
'Jock the leg and the merry mer-
chant' FL: As Jock the leg and
the merry merchant. 11
'Jock the leg and the merry mer-
chant' FL: Jock the leg an' the
merry merchant. 11
'Jockie o' Bridiesland' FL: O Jockie
rose up one May mornin'. 11
'Jody' FL: I've been workin' all day
long. 28
'Joe Bowers' FL: My name it is
Joe Bowers, I got a brother Ike.
25, 57
'Joe Hill' Alfred Hayes and Earl
Robinson. FL: I dreamed I saw
Joe Hill last night alive as you
and me. 4, 19
'Joe Turner' FL: They tell me Joe
Turner's come and gone. 57
'John and William' FL: O John and
William walked out one day. 11
'John B' FL: We come on the sloop
John B FLC: So hoist up the
John B sails. 57
'John Barbour' FL: What's the
matter with my daughter? the old
man said. 11
'John Blunt' FL: There was an old
couple lived under a hill. 11
John Brown had a little Indian see
'Ten little Indians'
'John Brown's body' FL: John
Brown's body lies amouldering in
the grave FLC: Glory, glory,
hallelujah. 1, 4, 19, 25, 38,
57, 66
John Bull don't remember now see
'Revolutionary times'
'John Dobber' FL: I married me a
wife and I sent her to milk FLC:
Ti rissle ti rassle. 11
'John Gobillips' FL: John Gobillips
take my fine shirt. 11
'John Hardy' FL: John Hardy was a
brave and desp'rate little man. 7
'John Hardy' FL: John Hardy was a
desperate little man. 14, 25,
56, 57
'John Hardy' FL: John Hardy was a
man, yes a hard hittin' man. 23
'John Henry' FL: John Henry said to
his captain. 25

'John Henry' FL: John Henry
told the captain. 28
'John Henry' FL: John Henry was a
little baby. 4
'John Henry' FL: John Henry was a
little, bitty boy, no bigger than
the palm of your hand. 7
'John Henry' FL: John Henry when
he was a little bitty boy. 14
'John Henry' FL: Well, every Monday morning. 27, 57
'John Henry' FL: When John Henry
was a little baby. 19, 23
'John Hielandman' FL: A hieland
lad me love was born FLC: Sing
hey, me braw John Hielandman.
57
'John Jacob Jingleheimer Schmidt'
FL: same. 57
'John o' the Hazelgreen' FL: As I
walked out one May morning. 11
'John of Haselgreen' FL: Why weep
'e by the tide, Ladye. 11
'John of Hazelgreen' FL: As I drew
out one May morning. 11
'John of Hazelgreen' FL: As I a-
walked out one fair May morning.
11
'John of Hazelgreen' FL: As I was
walking out one wondering morn.
11
'John of Hazelgreen' FL: As I were
walking down the road. 11
'John of Hazelgreen' FL: O on the
road one summer day. 11
'John of Hazelgreen' FL: An old
knight rode one summer's day.
11
'John of Hazelgreen' FL: While riding down that green wood road.
11
'John over the Hazel Green' FL: As
I walked out one fair May morning. 11
'John over the Hazel Green' FL:
As I walked out yonders green
wood tree. 11
'John Peel' FL: Do ye ken John
Peel with his coat so gray FLC:
Twas the sound of his horn
brought me from my bed. 23, 25,
57
'John Riley' FL: Fair young maid
all in the garden. 57
'John Riley' FL: On walking out on
a summer morning. 23, 25
John said the city was just four-
square see 'Walk in Jerusalem'

'Johnny Wedlock' FL: O Johnny Wedlock is my name. 11

Johnny's nae a gentleman and
Johnny's nae a laird see 'The
jolly beggar'

'Johnson' FL: Johnson, he was riding out as fast as he could ride.
57

'Johnson and the colonel' FL: As
Johnson and the young colonel.
11

'The Johnson Boys' FL: Johnson
boys were raised in the ashes.
56, 57

Johnson was a valiant man see
'The three butchers'

'Johnson's ale' FL: Five jolly
rogues of a feather walked o'er
the hill together FLC: When
Johnson's ale was new, my boys.
57

'Johnson's motor car' FL: Twas
down by Branigan's corner. 57

Join the CIO see 'I am a union
woman'

'Jolly' FL: Ol' master, don't you
whip me, I'll give you half a
dollar. 28

'Jolly beggar' FL: Ainst a beggar
cam out owre the lea FLC:
Raddle tee a tow row ree. 11

'The jolly beggar' FL: A beggarman
cam owre yon lea FLC: Larrity
a tow row ree. 11

'The jolly beggar' FL: It was the
jolly beggar--at the beginnin' he
had been FLC: Wi his hey daun-
tin airy, airy, airy an. 11

'The jolly beggar' FL: Johnny's nae
a gentleman and Johnny's nae a
laird. 11

'Jolly beggar' FL: Oh, an old beggarman comin' over the lea. 11

'The jolly beggar' FL: Oh, some
gaed on horse, anither gaed on
fute FLC: Raddlee a tow row ray.
11

'The jolly beggar' FL: There was a
jolly beggar, for beggin' he was
boun' FLC: And we'll gang nae
mair a-roving. 11

'The jolly beggar' FL: There wis a
auld beggar man FLC: Na mair
I'll gang a-rovin a-rovin in the
nicht. 11

A jolly bunch of cowboys on Franklin Slaughter ranch see 'Franklin Slaughter ranch'

A jolly fat frog lived in the river
swim O see 'The frog and the
crow'

'The jolly pinder of Wakefield' FL:
In Wakefield there lives a jolly
pinder. 11

'The jolly sailor' FL: When my
fortune does frown. 3

'Jordan is a hard road to trabel'
FL: I just arrived in town for to
pass de time away FLC: So take
off your coat boys and roll up
your sleeves. 36

Jordan's water is chilly and cold
see 'Wade in the water'

Joseph and Mary see 'The cherry
tree carol'

Joseph was a young man see 'The
cherry tree carol'

'Joseph was an old man' FL: O,
Joseph was an old man, and an
old man was he. 11

Joseph was an old man see 'The
cherry tree carol'

'Joshua fit the battle of Jericho'
FL: same. 25, 67

'Joshua fought the battle of Jericho'
FL: You may talk about your
kings of Gideon FLC: Joshua
fought the battle of Jericho. 34,
57

'The jovial beggar' FL: There was
a jovial beggar FLC: And a-begging we will go, will go, will
go. 25

The joy and tears that love endears
see 'Without you'

'Joy in thy hope' Robert Jones. FL:
Joy in thy hope, the earnest of
thy love. 26

'Joy to the world' Isaac Watts, G.
F. Handel. FL: Joy to the world;
the Lord is come. 34, 57

The joys of love seem like a moment or two see 'Plaisir
d'amour'

'J't'aim'rais mieux, mon mari?'
FL: Mon mari est bien malade
en grand danger de mourir FLC:
J't'aim'rais, mon mari mieux.
58

'Juanita' FL: Soft o'er the fountain.
25

'Jubilee' FL: It's all out on the old
railroad FLC: Swing and turn,
Jubilee. 57

Judge, he give me six months,
cause I wouldn't go to work see

'Been on the chain gang'
The judge says stand up boy and
dry your tears see 'Twenty-one
years'
The judge took his seat in the courthouse one day see 'His lordship
winked at the counsel'
'Judgment Day is rolling round' FL:
I've a good old mother in the
heaven, my Lord FLC: Judgment,
Judgment, Judgment day is rolling
around. 38
'Judgment will find you so' FL: O
brethren, brethren, watch and
pray FLC: Just as you live, just
so you die. 38
'The jug of punch' FL: As I was sit-
ting with a jug and spoon FLC:
Too ra loo ra loo. 35, 57
'Julie' FL: Julie, hear me when I
call you. 28
Jump down, turn around see
'Pick a bale of cotton'
'Jump Jim Crow' Thomas D. Rice.
FL: Come, listen, all you gals
and boys FLC: Wheel about, an'
turn about. 1
'Jumpin' Jack Flash' Mick Jagger
and Keith Richard. FL: I was
born in a crossfire hurricane.
16
'June in January' Leo Robin and
Ralph Rainger. FL: It's June in
January because I'm in love. 53
'June is bustin' out all over' Oscar
Hammerstein and Richard Rod-
gers. FL: March went out like
a lion FLC: June is bustin' out
all over. 1, 24, 67
Jungle drums were madly beating
see 'Babalu'
'A Junto song' FL: Tis money makes
the member vote FLC: And tax-
ing we will go. 49, 55
'Just a baby's prayer at twilight'
Sam Lewis, Joe Young and M.
K. Jerome. FL: There's a
mother there at twilight FLC:
Just a baby's prayer at twilight.
12, 31
'Just a closer walk with Thee' FL:
I am weak but Thou are strong
FLC: Just a closer walk with
Thee. 23, 27, 34, 57
'Just a gigolo' Irving Caesar and
Leonello Casucci. FL: Just a
gigolo, everywhere I go. 59
'Just a girl that men forget' Al

Dubin, Fred Rath and Joe Garren. FL: For when men settle
down FLC: You're the kind of
girl that men forget. 12
Just a little boy standing in the rain
see 'What have they done to the
rain?'
'Just a little lovin'' Zeke Clements
and Eddy Arnold. FL: Ever
since that time began love has
ruled the world FLC: Just a
little lovin' will go a long way.
10
Just a little rain falling all around
see 'What have they done to the
rain?'
Just a song at twilight see 'Love's
old sweet song'
Just a year ago today see 'Brown
eyes'
Just about a year ago see 'Lodi'
Just a-lookin' for a home see
'The boll weevil'
'Just as I am' Charlotte Elliott and
William B. Bradbury. FL: Just
as I am without one plea. 64
Just as you lived, just so you die
see 'Judgment will find you so'
'Just a-wearyin' for you' Carrie
Jacobs-Bond. FL: same. 25,
31
'Just before the battle, Mother'
George F. Root. FL: same FLC:
Farewell, Mother, you may never.
57
Just before the battle the general
hears a row see 'Goober peas'
Just behold that number see 'From
every graveyard'
Just break the news to mother see
'Break the news to mother'
Just down around the corner of the
street were I reside see 'Sweet
Rosie O'Grady'
Just hand me my old Martin see
'Franklin D. Roosevelt's back
again'
Just hang my cradle, Mammy mine
see 'Rock-a-bye your baby with
a Dixie melody'
'Just in time' Betty Comden,
Adolph Green and Jule Styne.
FL: I was resting comfortably
face down in the gutter FLC:
Just in time. 6, 42
Just kiss me once see 'It's been
a long, long time'
Just kiss me once, then kiss me

twice _see_ 'It's been a long,
   long time'
Just let a smile be your umbrella
   see 'Let a smile be your um-
   brella'
'Just like a woman' Bob Dylan. FL:
   Nobody feels any pain tonight as
   I stand inside the rain FLC: She
   takes just like a woman. 45
Just listen to this song I'm singin'
   brother _see_ 'Git back blues'
Just listen to this song I'm singing
   see 'Black, brown and white
   blues'
'Just one of those things' Cole
   Porter. FL: As Dorothy Parker
   once said to her boyfriend FLC:
   It was just one of those things.
   42, 46
'Just tell them that you saw me'
   Paul Dresser. FL: While stroll-
   ing down the street one evening
   upon mere pleasure bent FLC:
   Just tell them that you saw me.
   20
Just touch the harp gently, my
   pretty Louise _see_ 'Touch the
   harp gently'
Just walk on by _see_ 'Walk on by'
'Just walking in the rain' Johnny
   Bragg and Robert S. Riley. FL:
   same. 10, 52
Just yesterday mornin' they let me
   know you were gone _see_ 'Fire
   and rain'

                   - K -

'Kalinka' FL: Kalinka, Kalinka, Ka-
   linka moia. 57
'The kangaroo' FL: A kangaroo sat
   on an oak FLC: Kiminee kiddy
   kum keero. 57, 68
'Kansas City' Mike Stoller and Jerry
   Leiber. FL: I'm gonna be
   standin' on the corner FLC: I'm
   goin' to Kansas City. 52
'Kashmiri song' Laurence Hope and
   Amy Woodford-Finden. FL:
   Pale hands I loved beside the
   Shalimar. 31
'Katey Morey' FL: Come all you
   fair and tender ladies. 11
'Katey Morey' FL: Come young
   come old, come all draw nigh.
   11
'Katharine Jaffray' FL: Lochnagar

cam fae the West. 11
'Katharine Jaffray' FL: There was
   a squire of Edinboro town. 11
'Katherine Jaffrey' FL: There was
   a farmer lived in the east. 11
'Katherine Joffray' FL: It's of a
   farmer lived in the east. 11
'Katherine Janfarie' FL: There was
   a may and a weel far'd may. 11
'Kathleen Mavourneen' F. W. N.
   Crouch. FL: Kathleen Mavour-
   neen! the gray dawn is breaking.
   25, 57
'Kathy's song' Paul Simon. FL: I
   hear the drizzle of the rain. 60
'Katie Morie' FL: I went to her
   father's house. 11
'Katie Morey' FL: Come, all ye
   young and foolish lads FLC: Sing
   do ri iddle, sing do ri a. 11
'Katiusha' M. Isakovskii and M.
   Blanter. FL: Apple trees and
   pear trees were aflower. 58
'Katiushka' M. Isakovskii and M.
   Blanter. FL: Rastsvetali yablonii
   grushi. 57, 58
'Katy Cline' FL: Well now, who
   does not know Katy Cline FLC:
   Tell me that you love me, Katy
   Cline. 57
'Katy Cruel' FL: When I first came
   to town FLC: Oh, diddle lully
   day. 57, 58
'The keach i' the creel' FL: When
   the creel cam' to the top o' the
   lum. 11
'The keach in the creel' FL: Bonny
   Meg went out one day. 11
'The keach in the creel' FL: A fair
   maid doon thro' Collieston cam'.
   11
'The keach in the creel' FL: A fair
   young maid went up the street.
   11
'The keach in the creel' FL: Hey
   bonnie May went out one day. 11
'The keach in the creel' FL: Maisie
   she went oot tae buy FLC: Rickie
   doo dum day. 11
'The keach in the creel' FL: Oh,
   ye'll get a ladder, a long long
   ladder. 11
'The keach in the creel' FL: Pretty
   Polly went out one day. 11
'The keach in the creel' FL: They
   lad, they lay, in the bed they
   lay. 11
'The keach in the creel' FL: This

little maid went up the street.
11
Keedle up, a keedle up, a-turp,
turp tay see 'The cambric
shirt'
'The keel row' FL: As I came
through Sandgate. 25
'Keemo kimo' FL: In South Caro-
lina the darkeys go FLC: Keemo
kimo. 36
Keemo, kyemo, dah ro wah see
'The oppossum'
'Keemy Kyemo' FL: There was an
old frog and he lived in a spring
FLC: Sing song kitty catchee
kyemeeoh. 68
Keep a inching along see 'Inch-
ing along'
Keep a-movin' Dan see 'Cool
water'
'Keep me from sinking down' FL:
I tell you what I mean to do
FLC: Oh, Lord, oh, my Lord!
38
'Keep on the sunny side' FL:
There a dark and troubled side
of life FLC: Keep on the sunny
side. 14
'Keep the customer satisfied' Paul
Simon. FL: Gee but it's great
to be back home. 60
'Keep woman in her sphere' D.
Estabrook. FL: I have a neighbor, one of those. 57, 58
'Keep your feet still, Geordie Hin-
ney' Joe Wilson. FL: Wor Geor-
die and Bob Johnson byeth lay i'
one bed FLC: Keep yor fee still
Geordie Hinney let's be happy for
the neet. 17
'Keep your lamp trimmed and burn-
ing' FL: Brother, don't you get
a-worried FLC: Keep your lamp
trimmed and a-burning. 57
'Keep your lamps trimmed' FL:
Keep your lamps trimmed and
a-burning. 38
'Keep your saddle tight' FL: A
bunch of foaming mustangs. 43
'The keeper' FL: The keeper would
ahunting to FLC: Jackie boy,
Master! 57, 68
'The keeper would a-hunting go'
FL: same FLC: Jackie boy. 34,
72
'Keepin' out of mischief now' Andy
Razaf and Thomas Waller. FL:
Don't even go to a movie show

FLC: Keepin' out of mischief
now. 53
'Kellyburnbraes' FL: There lived a
carl in Kellyburnbraes. 11
'Kempion' FL: Come here, come
here, ye freely freed. 11
'Kempy Kane' FL: Kempy Kane's a
wooin' gane. 11
'Kentucky Babe' Richard Henry Buck
and Adam Geibel. FL: Skeeters
am a hummin' on de honeysuckle
vine FLC: Fly away, fly away,
Kentucky babe. 20
'Kentucky bootlegger' FL: Come all
you booze buyers if you want to
hear. 57
'Kentucky moonshiner' FL: I've been
a moonshiner for seventeen long
years. 57
'The Kerry recruit' FL: At the age
of nineteen I was diggin' the
land. 57
'Keven Barry' FL: Early on a Monday morning. 19, 57
'The kickin' mule' FL: As I went
down to the huckleberry picnic
FLC: Whoa there, mule, I tell
you. 14
'Kicking mule' FL: My uncle had an
old mule FLC: Well, whoa there
mule, I tell you. 72
Kids are different today I hear
every mother say see 'Mother's
little helper'
'Kilboggie' FL: First when I cam to
Kilboggie's toon. 11
'Kilgary Mountain' FL: As I was
awalking up on Kilgary Mountain
FLC: Mush-a ring um dur-um
dah. 57
'Killarney' FL: By Killarney lakes
and fells. 25
'Killyburn Braes' FL: It is true that
the women are worse than the
men? 11
Kiminee keddy kum keero see 'The
kangaroo'
Kind folks you will pity my horrible
tale see 'The dreary Black
Hills'
'Kind fortune' FL: One evening, one
evening, one evening in May. 30
Kind friends, gather near, I want
you to hear see 'Poor man's
heaven'
Kind friends, if you will listen
see 'Brown-eyed Lee'
Kind friends, you may ask what

makes me sad and still see
'Utah Carol'
Kind friends, your pity pray bestow
see 'Constantinople'
'Kind in unkindness' Thomas Campion and Philip Rosseter. FL:
Kind in unkindness, when will you
relent. 26
'Kind miss' FL: Kind miss, kind
miss, go ask your mother. 57
'Kind old husband' FL: What'll you
have for dinner, my kind old
husband. 37
'Kind wife' FL: Kind wife, loving
wife, how may it be. 11
'The king and the miller' FL: How
happy a state does the miller
possess. 25
'The king and the tinker' FL: An
now to be brief, let's pass over
the rest. 11
'The king and the tinker' FL: Oh,
the king and the tinker were at a
great fair FLC: Why why whack
the farrel the farrel la lay. 11
The king but and his nobles a' see
'Brown Robin'
King Hancock sat in regal state
see 'The Charleston song'; 'A
song about Charleston'
The king has wedden an ill woman
see 'The wedding of Robin Hood
and Little John'
The king he sits in Dumferling
town see 'Sir Patrick Spence'
The king he wrote a letter see
'Lord Ellenwater'
The king he wrote a love letter
see 'The king's love letter'
'King Henry' FL: Lat never a man
a wooing went. 11
'King Henry V. and the King of
France' FL: As our king lay
dreaming upon his bed. 11
'King Henry the 5th, his victory'
FL: A councel grave our king
did hold. 11
'King Henry V's conquest of
France' FL: As our king lay
musing on his bed. 11
'King Henry Fifth's conquest of
France' FL: A king was sitting
on his throne. 11
'King Henry, my son' FL: Oh,
where have you been wandering,
King Henry, my son! 11
King Henry was sent for see
'Queen Jane'

'King Herod and the cock' FL:
There was a star in David's land.
11
King Jesus in the chariot rides see
'He's the lily of the valley'
'King John' FL: An ancient story
I'll tell you anon. 11
'King John and the Abbot of Canter-
bury' FL: An ancient story I'll
tell you anon. 11
'King John and the Abbot of Canter-
bury' FL: I'll tell you a story,
a story anon. 11
'King John and the bishop' FL: A
story, a story, a story of one.
11
'The king lay musing on his bed'
FL: same. 11
The king luikit owre his castle wa
see 'Sir Colin'
'King Malcolm and Sir Colvin' FL:
There ance lived a king in fair
Scotland. 11
'King of the road' Roger Miller
FLC: Trailer for sale or rent.
10
'King Orfeo' FL: Der lived a king
into da aist. 11
'King Orfeo' FL: Will ye come in
into our ha'. 11
'King Pharim' FL: King Pharim sat
amusing. 11
King San of Senegal see 'San'
The king sat in Dumfermline town
see 'Sir Patrick Spens'
A king was sitting on his throne
see 'King Henry Fifth's conquest
of France'
The king will take the queen see
'The card song'
'King William' FL: King William
was King James' son. 7
'King William and Lady Margaret'
FL: There was such a man as
King William, there was. 11
'Kingdom coming' Henry C. Work.
FL: Say, darkies, hab you seen
de massa FLC: De massa run,
ha, ha. 1
'The king's daughter' FL: He was
mounted on a milk white steed.
11
'King's daughter' FL: My pretty
little crowin' chicken. 11
'The king's daughter' FL: You fol-
lowed me up, you followed me
down. 11
'The king's daughter fair' FL: There

'The laird o' Linne' FL: O yonder
he stands, and there he gangs.
11
'The laird o' Roslin's daughter' FL:
same. 11
The laird o' Roslin's daughter
walked through the wood her lane
see 'Captain Wedderburn's courtship'
'The laird of Cockpen' FL: The laird
o' Cockpen, he's proud an' he's
great. 25
'The laird of Drum' FL: The laird
o' Drum has a-hunting gane. 11
'The laird of Drum' FL: The laird
o' Drum a-wooing gane. 11
'The laird of Ochiltrie' FL: O listen
gude people to my tale. 11
'The laird of Roslin's daughter' FL:
see 'Captain Wedderburn'
The laird's Jock ane, the laird's
wat twa see 'Jock o' the Syde'
'Lambeth Walk' Noel Gay and Doug-
las Furber. FL: Every little
Lambeth gal FLC: Any time you're
Lambeth way. 12
'Lambkin' FL: Oh, Lamkin was a
mason. 11
'Lambkin' FL: Said the lord to the
lady. 11
'A lamentable ditty on the death of
Geordie' FL: Come, all you lusty
northern lads. 11
'Lamkin' FL: And where is the land-
lady. 11
'Lamkin' FL: Bold Dunkins were as
fine a mason. 11
'Lamkin' FL: It's Lamkin was a
mason good. 11
'Lamkin' FL: The landlord to his
lady. 11
'Lamkin' FL: Oh! lady, oh! lady;
I'm now going out. 11
'Lamkin' FL: Oh, wife, dear wife.
11
'Lamkin' FL: Old Lamkin was as
good a mason. 11
'Lamkin' FL: Said the lord to his
lady. 30
'Lamkin' FL: Says the lord to lady,
I'm going out from home. 11
'Lamkin' FL: There was a wealthy
merchant. 11
'Lamkin' FL: Where is the landlord?
11
'Lammikin' FL: A better mason than
Lammikin. 11
'Lampkin' FL: Why need I reward

Lampkin? 11
'Land of the silver birch' FL: same.
13
The landlord came home so late in
the night see 'The gypsy laddie'
'Landlord, fill the flowing bowl'
FL: same. 23, 57
The landlord to his lady see
'Lamkin'
'The Lane County bachelor' FL: My
name is Frank Bolar an ole
bachelor I am FLC: But hurrah
for Lane County, the land of the
free. 66
Lane he stands and lane he gangs
see 'The heir o' Lynne'
'Lang a-growing' FL: The trees they
are ivied, the leaves they are
green. 57
'Lang Johnnie Moir' FL: There
lived a man in Rhynie's land
FLC: The press gang came
quickly round. 11
'Lang Johnnie More' FL: There
lives a man in Rynie's land. 11
'Lang Johnny More' FL: There
lived a lad at Rhynie's town FLC:
A riddle a nil din adie. 11
'The lantern' Mick Jagger and Keith
Richard. FL: We in our present
life. 16
'The lark' FL: The lark it is a
handsome bird. 72
Larrity a tow row ree see 'The
jolly beggar'
'The lass from the low country' FL:
Oh she was a lass from the low
country FLC: Oh sorrow, deep
sorrow. 23, 25
'The lass of Lochroyan' FL: O who
will shoe my bonny feet. 11
'The lass of Richmond Hill' Leonard
McNally and James Hook. FL:
O Richmond Hill there lives a
lass FLC: This lass so neat,
with smile so sweet. 1, 25
'Lass of Roch Royal' FL: Adieu,
kind friend adieu, adieu. 11
'The lass of Roch Royal' FL: Oh,
who will shoe my little foot, foot,
foot? 11
'Lass of Roch Royal' FL: Who will
shoe your pretty little feet. 11
A lass that was loaden with care
see 'The dejected lass'
'The lass with the delicate air' FL:
Young Molly, who lived at the
foot of the hill. 25

'The lasses of Dublin' FL: The
meadows look cheerful, the birds
sweetly sing. 3
Lassie wi' your tow pow ree see
'The gaberlunzie man'
Last Easter I got married see
'The low low lands of Holland'
Last Easter I was married, that
night I went to bed see 'The
lowlands of Holland'
'Last fair deal gone done' FL: It's
the last fair deal gone down. 57
Last Friday morn when we set sail
see 'The mermaid'
Last Friday morning as we set sail
see 'The mermaid'
Last Friday night Lady Margaret
she lie see 'Young Hunting'
'The last great round-up' FL: When
I think of the last great round-up.
2
Last nicht there were four Maries
see 'Mary Mild'
Last night as I lay on the prairie
see 'The cowboy dream'; 'The
cowboy's dream'; 'The grand
roundup'; 'Roll on dogies'
'Last night I had the strangest
dream' Ed McCurdy. FL: same.
4
Last night I was a-married and on
my marriage bed see 'The lowlands of Holland'
Last night I was out rather late
see 'I've only been down to the
club'
Last night I went to a social club
see 'We all went home in a cab'
'Last night, last night Lady Margaret lay asleep see 'Young
Hunting'
Last night the gypsies came to my
door see 'Wraggletail gypsies'
Last night there were four Maries
see 'The four Maries'
Last night there were four Marys
see 'The four Marys'
Last night three gypsies came to
my door see 'The raggle taggle gypsies oh'
Last night Tom Snooks says he to
me see 'When we went out a
fishing'
Last night we met and I dream of
you yet see 'With the wind and
the rain in your hair'
'The last request' FL: Fast, fast
my life is fading. 57

'The last rose of summer' Thomas
Moore. FL: Tis the last rose
of summer. 25, 63
Last summertime I went away to
Dover by the sea see 'Seaweed'
Last Sunday mornin', Lord, Lord,
Lord see 'Gray goose'
'The last time' Mick Jagger and
Keith Richard. FL: I've told you
once. 16
'The last time I saw Paris' Oscar
Hammerstein and Jerome Kern.
FL: A lady known as Paris FLC:
The last time I saw Paris. 24,
67
The last train is nearly due see
'A poem on the underground wall'
'Last week I took a wife' M. Kelly.
FL: same. 1
'The last word in lonesome is me'
Roger Miller. FL: Too bad
what's happened to our good love.
47
Lat never a man a wooing wend
see 'King Henry'
Late at e'en, drinking the wine
see 'The dowie dens o' Yarrow'
Late last Friday night see 'Sir
Henry and Lady Margaret'
'Laugh! Clown! Laugh!' Sam M.
Lewis, Joe Young and Ted Fio-
rito. FL: Even though you're
only make believing. 54
'Laura' Johnny Mercer and David
Raksin. FL: Laura is the face
in the misty light. 59
'Lavender's blue' FL: Lavender's
blue, diddle, diddle. 25, 48
A law was made a distant moon
ago here see 'Camelot'
A lawyer, he went out one day see
'Mowing the barley'
'Lay dis body down' FL: I know
moonrise, I know starrise. 29
Lay down, lay down, lovin' Henry,
she said see 'Lord Henry and
Lady Margaret'
Lay him down, lay him down fine
see 'Giles Collins'
'Lay, lady, lay' Bob Dylan. FL:
Lay, lady, lay, lay across my
big brass bed. 45
Lay that pistol down, Babe see
'Pistol packin' Mama'
'Lazarus' FL: As it fell out upon
one day. 11
'Lazarus' FL: There was a man in
ancient times. 11

'Lazarus and Dives' FL: There was
a man in ancient times. 11
Lead her up and down, Rosabeckaliner see 'Rosabeckaliner'
'Leatherum thee-thou and a'' FL:
There was a knicht an' a lady
bricht. 11
'The leatherwing bat' FL: Hi, said
the little leatherwing bat. 57
'Leave her, Johnny' FL: I thought I
heard the old man say. 19
Leave your sheep and leave your
lambs see 'Rise up shepherd
and follow'
'Leaves that are green' Paul Simon.
FL: I was twenty-one years when
I wrote this song. 60
'Leaving on a jet plane' John Den-
ver. FL: All my bags are
packed FLC: So kiss me and
smile for me. 71
'Lee's ferry' FL: Come all you
roving cowboys, bound on these
western plains. 43
'Leezie Lindsay' FL: Will ye gang
to the Hielands, Leezie Lindsay.
11
Left a good job in the city see
'Proud Mary'
'Legacy' FL: When in death I shall
calm recline. 29
'Lemon tree' Will Holt. FL: When
I was just a little boy. 47
Lero, lero, Lilliburlero see
'Lilliburlero'
Less go down to Jordan! see
'Don't you want to go?'
'Let a smile be your umbrella' Irv-
ing Kahal, Francis Wheeler and
Sammy Fain. FL: Once I met a
happy little blue bird FLC: Just
let a smile be your umbrella.
54
'Let a smile be your umbrella' Irv-
ing Kahal, Francis Wheeler and
Sammy Fain. FL: Whenever skies
are gray FLC: Just let a smile
be your umbrella. 12
Let Bacchus' sons be not dismayed
see 'Garryowen'
'Let 'em eat cake' George and Ira
Gershwin. FL: Oh, comrades,
you deserve your daily bread.
21
Let every good fellow now join in
a song see 'Vive l'amour'
Let every good fellow now fill up
his glass see 'Vive la com-

pagnie'
Let every Pagan muse be gone see
'Romping Rosy Nell'
Let grasses grow and waters flow
see 'Real old mountain dew'
'Let him go, let him tarry' FL:
Farewell to cold winter now that
summer's come at last FLC: Let
him go, let him tarry, let him
sink or let him swim. 25
Let horrid jargon split the air see
'Jargon'
'Let it be' Lennon and McCartney.
FL: When I find myself in times
of trouble Mother Mary comes to
me. 44
'Let it bleed' Mick Jagger and
Keith Richard. FL: Well, we all
need someone we can lean on.
16
Let it rain and thunder see 'Who
cares?'
Let it rain, let it pour see 'Dee-
river blues'
Let me be your salty dog see
'Salty dog'
'Let me entertain you' Stephen
Sondheim and Jule Styne. FL:
Extra! Extra! Hey! look at the
headline FLC: Let me entertain
you. 6
'Let me fly' FL: Way down yonder
in the middle of the field FLC:
Now let me fly. 34, 35, 57
'Let me kiss him for his Mother'
John P. Ordway and L. O. Emer-
son. FL: same FLC: Sleep,
dearest, sleep. 63
'Let me rove free' FL: Come all
ye good people and listen to me.
25
Let me take you down 'cause I'm
goin' to Strawberry Fields see
'Strawberry Fields forever'
Let me thrill again to your caress
of yesterday see 'Take me in
your arms'
Let mirth appear, every heart
cheer see 'The bold volunteer'
'Let my little light shine' FL: On
Monday he gave me the gift of
love FLC: This little light of
mine. 34
'Let my little light shine' FL: This
little light of mine. 35
'Let not Cloris think' John Danyel.
FL: Let not Cloris think because.
26

'Let Simon's beard alone' FL: same.
68
Let the drums roll out see 'Strike
up the band'
Let the Midnight Special shine her
light on me see 'Midnight
Special'
'Let the sun shine forever' Alex-
ander Ostrovsky and Jerry Silver-
man. FL: Sun shining down, sky
all around. 57
'Let there be peace on earth' Sy
Miller and Jill Jackson. FL:
Let there be peace on earth and
let it begin with me. 47, 52
Let those brown eyes smile at me,
dear see 'Brown eyes'
Let tyrants shake their iron rod
see 'Chester'
'Let us all speak our minds' J. G.
Maeder and William Brough.
FL: Men tell us tis fit that wives
should submit to their husbands.
19, 57, 58
Let us be lovers see 'America'
'Let us break bread together' FL:
Let us break bread together on
our knees. 23, 57
Let us go to the sugar camp see
'The sugar camp'
Let us go to the woods says Richard
to Robin see 'Hunting the wren'
Let us move along, move along
see 'Move along'
Let us try to roll the R see
'Roll the R'
Let's all get up and dance to a song
that was hit before your mother
was born see 'Your mother
should know'
Let's go fishin', honey baby see
'The crawdad song'
'Let's call the whole thing off'
George and Ira Gershwin. FL:
Things have come to a pretty
pass FLC: You say eether and I
say eyether. 21
'Let's do it' Cole Porter. FL:
When the little bluebird FLC:
Birds do it, bees do it. 46
Let's drink to the hard-working
people see 'The salt of the
earth'
'Let's get away from it all' Tom
Adair and Matt Dennis. FL:
Let's take a boat to Bermuda.
59
Let's go down by the grapevine

see 'Sweet blindness'
Let's go hunting, says Risky Rob
see 'Billy Barlow'
'Let's have a dance a heath' Thomas
Middleton and Richard Leveridge.
FL: same. 40
'Let's live for today' Michael Julien
and D. Shapiro and Mogol. FL:
When I think of all the worries
that people seem to find. 47
'Let's sing of stage coaches' George
Farquhar and John Eccles. FL:
same. 40
'Let's spend the night together'
Mick Jagger and Keith Richard.
FL: Don't you worry 'bout what's
on your mind. 16
Let's take a boat to Bermuda see
'Let's get away from it all'
'Let's take the long way home'
Johnny Mercer and Harold Arlen.
FL: same. 70
'The letter' Wayne Carson Thomp-
son. FL: Give me a ticket for
an airplane. 10
'The liar's song' FL: When I was a
little baby, just able to walk
alone. 30
'The liberated woman's husband's
talking blues' Jerry Silverman.
FL: I gonna tell you a story of a
gal I know. 58
'Liberation now' Betty Friedan,
Jacquelyn Reinach and Jo Rene.
FL: Femininity, what's femininity
FLC: Liberation, now. 58
Liberté, égalité see 'Sororité'
'The liberty song' John Dickinson
and William Boyce. FL: Come
join hand in hand brave Ameri-
cans all FLC: In freedom we're
born and in freedom we'll live.
1, 49, 55, 65
'Liberty tree' FL: In a chariot of
light from the regions of day. 8
Lie down, lie down, Lord William
cried see 'Lord William and
Lady Margaret'
Lie still, my pretty young man see
'Little Musgrove'
'Liebster Meiner' Abarbenel and
Ben Yomen. FL: S'iz der Steppe
Shoin opgeshorn. 57
Life has just begun see 'S wonder-
ful'
Life is a book that we study see
'My buddy'
'Life is a toil' FL: One day as I

Raul Portela, J. Galhardo and A. do Vale. FL: Portugal, Lisbon was gay in the moonlight FLC: I gave my heart to you in Old Lisbon that night. 9

Listen, big boy <u>see</u> 'Button up your overcoat'

Listen to my tale of woe <u>see</u> 'Oh, lady be good'

'Listen to the angels' FL: Where do you think I found my soul. 38

Listen to the hissing sounds <u>see</u> 'The suicide song'

'Listen to the lambs' FL: Come on, sister, with your ups and downs FLC: Listen to the lambs, all a-cryin'. 25

'Listen to the mocking bird' Alice Hawthorne and Richard Milburn. FL: I'm dreaming now of Hallie FLC: Listen to the mocking bird. 1, 57

Listen to the rumble, hear the motor scream <u>see</u> 'Trading-out blues'

'Little Annie Rooney' FL: Every evening, rain or shine. 41

'Little Annie Rooney' FL: She's my sweetheart, I'm her beau. 25

'Little Annie Rooney' Michael Nolan. FL: A winning way, a pleasant smile FLC: She's my sweetheart, I'm her beau. 20

'Little April shower' Larry Morey and Frank Churchill. FL: Drip, drip, drop. Little April shower. 13

'Little Betty Anne' FL: Little Betty Anne, she pretty little girl FLC: I'm a-going away. 11

'Little Birdie' FL: Little birdie, little birdie. 14, 57, 72

'A little bit of cucumber' T. W. Connor. FL: I was weaned on cucumber FLC: I like pickled onions. 17

'Little bitty baby' FL: Children, go! I will send thee. 23

'Little bitty baby' FL: Children go where I send thee. 25

'The little black bull' FL: The little black bull went down to the meadow. 72

The little black bull came down the meadow <u>see</u> 'Hoosen Johnny'

'Little black train is a-comin'' FL: God told Hezekiah FLC: Little black train is acoming. 34

'Little Bo-peep' FL: Little Bo-peep, she lost her sheep. 48

'Little boxes' Malvina Reynolds. FL: Little boxes on the hillside. 4

A little boy about five years old <u>see</u> 'Sir Hugh'

'Little boy blue' FL: same. 48

Little boy Blue come blow your horn <u>see</u> 'Long gone'

'A little boy threw his ball so high' FL: same. 11

'Little brown dog' FL: I buyed me a little dog, its color it was brown FLC: Sing taddle-a day. 57

'Little brown jug' Joseph E. Winner. FL: My wife and I lived all alone FLC: Ha! ha! ha! you and me. 1, 23, 25, 57

'Little brown jug polka' FL: My wife and I lived all alone. 67

'The little cabin boy' FL: There was a ship in the Northern countrie. 11

'Little cabin home on the hill' FL: Tonight I'm alone without you my dear FLC: Oh, someone has taken you from me. 14

'Little child' Wayne Shanklin. FL: Daddy dear, tell me please. 52

'The little cock sparrow' FL: A little cock sparrow sat on a green tree. 48

'The little cradle rock tonight' FL: If anybody asks you who I am. 33

Little darling, it's been a long cold lonely winter <u>see</u> 'Here comes the sun'

'Little darling pal of mine' A. P. Carter. FL: In the night while you lay sleeping FLC: My little darling, oh how I love you. 14

'Little David' FL: Little David was a shepherd boy FLC: Little David, play on your harp. 57

'Little David, play on your harp' FL: same. 5

'Little devils' FL: There was an old man and he lived near Hell. 11

'The Little Eau Plaine' FL: One evening last June as I wandered. 4

'Little Eleanor' FL: Lord Thomas a bold officer. 11

'Little girl' Madeline Hyde and

cried little Musgrave. 11

'Little Musgrave' FL: Twas on one day and a high holiday. 11

'Little Musgrave and Lady Barnard' FL: The first come down was a raven white. 11

'Little Musgrave and Lady Barnard' FL: The first came in were lily white. 11

'Little Musgrave and Lady Barnard' FL: The first one came down was Lord Diner's wife. 11

'Little Musgrave and Lady Barnard' FL: Go home with me, little Matthy Groves. 11

'Little Musgrave and Lady Barnard' FL: Holiday, a holiday. 11

'Little Musgrave and Lady Barnard' FL: It's holi, holi, holiday. 11

'Little Musgrave and Lady Barnard' FL: Little Mathy Groves was going to church. 11

'Little Musgrave and Lady Barnard' FL: The next come down was dressed in red. 11

'Little Musgrave and Lady Barnard' FL: One day, one day, one high holiday. 11

'Little Musgrave and Lady Barnard' FL: One day, one day, one holi whole day. 11

'Little Musgrave and Lady Barnard' FL: There was four and twenty ladies there. 11

'Little Musgrove' FL: Lie still, my pretty young man. 11

'Little Musgrove' FL: Little Musgrove did went to church an' saw de young lady so gay. 11

'Little Musgrove and Lady Barnswell' FL: There were nine ladies o' the east. 11

Little old man lived in the West, dandoo see 'The wife wrapt in wether's skin'

'The little old sod shanty' FL: I am looking rather seedy now while holding down my claim FLC: Oh, the hinges are of leather. 2

'Little old sod shanty' FL: I'm lookin' kind-a seedy now while headin' down my claim FLC: Oh, the hinges are of leather. 4, 62

'Little old sod shanty' FL: There was a happy time to me not many years ago. 62

'Little old sod shanty on the plain' FL: I'm looking rather seedy now while holding down my claim FLC: Oh, the hinges are of leather and the windows have no glass. 57

'The little orphan girl' FL: No home, no home, said the little girl. 57

'The little page boy' FL: O stop and pull me on before. 11

'The little paggy-lad' FL: It's of a little paggy-lad came trippin' over the lea. 11

'Little Phoebe' FL: Equinoxial swore by the green leaves on the trees. 35

'Little Powder-monkey Jim' FL: A yarn I've got to spin, it's how I heard my old Dad tell. 41

Little Roberta, let your hair grow long see 'Roberta'

'Little Sally Racket' FL: same. 57, 58

'Little Sally Walker' FL: Little Sally Walker sitting in a saucer. 37

'Little Saloo' FL: Yesterday was a holiday. 11

A little school boy, he bounced his ball see 'Sir Hugh'

'The little sergeant' FL: Oh, father, if you will agree, then I will go and see. 8

'Little Sir Hugh' FL: Do rain, do rain in American corn. 11

'Little Sir Hugh' FL: I won't come back or I shall not come back. 11

'Little Sir Hugh' FL: It rained, it mist, it rained, it mist. 11

'Little Sir Hugh' FL: It rained a mist, it rained a mist. 11

'Little Sir Hugh' FL: It rains, it rains in merry Scotland. 11

'Little Sir Hugh' FL: The rain rins down through Mirry-land toune. 11

'Little Sir Hugh' FL: Send out, send out, her daughter dear. 11

'Little Sir Hugh' FL: Up in a dark hollow. 11

'Little Sir Hugh' FL: Yesterday was a high holiday. 11

'Little Sir William' FL: Easter Day was a holiday. 11

'Little snowflake' FL: Little snowflake, light snowflake. 13

'Little soldier boy' FL: There was a little soldier boy who lately came from over. 11

'A little street where old friends meet' Gus Kahn and Harry Woods. FL: Homesick, heartsick, nothing seems real FLC: It's just a little street where old friends meet. 53

'Little Tommy Tinker' FL: Little Tommy Tinker was burned by a clinker. 68

'The little tune' Rose Fyleman and Marlys Swinger. FL: He played his little tune. 13

'The little wee croodin' Doo' FL: Oh, where have you been this livelong day. 11

'Little wee dog' Barton Hill. FL: Oh where, and oh where is my little wee dog? 36

Little Willie, can't you throw a ball see 'The two brothers'

Little Willie Harris coming back from Paris see 'Now she knows how to parle-voo'

'Little Wind' Kate Greenaway and Marlys Swinger. FL: Little wind, blow on the hilltop. 13

'The little yellow dog' FL: Oh, what's that stain on your shirt sleeve. 11

'The little Yorkshire boy' FL: There was an old farmer in Yorkshire did dwell FLC: Timmy right, fol de dol de dol de right. 11

'Live and let live' FL: They tell me you are going away FLC: Live and let live, don't break my heart. 14

'Live with me' Mick Jagger and Keith Richard. FL: I've got nasty habits. 16

'Lived ance twa luver in yon dale' FL: same. 11

'Livery stable blues' Marvin Lee, Ray Lopez and Alcide Nunez. FL: Way down in Alabam' FLC: O honey, listen here. 31

'Liza' George and Ira Gershwin. FL: Moon shinin' on the river FLC: Liza, Liza, skies are gray. 21

'Liza in the summertime' FL: same FLC: Po' li'l Liza, po' gal. 57

'Liza Jane' FL: I'll go up on the mountain top FLC: O po' Liza, po' gal. 57

Liza, Liza, skies are gray see 'Liza'

'Lizae Baillie' FL: Lizae Baillie's to Gartartan gane. 11

'Lizzie Lindsay' FL: O lassie but ye ken little. 11

'Lizzie Wan' FL: Fair Lucy sitting in her father's room. 11

Llevo preso en mi see 'Si tú pudieras quererme'

'La llorona' FL: Si al cielo subir pudiera llorona. 57

Load up your gun and whistle up your dog see 'Ground hog'

'Loch Lomond' Lady John Scott. FL: By yon bonnie banks and by yon bonnie braes FLC: Oh, you take the high road. 25, 57, 67

Lochnagar cam fae the West see 'Katherine Jaffray'

'Lodi' J. C. Fogerty. FL: Just about a year ago. 71

'The lofty tall ship' FL: As we were gone sailing five cold frosty nights. 11

'The logger's boast' FL: Come all ye sons of freedom throughout the state of Maine FLC: O, we'll range the wild woods over. 66

'Lolly too dum' FL: As I went out one morning to take the morning air. 34, 57

'Lolly-too-dum-day' FL: As I went out one mornin' to take the pleasant air. 66

'The Londerry air' FL: My heart still yearns for my old Londerry home. 25

'London Bridge' FL: London Bridge is broken down. 48

'London Bridge' FL: London Bridge is falling up, falling up, falling up. 68

'London waits' FL: Past three o'clock on a cold and frosty morning. 25

'Londonderry air' FL: Would God I were the tender apple blossom. 57

'The lone pilgrim' FL: I came to the place where the lone pilgrim lay. 50

'Lonely again' Jean Chapel. FL: You told me that others before you. 10

Lonely as the desert breeze see 'One alone'

Lonely, lonely was a town see

'Barb'ry Allen'

'Lonesome and sorry' Benny Davis and Con Conrad. FL: When night time comes stealing FLC: I'm lonesome and sorry. 12

'Lonesome blues' FL: I woke up this mornin', feelin' sad and blue FLC: I'm lonesome and the blues is in my way. 57

'Lonesome cowboy' FL: I ain't got no father FLC: I'm a poor lonesome cowboy. 57

'Lonesome house blues' FL: I had a dream last night, all about my gal. 57

'Lonesome low' FL: He took to his breast and he swum and he swum. 11

'The lonesome road' FL: Look down, look down, that lonesome road. 23

'The lonesome road' Gus Austin and Nathaniel Shilkret. FL: Look down, look down that lonesome road. 34, 54

'The lonesome sea' FL: There was a little ship that sailed upon the sea. 11

'Lonesome valley' FL: Jesus walked this lonesome valley. 34

'Lonesome valley' FL: You got to walk that lonesome valley. 57

'Long ago and far away' Ira Gershwin and Jerome Kern. FL: same. 67

'The long and winding road' Lennon and McCartney. FL: The long and winding road that leads to your door. 44

Long before the rising sun see 'Stir the pudding'

'Long gone' FL: Little Boy Blue come blow your horn FLC: He's long gone, wasn't he lucky. 28

Long-haired preachers come out every night see 'Pie in the sky'; 'The preacher and the slave'

'Long have I been with grief opprest' Charles Coffey. FL: same. 40

'Long hot summer days' FL: Godamighty look-a yonder. 28

'Long hot summer days' FL: When old Hannah go to beaming. 28

'Long John' FL: One day, one day I was walking along. 57

'Long journey home, or two dollar bill' FL: Cloudy in the West and it looks like rain FLC: Lost all my money but a two-dollar bill. 14

'Long Lankin' FL: Said my Lord to his lady, as he mounted his horse. 11

'Long, long ago' Thomas H. Bayly. FL: Tell me the tales that to me were so dear. 12, 25, 57

'Long long while' Mick Jagger and Keith Richard. FL: Baby, baby, been a long, long time. 16

'Long lost love' FL: My sweet little one, with your winsome ways FLC: Dearer to me, none ever can be. 50

'Long tail blue' FL: I've come to town to see you all FLC: Oh, for the long tail blue. 1

'Long tall Sally' Enotris Johnson, Richard Penniman and Robert Blackwell. FL: Gonna tell aunt Mary 'bout Uncle John. 52

Long time ago, long time ago see 'Hoosen Johnny'

A long time ago why back in history see 'Charlie Mopps'

The longest train I ever saw see 'In the pines'

'Long-handled shovel' FL: It take a long handled shovel to dig a nine foot hole. 57

'Long-line skinner' FL: I've got a belly full of whisky and a head full of gin FLC: Long-line skinner and my home's out West. 57

'Longside of the Santa Fe Trail' FL: Say, pards, have you sighted a schooner. 43

'Looby Loo' FL: Here we come looby loo. 48

Look ahead, look astern, look a-weather and the lee see 'High Barbary'

Look at me, I'm as helpless as a kitten up a tree see 'Misty'

Look at the hair see 'Oooh! look-a-there, ain't she pretty'

Look at them shufflin', a-shufflin down see 'Muskrat ramble'

Look down, look down, by my bedside see 'Barbara Allan'

Look down, look down that lonesome road see 'The lonesome road'

'Look down that lonesome road' FL: Look down, look down, that lonesome road. 1, 57

'Look for the silver lining' Buddy

De Sylva and Jerome Kern. FL: same. 67

Look here, you rascal, see what you've done see 'White house blues'

Look, look, look to the rainbow see 'Look to the rainbow'

Look out! Look out! see 'Jack Frost'

Look, says the catkin see 'Time for rabbits'

'Look to the rainbow' E. Y. Harburg and Button Lane. FL: On the day I was born FLC: Look, look, look to the rainbow. 6

'Looking at the world thru rose-colored glasses' Tommy Malie and Jimmy Steiger. FL: Why do I feel so spry? FLC: Looking at the world thru rose-colored glasses. 12

'Looking back' Clyde, Otis, Brook Benton and Buford Hendricks. FL: Looking back over my life. 10

'Looking for a boy' George and Ira Gershwin. FL: If it's true that love affairs are all arranged in heaven FLC: I am just a little girl who's looking for a little boy. 21

'Looky, looky yonder' FL: Ax am a-walkin' FLC: Looky, looky yonder. 57

The Lord above, in tender love see 'Thanksgiving hymn'

'Lord Aboyne' FL: Aft hae'd played at the ring and the ba'. 11

'Lord Akeman' FL: Lord Akeman was a noble Lord. 11, 30

'Lord Arnold' FL: It was on one fine, one fine holiday. 11

'Lord Arnold's wife' FL: Twas a holy day, a high holiday. 11

Lord Bacon was a nobleman see 'Young Beichan'

'Lord Bakeman' FL: In India lived a noble lord. 11

'Lord Bakeman' FL: In India there lived a noble lord. 11

'Lord Bakeman' FL: Lord Bakeman, he was a noble lord. 11

Lord Bakeman was a noble lord see 'The Turkish Lady'

'Lord Banner' FL: Four and twenty fair maids. 11

'Lord Banner' FL: Four and twenty gay ladies. 11

'Lord Banner' FL: Four and twenty ladies. 11

'Lord Banner's wife' FL: Four and twenty ladies all being at a ball. 11

'Lord Bateman' FL: As they steered East and they steered West. 30

'Lord Bateman' FL: He sailed east and he sailed west. 11

'Lord Bateman' FL: I'll sing to you about Lord Bateman. 11

'Lord Bateman' FL: In England lived a noble lord. 11

'Lord Bateman' FL: In India lived a noble lord. 11, 29

'Lord Bateman' FL: Lord Bateman he was, he was, he was. 11

'Lord Bateman' FL: Lord Bateman lived in London town. 11

'Lord Bateman' FL: Lord Bateman was a noble lord. 11

'Lord Bateman' FL: Lord Bateman was aden noble lord. 11

'Lord Bateman' FL: She wears a gold ring on all of her fingers. 11

'Lord Bateman' FL: There was a man that lived in England. 57

'Lord Bateman' FL: There was a noble lord. 11

'Lord Bateman' FL: They bored a hole through his left shoulder. 11

'Lord Bateman and the Turkish Lady' FL: There was a man in bondage brought. 11

Lord Bateman lived in London town see 'Young Beichan'

Lord Bateman was a noble Lord see 'Lord Bateman's castle'; 'The loving ballad of Lord Bateman'

'Lord Bateman's castle' FL: Lord Bateman was a noble Lord. 11

'Lord Batesman' FL: Lord Batesman was a brave young man. 11

'Lord Batesman' FL: There was a man who lived in England. 11

'Lord Beechman' FL: A gentleman from the courts of England. 11

'Lord Beichan' FL: Lord Beichan was a noble lord. 11

'Lord Beichan' FL: Young Beichan was in London born. 11

'Lord Benner' FL: Four and twenty ladies being at the ball. 11

'Lord Benner's wife' FL: If this be a lie you are telling me. 11

'The Lord bless and keep you'
Peter C. Lutkin. FL: same. 64
'Lord Bonnie' FL: Lord Bonnie he
was a hunting man. 11
'Lord Brechin' FL: Lord Brechin
was a noble man. 11
'Lord Brechin' FL: Lord Brechin
was as great a lord. 11
'Lord Brechin' FL: Lord Brechin
was as high a lord. 11
The lord came home so late at
night see 'The lady's disgrace'
'Lord Daniel's wife' FL: Down came
a lady. 11
'Lord Daniel's wife' FL: Holly,
holly, holliday. 11
'Lord Darnell' FL: I walked out
one hallow day. 11
'Lord Derwentwater' FL: Our king
has wrote a long letter. 11
'Lord Donald' FL: Holi, holi, holiday. 11
'Lord Donald' FL: Whaur hae ye
been all the day. 11
Lord, don't I wish I was a single
girl again see 'Don't I wish I
was a single girl again'
'Lord Ellenwater' FL: The king he
wrote a letter. 11
'Lord George' FL: Go fetch to me
my little nephew. 11
'Lord Gregory' FL: Go back from
these windows, and likewise this
hall. 11
'Lord Gregory' FL: O wha will lace
my shoes sae small? 11
Lord He thought he'd make a man
see 'These bones goin' to rise
again'
'Lord Henry' FL: Come in come in,
Lord Henry, said she. 11
'Lord Henry and Lady Margaret'
FL: Lay down, lay down, lovin'
Henry, she said. 11
'Lord, I wish I had a come' FL:
Lord, I wish I had a come when
you called me FLC: Sitting by the
side of my Jesus. 38
Lord, I'm almost home see 'Dem
charming bells'
The Lord is on the giving hand see
'Po' me'
Lord, I've never lived where
churches grow see 'A cowboy's
prayer'
'Lord John' FL: I'll wager, I'll wag-
er, says Lord John. 11
Lord John stands in his stable door

see 'Lord John's murder'
'Lord John's murder' FL: Lord
John stands in his stable door.
11
Lord Joshuay, she cried see 'The
maid freed from the gallows'
'Lord Land' FL: O, little bird on
the bough so high. 11
'Lord Lovel' FL: He rode and he
rode on his milk white steed.
11
'Lord Lovel' FL: How long you be
gone, Lord Lovel, says she. 11
'Lord Lovel' FL: Lord Lovel he
stood at his castle gate. 11, 29,
57, 61
'Lord Lovel' FL: Lord Lovel he
stood at St. Pancras' gate. 11
'Lord Lovel' FL: Lord Lovel was
at his gateside. 11
'Lord Lovel' FL: Lord Lover stands
by his des castle gate. 11
'Lord Lovell' FL: Lord Lovell he
stood at his castle gate a comb-
ing his milk white steed. 7
'Lord Lovell' FL: Lord Lovell he
rode on his milk-white horse.
11
'Lord Lovell' FL: Lord Lovell, he
stood at his garden gate. 11
'Lord Lovell' FL: Lord Lovell he
stood at his own stable door. 11
'Lord Lovell' FL: Lord Lovell sat
at St. Charles Hotel. 11
'Lord Lovell' FL: Lord Lovel stood
at his castle gate. 11
'Lord Lovell' FL: Where are you
going, Lord Lovel, she said. 11
'Lord Lovel and Lady Nancy' FL:
Lord Lovel he stood at his castle
gate. 11
'Lord Lover' FL: Lord Lover, Lord
Lover stood at the castle gate.
11
Lord Lover stands by his des cas-
tle gate see 'Lord Lovel'
'Lord Loving' FL: Hold my horse,
little Marget, he said. 11
'Lord Lowell' FL: Lord Lowell rode
up to his lady's gate. 11
'Lord Maxwell's good night' FL:
Adieu, madame, my mother dear.
11
'The Lord of Gordon's three daugh-
ters' FL: The Lord of Gordon
had three daughters. 11
'The lord of the dance' Sidney Car-
ter. FL: I danced in the

morning FLC: Dance, then wherever you may be. 33

'The Lord of the North Country' FL: There was the lord lived in the North country, bow down. 7

'Lord Orland's wife' FL: The first came in was a gay ladye. 11

'Lord Ranald' FL: Faur hae ye been all the day, Lord Ranald, my honey? 11

'Lord Randal' FL: O what is the matter Henery my son. 11

'Lord Randal' FL: Oh, whaur hae ye been, Lord Randal, my son? 11

'Lord Randal' FL: O where have you been, Lord Randal my son? 11, 35

'Lord Randal' FL: Oh, where have you been, Taranty, my son? 11

'Lord Randal' FL: What did you have for your supper, Jimmy Randal, my son? 11

'Lord Randal' FL: What did your sweetheart give you. 11

'Lord Randal' FL: What had you for supper, Orlando, my son? 11

'Lord Randal' FL: What you will to your father Jimmy Randolph, my son? 11

'Lord Randal' FL: Where did you stay last night, O Randal, my son? 11

'Lord Randal' FL: Where have you been a-roving, Jimmy Randal my son? 11

'Lord Randal' FL: Where have you been, Randal, it's Randal my son. 11

'Lord Randall' FL: It's what did you eat for your breakfast, Jimmy Randal my son? 11

'Lord Randall' FL: Oh, where have you been, Fair Elson, my son? 11

'Lord Randall' FL: O where have you been, fair Randall, my son? 11

'Lord Randall' FL: O where have you been, O Billy, my son? 11

'Lord Randall' FL: Where have you been all the day, Randall my son? 57

'Lord Randall' FL: Where were you all day, my own pretty boy? 11

'Lord Rendel' FL: Jim Riley, Jim Riley, my son. 11

'Lord Rendel' FL: Where have you been a-roving my only son? 11

'Lord Rendal' FL: O where have you been to, Rendal my son? 11

'Lord Rendal' FL: Where have you been courting, Henry my son? 11

'Lord Rendal' FL: Where have you been to all the day, Henery my son? 11

'Lord Rendal' FL: Where have you been to all this day, Henry my son. 11

'Lord Rendle' FL: Where have you been, my fair pretty one? 11

'Lord Robinson's only child' FL: As I went out one evening down by my father's lawn. 11

'Lord Ronald' FL: Oh, where hae ye been, Lord Randal, my son. 11

'Lord Ronald' FL: What will ye leave for your brother, Lord Ronald, my son? 11

'Lord Ronald' FL: Where hae ye been huntin', Lord Ronald my son! 11

'Lord Ronald' FL: Where have ye been all the day, Lord Ronald my son? 11

'Lord Ronald MacDonald' FL: Here's a health to Lord Ronald Macdonald. 11

'Lord Ronald my son' FL: O where hae ye been, Lord Ronald, my son? 11

'Lord Ronald my son' FL: Whaur hae ye been a' day, Lord Ronald my son? 11

'Lord Ronald, my son' FL: Where hae ye been a' day, Lord Ronald, my son? 11

'Lord Saltoun and Annachie' FL: Oh, Buchan is bonnie and there lives my love. 11

The lord says to the lady <u>see</u> 'False Lamkin'

'Lord, this song ain't nothin' <u>see</u> 'Poor man's blues'

'Lord Thomas' FL: Come father, come mother come riddle my riddle. 29

'Lord Thomas' FL: Come riddle your rights, my mother dear. 11

'Lord Thomas' FL: It fell ance upon a time. 11

'Lord Thomas' FL: Lord Thomas he was a bold foreignman. 11

'Lord Thomas' FL: Lord Thomas
he was a bold young man. 11
'Lord Thomas' FL: Lord Thomas
he was a worthy man. 11
'Lord Thomas' FL: Lord Thomas,
Lord Thomas, a brave young
soldier. 11
'Lord Thomas' FL: Lord Thomas,
rose up one merry morning. 11
'Lord Thomas' FL: Lord Thomas
was a very young gentleman. 11
'Lord Thomas' FL: Oh, mother,
mother, Lord Thomas said. 11
'Lord Thomas' FL: O mother, O
mother, come riddle my sport.
11
'Lord Thomas' FL: Oh mother, oh
mother, come riddle us two. 11
'Lord Thomas' FL: Oh mother, oh
mother, go riddle this course.
11
Lord Thomas a bold officer see
'Little Eleanor'
'Lord Thomas and brown maid' FL:
A hundred of thy friends, dear
child. 11
'Lord Thomas and Fair Annet' FL:
same. 11
'Lord Thomas and Fair Annet' FL:
Lord Thomas he was a bold for-
ester. 61
'Lord Thomas and Fair Annet' FL:
Lord Thomas rode up to Fair
Elinor's gate. 61
'Lord Thomas and Fair Eleanor'
FL: Come riddle, come riddle
my own mother. 11
'Lord Thomas and Fair Eleanor'
FL: Lord Thomas, he was a bold
young man. 11
'Lord Thomas and Fair Eleanor'
FL: Lord Thomas he was a for-
ester bold. 11
'Lord Thomas and Fair Eleanor'
FL: Lord Thomas he was a gay
forester. 11
'Lord Thomas and Fair Eleanor'
FL: Lord Thomas he was a noble
lord. 11
'Lord Thomas and Fair Eleanor'
FL: Mother, O Mother, come tell
to me. 11
'Lord Thomas and Fair Eleanour'
FL: One was buried in the chan-
cel top. 11
'Lord Thomas and Fair Ellanor'
FL: Come near, come near me
now dear mother. 11

'Lord Thomas and Fair Ellen' FL:
Fair Ellen, fair Ellen was a
beautiful damsel. 11
'Lord Thomas and Fair Ellen' FL:
He dressed himself in the finest
of clothes. 11
'Lord Thomas and Fair Ellen' FL:
Lord Thomas he being a bold
young man. 11
'Lord Thomas and Fair Ellen' FL:
Lord Thomas he was a gay gen-
tleman. 11
'Lord Thomas and Fair Ellender'
FL: Come, Father, come father,
come riddle this riddle. 11
'Lord Thomas and Fair Ellender'
FL: Come father, come father,
riddle to me. 57
'Lord Thomas and Fair Ellender'
FL: Come, tell to me, dear
mother, he says. 11
'Lord Thomas and Fair Elender'
FL: O mother, O mother, come
rede me a riddle. 11
'Lord Thomas and Fair Ellendor'
FL: O mother, O mother, pray
what shall I do? 11
'Lord Thomas and Fair Ellinor'
FL: Come riddle me, riddle me,
my dear mother. 11
'Lord Thomas and Fair Ellinor' FL:
Fair Ellen, fair Ellen is a beau-
tiful damsel. 11
'Lord Thomas and Fair Ellinor' FL:
Lord Thomas he was a bold for-
ester. 11
'Lord Thomas and Fair Ellinor' FL:
Lord Thomas he was a brave
young man. 11
'Lord Thomas and Fair Ellinor' FL:
Lord Thomas he was a warrior
bold. 11
'Lord Thomas and Fair Ellinor' FL:
Lord Thomas he went to Fair
Ellender's gate. 11
'Lord Thomas and Fair Ellinor' FL:
Lord Thomas, Lord Thomas, is
this your wife? 11
'Lord Thomas and Fair Elinor' FL:
Lord Thomas rode up to Fair
Elinor's gate. 11
'Lord Thomas and Fair Ellinor' FL:
O mother, dear mother, come
riddle my sport. 11
'Lord Thomas and Fair Ellinor'
FL: O mother, O mother, come
riddle the sport. 11
'Lord Thomas and Fair Ellinor' FL:

O mother, O mother, come roll
us down. 11
'Lord Thomas and Fair Ellinor' FL:
O mother, O mother, go roll a
song. 11
'Lord Thomas and Fair Ellinor' FL:
O mother, O mother, O mother,
says he. 11
Lord Thomas he being a bold young
man see 'Lord Thomas and Fair
Ellen'
Lord Thomas rode up to Fair Eli-
nor's gate see 'Lord Thomas
and Fair Elinor'
Lord Thomas he was a bold foreign-
man see 'Lord Thomas'
Lord Thomas he was a bold forester
see 'The brown girl'; 'Lord
Thomas and Fair Annet'; 'Lord
Thomas and Fair Ellinor'
Lord Thomas he was a bold young
man see 'Lord Thomas'; 'Lord
Thomas and Fair Eleanor'
Lord Thomas he was a brave young
man see 'Lord Thomas and
Fair Ellinor'
Lord Thomas he was a forester
bold see 'Lord Thomas and
Fair Eleanor'
Lord Thomas he was a gay forester
see 'Lord Thomas and Fair
Eleanor'
Lord Thomas he was a gay gentle-
man see 'Fair Ellender'; 'Lord
Thomas and Fair Ellen'
Lord Thomas he was a noble lord
see 'Lord Thomas and Fair
Eleanor'
Lord Thomas he was a warrior
bold see 'Lord Thomas and
Fair Ellinor'
Lord Thomas he was a worthy man
see 'Lord Thomas'
Lord Thomas he went to Fair Ellen-
der's gate see 'Lord Thomas
and Fair Ellinor'
Lord Thomas, Lord Thomas, a
brave young soldier see 'Lord
Thomas'
Lord Thomas, Lord Thomas, is this
your wife? see 'Lord Thomas
and Fair Ellinor'
Lord Thomas, Lord Thomas, take
my advice see 'The brown
girl'
Lord Thomas, Lord Thomas, the
brave young soldier see 'The
brown girl'

'Lord Thomas of Winchbury' FL: It
fell once upon a day. 11
'Lord Thomas of Winesbury' FL:
As I looked over high castle wall.
11
'Lord Thomas of Winesbury' FL:
As I looked over the castle wall.
11
'Lord Thomas of Winesberrie' FL:
It fell upon a time, when the
proud king of France. 11
'Lord Thomas of Winesburry' FL:
There lived a girl in a far coun-
try. 11
'Lord Thomas of Winesburry' FL:
There was a lady in the north
country. 11
'Lord Thomas of Winesbury' FL:
Tis of a rich Irishman's daughter.
11
Lord Thomas rode up to Fair Eli-
nor's gate see 'Lord Thomas
and Fair Annet'
Lord Thomas rose up one merry
morning see 'Lord Thomas'
Lord Thomas was a very young
gentleman see 'Lord Thomas'
'Lord Thomas' wedding' FL: She
dressed herself all in her best.
11
'Lord Valley' FL: The first came in
was the scarlet red. 11
'Lord Vanover' FL: The first that
came in was scarlet red. 11
'Lord Wetram' FL: Lord Wetram
was a gentleman. 11
'Lord William' FL: He mounted her
on her milk-white steed. 11
'Lord William and Lady Margaret'
FL: Lie down, lie down, Lord
William cried. 11
'Lord William and Lady Margaret'
FL: Lord William stood at his
stable door. 11
Lord William down from the High-
lands rode see 'Lady Margaret'
Lord William he rose about four
o'clock see 'The seven brothers'
Lord William stood at his stable
door see 'Lord William and
Lady Margaret'
Lord, you know these cities are
burning see 'The cities are
burning'
A lord's house in London, great
merriment held see 'The wild-
erness lady, or A health to the
king'

'The Lord's my Shepherd' FL: The
Lord's my shepherd, I'll not
want. 25

'Lord's prayer' FL: Our Father
which art in Heaven. 38

Lordy, Lordy, my dear wife see
'The old man'

'Lorelei' George and Ira Gershwin.
FL: Back in the days of knights
in armor FLC: I want to be like
that gal on the river. 21

'The Lorelei' FL: I know not the why
and wherefore. 23

'The Lorelei' FL: Ich weiss nicht
was soll es bedeuten. 23, 25

'Lorena' H. D. L. Webster and J.
P. Webster. FL: The years
creep slowly by, Lorena. 4, 25,
57

'Lorendo' FL: Where have you been,
Lorendo, Lorendo, my son? 11

Lost all my money but a two-dollar
bill see 'Long journey home,
or Two-dollar Bill'

'The lost chord' Adelaide A. Procter
and Arthur Sullivan. FL: Seated
one day at the organ. 63

'Lost John' FL: Lost John settin' on
a railroad track. 28

'Lost John' FL: Old John, Old John.
28

'Lost my partner, what'll I do?
see 'Skip to my Lou'

A lot o' people say that kilt is not
the thing to wear see 'Tha's
the reason noo I wear a kilt'

'A lot of livin' to do' Lee Adams
and Charlest Strouse. FL: There
are girls just ripe for some kiss-
in'. 6

Loud roared the dreadful thunder
see 'The Bay of Biscay'

The loud wind roared, the rain fell
fast see 'A Negro song'

Loudly the bell in the old tower
rings see 'Asleep in the deep'

'Louise' Leo Robin and Richard A.
Whiting' FL: Wonderful! Oh, it's
wonderful FLC: Every little breeze
seems to whisper Louise. 54

'Louisiana hayride' Howard Dietz
and Arthur Schwartz. FL: What
kind o' fun do yo' fancy mos'
FLC: Get goin', Louisiana hayride. 46

'Louisville burglar' FL: Raised up
in Louisville, a city you all know
well. 57

'Lousy miner' FL: It's four long
years since I reached the land.
57

'Love alone' FL: I know King Edward was a noble and great FLC:
It's love and love alone. 56

Love and joy come to you see
'Here we come a-wassailing'

'Love, come home' FL: As you read
this letter I write to you FLC:
Sweetheart, I beg you to come
home tonight. 14

Love come along like a popular
song see 'I found a million
dollar baby'

'Love farewell' FL: Come now
brave boys, we're on for marching. 69

'Love for sale' Cole Porter. FL:
When the only sound in the empty
street FLC: Love for sale. 46

'Love Henry' FL: Get down, get
down, love Henry, she cried. 11

'Love Henry' FL: In Yorkshire lived
a noble knight. 11

'Love Henry' FL: Stop, oh stop,
love Henry she said, and stay
all night with me. 11

'Love in bloom' Leo Robin and
Ralph Rainger. FL: Blue night
and you alone with me FLC: Can
it be the trees that fill. 53

'Love is a pretty frenzy' Robert
Jones. FL: Love, love, love,
love is a pretty, pretty, pretty,
pretty frenzy. 26

Love is a queer little elfin sprite
see 'Because you're you'

'Love is blue' Andre Popp and
Bryan Blackburn. FL: Blue,
blue, my world is blue. 71

'Love is here to stay' George and
Ira Gershwin. FL: The more I
read the papers FLC: It's very
clear. 21

'Love is just around the corner'
Leo Robin and Lewis E. Gensler.
FL: Beautiful miracle FLC:
Love is just around the corner.
53

'Love is not blind' Michael Cavendish. FL: Love is not blind but
I myself am so. 26

'Love is pleasing' FL: O love is
pleasin' and love is teasin'. 57

Love is such a fantastic affair when
it comes to call see 'C'est
magnifique'

'Love is sweeping the country'
George and Ira Gershwin. FL:
Why are people gay FLC: Love is
sweeping the country. 21

'Love is the thing' Ned Washington
and Victor Young. FL: What good
is money if your heart isn't
light FLC: What does it matter if
we're rich or we're poor. 12

'Love Johnnie' FL: Love Johnnie's
on to England. 11

'Love letters' Edward Heyman and
Victor Young. FL: The sky may
be starless FLC: Love letters
straight from your heart. 70

Love! Love! Hooray for love see
'Hooray love'

Love, love, love, love, is a pretty,
pretty, pretty, pretty frenzy see
'Love is a pretty frenzy'

'Love me do' Lennon and McCartney.
FL: Love, love me do. 44

'Love me, my pet brunette see
'Negra consentida'

'Love me or leave me' Gus Kahn
and Walter Donaldson. FL: Love
me or leave me and let me be
lonely. 54

'Love me or not' Thomas Campion.
FL: Love me or not, love her I
must or die. 26

'Love me tender' Elvis Presley and
Vera Matson. FL: Love me
tender, love me sweet FLC: Love
me tender, love me true. 10

'Love me with all your heart' Mario
Rigual and Carlos Rigual. FL:
Cuando calienta el sol aquí en la
playa. 9

'Love me with all your heart' Sunny
Skylar and Carlos Rigual. FL:
same. 9

Love, oh love, oh careless love
see 'Careless love'

'Love Robbie' FL: A feathered fowl's
in your orchard, father. 11

'Love somebody' FL: Love somebody,
yes I do. 23

'Love somebody, yes I do' FL: same.
57

Love, sweet love is the poet's
theme see 'That is love'

The love that I have chosen, was to
my heart's content see 'The
lowlands of Holland'

'Love, the delight of all well-
thinking minds' Greville Fulke
and Michael Cavendish. FL:

same. 26

'Love walked in' George and Ira
Gershwin. FL: Nothing seemed
to matter any more FLC: Love
walked right in and drove the
shadows away. 21

'Love will find a way' FL: Here's
tae the blue and the bonny bonny
blue. 11

'Love will find out the way' FL:
Over the mountains and over the
waves. 25

'Lovefeast in heaven' FL: Oh! run
up, children, get your crown
FLC: There's a love feast in
heaven. 38

The loveliness of Paris see 'I
left my heart in San Francisco'

'The lovely creature' FL: There
she stands, the lovely creature.
25

'A lovely night' Oscar Hammerstein
and Richard Rodgers. FL: A
lovely night, a lovely night. 24

'The lovely Ohio' FL: Come all ye
brisk young fellows who have a
mind to roam. 57

'Lovely Stella' FL: Bright Sol at
length by Thetis wooed. 3

'Lovely to look at' Dorothy Fields,
Jimmy McHugh and Jerome Kern.
FL: Lovely to look at, delightful
to know and heaven to kiss. 67

'A lovely way to spend an evening'
Harold Adamson and Jimmy
McHugh. FL: This is a lovely
way to spend an evening. 67

'Lover' Lorenz Hart and Richard
Rodgers. FL: When you held
your hand to my heart FLC:
Lover, when I'm near you. 53

'Lover, come back to me' Oscar
Hammerstein and Sigmund Romberg. FL: You went away, I let
you FLC: The sky was blue, and
high above. 24, 46

Lover, when I'm near you see
'Lover'

'The lover's ghost' FL: I must be
going no longer staying. 11

'The lover's ghost' FL: Johnny is
the young man that lately promised he'd marry me. 11, 30

'The lover's ghost' FL: Oh, you're
welcome home again, said the
young man to his love. 11

'The lover's ghost' FL: She said
unto her mama, she said unto

her dada. 11, 30

'The lover's tasks' FL: O, can you make me a cambric shirt? 11

'The lover's tasks' FL: Say can you make me a cambric shirt. 11

'Love's a baby dat grows up wild see 'Dat's love'

'Love's a sweet and soft musician' George Colman. FL: same. 40

'Love's been good to me' Rod McKuen. FL: There was a girl in Denver FLC: I have been a rover. 71

'Love's god is a boy' Robert Jones. FL: same. 26

'Love's old sweet song' G. Clifton Bingham and James L. Molloy. FL: Once in the dear dead days beyond recall FLC: Just a song at twilight. 1, 20, 25, 57, 63

'The loving ballad of Lord Bateman' FL: Lord Bateman was a noble lord. 11

'Loving Henry' FL: Come in, come in, loving Henry, come in. 11

'Loving Henry' FL: Get down, get down, loving Henry, she cried. 11

'Loving her was easier than anything I'll ever do again' Kris Kristofferson. FL: I have seen the morning burning golden on the mountain in the skies. 10

Low, and low and low holiday see 'Sir Hugh'

'Low bridge, everybody down' FL: I've got a mule and her name is Sal FLC: Low bridge; everybody down. 19

Low bridge, everybody down see 'The Erie canal'

Low golden moon, blue tropic skies see 'Moonlight and shadows'

'Low in the lowlands, low' FL: There was a good ship from the north countrie. 11

'The low low lands of Holland' FL: Abroad as I was walking down by the riverside. 11

'Low low lands of Holland' FL: Come arise my bonnie lassie. 11

'The low low lands of Holland' FL: Last Easter I got married. 11

'The low low lands of Holland' FL: The very first day I got married. 11

'Lowe Bonnie' FL: Lowe Bonnie, Lowe Bonnie was a hunting young

man. 11, 29, 57

'The lowland of Holland' FL: The first night I was married, a happy happy bride. 11

'The lowland sea' FL: All on the Spanish Main the Turkish 'Shiveree'. 11

'Lowlands' FL: O was you ever in Mobile Bay? 57

'Lowlands lonesome low' FL: There was a little boat, all fitted for the sea. 11

'Lowlands low' FL: It's I have got a ship in the north of countery. 11

'The lowlands low' FL: It's of a little galley bark by the North America. 41

'Lowlands low' FL: Then he seized this auger and overboard jumped he. 11

'The lowlands low' FL: There was a ship from the Northern country. 11

'The lowlands low' FL: There was a ship of the North Countrie. 11

'The lowlands low' FL: There was a ship that was sailing on the sea. 11

'Lowlands low' FL: Twas on the Spanish Main that the Turkish Lavoree. 11

Lowlands, lowlands see 'The Golden Vanitee'

'The lowlands of Germany' FL: Oh, the very first night I was married, I laid down on my bed. 11

'The lowlands of Holland' FL: Last night I was a-married and on my marriage bed. 11

'The lowlands of Holland' FL: Last Easter I was married, that night I went to bed. 11

'The lowlands of Holland' FL: The love that I have chosen, was to my heart's content. 11

'The lowlands of Holland' FL: My love has built a bonny ship, and set her on the sea. 11

'The lowlands of Holland' FL: O the very first night I was married. 11

'Lowlands of Holland' FL: One evening as I walked out. 11

'The lowlands of Holland' FL: Yesterday I married a wife. 11

'Lowly Bethlehem' FL: Nicht Jerusalem sondern Bethlehem. 66

'Lowly Bethlehem' FL: Not Jerusa-
lem, lowly Bethlehem twas. 66
'The lowly stable' FL: See, there
stands a lowly stable. 13
'Luck be a lady' Frank Loesser.
FL: They call you Lady Luck but
there is room for doubt FLC:
Luck be a lady tonight. 6
'The lucky escape' FL: I that once
was a ploughman, a sailor am
now. 3, 4
'Lucy' FL: O what shall I do with
your houses and your lands. 11
'Lucy in the sky with diamonds'
Lennon and McCartney. FL:
Picture yourself in a boat on a
river with tangerine trees and
marmalade skies. 44
'Lucy Locket' FL: Lucy Locket lost
her pocket. 48
'Lullaby' FL: Hush, be still as any
mouse. 7
'Lullaby' FL: Peaceful slumbering
on the ocean. 3
Lullaby-lullaby lulla-by lullaby
see 'Russian lullaby'
'The lumberman in town' FL: When
the lumberman comes to town.
57
'Lydia Pinkham' FL: Mrs. Brown
had a female weakness FLC: Sing,
o sing of Lydia Pinkham. 39
'Lydia Pinkham' FL: Oh, it sells
for a dollar a bottle FLC: Then
we'll sing of Lydia Pinkham. 57
'Lydia Pinkham' FL: Then we'll
sing of Lydia Pinkham. 58
'Lyttle Musgrave' FL: One day, one
day, one fine holiday. 11

- M -

'Ma, he's making eyes at me' Sid-
ney Clare and Con Conrad. FL:
I'm beside him, mercy FLC: Ma,
he's making eyes at me. 12
'Ma, I won't have him' FL: My ma,
she told me to open the door. 7
Ma n'atu sole cchiù bello see 'O
sole mio'
'Mà Teodora' FL: ¿Donde está la
Mà teodora? FLC: Rajando la
leña está. 51
'MacArthur Park' Jimmy Webb.
FL: Spring was never waiting for
us. 45
McKinley called for volunteers see

'Battleship of Maine'
McKinley, hollered, McKinley
squalled see 'White House
blues'
'Mack's blues' FL: Say, I told the
captain, he don't worry me. 28
'MacPherson's farewell' FL: Farewell, ye dungeons dark and
strong FLC: Sae rantin'ly, sae
wantonly. 57
'MacTavish' FL: Oh, MacTavish is
dead and his brother don't know
it. 68
'Mad Anthony Wayne' Albert G.
Emerick. FL: His sword blade
gleams and his eyelight beams
FLC: And many a Redcoat here
tonight. 55
'Madam, I have come-a-courtin''
FL: same. 7
Madam, I have come acourting see
'You go to Old Harry!'
Madam, I have come for to court
you see 'Uh uh, no'
Madam, will you make me a cam-
bric shirt see 'The cambric
shirt'
'Madama Doré' FL: O quante bella
figlie Madama Doré. 48
'Maddy Gross' FL: I took her by
the lily-white hand. 11
'Mademoiselle from Armentieres'
Harold Ross. FL: Mademoiselle
from Armentieres, parlez vous.
1, 25, 31
Mad'moiselle from Armentieres
parley voo see 'Hinky Dinky
parlay-voo'
'Maggie Murphy's home' Edward
Harrigan and Dave Braham. FL:
Behind a grammar schoolhouse
FLC: On Sunday night, tis my
delight. 63
'Magic is the moonlight' Maria
Grever. FL: Te quiero, dijiste
FLC: Muñequita linda. 9
'Magic is the moonlight' Charles
Pasquale and Maria Grever. FL:
Te quiero, sweet heaven FLC:
Magic is the moonlight. 9
'Magical mystery tour' Lennon and
McCartney. FL: Roll up, roll
up for the mystery tour. 44
'The maid and the mill' FL: There
was a maid and she went to the
mill. 25
The maid came tripping down the
stairs see 'Hind Horn'

'Maid freed' FL: Moder, moder, is you brought me any gold an' silver too. 11

'The maid freed from the gallows' FL: Hangman, hangman, howd yo hand. 61

'The maid freed from the gallows' FL: Hangman, hangman, spare my life. 11

'The maid freed from the gallows' FL: Hangman, hangman, swing yer rope. 11

'The maid freed from the gallows' FL: Hold up your hands and Joshua, she cries. 11

'The maid freed from the gallows' FL: Lord Joshuay, she cried. 11

'The maid freed from the gallows' FL: O hang, o hang, o slack your rope. 11

'The maid freed from the gallows' FL: O hangsman, hangsman, slack your rope. 11

'The maid freed from the gallows' FL: Slack man, slack man, slack up your rope. 11

'The maid freed from the gallows' FL: Slack your rope, hangsman. 57, 61

'The maid of Amsterdam' FL: In Amsterdam there lives a girl FLC: A-roving, a-roving. 23

'The maid of Cowdenknowes' FL: O the broom and the bonnie, bonnie broom. 11

'Maid of Islington' FL: All the girls in Exeter town. 11

'Maid of Islington' FL: If he is dead, I'll sell my steed. 11

'The maid of Monterey' FL: The moon was shining brightly. 62

'The maid on the shore' FL: Twas of a young maiden who lived all alone. 57

A maid passed by the prison door see 'The flower o' Northumberland'

'The maid peept out at the window' FL: As I lay musing all alone. 11

'The maid saved' FL: Hangman, hangman, hold your rope. 11

A maid went to Dublin her markets to learn see 'The next market day'

A maiden from the Bosporus with eyes as bright as phosphorus see 'Bluebeard'

'The maiden who dwelt by the shore' FL: Twas of a young maiden who lived all alone. 11

'The maiden's lament' FL: As I roved out one evening in spring. 30

'Maids are simple, some men say' Thomas Campion. FL: same. 26

'Maids, when you're young never wed an old man' FL: Ah, an old man came a-courting me FLC: For they've got no fal-loo-rum. 57, 58

'Mairzy doats' Milton Drake, Al Hoffman and Jerry Livingston. FL: Mairzy doats and dozy doats and liddle lamzy divey. 59

Maisie she went oot tae buy see 'The keach in the creel'

'Major Andre' FL: Return enraptured hours. 3

'Make a longtime man feel bad' FL: Roberta, let your hair grow long. 28

'Make believe' Oscar Hammerstein and Jerome Kern. FL: The game of just supposing is the sweetest game I know FLC: We could make believe I love you. 24, 67

Make believe you're in a jungle movie see 'Baby elephant walk'

'Make me a bed on the floor' FL: same FLC: Bed on the floor, baby. 57

'Make me a cowboy again for a day' FL: Backward, turn backward oh time with your wheel. 2, 43

Make of our hands, one hand see 'One hand, one heart'

'Make someone happy' Betty Comden, Adolph Green and Jule Styne. FL: The sound of applause is delicious FLC: Make someone happy. 42

'Make the world go away' Hank Cochran. FL: Do you remember when you loved me FLC: Make the world go away. 10, 64

'Makin' whoopee' Gus Kahn and Walter Donaldson. FL: Every time I hear that march from Lohengrin FLC: Another bride, another June. 54, 59

'Malagueña' Ernesto Lecuona. FL: Ah ah, el amor me lleva hacia. 9

courted a Waxford girl.   41

Maria, the most beautiful sound I
ever heard see 'Maria'

'Marie Hamilton' FL: My mother
was a proud, proud woman.   11

'The Marines' Hymn' Jacques Offen-
bach.   FL: From the halls of
Montezuma.   1, 66

'Marion's men' FL: We follow where
the Swamp Fox guides.   8

'Marlborough's ghost' FL: Awful hero,
Marl-b'ro rife.   3

Married men will keep your secret
see   'Hey Lolly, Lolly'

'Marrying blue yodel' FL: Well, I
don't mind marryin'.   57

'La Marseillaise' Rouget de Lisle.
FL: Arise, ye sons of France to
glory.   19

'La Marseillaise' FL: Ye sons of
France, awake to glory.   25

'Marta' L. Wolfe Gilbert and Moises
Simons.   FL: Marta, now your
eyes beam at twilight FLC: Marta,
rambling rose of the wildwood.
12

'Martyr John' FL: It was Martyr
John who died of late.   11

'Martyrs Tune' FL: I said I will
look to my ways.   65

'The marvelous toy' Tom Paxton.
FL: When I was just a wee little
lad full of health and joy.   45

'Mary' FL: Mary have left her own
home.   41

Mary and Joseph together did go
see   'The cherry tree carol'

'Mary and Martha' FL: Mary and
Martha jus' gone 'long FLC:
Free grace, unadying love.   34

'Mary and Martha' FL: Mary and
Martha's just gone along FLC:
Crying free grace and dying love.
38

'Mary Ann' FL: Mary Ann, oh Mary
Ann FLC: All day, all night,
Mary Ann.   23

'Mary-Anne' FL: Oh fare you well,
my own true love, fare you well,
my dear.   25, 57

'Mary Ann McCarthy' FL: Mary Ann
McCarthy went fishing for some
clams FLC: All she got was in-
fluenza.   68

'Mary Goldan' FL: It's false Sir
John's a-courting gone.   11

'The Mary Golden tree' FL: There
was a little ship and she sailed

upon the sea.   11

'The Mary Golden Tree' FL: There
was a little ship that sailed out
on the sea.   11

'Mary had a baby' FL: same. 33, 57

'Mary had a little lamb' FL: Mary
had a little lamb, little lamb.   72

'Mary had a William Goat' FL:
Mary had a William goat, William goat, William goat FLC:
Whoop-dee-doo-den-doo-den-dah.
68

Mary had a William goat see
'William Goat'

'Mary Hamilton' FL: There lived a
knight in the north.   11

'Mary Hamilton' FL: They are talking in the kitchen.   23, 25

'Mary Hamilton' FL: Word has come
from the kitchen.   11

'Mary Hamilton' FL: Yestre'en the
queen had four Maries.   11

Mary have left her own home see
'Mary'

'Mary Lou' Abe Lyman and George
Waggner and J. Russel Robinson.
FL: Every bell in the steeple is
ready to ring FLC: Mary Lou,
Mary Lou.   12

'Mary Lou' Abe Lyman, George
Waggner and J. Russel Robinson.
FL: I have something on my mind
FLC: Mary Lou, Mary Lou.   54

'Mary Mary quite contrary' FL:
same.   48

'Mary Mild' FL: Last nicht there
were four Maries!   11

'Mary Mild' FL: Word went up, an'
word went doon.   11

'Mary of the wild moor' FL: It was
all on a cold winter's night.   7

'Mary on the wild moor' FL: One
night when the winds blew cold.
29

'"Mary" said St. Joseph' Seymour
Barab.   FL: same FLC: same.
33

Mary to the yowe-buchts has gane
see   'The broom of Cowdenknowes'

'Mary washed linen' FL: While Mary
washed linen.   48

'Mary, what you gonna name that
pretty little baby' FL: The Virgin
Mary had-a one son.   57

Mary wore three links of chain see
'Hold on'

'Maryland, my Maryland' James

Randall.   FL: The despot's heel
is on thy shore.   57
'The Maryland resolves' FL: On
Calvert's plains new faction
reigns.   8
'Mary's a grand old name' George
M. Cohan.   FL: My mother's
name was Mary FLC: For it was
Mary, Mary.   1, 12, 20, 31, 67
'Mary's dream' FL: The moon had a-
climbed the highest hill.   3
'Mary's questions' FL: Then Mary
took her young son.   11
Mas hoy que estoy tan solo   see
'The greatest performance of my
life'
'Mas que nada' Jorge Ben.   FL: O
ariá, raio obá obá, obá.   9
'Mas que hada' Loryn Deane and
Jorge Ben.   FL: O when your
eyes meet mine.   9
De massa run, ha ha   see   'Kingdom coming'
'Massachusetts liberty song' Benjamin Church.   FL: Come, swallow
your bumpers, ye Tories and
roar FLC: In freedom we're
born, and like sons of the brave.
55, 65
'Massa's in de cold ground' Stephen
Foster.   FL: Round de meadows
am a-ringing FLC: Down in de
cornfield.   63
Master bought some yellow girls
see   'Girls from the south'
'Matchmaker' Sheldon Harnick and
Jerry Bock.   FL: Matchmaker,
matchmaker, make me a match.
6, 64
'Matilda' FL: Five thousand dollar,
friend, I lost FLC: Matilda,
Matilda.   23
'Matilda Toots' FL: One frosty day
on pleasure bent I strolled in to
the park FLC: Oh! Matilda Toots,
you should have seen her boots.
36
Matt Casey formed a social club
that beat the town for style   see
'The band played on'
'Matthy Groves' FL: It being of a
day and a noble day.   30
'Matthy Groves' FL: Twas on one
day and a high holiday.   30
'Matty Groves' FL: One high, one
high, one high holiday.   23, 25,
57
'Maxwell's silver hammer' Lennon

and McCartney.   FL: Joan was
quizzical, studied pataphysical
science in the home.   44
Maxellton's braes are bonnie   see
'Annie Laurie'
'May Collean' FL: O heard ye e'er
o' a blood knight.   11
'May Colvin' FL: O! false Sir John
a wooing came.   11
'May Colvine and Fause Sir John'
FL: Heard ye ever of a bluidy
knight.   11
May God be with you my love   see
'Vaya con Dios'
'May Irwin's frog song' Charles E.
Trevathan.   FL: Away down a
yonder in Yankety Yank FLC:
An' jus' lots of folks is like dis
foolish frog of mine.   36
May Margery sat in her castle
tower   see   'Tam Lane'
'May the bird of paradise fly up
your nose' Neal Merritt.   FL:
One fine day as I was walking
down the street FLC: May the
bird of paradise fly up your nose.
10
May the Lord, He will be glad of
me   see   'Bright sparkles in the
churchyard'
'May you always' Larry Markes and
Dick Charles.   FL: This special
time, this special place FLC:
May you always walk in sunshine.
52
'Maybe' Richard Barrett.   FL:
Maybe, oh, if I could pray and I
try, dear.   15
'Maybe' Allan Flynn and Frank Mad-
den.   FL: Maybe you'll think of
me.   59
'Maybe' George and Ira Gershwin.
FL: Though today is a blue day
FLC: Soon or late, maybe.   21
Maybe, oh, if I could pray and I
try, dear   see   'Maybe'
Maybe the sun gave me the power
see   'Almost like being in love'
'Maybe this time' Fred Ebb and John
Kander.   FL: Maybe this time,
I'll be lucky.   6
Maybe you'll think of me   see
'Maybe'
Me an' my wife an' my wife's pap
see   'Cumberland Gap'
'Me and Bobby McGee' Kris Kris-
tofferson and Fred Foster.   FL:
Busted flat in Baton Rouge FLC:

Freedom's just another word for
nothin' left to lose. 10, 15, 45
'Me and Jesus' Tom T. Hall. FL:
Well, me and Jesus got our own
thing going. 10
'Me and Julio down by the school-
yard' Paul Simon. FL: The
mama pajama rolled out of bed
and she ran to the police station.
60
'Me and Mrs. Jones' K. Gamble,
L. Huff and C. Gilbert. FL:
Me and Misses Jones, we've got
a thing going on. 64
'Me and my captain' FL: Me and my
captain don't agree. 57
Me and my wife and my old grand-
pap see 'Cumberland Gap'
Me comee from Hong Kong Chinee
see 'The Chinee laundryman'
Me donkey walk, me donkey talk
see 'Tinga layo'
'Me father's a lawyer in England'
FL: same FLC: To-me-fang, to-
me-fing-o-lear-y. 57
Me han dicho que tus ojos see
'Cuando vuelas a mí'
'Meadowland' L. Kniper and Jerry
Silverman. FL: Open fields,
boundless plains. 57
'Meadowland' L. Kniper and V.
Gusev. FL: Poluishkopole dy.
57
The meadows look cheerful, the
birds sweetly sing see 'The
lasses of Dublin'
'Meet me in St. Louis, Louis'
Andrew B. Sterling and Kerry
Mills. FL: When Louis came
home to the flat FLC: Meet me
in St. Louis, Louis. 20, 31
Meeting at the building soon be
over see 'All over this world'
'Memo from Turner' Mick Jagger
and Keith Richard. FL: Didn't
I see you down in San Antone on
a hot and dusty night. 16
'Memories are made of this' Terry
Gilkyson, Rich Dehr and Frank
Miller. FL: Take one fresh and
tender kiss FLC: The sweet
memories you gave me. 52
'Memories of you' Andy Razaf and
Eubie Blake. FL: Waking skies
at sunrise. 59
Memories that linger in my heart
see 'When my blue moon turns
to gold again'

Men at arms shout, "Who goes
there?" see 'Citadel'
'Men of Harlech' FL: Men of Harlech
in the hollow. 25
'Men of the soil' Harold Hildreth,
Harold Hatcher and Gerald Patton.
FL: Men of the soil! We have
labored unending. 19
Men tell us tis fit that wives should
submit to their husbands see
'Let us all speak our minds'
A merchant ship in Bristol lay see
'The Turkish lady'
'The mermaid' FL: As I sailed out
one Friday night FLC: And the
sea is a-roar, roar, roar. 11
'The mermaid' FL: As I walked out
one evening fair. 11
'The mermaid' FL: Eight times
around went our gallant ship. 11
'The mermaid' FL: The first came
up was the carpenter of the ship
FLC: For the raging sea goes,
roar, roar, roar. 11
'The mermaid' FL: The first on
deck was the captain of the ship.
11
'The mermaid' FL: It was on Friday night when we set sail. 11
'The mermaid' FL: Last Friday
morn when we set sail. 11
'The mermaid' FL: Last Friday
morning as we set sail FLC:
The stormy winds do blow, blow,
blow. 11
'The mermaid' FL: O last Monday
morning as we set sail FLC: For
the stormy winds they do blow.
11
'The mermaid' FL: Oh see how she
looked, she looked around for
me. 11
'The mermaid' FL: O were my men
drunk or were my men mad. 11
'The mermaid' FL: O the first one
along was the captain of the ship.
11
'The mermaid' FL: On Friday
morning as we set sail. 11
'The mermaid' FL: On Good Friday
morning our ship set sail. 11
'The mermaid' FL: One Friday
morn, as we set sail FLC: Oh,
the stormy winds did blow. 25
'The mermaid' FL: One night as I
lay on my bed. 11
'The mermaid' FL: One night, as I
lay on my bed, I lay both warm

and at ease. 11
'The mermaid' FL: One stormy
night, when we set sail. 11
'The mermaid' FL: Three times
round went our gallant ship. 11
'The mermaid' FL: Twas Friday
morn, when we set sail FLC: Oh,
the ocean waves may roll. 68
'The mermaid' FL: Twas Friday
night when we set sail FLC: O
the ocean waves may roll. 11,
57
'The mermaid' FL: Twas nine
o'clock by the bells. 11
'The mermaid' FL: Up spoke the
boy of our gallant ship. 11
'The mermaid' FL: Up stepped a
man of our gallant ship FLC:
Round and round went our gallant
ship. 11
'The mermaid' FL: The wind was
still and the moon was clear. 11
'Merrily dance the Quaker's wife'
FL: same. 48
Merrily we roll along <u>see</u> 'Good
night, ladies'
'Merrimac at sea' FL: I will sing
you a song of the Merrimac at
sea FLC: O, the sea how it
roars, how it roars. 50
'The merry Broomfield' FL: As she
went to the merry green wood.
11
'The merry Broomfield' FL: It's of
a lord in the north countrie. 11
'The Merry Golden Tree' FL: There
was a little ship and she sailed
upon the sea. 11
Merry month of May <u>see</u> 'I've got
the world on a string'
Met her on the mountain <u>see</u> 'Tom
Dooley'
'Mexicali rose' Jack B. Tenney and
Helen Stone. FL: Mexicali rose,
stop crying. 54
'Mi caballo blanco' FL: Es mi ca-
ballo blanco FLC: Mi caballo, mi
caballo. 57
'Mi compadre mono' FL: same. 51
'Mi pollera' FL: Mi pollera, mi
pollera. 51
Mi rival es mi propio corazón <u>see</u>
'My rival'
'Mi vida' Ernesto Lecuona. FL:
Como azul sueño azul viniste
fugaz FLC: Mi vida, te amo
desde que yo te ví. 9
'Mi vida' Harry Ruby and Ernesto

Lecuona. FL: In some magic
way you came from afar FLC:
Mi vida, I loved you the moment
we met. 9
'Mi y'malel' FL: My y'malel g'vurot
Yisrael. 57
'Miami Beach rumba' Johnnie Cam-
acho and Irving Fields. FL:
De paso en mi viaje a Cuba. 9
'Miami Beach rumba' Albert
Gamse and Irving Fields. FL:
I started out to go to Haiti. 9
'Michael' FL: Sister help to trim
the sail, hallelujah FLC: Michael,
row the boat ashore Hallelujah.
23
'Michael Finnigin' FL: There was
an old man named Michael Finni-
gin. 57
'Michael, row the boat ashore' FL:
same. 1, 25, 29, 34, 57
'Michelle' Lennon and McCartney.
FL: Michelle, ma belle, these
are words that go together well.
44, 45
Mid pleasures and palaces though
we may roam <u>see</u> 'Home, sweet
home'
'Midnight cowboy' John Barry and
Jack Gold. FL: Once his hopes
were high as the sky. 71
'Midnight in Paris' Con Conrad and
Herb Magidson. FL: Sweet is
the madness of midnight in Paris.
47
'Midnight on the ocean' FL: Twas
midnight on the ocean. 68
'Midnight rambler' Mick Jagger and
Keith Richard. FL: Did you hear
about the midnight rambler. 16
'Midnight special' FL: Let the Midnight Special shine her light on
me. 28
'The Midnight Special' FL: Wake up
every morning FLC: Let the Midnight Special shine her light on
me. 23
'Midnight Special' FL: Well, you
wake up in the morning, hear the
ding dong ring FLC: Let the midnight special. 35, 57
'Midnight Special' FL: When you
wake up in the morning, hear the
ding dong ring FLC: Let the Midnight Special shine a light on me.
4
'The midnight sun will never set'
Dorcas Cochran, Quincy Jones

and Henri Salvador. FL: same.
47

'Mighty day' FL: I remember one
September FLC: Wasn't it a
mighty day. 57

'Mighty day' FL: Yes the Book of
Revolutions to be bro't forth on
that day FLC: O wasn't that a
mighty day? 5

'Mighty lak' a rose' Frank L. Stan-
ton and Ethelbert Nevin. FL:
Sweetest little feller. 1, 20, 31

'Mighty like a rose' FL: Sweetest
little fellow, everybody knows. 25

'Mighty rocky road' FL: Hit's a
mighty rocky road. 5

Mike Finnigan a patriot he swore
that he would raise see 'Finnigan's Musketeers'

'Milk and honey' Jerry Herman.
FL: This is the land of milk and
honey FLC: same. 6

'The mill mother's lament' Ella
Mae Wiggins. FL: We leave our
homes in the morning. 57, 58

'Mill o' Tiftie's Annie' FL: At Mill
o' Tiftie lived a man. 11

'The mill was made of marble' Joe
Glazer. FL: I dreamed that I
had died FLC: The mill was
made of marble. 19

Miller, O miller, there swims a
swan see 'The two sisters'

'The miller's daughter' FL: Oh,
hangman, o hangman, hang up
your rope. 11

The miller's daughter being dressed
in red see 'The swan swims
so bonny, O'

The miller's daughter went out one
day see 'The two sisters'

'The miller's daughters' FL: First
he bought her was a beaver hat. 11

'The miller's two daughters' FL:
The miller's two daughters brisk
and gay. 11

A million times I've asked you see
'Perhaps, perhaps, perhaps'

'Mimi' Lorenz Hart and Richard
Rodgers. FL: My left shoe's on my
right foot FLC: Mimi, you funny
little good for nothing Mimi. 53

'Mine' George and Ira Gershwin.
FL: Mine, love is mine. 21

Mine eyes are dim, I cannot see
see 'The quartermaster store'

Mine eyes have seen the glory of
the coming of the Lord see

'Battle hymn of the Republic'

'Miner's doom' FL: At five in the
morning as jolly as any. 57

'The miner's dream of home' Will
Godwin and Leo Dryden. FL: It
is ten weary years since I left
England's shore FLC: I saw the
old homestead and faces I love.
63

'Miner's farewell' FL: Poor hard
workin' miners, their troubles
are great FLC: Only a miner
killed under the ground. 57

'A miner's life' FL: A miner's life
is like a sailor's FLC: Union
miners, stand together. 19

Miner's life is like a sailor's see
'Miner's lifeguard'

'Miner's life guard' FL: Miner's
life is like a sailor's FLC: Union
miners stand together. 57

'Minnie the Moocher' Cab Calloway,
Irving Mills and Clarence Gaskell.
FL: Now here's a story 'bout
Minnie the Moocher. FLC: Ho
de ho de ho. 12, 59

'The minstrel boy' Thomas Moore
and the Moreen. FL: The minstrel boy to the war is gone.
23, 25, 57

'Miren, Cuántas luces' FL: same.
51

'Mischa, yascha toscha, sascha'
Arthur Francis and George Gershwin. FL: We really think you
ought to know FLC: Tempermental
Oriental gentleman are we. 21

'Misirlou' J. Pina and N. Roubanis.
FL: Cuando alegre tú sonries
mujer FLC: Oh, Misirlou. 9

'Misirlou' Fred Wise, Milton Leeds,
S. K. Russell and N. Roubanis.
FL: Desert shadows creep across
purple sands FLC: You, Misirlou.
9

'Miss Amanda Jones' Mick Jagger
and Keith Richard. FL: Down and
down she goes. 16

Miss Delia, she two timed her see
'Delia gone'

'Miss Mary Mack' FL: Miss Mary
Mack, Mack, Mack. 68

'Miss Wrinkle' FL: In a village
there lived an old maid. 36

'Mississippi mud' James Cavenaugh
and Harry Barris. FL: When
the sun goes down, the tide goes
out. 59

'J't'aim'rais mieux, mon mari!'

'Mona Lisa' Jay Livingston and Ray Evans. FL: In a villa in a little old Italian town FLC: Mona Lisa, Mona Lisa. 70

'Mona Lisa' Jay Livingston and Ray Evans. FL: Mona Lisa, Mona Lisa, men have named you. 47

Monday morning go to school see 'The two brothers'

'Money is king' FL: My mother was a soldier FLC: We are soldiers in the army. 57

'Monkey man' Mick Jagger and Keith Richard. FL: I'm a flea bit peanut monkey. 16

The monkey married the baboon's sister see 'Monkey's wedding'

'Monkey's wedding' FL: The monkey married the baboon's sister. 36

'Mood indigo' Duke Ellington, Irving Mills, and Albany Bigard. FL: You ain't been blue. 12, 59

The moon belongs to everyone see 'The best things in life are free'

Moon Deer, how near you soul divine see 'By the waters of Minnetonka'

The moon had climbed the highest hill see 'Mary's dream'

'The moon has raised her lamp above' John Oxenford and Julius Benedict. FL: same. 63

The moon is shining on the window sill see 'Who's that a-callin''

'Moon over Miami' Edgar Leslie and Joe Burke. FL: Tropical twilight descending FLC: Moon over Miami. 53

'Moon river' Johnny Mercer and Henry Mancini. FL: Moon River, wider than a mile. 71

The moon run down in a purple stream see 'Didn't my Lord deliver Daniel'

Moon shinin' on the river see 'Liza'

Moon shinin' bright along the pathway home see 'Stodola Pumpa'

The moon was shining bright in Carolina see 'Carolina moon keep shining'

The moon was shining brightly see 'The maid of Monterey'

'The moon was yellow' Edgar Leslie and Fred E. Ahlert. FL: same. 53

'Moonglow' Will Hudson, Eddie De Lange and Irving Mills. FL: I still hear you saying FLC: It must have been moonglow. 12, 59

'Moonlight and shadows' Leo Robin and Frederick Hollander. FL: Low golden moon, blue tropic skies FLC: Moonlight and shadows and you in my arms. 53

'Moonlight and skies' FL: Oh, come hear my story of heartaches and sighs. 43

'Moonlight becomes you' Johnny Burke and James Van Heusen. FL: Moonlight becomes you, it goes with your hair. 47, 70

'Moonlight gambler' Bob Hilliard and Philip Springer. FL: They call me the moonlight gambler. 52

'Moonlight mile' Mick Jagger and Keith Richard. FL: When the wind blows and the rain feels cold. 16

'Moonlight serenade' Mitchell Parish and Glenn Miller. FL: I stand at your gate. 59

The more I read the papers see 'Love is here to stay'

The more I reflect, the more plain it appears see 'Rivington's reflections'

'The more I see you' Mack Gordon and Harry Warren. FL: Each time I look at you is like the first time FLC: The more I see you. 70

'More pretty girls than one' FL: My mama told me last night FLC: There's more pretty girls than one. 57

The morn of life is past see 'My old dog Tray'; 'Old Dog Tray'

'The morning dew' FL: There's not one drop of morning dew. 30

The morning greets us with its coolness see 'Song of greeting'

'Morrissey and the Russian sailor' FL: Come all you sons of Erin, attention now I crave. 57

'Moscow Nights' V. Selovyev-Sedoy and M. Matusovsky. FL: Nye slyshny v sa du dazhe shorokhi. 57

'Moscow nights' V. Sedoy-Solovyev and Jerry Silverman. FL: Stillness in the grove not a rustling sound. 57

'The most beautiful girl' Norris
Wilson, Billy Sherrill and Rory
Bourke. FL: Hey, did you hap-
pen to see the most beautiful girl
in the world? 64
'The most beautiful girl in the world'
Lorenz Hart and Richard Rodgers.
FL: same. 67
The most chivalrous fish of the
ocean see 'The chivalrous
shark'
'A most peculiar man' Paul Simon.
FL: He was a most peculiar man.
60
Most people live on a lonely island
see 'Bali Ha'i'
'The moth and the flame' George
Taggart and Max S. Witt. FL:
At a gay reception given in a
mansion grand and old FLC: The
moth and the flame played a game
one day. 20
'Mother and child reunion' Paul
Simon. FL: No, I would not give
you false hope on this strange and
mournful day. 60, 64
A mother had two little babes see
'The cruel mother'
Mother, I long to get married see
'Whistle, daughter, whistle'
Mother I would marry, yes, I
would be a bride see 'Whistle
daughter, whistle'
'Mother Jones' FL: The world today
is mourning. 58
'Mother, make my bed soon' FL:
Where have you been my sweet,
my love? 11
Mother Mary, what is the matter
see 'Oh Jerusalem in the
morning!'
Mother, mother, mother, pin a
rose on me see 'Mother pin a
rose on me'
'Mother Nature's son' Lennon and
McCartney. FL: Born a poor
young country boy. 44
Mother, o mother, come riddle my
sport see 'Lord Thomas and
Fair Ellinor'
Mother, O Mother, come tell to me
see 'Lord Thomas and Fair
Eleanor'
Mother oh! why did you leave me
alone see 'Father's a drunkard
and mother is dead'
'Mother pin a rose on me' Dave
Lewis, Paul Schindler and Bob

Adams. FL: I love the country
air FLC: Mother, mother,
mother, pin a rose on me. 20
Mother raised three grown sons
see 'Didn't he ramble'
Mother told me always to follow the
golden rule see 'You'll never
get to heaven'
'Mother was a lady' Edward B.
Marks and Joseph W. Stern.
FL: Two drummers sat at dinner in a grand hotel one day
FLC: My mother was a lady.
20
'Motherless child' FL: O sometimes
I feel like a motherless child.
5
'Motherless children' FL: Mother-
less children have a hard time
when mother is dead. 57
'Mother's little helper' Mick Jagger
and Keith Richard. FL: Kids
are different today I hear every
mother say FLC: Doctor, please
some more of these. 16
'A motto for every man' Harry and
Charles Coote. FL: Some people
you've met in your time no doubt
FLC: So we will sing and banish
melancholy. 17
Mount up, mount up, my pretty
Polly see 'Pretty Polly'
'Mount Vernon' Stephen Jenks. FL:
What solemn sounds the ear invade. 65
'Mountain dew' FL: Down the road
here from me there's an old
hollow tree FLC: Oh, they call
it that good old mountain dew.
14, 56, 57
'Mountain greenery' Lorenz Hart
and Richard Rodgers. FL: Oh
the first of May. FLC: In a
mountain greenery. 46
'The mountains o' Mourne' FL: Oh,
Mary, this London's a wonderful
sight. 25, 57
'Mourn, Marcus, mourn' Michael
Cavendish. FL: Mourn, mourn,
mourn, Marcus, mourn and
mourning wish to die. 26
Mourn, saylan, mourn oh! see
'Saylan'
'Move along' FL: We are on the
ocean sailing FLC: Let us move
along, now move along. 38
'The mowing machine' Mac McClintock. FL: Oh, once in the

cavern in a canyon FLC: Oh my
darling. 23
My day in the hills has come to an
end see 'The sound of music'
'My days have been so wondrous
free' Francis Hopkinson and
Thomas Parnell. FL: same.
57, 65
My doll is as dainty as a sparrow
see 'Honey bun'
'My dolly was the fairest thing'
Isaac Bickerstaffe and G. F.
Handel. FL: same. 40
'My elusive dreams' Curly Putnam
and Billy Sherrill. FL: You fol-
lowed me to Texas FLC: I know
you're tired of following. 10, 47
'My evening sun is sinking fast see
'Angel band'
'My faith looks up to thee' Roy
Palmer and Lowell Mason. FL:
same. 1, 34
My father built me a dandy bower
see 'The famous flower of serv-
ing men'
My father built me a shady bower
see 'The flower of serving men'
'My father fain would have me take'
Robert Jones. FL: same. 26
My father feed me far far awa see
'The rantin laddie'
My father gave me an acre of land
see 'Sing Ivy'
My father had a ship in the North
countree see 'The Golden Van-
ity'
My father he left me a yacre of
land see 'A yacre of land'
My father he left me three acres of
lands see 'Sing Ivy'
My father he's a knight and a knight
of high renown see 'The dragoon
and the lady'
My father he's a lord and a lord of
high renown see 'The bold
dragoon and the lady'
My father is a knight see 'The
lady and the dragoon'
'My father is dead' FL: My father
is dead and I can't tell you how
FLC: With my whim, wham,
waddle. 48
My father left me an acre of land
see 'An acre of land'
My father married a pure Cherokee
see 'Half-breed'
My father owned a ship in the North
country see 'The Golden Vanity'

'My father shot a kangaroo' FL:
same. 72
My father was a lord see 'Dragoon
and the lady'
My father was a noble knight see
'Sweet William'
My father was as brave a lord see
'My husband built for me a
bower'
My father was the keeper of the
Eddystone Light see 'The
Eddystone Light'
'My father's apple tree' FL: Back
there, behind my father's. 48
My father's gone to glory see 'In
bright mansions above'
'My favorite things' Rodgers and
Hammerstein. FL: Raindrops on
roses and whiskers on kittens.
6, 24
My feet are in the stirrups, my
bridle's in my hand see 'Good-
bye old paint'
'My fiddle is my sweetheart' G. H.
Chirgwin and Harry Hunter. FL:
same FLC: same. 17
'My fiddle was my sweetheart' G.
H. Chirgwin and Charles Osborne.
FL: My fiddle was my sweetheart,
but now that's not the case FLC:
My fiddle was my sweetheart.
17
My foot in the stirrup, my pony
won't stand see 'Goodbye old
Paint'
'My friends and relations' FL: My
friends and relations they live in
the Nations. 43
My friends shall declare that my
time is misspent see 'The sweet
little girl that I love'
'My funny Valentine' Lorenz Hart
and Richard Rodgers. FL: Be-
hold the way our fine feathered
friend his virtue doth parade
FLC: My funny Valentine. 6, 42
'My gal is a high born lady' Barney
Fagan. FL: Thar' is gwine to
be a festival this evenin' FLC:
My gal is a high born lady. 36
'My gal on the Rio Grande' FL:
There's a little gal a livin' in a
shanty on a claim FLC: So hump
along yo' dogies, I ain't got long
to wait. 2
'My gal Sal' Paul Dresser. FL:
Everything is over and I'm feel-
ing bad FLC: They called her

frivolous Sal. 1, 20, 25, 31, 34, 67

'My gal's a corker' FL: My gal's a corker, she's a New Yorker. 68

My generous heart disdains the slave of love to be see 'Rondo'

'My golden ball' FL: Slack up the rope, slack up the rope. 37

'My good Lord's been here' FL: O brothers, where were you FLC: My good Lord's been here. 38

My good old auntie's gone along see 'Gone along'

My grandfather's clock was too large for the shelf see 'Grandfather's clock'

'My grandma's advice' FL: My grandma lives on yonder little green. 36

'My happiness' Betty Peterson and Borney Bergantine. FL: Evening shadows make me blue. 47

'My Harding County home' FL: Not so many years ago I left old Buffalo FLC: I can see the mustang band grazing by the river Grand. 43

'My heart belongs to Daddy' Cole Porter. FL: I used to fall FLC: While tearing off. 42

My heart is aching for someone see 'Wanting you'

My heart is sad and I am lonely see 'Bury me beneath the willow'

My heart is sad and lonely see 'Body and soul'

My heart still yearns for my old Londerry home see 'The Londerry air'

'My heart stood still' Lorenz Hart and Richard Rodgers. FL: I laughed at sweethearts I met at schools FLC: I took one look at you. 1, 42, 46

'My heart was so free' John Gay and Richard Leveridge. FL: same. 40

My heart's sad and I am all forlorn see 'A good man is hard to find'

My heavenly home is bright and fair see 'Wait a little while'

'My home's across the Smoky Mountains' FL: same. 34, 56, 57

'My home's in Montana' FL: My home's in Montana, I wear a bandana. 43

'My honey's lovin' arms' Herman Ruby and Joseph Meyer. FL:

Once caress, happiness FLC: I love your lovin' arms. 12

My, how I miss your tender kiss see 'Blue turning grey over you'

'My husband built for me a bower' FL: My father was as brave a lord. 11

'My ideal' Leo Robin, Richard A. Whiting and Newell Chase. FL: Will I ever find the girl in my mind. 47

My Lady Margaret sitting in her own chamber a-weeping see 'Lady Maisry'

'My lady's garden' FL: How does my lady's garden grow? 48

'My last gold dollar' FL: I wish I had never been born. 35

My left shoe's on my right foot see 'Mimi'

My life flower on in endless song above earth's lamentation see 'How can I keep from singing'

My little darling, oh how I love you see 'Little darling pal of mine'

My little Margie see 'Margie'

'My little pretty one' FL: same. 26

'My long tailed blue' FL: I've come to town to see you all. 36

'My lord and my master' Oscar Hammerstein and Richard Rodgers. FL: He is pleased with me. 24

My lord came home quite late one night see 'The gypsy Davy'

My lord calls me see 'Steal away'

'My Lord says there's room enough in Heaven for us all' FL: Backslider don't stay away FLC: My Lord says there's room enough. 28

'My Lord, what a morning!' Oh, you will hear the trumpet sound. FL: same. 33

'My Lord, what a mourning' FL: You'll hear the trumpet sound FLC: My Lord, what a mourning. 38

My Lord you know that you promise me see 'Set down, servant'

My lords with your leave see 'A new war song'; 'Sir Peter Parker'

My lords, with your leave an account I will give see 'Peter Parker'

'My love bound me with a kiss'

Robert Jones. FL: same. 26
My love built me a bonnie bower
see 'The border widow's lament'
My love don't give me presents see
'She's a woman'
'My love gave me a cherry' FL:
My love gave me a cherry, a
cherry without a stone. 11
My love has built a bonny ship, and
set her on the sea see 'The
lowlands of Holland'
My love he was as fine a fellow
see 'The gallows tree'
My love is a cowboy see 'Bucking
bronco'
'My love is a rider' FL: My love is
a rider, wild broncos he breaks.
43, 57, 62
My love is a rider, wild bronchos
he breaks see 'Bucking broncho'
My love is a vaquero see 'Bucking
bronco'
'My love is gone to sea' Francis
Hopkinson. FL: same. 65
'My love is like a red, red rose.
FL: Oh, my love is like a red,
red rose. 25
'My love is neither young nor old'
Robert Jones. FL: same. 26
My love, my pride, my treasure-o
see 'Christ Child lullaby'
My love sent me a chicken without
a bone see 'A paradox'
'My lover's a rider' FL: My lover's
a rider, a rider so fine. 62
'My luve she lives in Lincolnshire'
FL: same. 11
My ma, she told me to open the
door see 'Ma I won't have him'
My maiden's fair, yousels prepare
see 'The Earl of Aboyne'
My mama once gave me some blue
cheese to eat see 'Blue cheese'
My mama told me last night see
'More pretty girls than one'
'My Mammy' Walter Donaldson,
Sam Lewis and Joe Young. FL:
Mammy, Mammy, the sun shines
east. 31, 54
'My man's gone now' Du Bose Hey-
ward and George Gershwin. FL:
My man's gone now, ain't no use
a-listenin'. 21
My massa died a shouting see 'I'm
a traveling to the grave'
My master turned me out of doors
see 'The sleeping gamekeeper'
'My mother chose my husband' FL:

My mother chose my husband, a
lawyer's son was he FLC: Ah ha
ha, that's no way to. 57, 58
My mother chose my husband, a
lawyer's son was he see 'Ah-
hah-hah'
My mother she gave me an acre of
land see 'Sing Ivy'
My mother was a lady see 'Mother
was a lady'
My mother was a proud, proud
woman see 'Marie Hamilton'
My mother was a soldier see
'Money is king'
'My mother-in-law' R. A. Barnes.
FL: My mother-in-law with the
chattering jaw FLC: My mother-
in-law. 36
My mother's eyes are always wet
see 'Hind Etin'
My mother's name was Mary see
'Mary's a grand old name'
'My mother's old red shawl' FL:
It now lies on the shelf, it is
faded and torn FLC: It is useful
no more, yet I fondly adore. 57
My name is Charlie Brennan see
'The state of Arkansas'
My name is Frank Bolar an ole
bachelor I am see 'The Lane
County bachelor'
My name is Tom Hight, an old
bachelor I am see 'Starving to
death on a government claim'
My name is William Edwards, I
live down Cove Creek way see
'The TVA'
My name is William Guiseman see
'William Guiseman'
My name it is Joe Bowers, I got a
brother Ike see 'Joe Bowers'
My name it is Joe Seaven Orange
Blossom see 'Happy Darky'
My name it is Nell and quite candid
I tell see 'Nell Flaherty's
drake'
My name it is Sam Hall, chimney
sweep see 'Sam Hall'
'My new little sister' Marlys Swing-
er' FL: My new little sister
is tiny and small. 13
'My nose is blue, my teeth are
green. 68
My nose is very aquiline see 'The
handsome man'
'My obsession' Mick Jagger and
Keith Richard. FL: My obses-
sions, are your possessions. 16

11

The next come down was dressed in
red see 'Little Musgrave and
Lady Barnard'
'The next market day' FL: A maid
went to Dublin her markets to
learn. 57
'The next time it happens' Oscar
Hammerstein and Richard Rodgers.
FL: I leapt before I looked FLC:
The next time it happens. 24
Next time we sing this verse see
'Oh, the horse went around'
Neyn, manenyu, neyn see 'Yomi,
yomi'
'Niagara Falls' Winchell. FL:
From Buffalo my labor done. 36
'Nibble, nibble, nibble' Margaret
Wise Brown and Marlys Swinger.
FL: Nibble, nibble, nibble, goes
the mouse in my heart. 13
'Nice work if you can get it' George
and Ira Gershwin. FL: The man
who only lives for making money
FLC: Holding hands at midnight
neath a starry sky. 21
Nicht Jerusalem sondern Bethele-
hem see 'Lowly Bethlehem'
Nicodemus the slave was of African
birth see 'Wake Nicodemus'
Night after night I'm cryin' see
'Daddy won't you please come
home'
'Night and Day' Cole Porter. FL:
Like the beat, beat, beat of the
tom-tom FLC: Night and day, you
are the one. 1, 42, 46
Night and stars above that shine so
bright see 'Caravan'
Night and you, and blue Hawaii see
'Blue Hawaii'
'Night herding song' FL: Oh, slow
up dogies, quit moving around.
57
'Night herding song' FL: Slow down
dogies, quit your roving around.
18
A night in June see 'Coax me'
The night is bitter see 'The man
that got away'
'The night is young' Billy Rose,
Irving Kahal and Dana Suesse.
FL: The night is young and you're
so beautiful. 53
The night is young see 'It's-de-love-
ly'
The night sets softly with the hush
of falling leaves see 'Patterns'

'The night they drove old Dixie
down' J. Robbie Robertson. FL:
Virgil Caine is the name. 45
Night time, night time see 'Negra
consentida'
'Night train' Oscar Washington,
Lewis C. Simpkins and Jimmy
Forrest. FL: Night train that
woke my baby so far away. 52
The night was dark and stormy
see 'Little Jim'
'The nightingale' FL: One evening,
one evening, one evening so fair.
30
'The nightingale song' FL: One
morning, one morning, one
morning in May. 50
Nights are long since you went
away see 'My buddy'
'Nights of spendor' Harry D. Kerr
and J. S. Zamecnik. FL: Oh
nights of spendor, your charms
so tender. 47
'Nighty-night' Joe Davis. FL:
Nighty-night until tomorrow. 59
'Niña, nana' FL: A la nanita, nanita. 51
'Nine hundred miles' FL: I'm riding
on this train FLC: And I have to
hear the lonesome whistle blow.
57
'Nine hundred miles' FL: Well, I'm
walking down this track FLC:
And if this train runs me right.
34, 35
'Nine men slept in a boarding house
bed' FL: same. 34
Nine men slept in a boarding house
bed see 'Roll over, roll over'
'Nine-pound hammer' FL: This nine-
pound hammer is just a little
bit too heavy FLC: Roll on, Buddy, don't you roll so slow. 14,
27, 35, 57
'Nine questions' FL: Oh, what is
whiter than the milk? Sing fall-
de-rall-de-hall-de. 7
'19th nervous breakdown' Mick Jagger and Keith Richard. FL:
You're the kind of person you
meet at certain dismal dull affairs. 16
Ninety years without slumbering see
'Grandfather's clock'
'Nishi' FL: Nishi had a mater in
Chicockaneedle-o. 50
'No arms can ever hold you' Art
Crafer and Jimmy Webb. FL:

same. 52
No doubt you have heard of the
great fancy fair see 'O, Fred,
tell them to stop!'
'No expectations' Mick Jagger and
Keith Richard. FL: Take me to
the station and put me on a train.
16
No gal made has got a shade see
'Sweet Georgia Brown'
No harm, no harm see 'Tell
Brudder Lijah'
'No hiding place' FL: No hiding
place down there. 57
No home, no home, said an orphan
girl see 'The orphan girl'
No home, no home, cried the or-
phan girl at the door of the
princely hall see 'The orphan
girl'
No home, no home, said the little
girl see 'The little orphan girl'
No, I would not give you false hope
on this strange and mournful day
see 'Mother and child reunion'
'No ice so cold, so hard, as I'
David Garrick and Thomas A.
Arne. FL: same. 40
'No Irish need apply' J. F. Poole.
FL: I'm a decent boy just landed
from the town of Ballyfad FLC:
Some do count it a misfortune to
be christened Pat or Dan. 19,
57
No keepsakes have we of the days
that are gone see 'So far'
'No more auction block for me' FL:
same. 19
'No more booze' FL: There was a
little man and he had a little can.
57
'No more cane on the Brazos/God-
amighty' FL: Well, 'tain't no
more cane on the Brazos. 28
'No more cane on this Brazos' FL:
There ain't no more cane on this
Brazos. 4
'No more good time in the world for
me' FL: Well-a, no more good
time, poor boy in the world for
me. 28
No more moaning no more moaning
see 'Oh Freedom'
No more peck o' corn for me see
'Many thousand go'
No more peck of corn for me see
'Many thousand gone'
No more shall I work in the factory

see 'The factory girl'
No one to talk with, all by myself
see 'Ain't misbehavin'
'No other love' Oscar Hammerstein
and Richard Rodgers. FL: How
far away are you? FLC: No other
love have I. 42
No question about it see 'It's so
nice to have a man around the
house'
'No, sir' FL: Tell me one thing,
tell me truly. 41
No tears, no fears see 'We'll be
together again'
'No telephone in heaven' FL: Now I
can't fool with baby, the smiling
virgin said FLC: My child, the
virgin murmered, as she stroked
the anxious brow. 50
No use permitting some prophet of
doom see 'Cabaret'
'The noble lads of Canada' FL:
Come all ye British heroes. 55
A noble lord in Plymouth did dwell
see 'The half-hitch'
'The noble 24th' G. C. Anewick and
V. Davies. FL: A story came
one morning FLC: All honor to
the 24th. 69
A nobleman's fair daughter walked
down a narrow lane see 'Mr.
Woodburn's courtship'
'The nobleman's wedding' FL: Come
all you good people, I pray pay
attention. 30
'Nobody' FL: If to force me to sing
it be your intention. 3
'Nobody coming to marry me' FL:
The dogs began to bark FLC:
And it's oh! what will become of
me. 36
Nobody feels any pain tonight see
'Just like a woman'
'Nobody knows the trouble I see,
Lord!' FL: Brothers, will you
pray for me FLC: Nobody knows
the trouble I see, Lord. 38
'Nobody knows the trouble I've seen'
FL: same. 1, 23, 25
'Nobody knows the trouble I've seen'
FL: One morning I was a-walking
around FLC: Nobody knows the
trouble I've seen. 4
'Nobody knows the trouble I've seen'
FL: Sometimes I'm up, sometimes
I'm down FLC: Nobody knows the
trouble I've seen. 34, 57
Nobody knows what I know see

'Spring secret'
Nobody knows who I am see
  'Heaven bells ringin' in my soul'
'Nobody likes me' FL: Nobody likes
  me, everybody hates me. 68
'Nobody wins' Kris Kristofferson.
  FL: Anymore it doesn't matter
  what's right or wrong. 10
'Nobody's sweetheart' Gus Kahn,
  Ernie Erdman, Billy Meyers and
  Elmer Schoebel. FL: You're no-
  body's sweetheart now. 12, 47,
  54
'Noche azul' Ernesto Lecuona. FL:
  Noche azul que en mi alma reflejó
  la pasión. 9
'Noche azul' Carol Raven and Er-
  nesto Lecuona. FL: Starry blue
  night when branches bend and
  blow. 9
Noche, noche, ete llama el amor
  see 'Negra consentida'
Noche oscura nada veo see 'El
  tortillero'
'None can love like an Irishman'
  FL: The turbaned Turk, who
  scorns the world. 57
'None but the lonely heart' FL:
  Here in my twilight dreams, I
  dream of you dear. 25
None so dauntless and free on land
  or on sea see 'A son of the
  desert am I'
'Norham, down by Norham' FL:
  There were three ladies playing
  at the ba. 11
'North to Alaska' Mike Phillips.
  FL: Big Sam left Seattle in the
  year of ninety-two FLC: Where
  the river is windin'. 10
'The north wind' FL: The north
  wind doth blow. 48, 72
'Norwegian wood' Lennon and Mc-
  Cartney. FL: I once had a girl
  or should I say she once had me.
  44
Not from Joe see 'Winning the
  vote'
Not so many years ago I left old
  Buffalo see 'My Harding County
  home'
Not Jerusalem, lowly Bethelehem
  twas see 'Lowly Bethelehem'
Not that you are fair, dear see
  'Because you're you'
Not they who are determined see
  'Boys, keep your powder dry'
'Nothing else to do' FL: Away down

yonder in the Yankety Yank FLC:
  And just lots of folks are like
  that foolish frog o' mine. 68
'Nothing like grog' FL: A plague of
  those musty old lubbers. 3
Nothing seemed to matter any more
  see 'Love walked in'
'Nothing whatever to grumble at'
  FL: Wherever I poke sarcastic
  joke replete with malice spiteful.
  68
Nothing's impossible, I have found
  see 'Pick yourself up'
'Nottamun town' FL: As I rode out
  in Nottamun town. 57
Now a father had a young ploughboy
  see 'The dewy dens of Darrow'
Not a soul's down on the corner
  see 'Wedding bells'
Now after all my hard travelin'
  see 'Things about comin' my
  way'
Now, didn't it rain, chillun see
  'Didn't it rain'
Now down the road just a mile or
  two see 'Down the road'
Now ever since I tied the knot, and
  which it ain't a day see 'At my
  time of life'
Now, farewell, my Massa, my
  Missy, adieu see 'Good bye to
  America'
Now father, dear father, you have
  done me some harm see 'Still
  growing'
Now, for breakfast I never thinks
  of 'aving tea see 'Arf a pint
  of ale'
Now has come the hour sad of part-
  ing see 'Aloha oe'
Now he told you that he'd love you
  much more than I see 'Cry
  baby'
Now here's a story 'bout Minnie the
  Moocher see 'Minnie the
  Moocher'
Now how I came to get this hat tis
  very strange, and funny see
  'Where did you get that hat?'
Now I can't fool with baby, the
  smiling virgin said see 'No
  telephone in heaven'
'Now I know' Stanley Jay Gelber,
  Scott English and James Last.
  FL: Now I know why I've been
  lonely. 47
Now I would not marry a blacksmith
  see 'A railroader for me'

Now I pray you go fetch me my
little footboy see 'Come,
Mother, Mother, make my bed'
Now I'd a young lady lived up the
street see 'The gal that got
stuck on everything she saw'
Now if a man has money today see
'We are soldiers in the army'
Now if an elevator boy forgets to
close the door see 'Foolish
questions'
Now, if I should wander back to-
night see 'If I should wander
back tonight'
Now if you see that girl of mine
see 'Foggy mountain top'
Now if you want to get to heaven
see 'Talking blues'
Now, if you will listen, I'll sing
you a song see 'The story the
crow told me'
Now, if you're white, you're right
see 'Git back blues'
Now I'm troubled in mind see
'Troubled in mind'
Now in that bog there was a root
see 'Bog in the valley-o'
Now in the summer of life sweetheart see 'Will you love me in
December as you do in May'
Now is it not a pity such a pretty
girl as I see 'I won't be a nun'
'Now is the hour' Mauwa Kaihan,
Clement Scott and Dorothy Stew-
art. FL: While you're away FLC:
Now is the hour when we must
part. 12
'Now is the month of Maying' FL:
same. 25
Now it's my old man came home
one night see 'The cuckold's
song'
Now it's of a youth and a well-bred
youth see 'The bailiff's daughter
of Islington'
Now I've got heartaches by the num-
ber see 'Heartaches by the
number'
Now, I've got no use for the women
see 'I've got no use for the wo-
men'
Now Jim O'Shea was cast away see
'I've got rings on my fingers'
Now John came home all in a won-
der see 'Everyday dirt'
Now let me fly see 'Let me fly'
'Now let rich music sound' Thomas
Davies. FL: same. 3

Now Liddesdale has layen lang in
see 'Dick o' the cow'
Now Liddesdale has ridden a raid
see 'Jock o' the side'
Now listen all you maidens about to
choose a man see 'Get away
old man'
Now listen, honey, 'bout a new
dance craze see 'Walkin' the
dog'
Now neath the silver moon ocean is
glowing see 'Santa Lucia'
Now, O Lord, please lend thine
ear see 'The cowman's prayer'
Now old aunt Rebecca is rich see
'Bang went the chance of a life-
time'
Now over there across the sea
they've got another war see
'That crazy war'
Now poets may sing of the dear
Fatherland see 'Down where
the Wurzburger flows'
Now put your arms around me like
a circle round the sun see
'Stealin', stealin''
'Now, Robin, laugh and sing' Mar-
tin Peerson. FL: same. 26
'Now she knows how to parle-voo'
Edgar Leslie, Joe Young and
Harry Jentes. FL: Little Willie
Harris coming back from Paris
FLC: When he asked her to
parle-voo, parle-voo. 31
Now some folks like the summer
time see 'Footprints in the
snow'
Now steal me some of your father's
gold see 'The knight and the
chief's daughter'
Now sweet William's to get him a
wife see 'Jenny fair gentle
Rosemarie'
Now, sweetheart, you've done me
wrong see 'Sweetheart, you've
done me wrong'
Now that I have found you see
'He loves and she loves'
'Now that the buffalo's gone' Buffy
Sainte-Marie. FL: Can you re-
member the times. 4
Now that we're going to be married
see 'Sunday'
Now the Black Jack David come
riding through the plains see
'Black Jack David'
Now the curtain is going up see
'The entertainer'

'Now the day is over' Sabine Baring-
Gould and Joseph Barnby. FL:
same. 34
Now the golden sun can see us kiss
see 'When the snow is on the
roses'
Now the hacienda's dark, the town is
sleeping see 'Vaya con Dios'
Now the moon shines tonight on
pretty Red Wing see 'Red Wing'
Now things was looking rosy, baby
see 'Ups and down'
Now three gypsies once came beg-
ging at my door see 'The rag-
tail gypsies oh!'
Now turn your back on me see
'The false hearted knight'
Now twas of a fair maid was wand-
ering in love see 'Johnny Doyle'
Now twas twenty-five or thirty years
since Jack first saw the light
see 'Jack was every inch a sail-
or'
'Now we take this feeble body' FL:
same. 38
'Now we'll make the rafters ring'
FL: same. 34, 68
'Now what is love' Sir Walter
Raleigh and Robert Jones. FL:
Now, what is love I pray thee
tell? 26
Now what will you do, Lady Mar-
garet, he cried see 'Lady
Margaret and Lord William'
Now when I was a little lad, me
mother always told me see
'Haul away, Joe'
Now, when I waters the workers'
beer I puts in strychnine see
'The man who waters the work-
ers' beer'
Now will you love, me, little
darlin' see 'Will you be loving
another man?'
Now won't you listen dearie while
I say see 'After you've gone'
Now you can bring Pearl see
'Don't bring Lulu'
Now you want to play and then it's
no see 'Undecided'
Now your friends may be jolly see
'Don't go out tonight, my darling'
Nowell, Nowell, Nowell, Nowell
see 'The first Nowell'
'Nowhere man' Lennon and McCart-
ney. FL: He's a real nowhere
man. 44
Number one, number one see 'Old

John Braddleum'
'Number twelve train' FL: Number
twelve train took my baby. 57
'The nut brown bride' FL: Sweet
Willie and Fair Annie. 11
Nutmegs and cloves see 'The owl'
'Nuts in May' FL: Here we come
gathering nuts in May. 48
Nye slyshny v sa du dazhe shorokhi
see 'Moscow nights'

- O -

Oh, a frog a-courting he did ride
see 'A frog a-courting'
Oh, a gentle young lady was down
in yonders lane see 'A gentle
young lady'
Oh, a man there lives on the
western plains see 'The cowboy'
Oh, a shantyman's life is a weari-
some life see 'The shanty-
man's life'
Oh, a storm is threatening my very
life today see 'Gimme shelter'
O abre a cortina do passado see
'Brazil'
Oh! ain't I glad see 'I ain't going
to die no more'
Oh, all day long I'm lookin' for
trees see 'Deep sea blues'
'O all ye powers above' Henry
Fielding and John Eccles. FL:
same. 40
O all you little blackey tops see
'The scarecrow'
Oh, an old beggarman comin' over
the lea see 'Jolly beggar'
O and dear judge see 'The prickle
holly bush'
O, Annie dear, O Annie dear see
'Andrew Lammie'
Oh, answer me a question, love, I
pray see 'The sweetest story
ever told'
O ariá raio obá, obá see 'Mas
que nada'
'Oh, Babe, it ain't no lie' FL: One
old woman, Lord, in this town
FLC: Oh, babe, it ain't no lie.
57
O babes, o babes, if you was mine
see 'The cruel mother'
Oh, baby come on see 'Action'
O baby, O baby, if you were mine
see 'The greenwood siding'
Oh, Babylon's falling, falling,

falling see 'Babylon's falling'
Oh, beat the drum slowly and play
the fife lowly see 'The cowboy's
lament'
Oh, beat your drum slowly and play
your fife slowly see 'Tom Sher-
man's barroom'
O beautiful for spacious skies see
'America the beautiful'
O, Bessy Bell and Mary Gray see
'Bessy Bell'; 'Bessy Bell and
Mary Grey'
Oh, Billy, Billy, bonny Billy see
'The battle of Bothwell Brig';
'Earlistoun'
O Billy, O Billy you have come
home see 'Billy murdered John'
'Oh birthdays are fun' FL: Oh,
birthdays are fun throughout the
year. 13
Oh, black a Betty, black a Betty,
let your hammer ring see
'Hammer ring'
O Black Jack Davy crossed the
field see 'Black Jack Davy'
'O bless the Lord' Stephen Schwartz.
FL: O bless the Lord, my soul.
64
O blessed Savior, thou will guide
me see 'Life is like a mountain
railroad'
Oh, blow the man down, bullies
see 'Blow the man down'
Oh, blow the man down, bullies,
blow the man down see 'Blow
the man down'
'Oh, Brandy, leave me alone' FL:
same. 57
O brethren, brethren, watch and
pray see 'Judgment will find
you so'
Oh, brethren, do get ready see
'We are climbing the hills of
Zion'
Oh! brethren, my way, my way's
cloudy see 'My way's cloudy'
Oh, brethren, rise and shine, and
give God the glory, glory see
'Rise and shine'
Oh brillante estrella que anuncias la
aurora see 'Los reyes Oriental'
Oh, bring back my blue-eyed boy
see 'Blue-eyed boy'
Oh bring back to me my wandering
boy see 'Out in the cold world,
or bring back my wandering boy'
O bring down some of your father's
gold see 'Lady Isabel and the

elf knight'
Oh, bring me back my brown-eyed
boy see 'Likes likker better
than me'
Oh, bring me back the one I love
see 'Bring me back the one I
love'
O brother, can you toss the stone
see 'The two brothers'
Oh, brother, don't stay away see
'Room enough'
O brother, don't you want to go?
see 'Don't you want to go?'
O brother less go down see 'Down
in the valley to pray'
O brother, O brother, play ball
with me see 'The two brothers'
O! Brother Teague, dost hear the
decree see 'Lilliburlero'
O brothers, I love Jesus see 'I've
just come from the fountain'
'Oh Brothers now our meeting's
broke' FL: Oh, brothers now our
meeting's broke, and brothers
we must part. 7
Oh, brothers, oh brothers, can you
play ball see 'The two brothers'
O brothers, where were you see
'My good Lord's been here'
O brothers, won't you help me see
'I'm a rolling'
Oh, brothers, you oughta been there
see 'Roll, Jordan, roll'
Oh, Buchan is bonnie and there
lives my love see 'Lord Sal-
toun and Annachie'
'O bury me beneath the willow' FL:
Oh, bury me beneath the willow,
beneath the weeping willow tree.
7
'Oh bury me not on the lone prairie'
FL: same. 23, 25
Oh, bury me not on the lone prairie
see 'Bury me not on the lone
prairie'; 'The dying cowboy'
O cam ye frae the Hielands man
see 'Battle of Harlaw'; 'Harlaw'
O can ye sew cushions, and can ye
sew sheets see 'Can ye sew
cushions?'
O, can you make me a cambric
shirt? see 'The lover's tasks'
O can you rokka Romanes? see
'Can you rokka Romanes'
'O Canada' C. Lavallee, A. Routhier and R. S. Weir. FL: O Canada, our home and native land.
57

'O Canada' C. Lavallee and A. Routhier. FL: O Canada, terre de no aïeux. 57

O Cape Cod girls they have no combs see 'Cape Cod girls'

O Captain Glen's our skipper's name see 'Captain Glen'

O Charley he's a fine young man see 'Weev'ly wheat'

Oh! Charlie is my darlin' darlin', darlin' see 'Charlie is my darlin''

O childrens ain't you glad see 'When Moses smote the water'

Oh choppin' Charlie, great god-amighty see 'Choppin' Charlie'

'O Christmas tree' FL: O Christmas tree, O Christmas tree. 34

O clear running stream see 'Clear running stream'

O cold is the wind do blow, sweet-heart see 'The unquiet grave'

'O come, all ye faithful' John Francis Wade and J. Reading. FL: same FLC: O come let us adore Him. 34, 57

Oh, come all you young people and listen what I say see 'Naomi Wise'

Oh come along boys, and listen to my tale see 'The old Chisholm trail'

Oh, come along, brothers see 'We're almost done'

Oh! come back, sinner, and don't go there see 'Oh! sinner man'

O, come, come away from labor now reposing, let busy care awhile see 'Sweet Philomel'

Oh, come, come with me to the old churchyard see 'The old church-yard'

O come, dear sister, and let's take a walk see 'The two sisters'

Oh, come hear my story of heart-aches and sighs see 'Moonlight and skies'

O come let us adore Him see 'O come, all ye faithful'

'O come little children' Christoph von Schmid and J. A. P. Schulz. FL: same. 13

Oh, come to me in the evening when the sun hides the West see 'When the lights are soft and low'

Oh, come to the church in the wild-wood see 'The church in the wildwood'

Oh, come with me and we will go to the land where the mango apples grow see 'The wild gazelle'

Oh, come with me my little love, I will take you ten thousand miles see 'The turtle dove'

Oh, come with me to the kitchen see 'The suicide song'

Oh come you home, my own true love see 'The daemon lover'

Oh, comrades, you deserve your daily bread see 'Let 'em eat cake'

Oh, Danny boy, the pipes, the pipes are calling see 'Danny Boy'

Oh, darkies, give attention see 'Pretty Dinah Snow'

O Davy I'm so glad to meet you see 'The gypsy laddie'

Oh de boll weevil am a little black bug see 'De Boll Weevil'

O de heaven bells a-ringin' and I'm a-going home see 'Heaven bells ringin' and I'm a-goin' home'

O de heaven bells a-ringin' in my soul see 'Heaven bells ringin' in my soul'

Oh, dear John, stand here see 'The prick'ty bush'

O dear sister how could ye be sad see 'Castle Norie'

'Oh, dear what can the matter be' FL: He promised he'd buy me a beautiful fairing FLC: Oh, dear, what can the matter be? 25, 34, 48, 57

'Oh, dear, what can the matter be?' FL: same. 65, 67

Oh, deep in my heart see 'We shall overcome'

Oh, dem golden slippers see 'Golden slippers'

O did you ever hear of the brave Earl Brand see 'The brave Earl Brand and the King of England's daughter'

Oh, diddle lully day see 'Katy Cruel'

O didn't Jesus rule death in his arms see 'Rule death in his arms'

O dis union! see 'Big camp meeting in the Promised Land'; 'Stand on a sea of glass'

Oh, do you remember sweet Betsy from Pike see 'Sweet Betsy from Pike'

Oh, don't you remember a long
time ago see 'The orphans'

Oh, don't you remember sweet
Alice, Ben Bolt see 'Ben Bolt';
'Don't you remember sweet
Alice?'

Oh, don't you want to go to the
Gospel feast see 'Deep river'

Oh, down in the tules, a-wranglin'
around see 'Down in the tules'

Oh, down, oh down in rosemerry
Scotland see 'Christmas carol'

O down she threw her ivory comb
see 'Fair Margaret and Sweet
William'

Oh, Dunderbeck, Dunderbeck see
'Dunderbeck'

Oh, Dunderbeck, oh, Dunderbeck,
how could you be so, mean? see
'Dunderbeck'

O early in the month of May see
'Barbara Ellen'

Oh, Eliza, L'il Liza Jane see
'L'il Liza Jane'

Oh, esas palmeras murmurantes
see 'Brazil'

Oh, Eve, where's Adam see 'Adam
in the garden pinnin' leaves'

Oh, every morning at seven o'clock
there are twenty tarriers on the
rock see 'Drill, ye tarriers,
drill'

'O eyes, leave off your weeping'
Robert Hales. FL: same. 26

'O eyes, O mortal stars' Alfonso
Ferrabosco. FL: O eyes, o mortal stars! the authors of my
harms. 26

Oh fair Rosie Ann, oh Rosie Ann
see 'Fair Rosie Ann'

O! false Sir John a wooing came
see 'May Colvin'

Oh, fare thee well see 'Fare thee
well'

Oh fare you well, my own true love,
fare you well, my dear see
'Mary-Anne'

O fare you well, sweet Ireland see
'The sons of liberty'

Oh, father, if you will agree, then
I will go and see see 'The
little Sergeant'

Oh, father, oh father, come riddle
to me see 'Fair Ellender'

O Fernal up and down see 'Fernal
up and down'

O fetch to my aye a Holland shirt
see 'The elfin knight'

'O fir tree tall' FL: same. 13

O for my ain king, quo gude Wallace see 'Gude Wallace'

Oh, for the long tail blue see
'Long tail blue'

'O for the wings of a dove' William
Bartholomew and Felix M. Bartholdy. FL: O for the wings, the
wings of a dove. 63

'O, Fred, tell them to stop!'
George Meen. FL: No doubt you
have heart of the great fancy fair
FLC: Oh! Fred, tell them to
stop. 36

'Oh, freedom' FL: No more moaning, no more moaning. 19

'O freedom' FL: O freedom,
freedom, o freedom over me.
57

Oh, froggie went a-courtin' and he
did ride, uh-huh, uh-huh see
'Froggie went a-courtin''

'Oh! gee, Oh! gee, oh! golly, I'm
in love' Olson Johnson and Ernest
Breuer. FL: Oh! me, oh! my
FLC: Oh! gee, oh gosh. 12

O, Genevieve, I'd give the world
see 'Sweet Genevieve'

O, Genevieve, sweet Genevieve see
'Sweet Genevieve'

O Georgie shall be hanged in a
golden chain see 'Geordie'

Oh, give me a home where the buffalo roam see 'Home on the
range'

Oh, give me something to remember you by see 'Something to
remember you by'

O gley'd Argyll has written to
Montrose see 'Bonny house of
Airly'

Oh, glory be to me, says he, and
fame's unfadin' flower see
'Away up in the Mogliones'

Oh, go way, man, I can hypnotize
this nation see 'Maple leaf rag'

Oh, green grow the lilacs and so
does the rue see 'Green grow
the lilacs'

Oh, hallelujah to the Lamb see
'Down by the river'; 'The general roll'

O hang, o hang, o slack your rope
see 'The maid freed from the
gallows'

Oh hangerman, o hangerman, slack
on your rope see 'The hangerman's tree'

Kathleen'

O I winna grant thee thy son back again see 'Young Essex'

Oh, if I had another penny see 'Byker Hill'

Oh, I'll give you a paper of pins see 'A paper of pins'

Oh, I'll have a husband, ay!' see 'The romp's song'

Oh, I'll pawn you my gold watch and chain, love see 'Gold watch and chain'

Oh, I'll tell you of a soldier who lately came from war see 'A brave soldier'

O I'm a good old Rebel see 'The good old Rebel'

Oh, I'm a poor wayfarin' stranger see 'I'm a poor wayfarin' stranger'

Oh, I'm a Swede from Nort' Dakota see 'The Swede from North Dakota'

Oh, I'm a Texas cowboy far away from home see 'Texas cowboy'

O I'm goin' to sing see 'I'm goin' to sing'

Oh, I'm in love with a brown-eyed boy see 'Likes likker better than me'

O, I'm jes' a-goin' over on de other side of Jordan see 'Goin' over on de uddah side of Jordan'

Oh, I'm the man, the very fat man see 'The man who waters the workers' beer'

Oh! in Dixie's land I'll take my stand see 'Dixie's land'

Oh is it for my gold you weep see 'The house carpenter'

Oh it really is a wery pretty garden see 'If it wasn't for the 'ouses in between'

Oh, it sells for a dollar a bottle see 'Lydia Pinkham'

Oh, it was sad see 'The ship Titanic'

Oh, it's a long, long while see 'September song'

Oh, it's all for a pedlar and a pedlar boy see 'Robin Hood and the pedlar'

Oh, it's Brennan on the Moor see 'Brennan on the Moor'

O it's fetch me some water from a dungeon stone see 'The unquiet grave'

Oh! it's of a merchant's daughter dear see 'Tom the barber'

Oh, it's two gallant ships from England they did sail see 'Down around the coast of La Barbaree'

O it's where was you bred or where was you born? see 'Hind Horn'

Oh, I've got a ship in the North countree see 'The Spanish canoe'

O I've just returned from the salt water sea see 'The house carpenter'

Oh! Jaky shump der baby see 'Jakey jump der baby'

Oh, Jane was a neighbor for six months or more see 'Jane was a neighbor'

Oh! je vousdrais tant que tu te souvienes see 'Autumn leaves'

O, Jellon Graeme sat in good greenwood see 'Jellon Graeme'

'Oh Jerusalem in the morning' FL: Mother mother, what is the matter FLC: Oh Jerusalem in the morning. 33

O, Jesse leaves a wife, she's a mourner all her life see 'Jesse James'

O Jesus my Savior on thee I'll depend see 'I'm troubed in mind'

O Jimmy, lovely Jimmy, what you are saying is true see 'Jimmy and Nancy'

Oh! jingle bells, jingle bells, jingle all the way see 'Jingle bells'

O Jockie rose up one May mornin' see 'Jockie o' Bridiesland'

O John and William walked out one day see 'John and William'

Oh, Johnny, Johnny, John, come along, come along see 'Bang bang bang'

'Oh Johnny, oh Johnny, oh!' Ed Rose and Abe Olman. FL: All the girls are crazy 'bout a certain little lad FLC: Oh, Johnny, oh Johnny! how you can love! 59

O, Johnny Scot is huntin' gone see 'Johnny Scot'

O Johnny Wedlock is my name see 'Johnny Wedlock'

Oh Johnstone an' the young cornel see 'Young Johnstone'

O, Joseph was an old man, and an old man was he see 'The cherry tree carol'; 'Joseph was an old man'

'O Judges' FL: O judges, O judges
just hold your ropes. 11
Oh! just let me get up in the house
of God see 'Oh! let me get up'
Oh, keep your hat upon your head
see 'Gideon's band'
Oh, Kentucky, the hunters of Kentucky see 'The hunters of Ken-
tucky'
Oh, kind friend, you may ask me
what makes me sad, and still
see 'Utah Carroll'
Oh, kisses sweeter than wine see
'Kisses sweeter than wine'
Oh la la la chick a la le-o see
'La la la chick a la le-o'
Oh, ladee Yodelayhittee see 'Once
an Austrian went yodeling'
Oh! Ladies and gentlemen, please
to draw near see 'Down, down
derry down'
'Oh, lady be good' George and Ira
Gershwin. FL: Listen to my tale
of woe FLC: Oh, sweet and love-
ly, lady, be good. 21, 46
Oh! lady, oh! lady; I'm now going
out see 'Lamkin'
Oh, Lamkin was a mason see
'Lambkin'
O lassie but ye ken little see
'Lizzie Lindsay'
Oh lassie, oh lassie, ye're far owre
young see 'The gaberlunzie man'
O last Monday morning as we set
sail see 'The mermaid'
Oh, Lawd! Oh Lawd, I'm tired and
weary of pain see 'That lucky
old sun'
Oh, Lawdy, pick a bale of cotton
see 'Pick a bale of cotton'
'O let me be a blonde, Mother'
Grace H. Horr and F. W. Root.
FL: I know I'm called a gay
brunette FLC: Do Ma! Please
Ma! Now Ma! 36
'Oh! let me get up' FL: Oh! just
let me get up in the house of
God. 38
Oh, life is a toil and love is a
trouble see 'The housewife's
lament'; 'Life is a toil'
'Oh Lilly O' FL: There were three
sisters playing at ball. 11
Oh! Lilly, sweet Lilly see 'Lilly
Dale'
O listen gude people to my tale see
'The laird of Ochiltrie'
Oh listen, my lads, and I'll tell you

the tale see 'The parson and
the maid'
Oh listen now and I'll sing a song
see 'Gay young clerk in a dry
goods store'
Oh listen sister, I love my Mister
man see 'Can't help lovin' dat
man'
Oh, listen to the story see
'Copper kettle'
O, little bird on the bough so high
see 'Lord Land'
O, little did I think He was so nigh
see 'Who's dat youndah?'
Oh, little did my mother think see
'The four Marys'
'O little town of Bethlehem' Lewis
H. Redner and Phillips Brooks.
FL: same. 33, 34
Oh! Lizer! sweet Lizer! see 'The
future Mrs. 'Awkins'
Oh, Lord, oh, my Lord! see 'Keep
me from sinking down'
O, Lord our fathers oft have told
see 'New Plymouth'
O, Lord please lend me now, thine
ear see 'The cowman's prayer'
Oh, love, fare thee well see
'Whiskey, you're the devil'
O love is pleasin' and love is
teasin' see 'Love is pleasing'
Oh, MacTavish is dead and his
brother don't know it see
'MacTavish'
Oh, Mama, look! see 'The puppy
dog song'
O mamma, non no, no see 'Cara
Mamma, do sono malata'
Oh, Mandy, pick a bale of cotton
see 'Pick a bale of cotton'
Oh, many a bird did wake and fly
see 'The carol of the birds'
'Oh, Mary, don't you weep' FL: If
I could I surely would FLC: Oh,
Mary, don't you weep, don't you
mourn. 34, 57
Oh, Mary, this London's a wonder-
ful sight see 'The mountains o'
Mourne'
O Mary was a maid, when the birds
began to sing see 'The river in
the pines'
Oh, Mary, will you be there? see
'Roll, Jordan, roll'
Oh! Matilda Toots, you should have
seen her boots see 'Matilda
Toots'
Oh, Maybelle, drop 'em down see

'Drop 'em down'
Oh, Maysie she gaed oot ae nicht
see 'Wee toon clerk'
O, me master went to market as
farmers used to do see 'Rap
tap tap'
Oh me name is Dick Darby see
'Dick Darby'
Oh! me, oh! my see 'Oh! gee,
oh! gosh, oh! golly, I'm in love'
Oh, Misirlou see 'Misirlou'
Oh! Miss Bailey, unfortunate Miss
Bailey see 'The unfortunate
Miss Bailey'
'Oh, Mister Moon' FL: Oh, Mister
Moon, moon, bright and shiny
moon. 34
Oh, Mrs. McGrath, the sergeant
said see 'Mrs. McGrath'
O Mollie, O Mollie, it's for your
sake alone see 'Jack o' Dia-
monds'
Oh, Mother, dear Mother, come
here to me see 'The brown
girl'
O mother, dear mother, come rid-
dle my sport see 'Lord Thomas
and Fair Ellinor'
O mother, dear mother, come rid-
dle to me see 'Fair Ellen'
'Oh, Mother, go and make my bed'
FL: same. 11
O mother, mother, look under my
bed see 'Bob-ry Allen'
Oh, mother, mother, Lord Thomas
said see 'Lord Thomas'
O mother, O mother, come rede
me a riddle see 'Lord Thomas
and Fair Elender'
Oh mother, oh mother, come riddle
me this see 'The brown girl'
Oh mother, O mother, come riddle
my sport see 'Lord Thomas'
O mother, O mother, come riddle
the sport see 'Lord Thomas
and Fair Ellinor'
O Mother, o mother, come riddle
to me see 'Fair Ellender'
Oh, mother, o mother, come riddle
us down see 'The brown girl'
Oh mother, oh mother, come riddle
us two see 'Lord Thomas'
O mother, O mother, come roll us
down see 'Lord Thomas and
Fair Ellinor'
Oh mother, oh mother, go riddle this
course see 'Lord Thomas'
O mother, o mother, go roll a song

see 'The brown girl'; 'Lord
Thomas and Fair Ellinor'
O mother, O mother, O mother,
says he see 'Lord Thomas and
Fair Ellinor'
O mother, O mother, pray what
shall I do? see 'Lord Thomas
and Fair Ellendor'
Oh mother, oh mother, unriddle my
sport see 'The brown girl'
'Oh mother! take the wheel away'
Claribel. FL: Oh, mother, take
the wheel away, and put it out
of sight. 63
Oh, my brother, did you come for
to help me? see 'Sweet Canaan'
Oh my darling see 'My darling
Clementine'
Oh my darling, oh my darling see
'Clementine'
Oh, my fellow countrymen see
'Oleanna'
Oh, my golden slippers are laid
away see 'Golden slippers';
'Oh them golden slippers'
O my little soul's a going to shine,
shine see 'Shine, shine'
O my Lord, good and kind see
'New burying ground'
Oh, my love is like a red red rose
see 'My love is like a red, red
rose'
Oh my name is Captain Kidd see
'Captain Kidd'
Oh, my name it is Sam Hall see
'Sam Hall'
Oh, my old cottage home see 'My
old cottage home'
Oh my old man came home one
night see 'The cuckold'
Oh! my poor Nelly Gray see
'Darling Nelly Gray'
O my sonny and choose as you
please see 'The brown girl'
Oh, my soul, my soul am a-going
for to rest see 'Angel Gabriel'
Oh! my witching Dinah Snow see
'Pretty Dinah Snow'
Oh my yella yellow, yellow, yellow
gal see 'Yellow gal'
O Nancy Fat she was a gal see
'Nancy Fat'
O Nancy Fat what are you at see
'Nancy Fat'
O Nancy from London from a clear
purling stream see 'Nancy of
London'
O Nancy, lovely Nancy, I'm going

for to leave you see 'Farewell Nancy'
'O never to be moved' Thomas Campion. FL: same. 26
Oh nights of splendor, your charms
so tender see 'Nights of splendor'
'Oh, no, John' FL: On yonder hill
there stands a creature FLC: Oh,
no John, no, John, no, John, no.
34
Oh, now, brave boys, we'll run for
march see 'Whiskey, you're the
devil'
Oh, oh, how my thoughts do beat
me see 'Oh, how my thoughts
do beat me'
O on the road one summer day see
'John of Hazelgreen'
Oh, once I had a pretty girl see
'The rejected lover'
O once I had a ship in some foreign
country see 'The Golden Vanity'
'O once I loved a lass' FL: O once
I loved a lass but she loved not
me. 11
Oh once I was happy but now I'm
forlorn see 'Flying trapeze';
'The man on the flying trapeze'
Oh, once in the saddle I used to go
dashing see 'The mowing ma-
chine'
Oh, once there was a ship sailin'
the northern counteree see
'The Golden Furnity'
O, once upon a time in Arkansas
see 'Arkansas traveler'
Oh, once was a horse and his name
was Bill see 'A horse named
Bill'
'Oh ono chrio' FL: Even at the dead
time of the night. 11
'Oh open the door, Lord Gregory'
FL: same. 11
Oh, Paddy dear and did you hear
the news that's goin' round see
'Wearing of the green'
O Parcy Reed has crozer taen see
'Hey sae green as the rashes
grow'
Oh, pedlar, pedlar, what's in thy
pack? see 'Robin Hood and the
pedlar'
'O perfect love' D. F. Bloomfield
and J. Barnby. FL: O perfect
love, all human thought transcend-
ing. 64
Oh, Peter, go ring them bells see

'Peter, go ring them bells'
Oh, pity Reuben Ranzo! see 'Reu-
ben Ranzo'
O po' Liza, po' gal see 'Liza
Jane'
O Polly dear, O Polly see 'High
Germany'
O Polly, love, O Polly, the rout
has now begun see 'High Ger-
many'
Oh! Potatoes they grow small over
there see 'Over there'
'O precious time' Martin Peerson.
FL: O precious time, created by
thy might. 26
'Oh promise me' Clement Scott and
Reginald De Koven. FL: Oh
promise me that someday you and
I. 1, 20
'O rare Turpin' FL: On Hounslow
Heath as I rode o'er. 25
Oh, rattle your bones, you skinny
old cayute see 'Hard luck'
'O redeemed' FL: Although you see
me going along so FLC: O re-
deemed, redeemed. 38
O repent sinner see 'The Chris-
tian's hymn of the Crucifixion'
Oh, rise up, Betsy Gordon, and it's
bring tae me my gun see
'Baron of Brackley'
Oh! rise up children, get your
crown see 'Oh! Holy Lord'
O rise you up, my pretty Polly
see 'Pretty Polly'
O rise you up, ye seven brothers
see 'Earl Brand'
O Robin-a-thrush he married a wife
see 'Robin-a-Thrush'
Oh, Rock-a my soul in the bosom
of Abraham see 'Rock-a my
soul'
O Rose the Red and White Lilly
see 'Rose the Red and White
Lilly'
Oh, rum diddle dum, diddle du,
diddle dum see 'The gypsy laddie'
Oh! run up, children, get your
crown see 'Love feast in
heaven'
'O Sally, my dear' FL: O Sally my
dear, shall I come up to see you.
11
O Sally my dear will you come up
to me see 'Sally my dear'
Oh, Sally, oh Sally, oh Sally, said
she see 'Fair Sally'

'Stay in the field'

Oh, stir the pudding, Peggy see 'Stir the pudding'

Oh stop and pull me on before see 'The little page boy'

'Oh! Susanna' Stephen Foster. FL: I come from Alabama with my banjo on my knee FLC: Oh! Susanna, don't you cry for me. 1, 25, 57, 67

Oh, sweet and lovely, lady, be good see 'Oh, lady be good'

'O sweet flower' John Cooper. FL: O sweet flower, O sweet flower too quickly fading. 26

Oh, sweet heaven see 'Sweet heaven'

Oh, sweet is the vale where the Mohawk gently glides see 'Bonnie Eloise'

Oh, sweet Rose-Marie see 'Rose Marie'

Oh, sweetheart Lona see 'San'

Oh, tain't what you do, it's the way that cha do it see 'Tain't what you do'

Oh, take me back to the old Transvaal see 'Sarie Marais'

O tell my Willie to come down see 'Dewy dewy dens of Yarrow'

Oh that girl, that pretty little girl see 'The girl I left behind me'

Oh, the band of Gideon see 'Gideon's band'

O, the barrin' o' oor door, weel! see 'Get up and bar the door'

Oh, the birds were singing, it was morning see 'Kitty Wells'

Oh, the boll weevil is a little black bug see 'The boll weevil'; 'The boll weevil song'

O the broom and the bonnie, bonnie broom see 'The maid of Cowdenknowes'

Oh, the bulldog on the bank see 'Bulldog and the bullfrog'

Oh, the buzzin' of the bees in the cigarette trees see 'The big rock candy mountain'

Oh, the candidate's a dodger see 'The dodger song'

Oh, the candidate's a dodger yes a well-known dodger see 'The dodger'

Oh, the court of King Carraticus is just passing by see 'The court of King Carraticus'

Oh, the cuckoo is a pretty bird see

'The cuckoo'

Oh the day that Jones made up his mind that he would wed a girl see 'La-didily-idily, umti-umti ay'

Oh, the devil he came to the farmer one day see 'The devil and the farmer's wife'

O the devil he came to the farmer's gate see 'Farmer's curst wife'

Oh the Devil he cam tae the man at the plow see 'The farmer's curst wife'

Oh, the eagles they fly high over Mobile see 'The eagles they fly high'

Oh, the E-ri-e was a-risin' see 'E-ri-e Canal'

Oh, the farmer comes to town see 'The farmer is the man'

O the first one along was the captain of the ship see 'The mermaid'

Oh, the games people play see 'Games people play'

O the girls they do grow tall in Kansas see 'For Kansas'

Oh, the grizzly grizzly grizzly bear see 'Grizzly bear'

Oh, the hinges are of leather see 'The little old sod shanty'

Oh, the hinges are of leather and the windows have no glass see 'Little old sod shanty on the plain'

Oh the holly bears a berry as white as the milk see 'The holly bears a berry'

'Oh, the horse went around' FL: same FLC: Next time we sing this verse. 68

Oh, the king and the tinker were at a great fair see 'The king and the tinker'

Oh, the Ladies Auxiliary is the auxiliary see 'Ladies Auxiliary'

Oh, the land I am bound for see 'Sweet Canaan'

Oh, the minstrels sing of an English king see 'Barsted King of England'

Oh the moment was sad when my love and I parted see 'Savourneen Deelish'

Oh, the moonlight's fair tonight along the Wabash see 'On the banks of the Wabash, far away'

Oh, the night that I struck New

Oh who will shoe your pretty little foot? see 'Who will shoe your pretty little foot?'

O who's dat yondah see 'Who's dat yondah?'

Oh, who's going to shoe my pretty little foot? see 'I'll hang my harp'

O, why did you leave your house and home? see 'Gypsy laddie'

Oh, why don't you work like other men do? see 'Hallelujah, I'm a bum'

Oh, why you runnin', sinner see 'In that great day'

Oh, wife, dear wife see 'Lamkin'

O, wife dearest wife see 'Our goodman'

Oh, will you go to the rolling of the stones see 'The rolling away of the stones'

O Willie, my son, what makes ye sae sad see 'Among the blue flowers and the yellow'; 'The blue flowers and the yellow'

Oh, Willie, take my highland shirt see 'The dying soldier'

O Willie's fair and Willie's rare see 'Willie's drowned at Gamery'; 'Willie's drowned in Yarrow'

Oh, Windy Bill was a Texas boy, and he could rope, you bet see 'Windy Bill'

Oh, wisna she a wily wily wife see 'The Duke of Athole's nurse'

Oh, wonce ven I vas single see 'Jakey jump der baby'

O won't those mourners rise and tell see 'Been down into the sea'

O won't you come in, my pretty little bird see 'Young Hunting'

Oh, won't you hear me when I call you see 'Down the line'

Oh won't you leave your house carpenter see 'The house carpenter'

'Oh, won't you sit down?' FL: Who's that yonder dressed red? FLC: Oh, won't you sit down? 34, 68

Oh Yankee Doodle, Doodle Dandy see 'The dog-meat man'

Oh ye pinks and posies see 'Blood-red roses'

Oh yeah, I'll tell you something I think you'll understand see 'I want to hold your hand'

Oh, yeah, just to marry her daughter see 'Old Aunt Dinah'

Oh, ye'll get a ladder, a long long ladder see 'The keach in the creel'

Oh, yes I am a Southern girl see 'The homespun dress'

Oh yes, isn't it tarnation strange see 'Tarnation strange'

'Oh yes! Oh yes!' FL: I come this night for to sing and pray. 38

O yonder he stands, and there he gangs see 'The laird o' Linne'

Oh, you can kiss me on a Monday, a Monday see 'Never on Sunday'

'Oh, you can't get to heaven' FL: same FLC: I ain't gonna grieve my Lord no more. 68

Oh, you can't scare me, I'm sticking to the union see 'Union maid'

Oh, you must answer my questions nine see 'The devil's nine questions'

Oh, you ought to been uptown see 'Train forty-five'

Oh, you sweet thing! see 'Chantilly Lace'

Oh, you take the high road see 'Loch Lomand'

Oh, you will hear the trumpet sound see 'My Lord, what a morning!'

'O young woman, beautiful young woman' FL: O ven aeg, ven aalin aeg. 11

Oh, you're welcome, home again, said the young man to his love see 'The lover's ghost'

O Zion, O Zion see 'The ten virgins'

Oh! Zion's children coming along see 'Zion's children'

'Oats, peas, beans, and barley grow' FL: same. 37

'Ob-la-di Ob-la-da' Lennon and McCartney. FL: Desmond has his barrow in the market place. 44

'October and November' Clara Louise Kessler. FL: Many days are bright in October. 13

The odds were a hundred to one against me see 'They all laughed'

'Ode for American independence' Daniel George and Horatio Garnet. FL: Tis done, the edict passed FLC: Fly! Fly! fly, swift-

'Old Blue' FL: I had a dog and his name was Blue. 25

'Old Blue' FL: I had an old dog and his name was Blue. 23

'Old Blue' FL: I raised a dog and his name was Blue. 57, 66

'The old brigade' Fred E. Weatherly and Odoardo Barri. FL: Where are the boys of the old brigade FLC: Then steadily shoulder to shoulder. 63

'The old Chisholm trail' FL: Come along boys, and listen to my tale FLC: Come a ti yi yippy yippy yi yippi yea. 19

'The old Chisholm Trail' FL: Come gather round me boy and I'll tell you a tale FLC: Come ti yi youpy, youpy ya, youpy ya. 2

'The old Chisholm Trail' FL: Oh come along boys, and listen to my tale FLC: Comma, ti-yi-youpy, youpy ya, youpy ya. 25

'The old Chisholm trail' FL: Well, come along, boys and listen to my tale FLC: Come a ti yi yippy, yippy yay, yippy yay. 4, 23, 57

'The old church yard' FL: Oh come, come with me to the old church-yard. 50

'Old colony times' FL: In good old colony times FLC: Because they could not sing. 1, 4

'The old cow died' FL: Did you send for the doctor FLC: The old cow died. 57, 72

An old cowpoke went riding out one dark and windy day see 'Riders in the sky'

An old cowpoke went riding to a rodeo one day see 'Bull riders in the sky'

'Old Dan Tucker' Daniel D. Emmett. FL: I come to town the other night FLC: So git out of the way, Old Dan Tucker. 1, 25

'Old Dan Tucker' FL: Went to town the other night FLC: Get out the way, Old Dan Tucker. 57

'Old Dandoo' FL: Old Dandoo come home from the plow, Dandoo. 11

The old devil came into a field one day see 'The farmer's curst wife'

The old devil came to me one day at the plow see 'Devil doings'

'Old dog Tray' Stephen Foster. FL: The morn of life is past FLC:

Old Dog Tray's ever faithful. 72

'Old dogs, children and watermelon wine' Tom T. Hall. FL: I was sittin' in Miami pourin' blended whiskey down. 10

The old English cause knocks at every man's door see 'An appeal to Loyalists'

'The old family toothbrush' FL: same. 68

'The old farmer in the countree' FL: There was an old farmer lived in the countree. 11

'Old folks at home' Stephen Foster. FL: Way down, upon the Swanee River FLC: All the world is sad and dreary. 1, 25

'Old friends' Paul Simon. FL: Old friends, old friends. 60

'Old Gospel ship' FL: I have good news to bring and that is why I sing FLC: I'm gonna take a trip on that old gospel ship. 57

'Old gray mare' FL: Oh, the old gray mare she ain't what she used to be FLC: Many long years ago. 23, 25, 57, 72

'The old grey goose' FL: Go tell Aunt Rhody. 48

'Old grumbler' FL: Old Grumbler ripped, Old Grumbler swore. 37

'Old Hannah' FL: Won't you go down old Hannah? 57

The old home town looks the same see 'Green green grass of home'

'Old horse' FL: Old horse, old horse, we'd have you know. 68

'The old house at home' FL: Oh, the old house at home. 7

'Old Hundred' FL: All people that on earth do dwell. 57

'Old Hundredth' William Kethe and Louis Bourgeois. FL: All people that on earth do dwell. 1

'Old Jimmy Johnson' FL: Old Jimmy Johnson rolled a jug around the hill. 7

'Old Joe Clark' FL: I never did like Old Joe Clark. 7

'Old Joe Clark' FL: I went up to old Joe's house FLC: Round and round, old Joe Clark. 25

'Old Joe Clark' FL: Old Joe Clark, the preacher's son FLC: Round and around, old Joe Clark. 25, 57

'Old Joe Clark' FL: Old Joe Clark's a rough old man FLC: Git out of

hill, there is a still. 23

'The old navy' FL: Oh, we don't
have to march like the infantry.
68

Old Noah he built himself an ark
see 'One more river'; 'One
more river to cross'

'The old oaken bucket' Samuel Woodworth and George Kiallmark. FL:
How dear to my heart are the
scenes of my childhood. 1, 25

'The old orange flute' FL: In the
country Tyronne near the town of
Dungannon. 57

'Old Paint' FL: Goodbye, Old Paint,
I'm a-leavin' Cheyenne. 23

'Old Pike' FL: I once knew a man
by the name of Pike FLC: Haul
off your coat, roll up your
sleeves. 37

'Old rattler' FL: Old Rattler was a
good old dog FLC: Here, Rattler,
help, help. 27, 57

'Old Rosin the beau' FL: I live for
the good of my nation FLC: Resemble old Rosin the Beau. 1

'The old rustic bridge by the mill'
FL: I'm thinking tonight of the
old rustic bridge FLC: Beneath
it the stream gently rippled. 25

'The old salt sea' FL: Well met,
well met, my own true love. 11

Old Satan tho't he had me fast see
'Wake up, children'

'The old Scotch well' FL: Light,
light, light, my little Scotch-ee.
11

'Old settler's song' FL: I've traveled
all over this country. 25

'The old ship of Zion' FL: Take up
to the land of glory FLC: Tis the
old ship of Zion. 25

'The old ship of Zion' FL: Tis the
old ship of Zion, hallelujah FLC:
I'm no ways weary. 5

'Old ship of Zion' FL: What ship is
that asailing. 38

Old Simon, the cellarer keeps a
large store see 'Simon the
Cellarer'

'Old Slew Foot' FL: High on a
mountain, tell me what do you
see FLC: He's big around the
middle and broad across the
rump. 14

'Old Soldiers never die' FL: There
is an old cookhouse not far away
FLC: Old soldiers never die. 57

'The old soldiers of the king' FL:
Since you all must have singing
and won't be said nay FLC:
We're the old soldiers of the
king. 8

'Old time cowboy' FL: Come all
you melancholy folks, wherever
you may be. 43

Old time pals and old time gals
see 'I wonder what's become of
Sally?'

'Old time religion' FL: Gimme that
old time religion. 57

Old Vanamburgh is the man that
runs these 'ere shows see
'Vanamburgh's menagerie'

'Old wetherskin' FL: I married a
wife in the month of June. 11

'Old Wichet' FL: I went into my
stable to see what I might see.
11

'Old Wichet' FL: She beats me,
she bangs me. 11

'Old Wichet' FL: Whose horse is
that horse, where my horse ought
to be? 11

'Old Wichet' FL: You old fool you
blind fool. 11

Old Windy Bill was a Texas guy
see 'Windy Bill'

'The old woman and her pig' FL:
There was an old woman and she
had a little pig. 72

'The old woman and the pedlar' FL:
There was a little woman. 48

'Old woman in Slab City' FL: There
was an old woman in Slab City
FLC: Sing ti vi-tee ann vee i
vee ay. 37

'The old woman of the North countree' FL: There was an old woman lived in North Countree. 11

Old woman, old woman, will you do
my washing? see 'The deaf woman's courtship'

'The old woman tossed up in a
blanket' FL: There was an old
woman tossed up in a blanket.
48

'Old woman under the hill' FL:
There was an old woman lived
under the hill. 11

'Ole Bangum' FL: Ole Bangum will
you hunt an' ride? 11

'Ole Buttermilk sky' Hoagy Carmichael and Jack Brooks. FL:
Ole Buttermilk sky, I'm keeping
my eye peeled on you. 64, 70

'Ole Dan Tucker' FL: Twas 'n ole
woman in Tennessee. 41
O-le, Oleanna see 'Oleanna'
'Ole San Fannie' FL: Ole San Fannie
had a pig, uh huh. 7
'Oleanna' Jerry Silverman. FL: Oh,
my fellow countrymen FLC: O-le,
Oleanna. 57
'Omega' Supply Belcher. FL: Come
thou almighty king. 65
'Omie Wise' FL: I'll tell you all a
story about poor Omie Wise.
35, 57
On a bright and summer's morning
see 'The deer song'
'On a clear day' Alan Jay Lerner
and Burton Lane. FL: same
FLC: same. 6, 42
On a dark stormy night, as the
train rattled on see 'In the
baggage coach ahead'
On a high holiday, on a high holi-
day see 'Little Mathy Groves'
'On a Monday' FL: On a Monday,
Monday I was arrested FLC:
Well it's all, almost done. 57
On a Monday morning it began to
rain see 'Jay Gould's daughter'
'On a raven black horse' Vladimir
Zakharov. FL: Na kone voro-
nom. 57
'On a raven black horse' Vladimir
Zakharov and Jerry Silverman.
FL: same. 57
'On a raven-black horse' FL: same
FLC: Hey joining up with his
force. 56
On a stormy sea as we set sail
see 'Our gallant ship'
'On a summer morning' Antonia
Ridge and F. W. Möller. FL:
When on a summer morning. 13
On a summer's day in the month of
May see 'The big rock candy
mountain'
On a summer's day while the waves
were rippling see 'The ship
that never returned'
'On a Sunday afternoon' Andrew B.
Sterling and Harry von Tilzer.
FL: There's a day we feel gay
FLC: On a Sunday afternoon.
20, 31
On a Sunday morn, sat a maid for-
lorn see 'Wait till the sun
shines Nellie'
On Afric's wide plains where the
lion now roaring see 'The

desponding Negro'
'On and on' FL: Travelin' down this
long and lonesome highway FLC:
On and on I'll follow my darling.
14
On Armistice Day the Philharmonic
will play see 'Armistice Day'
On board of a ship and away sailed
he see 'The beggar man'
On board of the ship and away
sailed he see 'Hind Horn or
the beggarman'
'On board the Gallee' FL: In London
there dwelt a fair damsel. 30
On Calvert's plains new faction
reigns see 'The Maryland resolves'
On ching chong opium, taffy on a
stick see 'The Chinee laundryman'
On Christmas Day in '76 see 'The
battle of Trenton'
'On Erin's green shore' FL: One
evening for pleasure I rambled.
7
On Friday morning as we set sail
see 'The mermaid'
On Good Friday morning our ship
set sail see 'The mermaid'
On Houslow Heath as I rode o'er
see 'O rare Turpin'
'On Ilkla moor baht hat' FL: Where
hast thou been since I saw thee?
FLC: On Ilkla Moor baht hat.
25
On Ilkley Moor baht 'at see
'Ilkley Moor'
'On independence' Jonathan Mitchell
Sewall. FL: Come all you brave
soldiers, both valiant and free.
55
On Jordan's stormy banks I stand
see 'Bound for the Promised
Land'; 'I am bound for the
Promised Land'
On Monday he gave me the light of
love see 'Let my little light
shine'
On Monday morning at twelve
o'clock see 'Willie's drowned
in Gamrie'
On Monday morning going to school
see 'The two brothers'
'On Mondays I never go to work'
FL: same. 57
On mules we find two legs behind
see 'Mules'
'On music' FL: To music be the

ILGWU'

'One bottle of pop' FL: same. 68

One bright day in the month of May
see 'Barbara Allen'

One caress, happiness see 'My
honey's lovin' arms'

One Christmas Eve, the night was
dark see 'The wreck at Maud'

One cold and cloudy day in the
month of May see 'Barbara
Allen'

One dark and stormy winter's night
see 'The sailor boy'

One day a father to his little son
see 'Shall I be an angel, Daddy?'

One day a gypsy showed me golden
earrings see 'Golden earrings'

One day a little fat boy came walking in the store see 'Dunderbeck'

One day an honest working girl was
thirsty as could be see 'The
honest working girl'

One day as I rambled, down by the
sea shore see 'I never will
marry'

One day as I strolled down by the
Royal Albion see 'The young
sailor cut down in his prime'

One day as I wandered see 'Life
is a toil'

One day as I went o'er the plain
see 'The wee wee man'

One day I thought I'd have some fun
see 'Bronco buster'; 'The tenderfoot'

One day I was setting in my father's
hall see 'The cruel mother'

One day I was walking I heard a
complaining see 'The housewife's lament'

One day, I was walking in Strawberry Lane see 'Strawberry
Lane'

One day I'se a-walking along see
'Done been sanctified'

One day it rained in our town see
'Sir Hugh of Lincoln'

One day, one day I was walking
along see 'Long John'

One day, one day, one day, one
day see 'Crooked-foot John'

One day, one day, one fine holiday
see 'Lyttle Musgrave'

One day, one day, one high holiday
see 'Little Musgrave and Lady
Bana Barnard'

One day, one day, one holi whole

day see 'Little Musgrave and
Lady Barnard'

One day the Depression was over
see 'Soup song'

One day the old devil he came to
my plow see 'Hi lum day'

One day when I was sailing see
'The crocodile'

One day you'll look to see I've gone
see 'I'll follow the sun'

One dream in my heart see 'This
nearly was mine'

One duck on a pond see 'Ducks
on a pond'

One evening as a maid did walk
see 'The trooper and maid'

One evening as I walked out see
'Lowlands of Holland'

One evening for pleasure I rambled
see 'The blooming bright star
of Belle Isle'; 'On Erin's green
shore'

One evening last June as I wandered
see 'The little Eau Plaine'

One evening, one evening see
'The two brothers'

One evening, one evening, one evening, in May see 'Kind fortune'

One evening, one evening, one evening, so fair see 'The nightingale'

One evening two brothers was going
from school see 'The two
brothers'

One fine day as I was walking down
the street see 'May the bird
of paradise fly up your nose'

'One for my baby' Johnny Mercer
and Harold Arlen. FL: It's
quarter to three. 70

One Friday morn a ship set sail
see 'The stormy winds do blow'

One Friday morn, as we set sail
see 'The mermaid'

One frosty day on pleasure bent I
strolled into the park see 'Matilda Toots'

One great vision unites us see
'World youth song'

'One hand, one heart' Stephen Sondheim and Leonard Bernstein.
FL: Make of our hands, one hand.
6

'One happy Swede' Donna Shwarz-
rock. FL: Aye ban a farmer in
Minnesota. 19

One high, one high, one high holiday see 'Matty Groves'

One hogmany, at Glesca Fair see
'Rothesay-o'
'100 psalm tune new' John Tufts.
FL: With one consent let all. 65
148th Psalm' FL: From heaven O
praise the Lord! 65
'The one I love' Gus Kahn and Isham
Jones. FL: I'm unhappy, so un-
happy FLC: The one I love belongs
to somebody else. 54
One kiss from you, my own sweet-
heart see 'Cold blows the wind'
One little story that the crow told
me see 'The story the crow
told me'
One little, two little, three little
see 'Ten little kiddies'
One low, one low, one holiday see
'Little Mattie'
'One man shall mow my meadow'
FL: same. 32
'One meat ball' FL: There was a
man went up and down. 25
One misty moisty morning see
'The old man clothed in leather'
One Monday morn, in the month of
May see 'Barbara Allen'
One Monday morning, a landlord
went see 'Dry weather houses'
One Monday morning a-going to
school see 'The two brothers'
'One more day' FL: Only one more
day, my Johnny. 25
'One more river' FL: Old Noah he
built himself an ark FLC:
There's one more river to cross.
57, 68, 72
'One more river to cross' FL: Old
Noah, he built himself an ark
FLC: There's one more river.
25, 34
'One more try' Mick Jagger and
Keith Richard. FL: You need
some money in a hurry when
things ain't right. 16
One morning early in the May see
'Barb'ra Allen'
One morning I was a-walking around
see 'Nobody knows the trouble
I've seen'
One morning in a little tailor's shop
I saw see 'You've got a long
way to go'
One morning in June Sweet William
arose see 'Sweet William'
'One morning in May' FL: One
morning, one morning, one
morning in May. 7, 57

'One morning in May' Mitchell
Parish and Hoagy Carmichael.
FL: The world over was blue
clover FLC: One morning in May.
12
One morning in the month of May
see 'Barbara Allen'
One morning, one morning, just
before it was day see 'The
cruel ship's carpenter, or the
Gosport tragedy'
One morning, one morning, one
morning in May see 'The night-
ingale song'; 'One morning in
May'
One night as I lay on my bed see
'The mermaid'
One night as I lay on my bed a-
sleep see 'Go from my window'
One night, as I lay on my bed, I
lay both warm and at ease see
'The mermaid'
One night I went up in a balloon
see 'Up in a balloon'
One night just as the sun went
down see 'Big rock candy
mountain'
One night, one night Lady Margaret
was sitting by window see
'Sweet William's ghost'
One night when the winds blew cold
see 'Mary on the wild moor'
One of fair Scotland's daughters
see 'Captain Wedderburn's
courtship'
'One of the deathless army' T. W.
Thurban, Gilbert Wells, Will
Terry and V. R. Gill. FL: I am
a bolger sold--I mean I'm a
soldier bold FLC: For I'm a sol-
dier, a Territorial. 17
One of these mornings, bright and
fair see 'Great day'
One old woman, Lord, in this town
see 'Oh, babe, it ain't no lie'
One springtime I thought just for
fun see 'The tenderfoot'
One stormy night, when we set sail
see 'The mermaid'
One was buried in the chancel top
see 'Lord Thomas and Fair
Eleanour'
'Onkel Jakob' FL: Onkel Jakob,
Onkel Jakob. 34
Only a miner killed under the ground
see 'Miner's farewell'
'Only a rose' Brian Hooker and
Rudolph Friml. FL: Red rose

one night. 11
'Our goodman' FL: What's this man's
horse a-doing here. 11
'Our goodman came home at e'en'
FL: same. 11
Our king built a ship, twas a ship
of great fame see 'Captain
Ward and the rainbow'
Our king has wrote a long letter
see 'Lord Derwentwater'
Our lords are to the mountains gane
see 'Hughie Graham'
'Our old tom cat' W. Clifton. FL:
It oft was told me by my dad. 36
Our 'prentice Tom may now refuse
see 'Over the hills and far away'
'Out in the meadows' FL: Out in the
meadows the grain has been crad-
led. 13
Our romance won't end on a sorrow-
ful note see 'They can't take
that away from me'
Our ship she was a-sailing to some
foreign counteree see 'The
Golden Vanity'
Ours was a love song that seemed
constant as the moon see 'The
breeze and I'
Out amongst the flowers sweet see
'Hearts and flowers'
'Out in the cold world, or Bring
back my wandering boy' FL: Out
in the cold world and far away
from home FLC: Oh bring back
to me my wandering boy. 14
Out from the lands of Orient see
'Sir Donkey'
Out in the gloomy night, sadly I
roam see 'Father's a drunkard
and mother is dead'
Out in the west Texas town of El
Paso see 'El Paso'
Out of doorways black umbrellas
come to pursue me see 'Yesterday I heard the rain'
'Out of nowhere' Edward Heyman
and Johnny Green. FL: When I
least expected FLC: You came to
me. 53
Out of the tree of life I just picked
a plum see 'The best is yet to
come'
'Out of this world' Johnny Mercer
and Harold Arlen. FL: You're
clear out of this world. 70
'Out of time' Mick Jagger and Keith
Richard. FL: You don't know
what's going on FLC: You thought

you were a clever girl. 16
Out on the plains see 'Cow-cow
boogie'
Out then spak his auld father see
'Johnie Scot'
'The outlandish knight' FL: From
the North lands there came a
Northering knight. 11
'The outlandish knight' FL: Give me
some of your dada's gold. 30
'The outlandish knight' FL: He fol-
lowed me up and he followed me
down. 11
'The outlandish knight' FL: O the
outlandish knight came from the
North land. 11
'The outlandish knight' FL: An out-
landish knight came from the
North lands. 11
'The outlandish knight' FL: An out-
landish knight from the northern
land. 11
'The outlandish knight' FL: There
was a knight came from the
Northland. 11
'The outlandish knight' FL: There
was a rich nobleman I've heard
tell. 11
An outlandish knight from the North
counterie see 'The robber and
the lady'
'The over courteous knight' FL:
Yonder comes a courteous knight.
11
Over hill, over dale see 'The
caissons go rolling along'
Over the ground lies a mantle of
white see 'Winter wonderland'
Over the ground there comes a
sound see 'The riff song'
'Over the hills and far away' FL:
Our 'prentice Tom may now re-
fuse FLC: Over the hills and
o'er the main. 40
'Over the hills and far away' FL:
Tom he was a piper's son. 48
'Over the hills and far away' John
Gay. FL: Were I laid on Green-
land's coast FLC: And I would
love you all the day. 1
Over the hills, beautiful hills see
'West Virginia hills'
Over the hills I went one day see
'The foggy dew'
'Over the meadows' Augustus D.
Zanzig. FL: Over the meadows,
green and wide. 13
Over the mountains and over the

Peter on the sea, sea, sea. 5
'Peter Parker' FL: My lords, with
your leave an account I will give.
8
Peter, Peter, Peter on the sea,
sea, sea see 'Peter on the sea'
'Petticoats of Portugal' Michael Durso, Mel Mitchell and Murl Kahn.
FL: When the breezes blow petticoats of Portugal. 52
'Phfft! you are gone' (gospel version) Susan Heather. FL: Take
money or God you can't serve
two masters FLC: Where, oh
where where would I be! 14
'Phfft! you were gone!' Susan Heather. FL: I miss you so much
the 'taters need diggin' FLC:
Where, oh, where are you tonight? 14
'Photograph' George Harrison and
Richard Starkey. FL: Every
time I see your face. 64
'Piccolo Pete' Phil Baxter. FL:
Did you ever hear Peter go FLC:
same. 12
'Pick a bale a cotton' FL: Well it's
never will I pick a bale a cotton
FLC: How in the world can I pick
a bale a cotton? 28
'Pick a bale of cotton' FL: Gonna
jump down, turn around. 57
'Pick a bale of cotton' FL: You got
to jump down FLC: Jump down,
turn around. 66
'Pick a bale of cotton' FL: You got
to jump down, turn around FLC:
Oh, Lawdy, pick a bale of cotton.
25
'Pick a bale of cotton' FL: You got
to jump down, turn around FLC:
Oh, Mandy, pick a bale of cotton.
34
'Pick yourself up' Dorothy Fields
and Jerome Kern. FL: Nothing's
impossible, I have found. 67
Picture you upon my knee see 'Tea
for two'
Picture yourself in a boat on a river
with tangerine trees and marmalade skies see 'Lucy in the sky
with diamonds'
'Pie in the sky' Joe Hill. FL: Long-
haired preachers come out every
night FLC: You will eat by and by.
4
'Piece of my heart' Bert Berns and
Jerry Ragovoy. FL: Come on,

come on, come on, come on.
15
'Piece of my heart' Bert Berns and
Jerry Ragovoy. FL: Didn't I
make you feel like you were the
only man. 45
'Pig in a pen' FL: Goin' up on a
mountain FLC: I got a pig at
home in a pen. 14
'Pinkville helicopter' Tom Parrott.
FL: As they flew over Pinkville
the choppers could see. 4
'The pirate ship' FL: There was a
little ship and she sailed on the
sea. 11
'The pirates' FL: Down in old England there lived three brothers.
11
'Pistol packin' Mama' Al Dexter.
FL: Drinkin' beer in a cabaret
FLC: Lay that pistol down, Babe.
67
'Pitty patty polt' FL: same. 48
Pity me, my darling see 'The
factory girl'
'The place where my love Johnnie
dwells' FL: The sun shines high
on yonder hill. 11
A plague of those musty old lubbers
see 'Nothing like grog'
'Plaisir d'amour' FL: Delights of
love endure only for a day. 25
'Plaisir d'amour' Giovanni Martini.
FL: The joys of love seem like
a moment or two. 23
'Plaisir d'amour' Jean Paul Martino.
FL: Plaisir d'amour ne dure qu'un
moment. 23, 57
'Planting rice' FL: Planting rice is
never fun FLC: Planting rice is
no fun. 19
'Plastic Jesus' FL: I don't care if
it rains or freezes. 57
'Platonia' FL: You gaze at this pic-
ture with wondering eyes. 43
'Plato's advice' FL: Says Plato, why
should man be vain? 3
'Play, fiddle, play' Jack Lawrence,
Emery Deutsch and Arthur Alt-
man. FL: Sing my loved one a
rhapsody FLC: Play, fiddle, play.
12
Play it once and once again see
'Two guitars'
'Play with fire' Nanker Phelge.
FL: Well, you've got your dia-
monds. 16
'Please' Leo Robin and Ralph Rainger.

FL: Are you listening FLC:
Please lend your ear to my pleas.
53
Please allow me to introduce myself
see 'Sympathy for the Devil'
'Please don't talk about me when I'm
gone' Sidney Clare, Sam H. Stept
and Bee Palmer. FL: Years
we've been together FLC: Please
don't talk about me when I'm
gone. 46
'Please don't tell me how the story
ends' Kris Kristofferson. FL:
This could be our last goodnight
together. 10
Please forgive this platitude see
'Fine and dandy'
Please give me your attention and
I'll introduce you see 'Mister
Black'
'Please go home' Mick Jagger
and Keith Richard. FL:
Well, maybe I'm talking too
fast. 16
'Please help me I'm falling' Don
Robertson and Hal Blair. FL:
Please help me I'm falling in
love with you. 10
Please lend your ear to my pleas
see 'Please'
Please lock me away and don't al-
low the day see 'World without
love'
Please, pretty little dove see
'Cu-cu-rru-cu-cu, Paloma'
Please release me, let me go see
'Release me'
Please take your shoes off and make
yourself comfortable see 'Don't
go out into the rain'
Please tell me why the stars do
shine see 'Tell me why'
Pleased to meet you, hope you
guess my name see 'Sympathy
for the Devil'
'Plumb the line' FL: Well-a I'm
so glad I can plumb the line.
28
Po' li'l Liza, po' gal see 'Liza
in the summertime'
'Po' me' FL: The Lord is on the
giving hand FLC: Why brthering,
po' me. 5
'The poacher' FL: When I was bound
apprentice in famous Lincolnshire.
25
'A poem on the underground wall'
Paul Simon. FL: The last train

is nearly due. 60
Poets may sing of their Helicon
streams see 'The federal con-
stitution and liberty forever'
Pois eu fazeruma prece see 'The
constant rain'
'Poisoning the students' minds' FL:
The student Y has found a new
vocation. 57
Poll, dang it, how d'ye do? see
'The sailor boy capering ashore'
'Polly Ply' FL: If ever a tailor was
fond of good sport. 3
Polly, pretty Polly, come go along
with me see 'Pretty Polly'
'Polly put the kettle on' FL: same.
25, 48
'Polly said she loved me' FL:
Polly said she loved me, but yet
she told a fib! 22
'Polly Wolly Doodle' FL: I went
down south to see my Sal FLC:
Fare thee well, fare thee well.
57
'Polly Wolly Doodle' FL: Oh, I
went down South for to see my
Sal FLC: Fare thee well, fare
thee well. 25, 68
Poluishkopoli dy see 'Meadowland'
'A poor anxious woman' FL: A poor
anxious woman sat watching one
day her husband. 41
'Poor boy' FL: As I walked into the
depot, boy. 28
'Poor boy' FL: As I went down to
the river, poor boy FLC: Bow
down your head and cry, poor
boy. 23
'Poor boy' FL: As I went down to
the river, poor boy FLC: Hang
down your head and cry, poor
boy. 57
Poor city, Babylon's falling to rise
no more see 'Babylon's falling'
'Poor Ellen Smith' FL: Poor Ellen
Smith, how she was found. 57
'Poor gal didn't know' John Cooke.
FL: My sister's about the most
simple of girls FLC: But the
poor girl didn't know. 36
'Poor hard workin' miners, their
troubles are great see 'Miner's
farewell'
'Poor Howard' FL: Poor Howard's
dead and gone. 57
'Poor Jack' FL: Go patter to lubbers and swabs, do ye see. 3
Poor Jesse had a wife to mourn for

his life see 'Jesse James'
'Poor Lazarus' FL: High sheriff he
tol' the deputy. 57
'Poor little Jesus' FL: Poor little
Jesus, yeah Lord FLC: Ain't that
a pity and a shame, O Lord. 33
Poor little turtle dove settin' on a
pine see 'Turtle dove'
'Poor man's blues' FL: I never had
a barrel of money FLC: Lord,
this son ain't nothin'. 57
'Poor man's heaven' FL: Kind friends,
gather near, I want you to hear
FLC: In poor man's heaven we'll
have our own way. 57
Poor Sally was sick see 'The
death of Queen Jane'
'The poor soldier' FL: I'll tell you
of a soldier who lately came
from sea. 11
'The poor soldier' FL: There was a
bold soldier that lately came from
sea. 11
A poor soul say sighing by a sycamore see 'The willow song'
The poor soul sat sighing see
'Willow willow'
'Poor Tom or the sailor's epitaph'
FL: Here, a sheer hulk lies poor
Tom Bowling. 3
A poor unworthy son who dared
see 'Gambling on the Sabbath
day'
'Poor wayfaring stranger' FL: I'm
just a poor wayfaring stranger.
1, 34
'The poor working girl' FL: The
poor working girl, may heaven
protect her. 4
'Pop! goes the weasel' FL: All
around the cobbler's bench. 1,
57, 72
'Pop goes the weasel' FL: All around
the mulberry bush. 4
'Pop goes the weasel' FL: When de
night walks in as black as a
sheep FLC: Pop goes the weasel.
36
'Popcorn song' Nancy Byrd Turner
and Marlys Swinger. FL: Sing a
song of popcorn. 13
'The popular Wobbly' T. Bone Slim.
FL: I'm as mild mannered man
as can be. 57
Por aquí pasó una pava see 'Jeu,
Jeu!'
'Pore Jud' Oscar Hammerstein and
Richard Rodgers. FL: Pore Jud

is daid. 24
'The Portland County jail' FL: I'm
a stranger to your city. 57
Portugal, Lisbon was gay in the
moonlight see 'Lisbon Antigua'
'Potato harvest' Constance Rumbough. FL: Dig, oh dig with
pick and spade. 13
'Powder River, let 'er buck' FL:
Powder River, let 'er buck, a
surgin' mass of cattle. 43
Praise God, from whom all bless-
ings flow see 'The Doxology'
'Praise the Lord and pass the am-
munition!' Frank Loesser. FL:
Down went the gunner, a bullet
was his fate FLC: Praise the
Lord and pass the ammunition.
70
'The praties they grow small' FL:
Oh, the praties they grow small
over here. 57
Pray, can you buy me an acre or
more see 'A true lover of
mine'
'Pray on' FL: I washed my head in
the midnight dew FLC: Pray on,
brothers. 5
Pray on, pray on, pray on see
'In the river of Jordan'
'Prayer of Thanksgiving' Theodore
Baker. FL: We gather together
to ask the Lord's blessing. 1,
25
'The preacher and the slave' Joe
Hill. FL: Long-haired preachers
come out every night FLC: You
will eat by and by. 19, 57
'Prehistoric man' Richard Temple,
Jr. and C. G. Cotes. FL: I'm
really very harmless, no one
need have any fears FLC: And
I'm on show in the daytime, I'm
off show at night. 17
'Prepare us' FL: As I go down the
stream of time FLC: Prepare me,
prepare me. 38
'Prepare ye' Stephen Schwartz. FL:
Prepare ye the way of the Lord.
64
Press along, cowboy, press along
see 'The big corral'
'The press gang' FL: There was a
rich merchant in London did
dwell. 30
The press gang came quickly round
see 'Lang Johnnie Moir'
The prettiest gal I ever saw see

'Sucking cider through a straw'
The prettiest girl I ever saw see
'Sippin' cider thru a straw'
'Prettiest little baby in the country-
o' FL: What are we gonna do
with the baby-o. 57
'Pretty Dinah Snow' M. H. Drummond. FL: Oh, darkies, give
attention FLC: Oh! my witching
Dinah Snow. 63
A pretty fair maid out in the garden
see 'The sailor and the maid'
'A pretty fair miss' FL: A pretty
fair miss, all in a garden. 7,
61
'The pretty girl milking her cow'
FL: Twas on a bright morning in
summer. 25
Pretty is the story I hae to tell
see 'Young Logie'
Pretty little Flo was jealous of her
beau see 'When grown up
ladies act like babies'
'Pretty little horses' FL: Hush you
by. 48
'The pretty Mohea' FL: As I went
out walking for pleasure one day.
7
'Pretty Nancy' FL: As I sat down
to muse awhile. 11
'Pretty Polly' FL: Go bring me
some of your father's gold. 11
'Pretty Polly' FL: Go get me some
of your father's gold. 11
'Pretty Polly' FL: He followed her
up, he followed her down. 11
'Pretty Polly' FL: He mounted on
his milk white steed. 11
'Pretty Polly' FL: Hush, hush, my
pretty Polly dear. 11
'Pretty Polly' FL: I courted pretty
Polly the livelong night. 57
'Pretty Polly' FL: Mount up, mount
up, my pretty Polly. 11
'Pretty Polly' FL: O rise you up,
my pretty Polly. 11
'Pretty Polly' FL: Polly, pretty
Polly, come go along with me.
14
'Pretty Polly' FL: There was a
lord in Ambertown. 11
'Pretty Polly Ann' FL: He follered
me up, he follered me down.
11
Pretty Polly hadn't been married
but a very short time see 'The
wife of Usher's well'
'Pretty Polly, or the Scotland man'

FL: Come in, come in, my pret-
ty little bird. 11
Pretty Polly, she mounted her milk
white steed see 'Lady Isabel
and the elf knight'
Pretty Polly went out one day see
'The keach in the creel'
'Pretty Sally' FL: A beautiful damsel, from London came she. 7
'Pretty Sally' FL: A sailor came
over, came over he came. 30
'Pretty Sally' FL: A squire from
Dover, a squire he came. 30
'Pretty Sally' FL: There was a
beautiful damsel, from London
she came. 11
'Pretty Sally' FL: There was a rich
lady, from, Ireland she came.
11
'Pretty Sally' FL: There was a rich
lady, from London she came.
11
'Pretty Sally of London' FL: There
was a young lady. 11
'Pretty Saro' FL: Down in some
lone valley. 57
Prices goin' higher, yes, way up
higher see 'High-price blues'
'The prickle holly bush' FL: O and
dear judge. 11
'The prickly bush' FL: O hangman,
hold thy hand, he cried FLC:
Oh the prickly bush, the prickly
bush. 11
'The prickly briar' FL: O the prickly briar. 11
'The prick'ty bush' FL: Oh, dear
John, stand here FLC: Oh, the
prick'ty bush. 11
'The pride of Glencoe' FL: As I
went out walking one evening of
late. 30
'Pride of the prairie' FL: On the
wild and woolly prairie FLC:
Pride of the prairie, Mary, my
own. 43
'The primrose girl' FL: Come buy
of poor Kate primroses I sell.
3
'Primroses' James Hewitt. FL:
Come, buy of poor Kate, primroses I sell. 65
'Prince Charlie' FL: What loo is
that, quoth the brave Lor' Heel.
11
Prince or pauper, beggarman or
king see 'Dandelion'
'Prison bound' FL: It was early one

mornin'. 57

'A prisoner for life' FL: Farewell, green fields, soft meadows adieu! 23, 57

'Prisoner of love' Leo Robin, Clarence Gaskell and Russ Columbo. FL: Someone that I belong to FLC: Alone from night to night, you'll find me. 47, 53

'Promises, promises' Hal David and Burt Bacharach. FL: same. 6, 42

'Proshchai' FL: Proshchai ty novaya derevnya. 57

'A proud Irish lady' FL: A proud Irish lady from London she came. 11

Proud Maisrie stands at her bower door see 'The Gairdner child'

'Proud Mary' J. C. Fogerty. FL: Left a good job in the city FLC: Big wheel keep on turnin'. 71

'Proud Nancy' FL: As I roved out one evening, it happened in the month of May. 30

'The provost's dochter' FL: The provost's dochter went out a walking. 11

'The public spirit of the women' FL: Though age at my elbow has taken his stand. 49

'Puff, the magic dragon' Peter Yarrow and Leonard Lipton. FL: Puff the magic dragon lived by the sea FLC: same. 45

Pull off, pull off, the haulin' shirt see 'The two brothers'

Pull off that silk, my pretty Polly see 'Lady Isabel and the elf knight'

The puncher being cold, he went up to bed see 'Button Willow tree'

'Punchin' the dough' Henry Herbert Knibb and Jules Verne Allen. FL: Come all you young waddies I'll sing you a song. 2

'Punky's dilemma' Paul Simon. FL: Wish I was a Kellogg's cornflake. 60

'The puppy dog song' Plough Boys. FL: Oh, Mama, look. 13

'The purple people eater' Sheb Wooley. FL: Well, I saw the thing a-comin' out of the sky FLC: It was a one-eyed, one-horned, flyin', purple, people eater. 10

'Pussy cat high, Pussy cat low' FL: same. 48

'Pussy cat, pussy cat' FL: Pussy cat, pussy cat, where have you been. 72

'Pussy cat, pussy cat where have you been?' FL: same. 48

Pussycat, Pussycat, I've got flowers and lots of hours see 'What's new pussycat?'

'Put my little shoes away' FL: Come and bathe my forehead, Mother. 14

'Put on a happy face' Lee Adams and Charles Strouse. FL: Gray skies are gonna clear up FLC: same. 6, 42

Put on the skillet, put on the led see 'Short'nin' bread'

'Put your little foot' FL: Put your little foot, put your little foot. 43

Put your sweet lips a little closer to the phones see 'He'll have to go'

'Putting on the style' FL: Two wheels around a corner FLC: Putting on the agony. 34

'Putting on the style' FL: Young man in a roadster FLC: Puttin' on the agony. 23, 57

- Q -

'The Quaker's courtship' FL: Once there was a Quaker lover 57

'The Quartermaster's store' FL: There is beer, beer, beer that makes you feel so queer FLC: Mine eyes are dim, I cannot see. 57

'Que bonita bandera' FL: Azul blanca y colorada FLC: Que bonita bandera. 56, 57

Que bonitos ojos tienes see 'Malagueña salerosa'

Que será, será see 'Whatever will be, will be'

Queen Eleanor was a sick woman see 'Earl Marshall'

'Queen Jane' FL: King Henry was sent for. 11

'Queen Jane' FL: Queen Jane lay in labor for six weeks. 57

'Queen Jane' FL: Queen Jane, O! Queen Jane O! what a lady was she! 11

'Queen Jane' FL: Queen Jane sat at her window one day. 11

'Queen Jane' FL: Queen Jane was in

labor. 11

Queen Jane lay in labor full nine days or more see 'The death of Queen Jane'

Queen Jane was in labor see 'The death of Queen Jane'

'Queen Jean' FL: Queen Jean, she was sick and they thocht she was dee. 11

'Queen Jeanie' FL: Queen Jeanie, Queen Jeanie, traveled six weeks or more. 11

'Queen Mary's farewell to France' FL: O! thou loved country, where my youth was spent. 3

'The Queen of Elfan's nourice' FL: I heard a cow low, a bonnie cow low. 11

'Queen of Hearts' FL: She's the Queen of Hearts. 23

'The Queen of Hearts' FL: To the Queen of Hearts goes the Ace of Sorrow. 57

'The 'Queen of Russia' and the 'Prince of Wales'' FL: There was two ships from old England came. 11

Quiéreme mucho dulce amor mío see 'Yours'

Quiero cantarte, mujer, mi más bonita canción see 'Marie Elena'

Quiero que vivas sóla see 'Frenesi'

- R -

Ra diddle ding, diddle ding, ding dey see 'The lady's disgrace'

'Rabbit ain't got' FL: Rabbit ain't got no tail at all. 72

Rabbit twitched his twichety ears see 'Hurry, hurry, hurry'

'Rabbit-foot blues' FL: Blues jumped a rabbit and he ran a solid mile. 57

Raccoons up in the simmon tree see 'Bile them cabbage down'

'The race horse' FL: See the course thronged with gazers. 3

'The race is on' Don Rollins. FL: I feel tears wellin' up cold and deep inside. 10

'Racing with the moon' Vaughn, Monrie, Pauline Pope and Johnny Watson. FL: Racing with the moon high up in the midnight blue.

59

Raddle, daddle, ding ding, ding, ding, ding see 'Gypsy Davy'

Raddle tee a tow row ree see 'Jolly beggar'

Raddle up a dinklium, a dinktum, a dinktum see 'It was late in the night when Johnny came home'

Raddleee a tow row ray see 'The jolly beggar'

'The ragged beggarman' FL: It's of a ragged beggarman came tripping o'er the plain. 11

'The raggle taggle gypsies oh' FL: Last night three gypsies came to my door. 11

'The raging sea, how it roars' FL: It's nine times around, said the captain of the ship. 11

'The ragtail gypsies oh!' FL: Now three gypsies once came begging at my door. 11

'Railroad Bill' FL: Once he got himself a B.B. gun FLC: Railroad Bill, Railroad Bill. 23, 25

'Railroad Bill' FL: Railroad Bill, Railroad Bill. 14, 35, 57

'A railroader for me' FL: Now I would not marry a blacksmith FLC: A railroader, a railroader. 57

'Rain' Lennon and McCartney. FL: If the rain comes they run and hide their heads. 44

The rain is cold and slowly falling see 'I wonder where you are tonight'

'The rain rins down' FL: The rain rins down thro' Mirry-lant toune. 11

'The rain rins down through Mirry-land toune see 'Little Sir Hugh'

The rain was a song see 'With the wind and the rain in your hair'

'Raindrops keep fallin' on my head' Hal David and Burt Bacharach. FL: same. 71

Raindrops on roses and whiskers on kittens see 'My favorite things'

'Raise a ruckus' FL: My old master said to me FLC: Come along, little children, come along. 35

'Raise a ruckus tonight' FL: My old master promised me FLC: Come along, little children, come along. 57, 58

'Raise 'em up higher' FL: Raise 'em
up higher, higher, drop 'em down.
28
Raised up in Louisville, a city you
all know well see 'Louisville
burglar'
'Raisin and almonds' FL: I was only
a tiny sleepy head. 23
Rajando la leña está see 'Má
Teodora'
'Rake and rambling boy' FL: Well,
I'm a rake and a rambling boy.
57
'Rakes of Mallow' FL: Beauing,
belleing, dancing, drinking. 25
Rally cum a ringum ringum ray
see 'Gypsy Davy'
'Rambling blues' FL: Rambling
around your city. 57
'The rambling gambler' FL: I'm a
rambling gambler FLC: I'm a
rambler, I'm a gambler. 23, 25
'El rancho grande' FL: Allá en el
rancho grande. 51
'El rancho grande' Bartley Costello
and Silvano R. Ramos. FL:
Give me my ranch and my cattle
FLC: I love to roam out yonder.
9
'El rancho grande' Silvano R. Ramos.
FL: Te voy hacer tus calzones
FLC: Allá en el rancho grande.
9
The ranks of the prophet are hardy
and bold see 'Abdullah Bulbul
Amir'
'The rantin laddie' FL: Aften hae I
played at the cards and the dice.
11
'The rantin laddie' FL: My father
feed me far far awa. 11
'The rantin laddie' FL: Oft hae I
played at the cards and dice. 11
'Rap tap tap' FL: O, me master went
to market as farmers used to do.
57
'Rare Willie drowned in Yarrow'
FL: Willie's fair, and Willie's
rare. 50
Rastsvetali yablonii grushi see
'Katiushka'
'Ration blues' FL: Well, I wonder
what's the matter, what's the
matter with Captain Mac. 28
Rattle dattle dum, dattle dum, dattle dum see 'Gypsy Daisy'
'Rattler' FL: Whoa, Rattler was a
mighty dog. 28

'Rattler' FL: Won't you here, here,
Rattler. 28
'Razors in the air' B. Maxwell.
FL: Come, my love, and go with
me FLC: Hoe de corn. 69
'The real American folk song'
George and Ira Gershwin. FL:
Near Barcelona the peasant
croons FLC: The real American
folk song is a rag. 21
'Real old mountain dew' FL: Let
grasses grow and waters flow.
57
Reared midst the war empurpled
plain see 'Death song of an
Indian chief'
'The rebel girl' Joe Hill. FL:
There are women of many de-
scriptions FLC: That's the rebel
girl. 57, 58
'The rebels' FL: Ye brave, honest
subjects, who dare to be loyal.
49
'The recess' FL: And now our senators are gone. 49
Recuerda aquel beso see 'What a
difference a day made'
'Red apple juice' FL: Ain't got no
use for your red apple juice.
35
'Red apple juice' FL: I ain't got no
use for your red apple juice.
57, 58
'The red flag' Jim Connell. FL:
The people's flag is deepest red
FLC: Then raise the scarlet
standard high. 19
'Red iron ore' FL: Come all you
bold sailors that follow the Lakes.
57
'The red light saloon' FL: It was
early one morning I strolled into
town. 57, 58
'Red River Valley' FL: From these
prairies of life I'll be leaving.
18
'Red River Valley' FL: From this
valley they say you are going
FLC: Come and sit by my side
if you love me. 1, 4, 23, 25
'Red River Valley' FL: Won't you
think of this valley you're leaving FLC: Come and sit by my
side if you love me. 57
'Red rocking chair' Charlie Monroe.
FL: I've got no use for a red
rockin' chair. 14, 56
Red rose out of the east see 'Only

a rose'
'Red rosey bush' FL: Wish I was a
red rosey bush on thee banks of
thee sea. 7
'The red rover' FL: He called his
servants one by one. 11
'Red rubber ball' Paul Simon. FL:
I should have known you'd bid me
farewell FLC: And I think it's
gonna be all right. 60
'Red wing' Thurland Chattaway and
Kerry Mills. FL: There once
lived an Indian maid FLC: Now
the moon shines tonight on pretty
Red Wing. 14
'Redesdale and Wise William' FL:
Roudesdales and Clerk William.
11
'Redio-tedio' FL: I want you to
make me a cambric shirt. 11
'A refugee song' FL: Here's a bumper, brave boys, to the health of
our king. 49
'Reign, oh! reign' FL: Take a humble soul to join up in the service
of the Lord FLC: Reign, oh!
reign. 38
'Reilly the fisherman' FL: As I
roved out one evening down by a
riverside. 30
'The rejected lover' FL: Oh, once I
had a pretty girl. 7
Rejoice, Columbia's sons, rejoice
see 'Jefferson and liberty'
'Release me' Eddie Miller, Dub
Williams and Robert Yount. FL:
Please release me, let me go.
10
Remember, dear, when your heart
was mine see 'Lady Isabel and
the elf knight'
'Remember September' May Justus
and Marlys Swinger. FL: same.
13
The report of the Commissioner of
Enquiry has arrived see 'The
commissioner's report'
'The request to the nightingale' FL:
Bird of May, leave the spray.
25
'The rescue of Will Stutly' FL: As
Robin Hood in the green wood
stood. 11
Resemble old Rosin the Beau see
'Old Rosin the beau'
'A restless night' FL: Come all you
good people, I pray you draw
near. 50

Return enraptured hours see 'Ma-
jor Andre'
'Reuben and Rachel' Harry Birch
and William Gooch. FL: Reuben,
I have long been thinking. 36
'Reuben Ranzo' FL: Oh, pity Reu-
ben Ranzo! 35
Reuben, Reuben, I've been thinking
see 'How you gonna keep 'em
down on the farm?'
'Reuben Wright and Phoebe Brown'
Sam Cowell. FL: In Manchester
a maid dwelt whose name was
Phoebe Brown. 36
'Reuben's train' FL: Reuben's coming down the track. 56, 57
'Revolution' Lennon and McCartney.
FL: You say you want a revolution. 44
'The Revolutionary alphabet' FL:
A stands for Americans, who
never will be slaves FLC: Stand
firmly, A to Z. 8
'Revolutionary tea' FL: There was
an old lady lived over the sea.
4, 55, 57
'Revolutionary times' FL: John Bull
don't remember now FLC: Ha,
ha, ha. 36
'Los Reyes Oriente' FL: De tierra
lejana venimos a verte nos sirve
de guía la FLC: Oh brillante
estrella que anuncias la aurora.
33
Ri tu, di ni, ri tu, di nu, ri na
see 'The cork leg'
'Ricardo' FL: The farmer's daughter
gade to the market. 11
'Rich banker thieves' FL: The California people are determined if
they find FLC: So be careful all
you rowdies. 25
'Rich gal, poor gal' FL: Rich gal
she wears the best perfume. 35
'A rich Irish lady' FL: A rich
Irish lady from Ireland came.
57
'A rich Irish lady' FL: A rich
Irish lady from London she came.
11
'A rich lady from London' FL:
There was a rich lady from
London she came. 11
'Rich lady from London' FL: There's
a fair English lady from London
she came. 11
'The rich man and Lazarus' FL:
There was a man in ancient time.

11

'The rich man and the poor man'
FL: There was a rich man and
he lived in Jerusalem FLC: Hi-
ro-ji-rum. 19, 57

'The rich man came from o'er the
sea see 'The gypsy davie'

'The rich merchant' FL: In London
there lived a rich merchant. 41

'The rich merchant's daughter' FL:
Twas of a rich merchant in London did dwell. 30

'The rich old lady' FL: There was
an old woman in our town. 30

'Richard Cory' Paul Simon. FL:
They say that Richard Cory owns
one half of this whole town. 60

'Richest girl in our town' FL: The
richest girl in our town. 11

Richie doo dum day see 'The
keach in the creel'

'Richie story' FL: Here's a letter
to you madam. 11

'Richie's lady' FL: There were
seven ladies in yon ha'. 11

'Rickety tickety tin' FL: About a
maiden I'll sing a song. 68

'Ricky doo dum day' FL: Mysie she
gaed out ae nicht FLC: Ricky doo
dum day, doo dum day. 11

'Ricky doo dum day' FL: 'S oh bonny
May's gane oot one nicht FLC:
Ricky doo dum day, doo dum day.
11

Ricky doo dum day, doo dum day
see 'Wee toon clerk'; 'The wee
town clerk'

A riddle a nil din adie see 'Lang
Johnny More'

'The riddle song' FL: I brought my
love a cherry without any stone.
11

'The riddle song' FL: I gave my
love a cherry that has no stone.
1, 11, 34, 57

'The riddle song' FL: I gave my
love a cherry without a stone.
4, 11

'A riddle wittily expounded!' FL:
There was a lady in the North
country. 11

'Ride a cock-horse' FL: Ride a
cock-horse to Banbury cross. 48

Ride around, little dogies, ride
around them slow see 'I ride
an Old Paint'

'Ride on, baby' Mick Jagger and
Keith Richard. FL: A smile on

your face. 16

'Riders in the sky' Stan Jones. FL:
An old cowpoke went riding out
one dark and windy day. 70

'Ride on, King Jesus' FL: I was
but young when I begun FLC:
Ride on, King Jesus. 38

Riding the night on the high cold
wind see 'How mountain girls
can love'

'The riff song' Otto Harbach, Oscar
Hammerstein, and Sigmund Romberg. FL: Over the ground there
comes a sound FLC: Ho! So we
sing as we are riding. 24

'The rifle' FL: Why come ye hither,
Redcoats? FLC: For the rifle.
57

'Riflemen of Bennington' John Allison. FL: Why come ye hither
Redcoats FLC: For the rifle. 55

'Rig a jig jig' FL: As I was walking
down the street FLC: Rig a jig
jig and away we go. 57

Right to the end see 'Who's sorry
now?'

'Ring around the rosy' FL: same.
66

Ring, ching, ching, ring ching,
ching see 'The Spanish guitar'

'Ring the bell softly' W. D. Smith
and E. N. Catlin. FL: Someone has gone from this strange
world of ours FLC: Weary with
mingling life's bitter and sweet.
63

'Ring the bell, watchman' Henry C.
Work. FL: High in the belfry,
the old sexton stands FLC: Ring
the bell, watchman, ring, ring,
ring. 63

'Ring-a-ring-a-round O' FL: same.
48

'Ring-a-ring o' roses' FL: same.
48

'Ringeltanz' FL: Es regnet auf der
Brücke, und es werd nass. 48

'Ringo's theme' Lennon and McCartney. FL: That boy took my
love. 44

Rink to my dink to my diddle diddle
dum see 'How old are you, my
pretty little miss?'

'Rio Grande' FL: Oh say were you
ever in Rio Grande? FLC: Then
away, love, away. 25, 57

'Ripe is the apple, love' FL: Ripe
is the apple that'll soon get a

rotten love. 22
'Rise and shine' FL: Don't you want
to be a soldier, soldier, soldier
FLC: Oh, brethren, rise and
shine, and give God the glory,
glory. 34, 38, 57
'Rise Columbia!' Thomas Paine.
FL: When first the sun o'er the
ocean glowed FLC: Rise Columbia,
Columbia brave and free. 3
'Rise, mourners' FL: Yes, He's
taken my feet out of the miry
clay FLC: Rise, mourners, rise
mourners. 38
Rise, my Delia, heavenly charmer
see 'A new song for a serenade'
Rise up, rise up, Lord Douglas,
she says see 'The Douglas
tragedy'
Rise up, rise up, ye seven brothers
all see 'The seven brothers'
'Rise up shepherd, and follow' FL:
There's a star in the East on
Christmas morn FLC: Leave
your sheep and leave your lambs.
33, 57
'Rise ye up' FL: Rise ye up, rise
ye up, ye drowsy old churls.
11
'The rising of the moon' FL: Oh!
then tell me Sean O'Farrell. 57
Risslety rosslity he John Dosslety
see 'Ti risslety rosslety'
'Ritchie's lady' FL: There were
seven bonnie ladies in yonder ha'.
11
Rite fal le riddle ral de rido see
'The knight and the shepherd's
daughter'
Rival de mi cariño el viento que te
besa see 'My rival'
'River deep, mountain high' Jeff
Barry, Ellie Greenwich and Phil
Spector. FL: When I was a
little girl I had a rag doll. 45
'The river in the pines' FL: O Mary
was maid when the birds began to
sing. 57
'Rivington's Reflections' FL: The
more I reflect, the more plain it
appears.
The road is long, with many a winding turn see 'He ain't heavy...
he's my brother'
'Road is rugged, but I must go' FL:
same. 29
'The road to Gundagai' FL: Oh, we
started out from Roto when the

sheds had all cut out. 57
The roadhouse in Cheyenne is filled
every night see 'The dreary
Black Hills'
'Rob Roy McGregor' FL: Rob Roy
frae the Highlands cam. 11
'The robber and the lady' FL: An
outlandish knight from the North
Countrie. 11
'The robber song' FL: Come listen
unto me and a story I shall tell.
11
'Roberta' FL: Little Roberta, let
your hair grow long. 28
Roberta, let your hair grow long
see 'Make a longtime man feel
bad'
'Robertin Tush' FL: Robertin Tush,
he married a wife. 11
'Roberty Boberty' FL: I see a wren,
said Roberty Boberty. 7
'Robin Adair' FL: What's this dull
town to me? 25
Robin dresses himself in a shep-
herd's long cloak see 'Robin
Hood rescuing the three squires'
Robin he married a wife in the
west see 'Robin-a-Thrush'
'Robin Hood' FL: As Robin Hood
ranged the woods all around. 11
'Robin Hood' FL: Bold Arden walked
forth one summer morning. 11
'Robin Hood' FL: When Phoebus had
melted the shackles of ice. 11
'Robin Hood and Little John' FL:
Then Robin he went to a tree
cutter's tree. 11
'Robin Hood and Little John' FL:
When Robin Hood was about
twenty (eighteen) years old. 11
'Robin Hood and the Bishop of Here-
ford' FL: O some they do talk
of bold Robin Hood. 11
'Robin Hood and the Bishop of Here-
ford' FL: Some will talk of bold
Robin Hood. 11
'Robin Hood and the curtall friar'
FL: In summer time when leaves
grow green. 11
'Robin Hood and the keeper' FL:
When Phoebus had melted the
ic'les of ice. 11
'Robin Hood and the pedlar' FL:
Oh it's all for a pedlar and a
pedlar boy. 11
'Robin Hood and the pedlar' FL:
Oh, pedlar, pedlar, what's in thy
pack? 11

'Robin Hood and the pedlar' FL: Tis of a pedlar, and pedlar trim. 11
'Robin Hood and the pedlar' FL: Twas of a pedlar stout and bold. 11
'Robin Hood and the Prince of Aragon' FL: Robin Hood and Will Scarlot and Little John. 11
'Robin Hood and the tanner' FL: Twas of a bold tanner in old Devonshire. 11
'Robin Hood and the three squires' FL: Bold Robin Hood ranged the forest all around. 11
'Robin Hood and the widow's three sons' FL: Bold Robin he marched the forest along. 11
Robin Hood and Will Scarlet and Little John see 'Robin Hood and the Prince of Aragon'
Robin Hood he bent his noble good bow see 'Robin Hood's progress to Nottingham'
'Robin Hood rescuing three squires' FL: Robin dressed himself in a shepherd's long cloak. 11
Robin Hood, Robin Hood, said Little John see 'A round of three country dances in one'
'Robin Hood's death' FL: As Robin Hood and Little John. 11
Robin Hood's father was the earl's own steward see 'The birth of Robin Hood'
'Robin Hood's men' FL: Three hundred and ten of bold Robin Hood's men. 11
'Robin Hood's progress to Nottingham' FL: Robin Hood he bent his noble good bow. 11
'Robin-a-Thrush' FL: O Robin-a-Thrush he married a wife. 11
'Robin-a-Thrush' FL: Robin he married a wife in the West. 11
'Rock about my Saro Jane' FL: I've got a wife and-a five little children FLC: O there's nothing to do but to set down and sing. 57
'The Rock Island Line' FL: I know I'm right when I say it's fine FLC: I say the Rock Island Line is a mighty good road. 23
'The Rock Island Line' FL: I may be right and I may be wrong FLC: I say the Rock Island Line is a mighty good road. 34
'Rock Island Line' FL: Oh the Rock Island line it's a mighty good road. 25

'Rock me to sleep' Elizabeth A. Allen and Julius Benedict. FL: Backward, turn backward, oh time in your flight. 63
'Rock of ages' Augustus M. Toplady and Thomas Hastings. FL: Rock of ages, cleft for me. 1
'Rock-a my soul' FL: When I went down to the valley to pray FLC: Oh, rock-a my soul in the bosom of Abraham. 23, 25
'Rock-a-bye, baby' Effie I. Canning. FL: Baby is sleeping so cozy and fair FLC: Rock-a-bye baby, on the tree top. 20
'Rock-a-bye your baby with a Dixie melody' Sam M. Lewis, Joe Young and Jean Schwartz. FL: Just hang my cradle, Mammy mine FLC: Rock-a-bye your baby with a Dixie melody. 12
'Rock-a-bye your baby with a Dixie melody' Sam M. Lewis, Joe Young and Jean Schwartz. FL: Mammy mine, your little rollin' stone that rolled away FLC: Rock-a-bye your baby with a Dixie melody. 31
'Rocked in the cradle of the deep' Emma H. Willard and Joseph P. Knight. FL: same. 63
'Rocking' FL: Little Jesus, sweetly sleep, do not stir. 13
'Rocks and gravel' FL: Rocks and gravel make a solid road. 57
'The rocks and the mountains' FL: Seeker, seeker, give up your heart to God FLC: Oh, the rocks and the mountains shall all flee away. 38
'Rocky raccoon' Lennon and McCartney. FL: Rocky Raccoon, checked into his room. 44
'Roddy McCorley' FL: Ho, see the fleet foot hosts of men. 57
'Roll, Alabama, roll' FL: When the Alabam's keel was laid. 57
'Roll in my sweet baby's arms? FL: Ain't gonna work in the city. 56
'Roll in my sweet baby's arms' FL: Ain't gonna work on the railroad FLC: Roll in my sweet baby's arms. 27, 57
'Roll in my sweet baby's arms' Lester Flatt. FL: I ain't gonna work on the railroad FLC: Roll

in my sweet baby's arms. 14

'Roll, Jordan, roll' FL: Oh, brothers, you oughta been there FLC: Roll, Jordan, roll. 34, 38

'Roll, Jordan, roll' FL: Oh, Mary, will you be there? FLC: Roll, Jordan, roll. 68

Roll on, Buddy, don't you roll so slow see 'Nine-pound hammer'

'Roll on, Columbia' Woody Guthrie, Huddie Ledbetter and John A. Lomax. FL: Green Douglas firs where the waters cut through FLC: Roll on, Columbia, roll on. 4

'Roll on dogies' FL: Last night as I lay on the prairie. 18, 62

Roll on, roll on, roll on little dogies see 'The cowboy dream'

'Roll on the ground' FL: Work on the railroad FLC: Roll on the ground, boys. 57

'Roll out, heave dat cotton' FL: I hear de bell a-ringin', I see de captain stand. 66

Roll out the barrel see 'Beer barrel polka'

'Roll over roll over' FL: Nine men slept in a boarding house bed. 68

'Roll the R' FL: Let us try to roll the R. 68

'Roll the union on' John Handcox and Lee Hays. FL: If the boss is in the way, we're gonna roll it over him FLC: We're gonna roll, we're gonna roll. 19, 57

Roll up, roll up for the mystery tour see 'Magical mystery tour'

'Rollicking rams' Charles J. Miers. FL: Button up your waistcoat. 36

'The rolling away of the stones' FL: Oh, will you go to the rolling of the stones. 11

'Rolling home' FL: Call all hands to man the capstan FLC: Rolling home, rolling home. 25

Romance is a game for fools see 'Fools rush in'

'Rome County' FL: In the beautiful hills way out in Rome county. 50

'Romping Rosy Nell' FL: Let every pagan muse be gone. 3

'The romp's song' Henry Carey. FL: Oh, I'll have a husband, ay! 40

'Ronald' FL: Oh what's that red upon your blade? 11

'Rondo' Francis Hopkinson. FL: My generous heart disdains the slave of love to be. 65

'Room enough' FL: Oh, brothers, don't stay away FLC: For my Lord says there's room enough. 38

'Root, hog or die' FL: I'm a lonely bullwhacker. 57

'Ropesman' FL: Ropesman, ropesman, slack up your rope. 11

'Rop'ry' FL: Rop'ry, Rop'ry, slack your rope, slack it for awhile. 7

'Rosabeckaliner' FL: Lead her up and down, Rosabeckaliner. 37

'Rosalie, the prairie flower' George F. Root. FL: On the distant prairies, where the heather wild. 1

'Rosanna' FL: My Rosanna, Rosanna, says he. 11

'The Rosary' Robert C. Rogers and Ethelbert Nevin. FL: The hours I spent with thee, dear heart. 1, 20, 63

'The rosary' FL: Tho' oft we meet severe distress. 3

'Rose de Marian time' FL: As you go through yonder town. 11

'Rose Marie' Otto Harbach, Oscar Hammerstein and Rudolf Friml. FL: Oh, sweet Rose-Marie FLC: Rose-Marie, I love you. 24, 46

A rose must remain with the sun and the rain see 'To each his own'

'The rose o' Malindie O' FL: She leant her back against a thorn. 11

'The rose of Britain's Isle' FL: Come all you people young and old. 30

'The rose of Tralee' Mordant Spencer and Charles W. Glover. FL: The pale moon was rising above the green mountain FLC: She was lovely and fair as the rose of the summer. 25, 57

'Rose, Rose' FL: Rose, Rose, Rose, Rose. 57

'The rose that all are praising' FL: The rose that all are praising is not the rose for me. 7

'Rose the Red and White Lilly' FL: O Rose the Red and White Lilly. 11

'Rosemary and thyme' FL: When you go down to yonder town. 11

Rosered is the evening sky see 'Winter walk'

'The rosewood casket' FL: In a little rosewood casket, that lies resting on the stand. 7

'Rosewood casket' FL: There's a little rosewood casket lying on a marble stand. 57

Rosy cheeks and turned up nose and curly hair see 'Baby face'

'Rotation blues' Jerry Silverman. FL: I'm a lonely soldier sitting here in Korea. 57

'Rothesay-O' FL: One hogmany at Glesca Fair FLC: A dir-rum a doo a dum a day. 57

Roudesdales and Clerk William see 'Redesdale and Wise William'

Round and round, old Joe Clark see 'Old Joe Clark'

Round and round went our gallant ship see 'The mermaid'

'Round dance' FL: Upon the bridge it's raining and we'll get wet. 48

'Round her neck she wore a golden locket' FL: same FLC: Far away, far away. 25

Round de meadows am a-ringing see 'Massa's in de cold ground'

Round my Indian homestead wave the cornfields see 'On the banks of the Wabash, far away'

'A round of three country dances in one' FL: Robin Hood, Robin Hood, said Little John. 11

'Round the bay of Mexico' FL: Been to sea for a month or more FLC: Round the bay of Mexico. 25

'Round the bay of Mexico' FL: When I was a young man in my prime FLC: Then, round the Bay of Mexico. 57

Round the bend, beyond the island see 'Stenka Razin'

'Rounded up in glory' FL: I've been thinking today FLC: He will round us up in glory by and by. 18

'Roundup in the spring' FL: In the lobby of a big hotel in New York town one day FLC: I can see the cattle grazing on the hills at early morn. 43

'Rouse, Britons' FL: Rouse, Britons at length and put forth your strength. 8

Rouse up, rouse up, my seven sleepy sons see 'The seven sons'

'The roving gambler' FL: I'm a roving gambler. 35, 57

'Row, row, row' William Jerome and Jimmy V. Monaco. FL: And then he'd row, row, row. 67

'Row row, row your boat' FL: same. 34

'Rozinkes mit mandlen' FL: In dem beys hamikaash in a vinkl cheyder. 57

'Ruby Tuesday' Mick Jagger and Keith Richard. FL: She would never say where she came from FLC: Goodbye Ruby Tuesday. 16

'Rue' FL: Come all you fair and tender girls. 57

Rufus Rastus Johnson Brown see 'What you goin' to do when the rent comes round'

'Ruggleton's daughter of Iero' FL: There was a man lived in the West. 11

El ruiseñor no canta ya see 'Cuando vuelas a mí'

'Rule death in his arms' FL: When God commanded Michael in the morning FLC: O didn't Jesus rule death in his arms. 5

'Rules' Alexander Soames and Karla Kuskin. FL: Do not jump on ancient uncles. 68

'Rumsty-o' FL: A beggarman laid himself down to sleep. 25

'Run come see Jerusalem' FL: It was in nineteen hundred and twenty-nine. 57

'Run that body down' Paul Simon. FL: Went to my doctor yesterday. 60

'Run to Jesus' FL: He will be our dearest friend FLC: Run to Jesus, shun the danger. 38

'Russian lullaby' FL: Lullay-lull-a by, lull-a by lulla-by. 57

'Rye whiskey' FL: It's whiskey, rye whiskey FLC: Rye whiskey, rye whiskey. 27, 57

- S -

'S I went down in the valley to pray

'Scatter-brain' Johnny Burke, Kahn
Keene, Carl Bean and Frankie
Masters. FL: You're as pleasant
as the morning and refreshing as
the rain. 59
Scenes of life are swiftly fading
see 'Kiss me, mother, kiss
your darling'
'Schlaf, kindlein, schlaf' FL: same.
48
'School days' Will D. Cobb and Gus
Edwards. FL: You were my
queen in calico FLC: School days,
school days. 12
'The schoolhouse fire' John Duffey,
Dorsey Dixon and Peter Roberts.
FL: Twas an afternoon in springtime FLC: You could hear those
children singing. 14
'The schoolmaster' FL: Come,
come my children, I must see.
36
Scintillate, scintillate, globule au-
rific see 'Mixed up Mother
Goose'
'The scolding wife' FL: He yoked
up his pigs one day for to plow.
11
'Scotland's burning' FL: Scotland's
burning, Scotland's burning. 34,
57
'Scots wha hae' Robert Burns. FL:
Scots wha hae wi' Wallace bled.
57
'The sea captain' FL: It was of a
sea captain that followed the sea.
11
'The sea captain' FL: It's of a fair
maiden that lived on the shore.
30
'The sea captain' FL: It's of a sea
captain that ploughs the salt seas.
11
'The sea captain' FL: Twas of a sea
captain twas deep in love. 11,
30
'The sea captain, or the maid on the
shore' FL: It's of a sea captain
that ploughs the salt seas. 30
Sea captain, sea captain, down by the
banks of the willow see 'Banks
of green willow'
'The sea hath many thousand sands'
Robert Jones. FL: same. 26
'The sea shore' FL: Dear sister,
dear sister let's take a walk. 11
'The sea side' FL: As I roved out
by the sea side. 11

'The sea-faring man' FL: What a
life, what a life, says the sea-
faring man. 11
' ''Seagull'' the maiden is named' M.
Lisianskii and A. Doplukhanian.
FL: Far out in space endless
highways are glowing. 58
'The season for singing' Seymour
Barab. FL: The season for
singing a joyous refrain. 33
Seated one day at the organ see
'The lost chord'
'Seaweed' Fred Earle. FL: Last
summertime I went away to Dov-
er by the sea FLC: With my
seaweed in my hand I got into
the train. 17
'Secret agent man' P. F. Sloan and
Steve Barbi. FL: There's a man
who leads a life of danger. 47
See Alberta comin' down that road
see 'Alberta'
See now the flustering Boreas blows
see 'How cold it is'
See that host all dressed in white
see 'Wade in the water'
See that train comin' round the bend
see 'Goodbye, my lover, good-
bye'
See the course thronged with gazers
see 'The race horse'
See the pyramids along the Nile
see 'You belong to me'
See the setting sun see 'Be mine
tonight'
See the star of Bethlehem see
'Star of Bethlehem'
See the tree, how big it's grown
see 'Honey'
See, there stands a lowly stable
see 'The lowly stable'
See who comes over the red blos-
somed heather see 'The bold
Fenian men'
'Seeing Nellie home' FL: In the sky
the bright stars glittered FLC:
I was seeing Nellie home. 57
Seeker, seeker, give up your heart
to God see 'The rocks and the
mountains'
'See-saw, Margery Daw' FL: same.
48
'Send me the pillow you dream on'
Hank Locklin. FL: Each night
while I'm sleeping, oh, so lone-
ly FLC: Send me the pillow that
you dream on. 10
Send out, send out, her daughter

seen better days. 20

She mounted on her bonny, bonny
brown see 'Tell-tale Polly'

She mounted on her milk-white
steed see 'The false hearted
knight'; 'Lady Isabel and the elf
knight'

She never saw the streets of Cairo
see 'Streets of Cairo'

She picked him up so shyly see
'The seven king's daughters'

She pressed herself against the wall
see 'The cruel mother'

She pulled out a pretty yellow apple
see 'Sir Hugh'

She rode up in the court house yard
see 'Geordie'

She said unto her mama, she said
unto her dada see 'The lover's
ghost'

She sat down below a thorn see
'Fine flowers in the valley'

She says the coffin to be opened
see 'George Collins'

She sharpened her knife both sharp
and keen see 'Young Hunting'

'She smiled sweetly' Mick Jagger
and Keith Richard. FL: Who do
my thoughts loom so large on
me? 16

She taken her little babe on her
knee see 'The daemon lover'

She takes just like a woman see
'Just like a woman'

She took her babe upon her knee
see 'The house carpenter's wife'

She took the baby on her knee see
'The house carpenter'

She tossed it high, she tossed it
low see 'Sir Hugh'

'She touched me' Ira Levin and Milton Schafer. FL: She touched
me, she put her hand near mine.
6

She wadna bake, an she wadna brew
see 'Hollin green Hollin'

She wadna' be a bride see 'Eppie
Morrie'

'She walks as she dreams' Nathaniel
Lee and Daniel Purcell. FL:
She walks as she dreams in a
garden of flowers. 40

She was a dame in love with a guy
see 'True blue Lou'

She was a working girl north of
England way see 'Honey pie'

'She was bred in old Kentucky'
Harry Braisted and Stanley Carter.

FL: When a lad, I stood one day
by a cottage far away FLC: She
was bred in old Kentucky. 20

She was loved by a poor young
house carpenter see 'The house
carpenter'

She was lovely and fair as the rose
of the summer see 'The rose
of Tralee'

She was poor, but she was honest
see 'It's the same the whole
world over'

She wears a gold ring on all of her
fingers see 'Lord Bateman'

She went upstairs to make her bed
see 'The butcher boy'

'She wore a wreath of roses'
Thomas H. Bayly and Joseph P.
Knight. FL: same. 63

She wore blue velvet see 'Blue
velvet'

She would never say where she
came from see 'Ruby Tuesday'

Shee ne sha shee na sha see 'Navajo happiness song'

'Sheep in the clusters' FL: Her
sheep had in clusters crept close
by the grove. 3

'Sheep shearing' FL: How delightful
to see. 72

The sheep's in the meadow see
'Crow on the cradle'

'The sheik of Araby' Harry B.
Smith, Francis Wheeler and Ted
Snyder. FL: The stars that
shine above FLC: I'm the sheik
of Araby. 12

'She'll be comin' round the mountain'
FL: She'll be comin' round the
mountain when she comes. 1,
23, 25, 34, 57, 67, 68

'Shenandoah' FL: Oh, Shenandoah, I
long to hear you. 1, 4, 23, 25,
34, 57, 66, 67

'The shepherd lad' FL: There was
a bonnie shepherd lad. 11

'The shepherd laddie' FL: There
was a shepherd laddie kept sheep
on yonder hill. 11

'Shepherd's daughter' FL: It's of a
shepherd's daughter. 11

'The shepherd's daughter' FL:
There was a shepherd's daughter.
11

'The shepherd's daughter' FL: Twas
of a shepherd's daughter. 11

A shepherd's daughter dear see
'Earl Richard'

A shepherd's daughter watching sheep see 'The knight and the shepherd's daughter'

'Shepherds in Judea' Jeremiah Ingalls. FL: As shepherds in Jewry were guarding their sheep. 33

The shepherds kept their watching see 'Go, tell it on the mountain'

'She's a rainbow' Mick Jagger and Keith Richard. FL: She comes in colors everywhere FLC: She combs her hair. 16

'She's a woman' John Lennon and Paul McCartney. FL: My love don't give me presents. 47

'She's leaving home' Lennon and McCartney. FL: Wednesday morning at five o'clock as the day begins. 44

'She's like the swallow' FL: She's like the swallow that flies so high. 30, 57

She's ma lady love, she is ma dove, my baby, love see 'Lily of Laguna'

'She's more to be pitied' FL: She's there at the bar every evening FLC: She's more to be pitied than scolded. 14

She's my sweetheart, I'm her beau see 'Little Annie Rooney'

She's not the only pebble on the beach see 'You're not the only pebble on the beach'

She's only a bird in a gilded cage see 'A bird in a gilded cage'

She's so affectionate I'll say this see 'When my sugar walked down the street'

She's the Queen of Hearts see 'Queen of Hearts'

She's the sweetest rose of color a feller ever knew see 'The yellow rose of Texas'

She's there at the bar every evening see 'She's more to be pitied'

She's very wealthy it's true see 'Cool, calm and collected'

Shine, little glow worm, glimmer see 'Glow worm'

'A Shine on your shoes' Howard Dietz and Arthur Schwartz. FL: Don't you be a good for nothin' FLC: When there's a shine on your shoes. 46

'Shine, shine' FL: I don't care where you bury my body FLC: O my little soul's going to shine, shine. 38

'Shine, shine' FL: I'm going to sit at the welcome table FLC: Shine, shine, I'll meet you in the morning. 38

'A ship a-sailing' FL: A ship, a ship a-sailing. 48

'A ship came sailing' FL: A ship came sailing over the sea. 11

'The ship carpenter' FL: Well met, well met, my old true love. 11

A ship I have got in the North Countree see 'The Golden Vanity'

'The ship I love' Felix McGlennon. FL: A gallant ship was lab'ring FLC: I'll stick to the ship, lads. 63

The ship is sailing down the bay see 'Goodbye, my lover, goodbye'

'A ship set sail for North America' FL: same. 11

'The ship that never returned' Henry C. Work. FL: On a summer's day while the waves were rippling FLC: Did she ever return? 4, 57

'The ship that never returned' FL: Says a pale face youth to his loving mother. 41

'The ship Titanic' FL: Oh, they built the ship Titanic to sail the ocean blue FLC: Oh, it was sad. 68

'The ship's carpenter' FL: I've just returned from the salt, salt sea. 11

Ships may come and ships may go see 'Get up, Jack'

'The shipwrecked sailors' FL: On the first of May as we set sail FLC: Oh, the raging sea how she roar, roar, roared. 11

'Shoe-lie-low' FL: Stole my partner shoe lie low. 29

'Shoo, fly don't bother me' FL: same. 72

'Shoo purp don't bodder me' Henry Ward Beecher. FL: Ho Sergeant Kick that nasty purp FLC: Shoo purp, shoo purp. 36

'Shoot the buffalo' FL: Stand you up, my dearest dear. 4

'Shootin' with Rasputin' FL: An intimate friend of the Czar was I FLC: But all that seems distant

and all that seems far. 57, 68
'Shooting of his dear' FL: Come all
  you young gallants, take delight
  in a gun. 30
'Short Creek raid' FL: In the good
  old town of Short Creek, in the
  year of '53. 43
'Short rations' FL: Fair ladies and
  maids of all ages FLC: For we
  soldiers have seen something
  rougher. 25
'Short'nin' bread' FL: Put on the
  skillet, put on the led FLC:
  Mammy's little baby loves short'-
  nin' short'nin'. 1, 23, 25
'Short'nin' bread' FL: Three little
  babies lyin' in bed FLC: Mammy's
  little baby loves short'nin',
  short'nin'. 57
'Shorty George' FL: Oh well, it's
  Shorty George, he wasn't no
  friend a mine. 28
'Shorty George' FL: Oh, well-a
  Shorty George. 57
'Shorty George' FL: Shorty George,
  you ain't a friend of mine. 23
'Should a been on the river in 1910'
  FL: Well, you should a been on
  the river in 1910. 28
Should auld acquaintance be forgot
  see 'Auld lang syne'
'Show me the way' FL: Brother,
  have you come to show me the
  way? 38
'Shrimp boats' Paul M. Howard and
  Paul Weston. FL: They go to
  sea with the evening tide FLC:
  Shrimp boats is a-comin'. 52
Sh-ta-ra-day-dey, ash-ta-day see
  'Times is mighty hard'
Shtet a bocher und er tracht see
  'Tumbalalaika'
Shteyt a bocher oon er tracht see
  'Toom Balalaika'
'Shtil, di nacht' Hirsh Glik. FL:
  Shtil, di nacht iz oysgeshternt.
  57
'Shuckin' sugar blues' FL: I've got
  your picture and I'm gonna put in
  a frame. 57
'The Shushai' FL: We all went on a
  Christmas Day. 22
Si al cielo subir pudiera llorona
  see 'La llorona'
'Si me quieres escribir' FL: same.
  57
'Si tú pudieras quererme' Johnnie
  Camacho and Arthur Schwartz.

FL: Llevo preso en mi FLC: Si
  tú pudieras quererme. 46
Si tu supieras lo que he pecado
  see 'The four winds'
'Sick, sick and very sick' FL: It
  befell at Martinmas. 11
'The sidewalks of New York' Charles
  B. Lawlor and James W. Blake.
  FL: Down in front of Casey's
  FLC: East side, west side. 1,
  20, 25, 34, 67
Siempre fuiste la razón de mi exi-
  stir see 'The story of love'
Siempre que te pregunto see
  'Perhaps, perhaps, perhaps'
'The Sierry Petes' FL: Away up
  high in the Sierry Petes. 43
'Sings of spring' May Justus and
  Marlys Swinger. FL: I know, I
  know, I know it. 13
Silent evening falls in a mist see
  'In the heart of the dark'
'Silent night' Joseph Mohr and
  Franz Gruber. FL: Silent night,
  holy night. 34, 57
Silent night holy night see '7
  o'clock news/Silent night'
'Silicosis blues' Jerry Silverman.
  FL: I said, silicosis you made a
  mighty bad break of me. 57
'Silkie' FL: The silkie be a creature
  strange. 23, 25
'The silly old man' FL: Aw! come
  now I'll sing you a song. 11
'The silly old man' FL: Come,
  neighbors, I'll sing you a song.
  11
'The silly old man' FL: It's of and
  a silly old man. 11
'Silver dagger' FL: Don't sing love
  songs, you'll wake my mother.
  35
'The silver dagger' FL: Sing no love
  songs, you'll wake my mother.
  23, 25
Silver sage a-settin' in the pale
  twilight see 'Cowboy lullaby'
'Silver threads among the gold'
  Eben E. Rexford and Hart P.
  Danks. FL: Darling, I am growing old FLC: Darling, I am growing, growing old. 1, 57
'Simon the cellarer' FL: Old Simon
  the cellarer keeps a large store.
  25
'A simple desultory philippic' Paul
  Simon. FL: I been Norman
  Mailered, Maxwell Taylored. 60

'Simple gifts' FL: Tis a gift to be simple. 57

'The simple ploughboy' FL: Do you see my little ploughboy ploughing on the lea. 30

Since I found you see 'Amapola'

Since I was young I've been very hard to please see 'Sittin' on a fence'

Since Mother Eve in the garden long ago see 'When I take my morning promenade'

Since my baby left me found a new place to dwell see 'Heartbreak Hotel'

Since my soul's got a seat see 'That's all right'

Since then I'm doomed this sad reverse to prove see 'Song in the spoiled child'

Since you all must have singing and won't be said nay see 'The old soldiers of the king'

Since you all will have singing and won't be said nay see 'The king's own regulars'

Since you and I have drifted apart see 'I let a song go out of my heart'

Since you've gone away see 'When day is done'

Sing a song of popcorn see 'Popcorn song'

'Sing a song of sixpence' FL: same. 48

'Sing a song of spring' Edith Moller, Antonia Ridge and F. W. Möller. FL: When the green buds show. 13

Sing courting, courting, courting, cane see 'The Suffolk miracle'

Sing do ri iddle, sing do ri a see 'Katie Morey'

Sing hallelujah, hallelujah see 'Hallelujah'

Sing hey, me braw John Hielandman see 'John Hielandman'

'Sing I for a brave and a gallant barque see 'Ten thousand miles away'

'Sing Ivy' FL: My father gave me an acre of land. 11

'Sing Ivy' FL: My father he left me three acres of land. 11

'Sing Ivy' FL: My mother she gave me an acre of land. 11

Sing my loved one a rhapsody see 'Play, fiddle, play'

Sing no love songs, you'll wake my mother see 'The silver dagger'

Sing, o sing of Lydia Pinkham see 'Lydia Pinkham'

Sing song kitty cathcee kyemeeoh see 'Keemy kyemo'

Sing taddle-o day see 'Little brown dog'

Sing tan-ta-ra-ra-ra see 'The halcyon days of Old England'

'Sing this all together' Mick Jagger and Keith Richard. FL: Why don't we sing this song all together? 16

Sing ti vi-tee ann vee i vee ay see 'Old woman in Slab City'

Sing to joy and gladness now and evermore to freedom's song see 'Ode to joy'

Sing too-ra-li, oo-ra-li see 'Sweet Betsy from Pike'

'Sing we the Virgin Mary' FL: same. 33

Sing whack faloora, loora lay see 'Old jokey song'

Sing willow, willow, willow, willow see 'The willow song'

'Sing you sinners' Sam Coslow and W. Franke Harling. FL: Brothers and sisters, my sermon today FLC: You sinners, drop everything. 47, 53

'Sing your way home' FL: Sing your way home at the close of the day. 34

'Singa hipsy doodle' FL: There was an old woman and in our town did dwell. 7

'The singer, not the song' Mick Jagger and Keith Richard. FL: Everywhere you walk I always go. 16

Singing a bye low, my baby see 'Goodbye, my lover, goodbye'

Singing blow ye winds in the morning see 'Blow ye winds in the morning'

Singing, blow ye winds of the morning see 'The baffled knight'

Singing to la lol la rol lall to ral lal la see 'Vilikins and his Dinah'

Singing too ra li, too ra li see 'Toorali'

Singing too ral, lal loo ral see 'Villikins and his Dinah'

Singing, tra la la la la la see 'Bulldog and the bullfrog'

'Single girl' FL: Single girl, oh
single girl. 57, 58
'Single girl' FL: When I was single,
go dressed neat and fine FLC: I
wish I were a single girl again.
4
'Sinking in the lonesome sea' FL:
There was a little ship and she
sailed upon the sea. 11
'Sinner man' FL: Oh, sinner, man,
where you gonna run to? 34
'Sinner, you better get ready' FL:
The tallest tree in Paradise FLC:
Sinner, you better get ready. 5
'The Sioux Indians' FL: I'll sing you
a song, though it may be a sad
one. 57, 66
'Sippin' cider thru a straw' FL:
The prettiest girl I ever saw.
23, 34, 68
'Sir Colin' FL: The king luikit owre
his castle wa. 11
'Sir Donkey' FL: Out from the lands
of Orient FLC: Heigh, Sir Don-
key oh heigh. 72
'Sir Eglamore' FL: Sir Eglamore,
that valiant knight. 11, 25
'Sir Eglamore and the dragon' FL:
Sir Eglamore, that valiant knight.
35
'Sir Henry and Lady Margaret' FL:
Late last Friday night. 11
'Sir Hugh' FL: All the scholars in
the school. 11
'Sir Hugh' FL: As I walked tout one
holiday. 11
'Sir Hugh' FL: Dark and dark some
drizzling day. 11
'Sir Hugh' FL: Down come a Jewess.
11
'Sir Hugh' FL: Go bury my Bible at
my head. 11
'Sir Hugh' FL: It rained a mess, it
rained a mess. 11
'Sir Hugh' FL: It rained a mist, it
rained a mist. 11
'Sir Hugh' FL: It rained, alas! it
rained, alas! 61
'Sir Hugh' FL: It rains, it rains in
merry Scotland. 11
'Sir Hugh' FL: A little boy about
five years old. 11
'Sir Hugh' FL: A little school boy,
he bounced his ball. 11
'Sir Hugh' FL: Low and low and low
holiday. 11
'Sir Hugh' FL: O she tossed it high,
she tossed it low. 11

'Sir Hugh' FL: She pulled out a
pretty yellow apple. 11
'Sir Hugh' FL: She tossed it high,
she tossed it low. 11
'Sir Hugh' FL: Twas on a dark and
holiday. 11
'Sir Hugh and the Jew's daughter'
FL: Young Hugh he was the best
of all. 11
'Sir Hugh of Lincoln' FL: One day
it rained in our town. 11
'Sir James the Rose' FL: Failin fa,
Sir James the Rose. 11
'Sir James the Ross' FL: It's all
those Scottish lords and chiefs.
11, 30
'Sir James the Ross' FL: Of all
the Scottish northern chiefs of
high and warlike name. 11, 30
'Sir Lionel' FL: Bangry Rewey a-
courting did ride. 11
'Sir Lionel' FL: I went out a-hunting one day. 11
'Sir Lionel' FL: There is a wild
boar in these woods. 11
'Sir Lionel' FL: Tom and Harry
went to plough. 11
Sir Patrick dressed in best array
see 'Burd Isabel and Sir Patrick'
'Sir Patrick Spence' FL: The king
he sits in Dumferling town. 11
'Sir Patrick Spens' FL: Hie sits oor
king in Dumferline. 11
'Sir Patrick Spens' FL: The king sat
in Dumfermline town. 11
'Sir Peter Parker' FL: My lords,
with your leave. 55
'Sir William Gower' FL: I'm a gay
young sailor stout and strong.
11
Sister, dear sister, let's walk the
seashore see 'The two sisters'
Sister help to trim the sail hallelu-
jah see 'Michael'
Sister Mary came a-running see
'The angel rolled the stone away'
'Sister Mary had but one child' FL:
O three wise men to Jerusalem
came FLC: Sister Mary had-a
but one Child. 33
'Sister Morphine' Mick Jagger,
Keith Richard and Marianne Faith-
full. FL: Here I lie in my hos-
pital bed. 16
Sister, o sister, let's take a walk
out see 'The two sisters'
Sit alone every night see 'Abilene'
Sit doon, my weary workin' man

Britons always loyally declaim,
about the way we rule the waves
FLC: It's the soldiers of the
Queen, my lads. 69

'The soldier's poor little boy' FL:
The snow was fastly falling. 7

'The soldier's tear' Thomas H.
Bayly and Alexander Lee. FL:
Upon the hill he turned. 63

'The soldier's wooing' FL: I will
tell you of a soldier who lately
came from war. 11

'Solemn dirge' Thomas A. Arne.
FL: Ah, hapless maid. 40

'Solidarity forever' Ralph Chaplin.
FL: When the union's inspiration
through workers' blood shall run
FLC: Solidarity forever! 19

'Solitude' Eddie De Lange, Irving
Mills and Duke Ellington. FL: I
sit in my chair FLC: In my solitude. 12

Some bright morning when this life
is over see 'I'll fly away'

Some cowboys once told me about
the horse I drew see 'Average
rein'

Some dare to say that Irishmen
should refuse to fight for Britain's crown see 'Bravo, Dublin Fusiliers'

'Some day' Brian Hooker and Rudolf
Friml. FL: Some day you will
seek me and find me. 54

Some day we'll build a home on a
hill top high see 'The folks
who live on the hill'

Some do call me Jim and some do
call me John see 'Earl Richard'

Some do count it a misfortune to be
christened Pat or Dan see 'No
Irish need apply'

'Some enchanted evening' Oscar Hammerstein and Richard Rodgers.
FL: same. 6, 42

Some fellers love to 'Tiptoe through
the tulips' see 'Bidin' my time'

Some go to church for to sing and
shout see 'Ezekiel saw the
wheel'

Some people think that I have no
grace see 'Sweet heaven'

Some people you've met in your
time no doubt see 'A motto for
every man'

Some say it's one thing see 'What
you gonna call yo' pretty little
baby'

Some say that John the B. was
nothing but a Jew see 'Been a
listening'

Some talk of Alexander see 'The
British grenadiers'

Some they will talk of bold Robin
Hood see 'The Bishop of Hereford's entertainment'

'Some things just stick in your
mind' Mick Jagger and Keith
Richard. FL: Why does the sky
turn grey every night? 16

Some think the world is made for
fun and frolic see 'Funiculi
Funicula'

Some time ago, three months or
more, if I remember well see
'Cowboy in church'

Some were playing cards and others
were playing dice see 'The
Golden Vanity'

Some will talk of bold Robin Hood
see 'Robin Hood and the Bishop
of Hereford'

'Somebody' FL: Was I reduced to
beg my bread. 3

'Somebody bad stole de wedding
bell' Bob Hilliard and David
Mann. FL: All day de people
look at de steeple. 52

'Somebody bigger than you and I'
Johnny Lange, Hy Heath and
Sonny Burke. FL: Who made
the mountain. 64

'Somebody else is taking my place'
Dick Howard and Bob Ellsworth
and Russ Morgan. FL: same.
59

'Somebody got lost in a storm' FL:
same. 23

'Somebody loves me' Ballard Macdonald, B. G. De Sylva, and
George Gershwin. FL: When
this world began FLC: Somebody
loves me. 21, 42

'Somebody's knocking at your door'
FL: same. 23, 25

'Somebody's sweetheart I want to
be' Cobb and Edwards. FL: I
am so lonely, I am so blue FLC:
Somebody's sweetheart I want to
be. 20

'Someday' Jimmie Hodges. FL:
Someday you'll want me to want
you FLC: I know that someday
you'll want me to want you. 12

Someday he'll come along, the man
I love see 'The man I love'

Someday, some way, you'll realize you've been blind see 'It's just a matter of time'

Someday we'll meet again, sweetheart see 'We'll meet again, sweetheart'

Someday when I'm awfully low see 'The way you look tonight'

Someday you'll want me to want you see 'Someday'

Someone has gone from this strange world of ours see 'Ring the bell softly'

Someone that I belong to see 'Prisoner of love'

'Someone to watch over me' George and Ira Gershwin. FL: There's a saying old, says that love is blind FLC: There's a somebody I'm longing to see. 21, 42, 46

Someone told me it's all happening at the zoo see 'At the zoo'

Someone woke me up this mornin' and I lit a cigarette see 'Sad day'

Someone's crying, Lord, kum ba ya see 'Kum ba ya'

'Something' George Harrison. FL: Something in the way she moves. 45

'Something happened to me yesterday' Mick Jagger and Keith Richard. FL: same. 16

Something in the way she moves see 'Something'

'Something to remember you by' Howard Dietz and Arthur Schwartz. FL: You are leaving me and I will try to face the world alone FLC: Oh, give me something to remember you by. 46

Sometime ago I wandered into old Mexico see 'Frenesi'

Sometime ago, two weeks or more see 'A cowboy at church'

Sometimes I feel discouraged see 'Balm in Gilead'

'Sometimes I feel like a motherless child' FL: same. 1, 23, 25, 57, 66

Sometimes I plow my old gray horse see 'Whoa buck'

Sometimes I wonder why I spend the lonely night see 'Star dust'

'Sometimes I'm happy' Irving Caesar and Vincent Youmans. FL: Every day seems like a year FLC: Some-times I'm happy. 46

Sometimes I'm up, sometimes I'm down see 'Nobody knows the trouble I've seen'

Sometimes in the morning when shadows are deep see 'My cup runneth over'

Sometimes it's hard to be a woman see 'Stand by your man'

Sometimes they call me Jockie see 'The knight and the shepherd's daughter'

'Somewhere' Stephen Sondheim and Leonard Bernstein. FL: There's a place for us. 6

'Somewhere along the way' Sammy Gallop and Kurt Adams. FL: I used to walk with you along the avenue. 47

Somewhere beyond the sea see 'Beyond the sea'

Somewhere, somewhere see 'Beautiful isle of somewhere'

Somewhere the sun is shining see 'Beautiful isle of somewhere'

'Somewhere they can't find me' Paul Simon. FL: I can hear the soft breathing of the girl that I love FLC: But I've got to creep down the alleyway. 60

'Son David' FL: O, what's the blood that's on your sword? 11

'The son of a gambolier' FL: I'm a rambling wretch of poverty from Tip'ry town I came FLC: Then combine your humble ditties as from tavern to tavern we steer. 57

'Son of a preacher man' John Hurley and Ronnie Wilkins. FL: Jimmy Ray was a preacher's son. 71

'A son of the desert am I' John P. Wilson and Walter A. Phillips. FL: same FLC: None so daunt-less and free on land or on sea. 63

Soñar en noche de luna see 'Full moon'

'A song' FL: There was a knight and he was young. 11

The song a robin sings see 'Stella by starlight'

'A song about Charleston' FL: King Hancock sat in regal state. 49

'Song for the asking' Paul Simon. FL: Here is my song for the asking. 60

A song I will sing unto you see
'Saddle to rags'
'Song in the spoiled child' FL: Since
then I'm doomed this sad reverse
to prove. 3
Song is in the air see 'You and
and the night and the music'
'The song is you' Oscar Hammerstein and Jerome Kern. FL: I
hear music when I look at you.
24, 67
'A song made upon the election of
new magistrates for this city'
FL: To you good lads that dare
oppose. 55
'A song made upon the foregoing occasion' FL: Come on brave boys,
let us be brave. 55
'Song of a soldier' FL: My song is
of a soldier just lately come
from war. 11
'Song of greeting' D. Shostokovich
and Jerry Silverman. FL: The
morning greets us with its coolness. 57
'Song of greeting' D. Shostakovich
and B. Kornilov. FL: Nas utro
vstrechaet prokhladoi. 57
'A song of liberty' Joseph Warren.
FL: That seat of science, Athens.
49
'Song of the freedmen' FL: We are
coming from the cotton fields
FLC: Then come along, my
brothers. 4
'Song of the guaranteed wage' Ruby
McDonald and Joe Glazer. FL:
I'll tell you the story of Jonathan
Tweed. 19
'Song of the heads' FL: Ye wrong
head, ye strong heads, attend to
my strains FLC: Derry down,
down, hey derry down. 8
'Song of the islands' Charles E.
King. FL: When the lime flower
white is gleaming FLC: Hawaii,
isles of beauty. 12
'The song of the Salvation Army'
FL: We're coming, we're coming,
our brave little band FLC: Away,
away, with rum, by gum. 68
'Song of the vagabonds' Brian Hook-
er and Rudolf Friml. FL: Come
all you beggars of Paris town
FLC: Sons of toil and danger. 54
'Song of the Wise Men' Seymour
Barab. FL: We have traveled
far, all thought of rest forsaken.

33
'A song to the Sons of Liberty' FL:
Come jolly Sons of Liberty. 49
A song unto Liberty's brave bucca-
neer see 'Paul Jones'
Sons of freedom, listen to me see
'James Bird'
'The Sons of Liberty' FL: O fare
you well, sweet Ireland. 55
The sons of the prophet are brave
men and bold see 'Abdullah
Bulbul Amir'
Sons of toil and danger see 'Song
of the vagabonds'
'Soon' George and Ira Gershwin.
FL: I'm making up for all the
years that I waited FLC: Soon,
the lonely nights will be ended.
21
'Soon' FL: The time is quite near
for our Lord to appear. 18
Soon ez we all cook swee' petatehs
see 'Sweet Potatoes'
'Soon in de morning' FL: I dunno
what my brother wants to stay
here for FLC: I'm goin' up home
soon in de mornin'. 5
Soon or late, maybe see 'Maybe'
Soon, the lonely nights will be ended
see 'Soon'
Sooner in the morning see 'Gwine
to ride up in the chariot'
'Sophisticated lady' Irving Mills,
Mitchell Parish and Duke Ellington. FL: The years have changed
you somehow FLC: They say into
your early life romance came.
12
'Sophronia' FL: Forbear my friends,
forbear and ask no more. 3
'Sororité' Joyce Suskind. FL: We
were divided for years and years
FLC: Liberté, égalité. 58
'Sorrow, stay' John Dowland. FL:
Sorrow, sorrow, stay, lend true
repentant tears. 26
The sound of applause is delicious
see 'Make someone happy'
'The sound of music' Oscar Hammerstein and Richard Rodgers.
FL: My day in the hills has come
to an end FLC: The hills are
alive with the sound of music. 6
'The sound of silence' Paul Simon.
FL: Hello darkness, my old
friend. 60
'Soup song' Joe Glazer. FL: One
day the Depression was over

FLC: Sooop, sooop. 19
'Sourwood Mountain' FL: Chickens
a-crowin' on Sourwood Mountain.
23, 25, 57
'Sourwood Mountain' FL: I've got a
girl in the Sourwood Mountain.
7
'The Souters o' Selkirk' FL: It's up
wi' the Souters o' Selkirk. 69
'South Australia' FL: In South Australia I was born FLC: Haul
away, you rolling kings. 57
'Southwel new' Thomas Walter.
FL: Bow down, O Lord, thine
near. 65
'The sow got the measles' FL: How
do you think I started in life.
57, 72
'The sow took the measles' FL:
What do you think I made of her
hide? FLC: How do you think I
began in this world? 66
'Sowing on the mountain' FL: same.
57
'Spacey Jones' Don Jacobs and Eddie
Newton. FL: Come all ye spacemen in if you want to hear FLC:
Spacey Jones mounted his cabin.
4
Spaniens Himmel breitet seine see
'Freiheit'
'The Spanish canoe' FL: Oh, I've
got a ship in the North countree.
11
'The Spanish gambaleer' FL: The
Spanish gambaleer sat under a
tree. 41
'The Spanish guitar' FL: When I was
a student at Cadiz FLC: Ring,
ching, ching, ring ching, ching.
25
'Spanish ladies' FL: Goodbye, and
adieu to you, Spanish ladies. 30
'The Spanish Main' FL: I was scarce
eighteen, when I started roving.
30
Spanking Jack was so comely, so
pleasant, so jolly see 'The
sailor's consolation'
Spare, me, spare me, Clyde's
waters see 'Clyde's water'
'Sparrow' Paul Simon. FL: Who
will love a little sparrow. 60
Spendin' too much time away see
'Goin' home'
Spending these lonesome evenings
see 'Why was I born?'
'The spider and the fly' Mick Jagger

and Keith Richard. FL: Sittin',
thinkin', sinkin', drinkin'. 16
'The spider and the fly' FL: Will
you walk into my parlor said a
spider to a fly FLC: Will you,
will you. 36
'Spiders and snakes' Jim Stafford.
FL: And so we took a stroll. 64
'The spinning wheel' FL: To ease
his heart, and own his flame. 3,
4
'Spinning wheel' FL: David C.
Thomas. FL: What goes
must come down. 71
'Sportin' life blues' FL: I got a
letter from my home. 57
'The sporting bachelors' FL: Come
all you sporting bachelors. 57
'Sporting cowboy' FL: When I was a
cowboy I learned to throw the
line. 43
'S'posin'' Andy Razaf and Paul
Denniker. FL: I know something
but I can't express it FLC:
S'posin' I should fall in love with
you. 54
'Spring secret' May Justus and Vonnie Burleson. FL: Nobody knows
what I know. 13
Spring was never waiting for us
see 'MacArthur Park'
'Springfield Mountain' FL: On Springfield Mountain there did dwell
FLC: Too-roo-dee-nay. 1, 25,
57, 68
'Springtime in the Rockies' FL: It
was springtime in the Rockies.
68
The springtime returns and clothes
the green plains see 'Alloa
House'
'The squid jiggin' ground' FL: Oh,
this is the place where the fish-
ermen gather. 57
A squire, a squire, he lived in the
wood see 'Broomfield wager'
The squire came home late at night
see 'The davy'
The squire came home late in the
night see 'The gypsy laddie'
A squire from Dover, a squire he
came see 'The brown girl';
'Pretty Sally'
The squire he came home at night
see 'The gypsy laddie'
'The squire in the North Countree'
FL: It's of a rich squire in the
North country. 11

'The squire of Edinbro's town' FL:
There was a squire of Edinbro'
town. 11

'Squire Relantman' FL: Squire Relantman was a fine mason. 11

'The squire who lived in the West'
FL: Tis of a young squire who
lived in the West. 11

'The squirrel' FL: Squirrely is a
pretty thing. 72

Squirrel he's got a bushy tail see
'Git along home, Sally gal'

'Stag O'Lee' FL: It was early,
early one morning. 23

Stained with alkali, sand and mud
see 'My Stetson hat'

'Stand by your man' Tammy Wy-
nette and Billy Sherrill. FL:
Sometimes it's hard to be a woman. 10

Stand firmly, A. to Z. see 'The
revolutionary alphabet'

'Stand on a sea of glass' FL: Satan
tried my soul to stay FLC: O dis
union. 5

Stand you up, my dearest dear see
'Shoot the buffalo'

Standin' on the corner with the low-
down blues see 'Salty dog'

Standing in the dock at Southampton
see 'The ballad of John and
Yoko'

'Standing in the need of prayer' FL:
Ain't my brother or my sister
FLC: It's me, it's me, it's me,
oh Lord. 23, 25, 34, 57

'Star dust' Michael Parish and
Hoagy Carmichael. FL: And now
the purple dusk of twilight time
FLC: Sometimes I wonder why I
spend the lonely night. 1, 12, 59

'Star in the East' FL: Hail, blessed
morn FLC: Brightest and best of
the sons of the morning. 33

'Star of Bethlehem' Louis Haber and
Seymour Barab. FL: See the
star of Bethlehem. 33

The star of empire poets say see
'Ho! westward ho!'

Starry blue night when branches
bend and blow see 'Noche azul'

The stars at night are big and
bright see 'Deep in the heart of
Texas'

'Stars fell on Alabama' Mitchell
Parish and Frank Perkins. FL:
I can't forget the glamour FLC:
We lived our little drama. 12

The stars that shine above see
'The sheik of Araby'

'The star-spangled banner' Francis
Scott Key and J. S. Smith. FL:
O say can you see, by the
dawn's early light. 1, 25, 34,
55, 67

'Stars begin to fall' FL: I tink I
hear my brudder say. 29

'Starving to death on a government
claim' FL: My name is Tom
Hight, an old bachelor I am FLC:
Hurray for Greer County! the
land of the free. 57

'The state of Arkansas' FL: My
name is Charlie Brennan. 57

'A stately song' FL: If Mary goes
far out to sea. 68

'Stay, cruel, stay' John Danyel.
FL: same. 26

'Stay in the field' FL: I've got my
breast plate, sword, and shield
FLC: O stay in the field childe-
renah. 5

Stay, mighty love, and teach my
song see 'Holland'

'Steal away' FL: My Lord calls me
FLC: Steal away, steal away,
steal away to Jesus. 25, 34,
38, 66

'Stealin', stealin'' FL: Now put
your arms around me like a
circle round the sun FLC: Stealin', stealin', pretty mama. 57

'Stella by starlight' Ned Washington
and Victor Young. FL: Have
you seen Stella by starlight FLC:
The song a robin sings. 70

'Stenka Razin' FL: Izza ostrova na
strezhen. 57

'Stenka Razin' Jerry Silverman.
FL: Round the bend, beyond the
island. 57

Step for two the weevily wheat see
'Weevily wheat'

'Step it up and go' FL: With a girl,
havin' a little fun FLC: I had to
step it up and go. 57

Step up buddies and listen to my
song see 'Otto Wood'

'Sterne's Maria' FL: Twas near a
thickets calm retreat. 3

'Stewball' FL: It's good mornin',
you young ladies FLC: It's good
mornin' you young men. 28

'Stewball' FL: Stewball was a good
horse. 23, 25, 56

'Stewball' FL: There's a big day in

Dallas. 57

'Stick close to your bedding ground' FL: When the night is black and the storm clouds crack. 18

'Still growing' FL: Now father, dear father, you have done me some harm. 30

Still she cried, "I love him the best" see 'I know my love'

'Stille nacht' Joseph Mohr and Franz Gruber. FL: Stille nacht, heilige nacht. 34

Stillness in the grove not a rustling sound see 'Moscow nights'

'Stir the pudding' FL: Long before the rising sun FLC: Oh, stir the pudding, Peggy. 57, 58

'Stodola Pumpa' Robert E. Nye. FL: Moon shining bright along the pathway home FLC: Stodola stodola, stodola pumpa. 34

Stole my partner shoe lie low see 'Shoe-lie-low'

'Stompin' at the Savoy' Andy Razaf, Benny Goodman, Chick Webb and Edgar Sampson. FL: Savoy, the home of sweet romance. 53

'Stoned soul picnic' Laura Nyro. FL: Can you surry? Can you picnic? 45

Stop and lemme tell you 'bout the coming of the Savior see 'Great gettin' up mornin''

'Stop it!' Harry D. Kerr and Mel B. Kaufman. FL: Hurry, honey, come with me FLC: Oh when the band begins a-jazzin' in the blues. 54

Stop, oh stop, Love Henry she said, and stay all night with me see 'Love Henry'

'The storm' FL: Cease, rude Boreas, blustering railer. 3

'The storm of Heber Springs, November 25, 1926' FL: Twas on Thanksgiving Day. 50

'The storms are on the ocean' FL: I'm going away for to leave you FLC: The storms are on the ocean. 56

Stormy the night and the waves roll high see 'Asleep in the deep'

'Stormy weather' Ted Koehler and Harold Arlen. FL: Don't know why there's no sun up in the sky. 53, 64

'The stormy winds' FL: Twas Friday morn when we sot sail FLC: The stormy winds do blow, blow, blow. 11

'The stormy winds do blow' FL: One Friday morn a ship set sail FLC: For the raging seas do roar. 11

'The stormy winds do blow' FL: Then up spoke the captain of our gallant ship. 11

The stormy winds do blow, blow, blow see 'The mermaid'; 'The stormy winds'

A story, a story, a story anon see 'The Bishop of Canterbury'

A story, a story, a story of one see 'King John and the bishop'; 'The king's three questions'

A story came one morning see 'The noble 24th'

'A story of love' Carlos Almaran. FL: Siempre fuiste la razón de mi existir FLC: Ya no estás a mi lado corazón. 9

'The story of love' George Thorn and Carlos Almaran. FL: When he tells you with his soft appealing ways FLC: All at once you find your dreams are coming true. 9

'The story of the rose' 'Alice' and Andrew Mack. FL: A youth one day in a garden fair FLC: Heart of my heart I love you. 20

'The story the crow told me' FL: Now, if you will listen, I'll sing you a song FLC: One little story that the crow told me. 68

'Stouthearted men' Oscar Hammerstein and Sigmund Romberg. FL: You who have dreams FLC: Give me some men who are stouthearted men. 24, 46

Strange, dear, but true, dear see 'So in Love'

A strange young man from the north country see 'Barbery Ellen'

'Stranger in Paradise' Robert Wright and George Forrest. FL: Take my hand, I'm a stranger in Paradise. 6

Strangers, and we were sweethearts for so long see 'Perfidia'

'Strawberry Fields forever' Lennon and McCartney. FL: Let me take you down 'cause I'm goin' to Strawberry Fields. 44

'Strawberry Lane' FL: As I was a-walking up Strawberry Lane. 11, 57

'Strawberry Lane' FL: One day I was walking in Strawberry Lane. 11

'The strawberry roan' FL: I was hangin' round town just a-spending my time FLC: Well, it's oh that Strawberry roan. 43, 57

'The stray' FL: We are like some human folks who through this world must roam. 43

'Stray cat' Mick Jagger and Keith Richard. FL: I hear the click clack of your feet on the stairs. 16

'The streamlet that flowed round her cot' FL: same. 3

'Street fighting man' Mick Jagger and Keith Richard. FL: Everywhere I hear the sound of marching, charging feet. 16

'Streets of Cairo' G. M. Rosenberg and James Thornton. FL: I will sing you a song FLC: She never saw the streets of Cairo. 20

'The streets of glory' FL: I'm gonna walk the streets of glory. 57

'Streets of Laredo' FL: As I passed by Ben Sherman's barroom. 62

'The streets of Laredo' FL: As I walked out in the streets of Laredo. 23, 25, 34, 57

'The streets of Laredo' FL: As I was a-ridin' the streets of Laredo. 66

'Streets of Laredo' FL: As I was riding down past Tom Sheridan's barroom. 62

'The streets of New York' Henry Blossom and Victor Herbert. FL: In dear old New York, it's remarkable--very. 20

Stretch your lovin' arms straight out in space see 'Ballin' the jack'

'Strew the sweet roses of pleasure between' FL: If life's a rough path, as the sages have said. 3

'Strike up the band' Andrew B. Sterling and Charles B. Ward. FL: Jack is the king of the dark blue sea FLC: Strike up the band. 31

'Strike up the band' George and Ira Gershwin. FL: We fought in 1917 FLC: Let the drums roll out. 21, 46

'Strolling through Norfolk' FL: While strolling thro' Norfolk one day on a spree FLC: Over the ocean I've sailed merrily. 35

The student Y has found new vocation see 'Poisoning the students' mind'

'Stung right' Joe Hill. FL: As I was walkin' round the town FLC: Well I was stung right! 57

'Stupid girl' Mick Jagger and Keith Richard. FL: I'm not talkin' about the kind of clothes she wears. 16

'Stuttering song' Walter Jones. FL: There are p-p-p-points in the singing of a s-s-s-song. 36

Such captivating green eyes see 'Green eyes'

'Sucking cider through a straw' FL: The prettiest gal I ever saw. 25, 57

Sue wants a barbecue see 'In the cool, cool, cool, of the evening'

'The Suffolk miracle' FL: Come you people, old and young. 11

'The Suffolk miracle' FL: Sing courting, courting, courting, cane. 11

'The Suffolk miracle' FL: There was a squire lived in this town. 11

'The Suffolk miracle' FL: There was an old and wealthy man. 11

'The Suffolk miracle' FL: Twelve months he rose put on his clothes. 11

Sugar, ah, honey, honey see 'Sugar, sugar'

'Sugar babe blues' FL: Take your arm from round me neck, Sugar Babe. 57

'The sugar camp' Frances Densmore. FL: Let us go to the sugar camp. 13

'Sugar lips' Billy Sherrill and Buddy Killen. FL: same. 47

'Sugar, sugar' Jeff Barry and Andy Kim. FL: Sugar, ah honey, honey. 45

'The suicide song' Pat Blanke, James Leisy and Alice Hawthorn. FL: Oh, come with me to the kitchen FLC: Listen to the hissing sounds. 35

Sul mare luccia see 'Santa Lucia'

'Suliram' FL: Suliram, suliram, suliram. 57

Sum speikis of lords, sum speikis

of lairds see 'Johnie Arm-
strang'
'Summer fun' FL: In summer when
the sky is blue. 13
'Summertime' Du Bose Heyward
and George Gershwin. FL: Summertime an' the livin' is easy.
6, 21, 42, 64
The sun sets at night and the stars
shun the day see 'Alknomook';
'The Indian chief'
The sun shines bright in the old
Kentucky home see 'My old
Kentucky home'
The sun shines high on yonder hill
see 'The false lover won back';
'The place where my love John-
nie dwells'
Sun shining down, sky all around
see 'Let the sun shine forever'
Sun turning 'round with graceful
motion see '2000 light years
from home'
The sun was sinking in the west
see 'The dying ranger'
'Sunbonnet Sue' Will D. Cobb and
Gus Edwards. FL: You looked so
nice FLC: Sunbonnet Sue, Sunbon-
net Sue. 12
'Sunday' Oscar Hammerstein and
Richard Rodgers. FL: Now that
we're going to be married FLC:
Sunday, sweet Sunday, with noth-
ing to do. 24
'Sunday mornin' comin' down' Kris
Kristofferson. FL: Well, I woke
up Sunday mornin' with no way to
hold my head that didn't hurt
FLC: On the Sunday mornin' side-
walk. 10, 15
Sunday morning just at nine see
'Down went McGinty'
Sunday, sweet Sunday, with nothing
to do see 'Sunday'
'Sunday will never be the same'
Gene Pistilli and Terry Cashman.
FL: I remember Sunday morning.
47
'Sung at harvest time' Christine
Turner Curtis. FL: Come, my
sisters, come, my brothers. 13
'Sunrise, sunset' Sheldon Harnick
and Jerry Bock. FL: Is this the
little girl I carried? FLC: Sun-
rise, sunset. 6, 42, 64
The sunrise tints the dew see
'Crocuses'
Sunshine came softly through my

window today see 'Sunshine
superman'
'Sunshine, lollipops and rainbows'
Howard Liebling and Marvin Ham-
lisch. FL: same. 47
'The sunshine of Paradise Alley'
Walter H. Ford and John W.
Bratton. FL: There's a little
side street such as often you
meet FLC: Every Sunday down
to her home we go. 20
'Sunshine superman' Donovan Leitch.
FL: Sunshine came softly through
my window today. 45
'Superstar' Tim Rice and Andrew
L. Webber. FL: Every time I
look at you I don't understand.
45
'Sur le pont d'Avignon' FL: Les
beaux messieurs font comm ci
FLC: Sur le pont d'Avignon. 25,
34, 48
Sure, I've got rings on my fingers,
bells on my toes see 'I've got
rings on my fingers'
'Sure make a man feel bad' FL:
Sure hate to see poor mother go.
28
'Surprise, surprise' Mick Jagger
and Keith Richard. FL: Well,
I told friends of mine. 16
'The surrey with the fringe on top'
Oscar Hammerstein and Richard
Rodgers. FL: When I take you
out tonight with me FLC: Chicks
and ducks and geese better scur-
ry. 42
'Susan Brown' FL: Choose your
partner as we go around. 37
'Susani' Katherine F. Rohrbough.
FL: From heaven high, bright
angels, come. 13
'Susie Cleland' FL: There lived a
lady in Scotland. 11
'The swan swims so bonny, O' FL:
The miller's daughter being
dressed in red. 11
'Swanee' Irving Caesar and George
Gershwin. FL: I've been away
from you a long time FLC:
Swanee, how I love you. 21
'Swanee River' Stephen Foster. FL:
Way down upon the Swanee River
FLC: All the world is sad and
dreary. 57
'Swannonoa Tunnel' FL: Ashville
Junction, Swannonoa Tunnel. 57
'Sway' Mick Jagger and Keith

Sweet Rosie O'Grady. 20, 31, 67

Sweet summer breeze, whispering trees see 'Kiss me again'

Sweet, sweet, sweet, let me go! see 'Sweet, let me go'

'Sweet the evening air of May' FL: same. 57

'Sweet thing' FL: Sweet thing, I'm writing this letter to you FLC: Sweet thing, I love you. 14

A sweet Tuxedo girl you see see 'Ta-ra-ra-boom-der-e'

'Sweet Violets' J. K. Emmett. FL: Sweet violets, sweeter than all the roses. 67

'Sweet violets' Cy Coben and Charles Grean. FL: There once was a farmer who took a young miss FLC: Sweet violets. 52

'Sweet William' FL: Before the rising of the sun. 11

'Sweet William' FL: Come, all ye ladies great and small. 11

'Sweet William' FL: In Scarlet town where I was born. 11

'Sweet William' FL: It's early, early all in the spring. 30

'Sweet William' FL: My father was a noble knight. 11

'Sweet William' FL: One morning in June sweet William arose. 11

'Sweet William' FL: Sweet William arose on last May morning. 11

'Sweet William' FL: Sweet William rode up to the old man's gate. 11

'Sweet William' FL: Sweet William's gane over seas. 11

'Sweet William and Fair Ellen' FL: Sweet William rode up to Fair Ellen's gate. 11

'Sweet William and Lady Margaret' FL: Lady Margaret was sitting in the new church door. 11

'Sweet William and Lady Margaret' FL: Lady Margaret was standing in her drawing room door. 11

'Sweet William and Lady Margaret' FL: O twas on one merry May morning. 11

'Sweet William and Lady Margaret' FL: Sweet William arose one May May morning. 11

'Sweet William and Lady Margaret' FL: Sweet William arose one May misty morning. 11

'Sweet William and Lady Margaret'

FL: Sweet William arose one merry morn. 11

'Sweet William and Lady Margaret' FL: Sweet William he rose one May morning. 11

'Sweet William and Lady Margaret' FL: Sweet William he said he was troubled in his head. 11

'Sweet William and Lady Margery' FL: Sweet William rose one early morning. 11

Sweet William arose and he put on his clothes see 'Fair Margaret and Sweet William'

Sweet William arose on last May morning see 'Sweet William'

Sweet William arose one May May morning see 'Sweet William and Lady Margaret'

Sweet William arose one May misty morning see 'Sweet William and Lady Margaret'

Sweet William arose on May morning see 'Fair Margaret and Sweet William'; 'Lady Margaret'; 'Lady Margaret and Sweet William'

Sweet William arose one merry morn see 'Sweet William and Lady Margaret'

Sweet William he married him a wife see 'The wife wrapt in wether's skin'

Sweet William he rose in the month of May see 'Fair Margaret and Sweet William'

Sweet William he rose one May morning see 'Fair Margaret and Sweet William'; 'Sweet William and Lady Margaret'

Sweet William he rose one merry, merry morning see 'Fair Margaret and Sweet William'

Sweet William he said he was troubled in his head see 'Sweet William and Lady Margaret'

'Sweet William, my son' FL: Oh, where have you been, Sweet William my son? 11

Sweet William rode up to fair Ellen's gate see 'Sweet William and Fair Ellen'

Sweet William rode up to the old man's gate see 'Sweet William'

Sweet William rose on early morning see 'Sweet William and Lady Margery'

Sweet William rose one Easter

Tam Pierce, lead me your gray
mare FLC: With Bill Brewer,
Jane Stewer, Peter Guerney. 57
'Tampa' FL: I got a long tall yellow
gal in Georgia. 28
'Tammany' Gus Edwards and Vincent
Bryan. FL: Hiawatha was an In-
dian, so was Navajo FLC: Tam-
many, Tammany. 57
'Tangerine' Johnny Mercer and Vic-
tor Schertzinger. FL: Tangerine,
she is all they claim. 47, 59
'Taps' FL: Day is done, gone the
sun. 34, 66
'Ta-ra-ra-boom-de-ay!' Angelo A.
Asher and Lottie Collins. FL:
A smart and stylish girl you see
FLC: Ta-ra-ra-boom-de-ay. 36
'Ta-ra-ra Boom-der-é' Henry J.
Sayers. FL: A sweet Tuxedo
girl you see FLC: Ta-ra-ra-boom-
der-é. 1, 25
'Tarnation strange' J. Blewitt. FL:
Yankee wonders are now all the
rage FLC: Oh yes, isn't it tar-
nation strange. 36
'Tarranty, my son' FL: Oh, where
have you been, Tarranty, my
son? 11
'The tasks' FL: Thou must buy me
my lady a cambrick shirt. 11
'A taste of honey' Rick Marlow and
Bobby Scott. FL: Winds may
blow over the icy sea. 71
'Tatters' Gerald Lane. FL: Tatters,
with his little broom FLC: Ah!
rags and tatters. 63
Te quiero, dijiste see 'Magic is
the moonlight'
Te quiero, sweet heaven see
'Magic is the moonlight'
Te voy hacer tus calzones see 'El
Rancho grande'
'Tea for two' Irving Caesar and
Vincent Youmans. FL: I'm dis-
contented with homes that are
rented FLC: Picture you upon my
knee. 1, 42, 46
'The tea party' FL: I snum I am a
Yankee man and I'll sing to you
a ditty FLC: Folderal deray,
folderal deray. 8
'A tea party song' FL: As near beau-
teous Boston lying. 49
Tea ships near to Boston lying see
'The ballad of the tea party'
'The tea tax' FL: I snum I am a
Yankee lad and I guess I'll sing

a ditty. 36
Teacher, teacher, why are you so
poor see 'Teacher's blues'
Teachers are on strike no school
today see 'Skip a rope'
Teacher's blues' FL: Teacher,
teacher, why are you so poor.
57
'The teacher's lament' Merle Travis.
FL: I woke one morning, it was
cloudy and cool. 19
'Tears on my pillow' Gene Autry
and Fred Rose. FL: Tears on
my pillow each morning. 10
'Teasing' Cecil Mack and Albert
von Tilzer. FL: I feel so awful
blue FLC: Teasing, teasing. 20
'The teensy weensy spider' FL:
The teensy weensy spider went
up the water spout. 72
Teet tee dee dee dee see 'Willie
the Weeper'
'The tee-to-tal society' FL: I'm
come to exhort you so free. 36
'Tell bruddah Lijah' FL: O sinner,
ain' you tired of sinnin' FLC: No
harm, no harm. 5
'Tell me boys' FL: When I joined
the army a few weeks ago FLC:
Tell me, boys, have you any
complaints. 57
Tell me, do you love me? see
'The sweetest story ever told'
Tell me how long do I have to wait?
see 'Hesitation blues'
Tell me one thing tell me truly
see 'No, sir'
'Tell me pretty maiden' Leslie
Stuart. FL: same. 20
Tell me that you love me, Katy
Cline see 'Katy Cline'
'Tell me that you love me tonight'
Al Silverman and C. A. Bixio.
FL: same. 67
Tell me the tales that to me were
so dear see 'Long, long ago'
'Tell, me what month my Jesus was
born in' FL: same FLC: Well,
you got January, February,
March. 57
'Tell me why' FL: Please tell me
why the stars do shine. 34
'Tell old Bill' FL: Tell old Bill
when he comes home. 35, 57
'Tell-tale Polly' FL: She mounted
on her bonny, bonny brown. 11
'Temperance Bells' FL: Hark the
temperance bells are ringing

FLC: Hear the bells, joyous
bells. 63
Tempermental Oriental gentleman
are we see 'Mischa, Yascha,
Toscha, Sascha'
Tempted and tried we're oft made
to wonder see 'Farther along'
'Ten cents a dance' Lorenz and
Richard Rodgers. FL: I work at
the Palace Ballroom FLC: Ten
cents a dance. 46
'Ten green bottles' FL: Ten green
bottles hanging on the wall. 34
'Ten little Indians' FL: John Brown
had a little Indian. 57
'Ten little kiddies' FL: Ten little
kiddies going out to dine FLC:
One little, two little, three
little. 25
'Ten minutes ago' Oscar Hammer-
stein and Richard Rodgers. FL:
Ten minutes ago I saw you. 24
'Ten thousand cattle' FL: Ten thou-
sand cattle gone astray FLC:
Ten thousand cattle straying. 43,
57
'Ten thousand miles away' FL: On
the banks of a lonely river, ten
thousand miles away. 50
'Ten thousand miles away' FL: Sing
I for a brave and a gallant
barque. 57
'The ten virgins' FL: Five of them
were wise when the bridegroom
came FLC: O Zion, O Zion. 38
'The tenderfoot' FL: I thought one
day that just for fun. 57
'The tenderfoot' FL: One day I
thought I'd have some fun. 62
'The tenderfoot' FL: One springtime
I thought just for fun. 66
'Tenderly' Jack Lawrence and Walter Gross. FL: The evening
breeze caressed the trees tenderly. 59, 70
'The Tennessee wig-walk' Norman
Gimbel and Larry Coleman. FL:
I'm a bowlegged chicken. 67
'Tenting tonight' Walter Kittredge.
FL: We're tenting tonight on the
old camp ground FLC: Many are
the hearts that are weary tonight.
1, 4, 57
'Terence, my son' FL: Oh, where
have you been today, Terence,
my son? 11
'Texarkana Mary' FL: Wo, Texarkana Ida, Holl'rin' wo, Lord. 28

'Texas cowboy' FL: Oh, I'm a Texas cowboy far away from home.
62
A Texas cowboy lay down on a
barroom floor see 'The Hell-
bound train'
'The Texas rangers' FL: Come all
ye Texas Rangers wherever you
may be. 43, 50, 57
'The Tex-i-an boys' FL: Come
along, girls, and listen to my
noise. 57, 58
Thank God, she's got religion see
'Gone along'
'Thanks for the memory' Leo Robin
and Ralph Rainger. FL: Thanks
for the memory of candelight and
wine. 53
'Thanksgiving hymn' FL: The Lord
above in tender love. 49
Thar' is gwine to be a festival this
evenin' see 'My gal is a high
born lady'
That big eight wheeler rollin' down
the track see 'I'm movin' on'
That boy took my love see 'Ringo's theme'
'That certain feeling' George and
Ira Gershwin. FL: Knew it from
the start FLC: That certain feeling. 21
'That crazy war' FL: Now over there
across the sea they've got another
war. 57
'That doggie in the window' Bob
Merrill. FL: How much is that
doggie in the window. 10
'That is love' Felix McGlennon.
FL: Love, sweet love is the
poet's theme. 63
'That lucky old sun' Haven Gillespie and Beasley Smith. FL: Oh
Lawd! Oh Lawd, I'm tired and
weary of pain FLC: Up in the
mornin' out on the job. 10
'That old black magic' Johnny Mercer and Harold Arlen. FL: That
old black magic has me in its
spell. 47, 70
That seat of science, Athens see
'Free America'; 'A song of lib-
erty'
That sweet little gal see 'The gal
I left behind me'
'That's a plenty' Ray Gilbert and
Lew Pollack. FL: That's a
plenty gotta beat in it FLC:
same. 31

'That's all right' FL: same FLC:
    Since my soul's got a seat. 57
'That's amore' Jack Brooks and
    Harry Warren. FL: In Napoli
    where love is king FLC: When
    the moon hits your eye like a
    pizza pie. 52
'That's how much I love you' Eddy
    Arnold, Wally Fowler and J.
    Graydon Hall. FL: If I had a
    nickel I know what I would do.
    67
'That's my desire' Carroll Loveday
    and Helmy Kresa. FL: To spend
    one night with you. 12
'That's the reason noo I wear a
    kilt' Harry Lauder and A. B.
    Kendall. FL: A lot o' people
    say the kilt is not the thing to
    wear FLC: Every nicht I used to
    hing my troosers up. 17
That's the rebel girl see 'The
    rebel girl'
'That's where my money goes' FL:
    same. 23, 25
Them Methodists and Baptists can't
    agree see 'The winter soon be
    over'
Then away, love, away see 'Rio
    Grande'
Then away you Santy see 'Can't
    you dance the polka?'
Then beat the drum lowly and play
    the fife merrily see 'The
    young sailor cut down in his
    prime'
Then blow ye winds westerly, west-
    erly blow see 'Blow ye winds
    westerly'
Then by there cam' twa gentlemen
    see 'Barrin' o' the door'
Then cheer, cheer, the Green
    Mountaineer see 'The Green
    Mountaineer'
Then cherish her with care see 'A
    boy's best friend is his mother'
Then combine your humble ditties
    as from tavern to tavern we steer
    see 'The son of a gambolier'
Then come along, my brothers see
    'Song of the freedman'
Then come along, my hearties, to-
    gether we will ride see 'Bur-
    mese tune'
Then come sit here awhile ere you
    leave us see 'The cowboy love
    song'
Then come with your cash everyone

see 'Uncle Sam's menagerie'
Then drill, ye tarriers, drill see
    'Drill, ye tarriers, drill'
Then forward, you workers, free-
    dom awaits you see 'Whirlwinds
    of danger'
Then he seized this auger and over-
    board jumped he see 'Lowlands
    low'
Then I wish I was in Dixie see
    'Dixie'
Then Joseph took Mary upon his
    right knee see 'The cherry tree
    carol'
Then let the bells of Dublin ring
    see 'One and all'
Then let us be merry see 'A
    virgin unspotted'
Then Mary took her young Son see
    'Mary's questions'
Then only say that you'll be mine
    see 'Banks of the Ohio'
Then one day when cook was baking
    see 'La cucaracha'
Then raise the scarlet standard high
    see 'The red flag'
Then Robin he went to a tree cut-
    ter's tree see 'Robin Hood and
    Little John'
Then, round the bay of Mexico see
    'Round the bay of Mexico'
'Then say my sweet girl, can you
    love me?' FL: Dear Nancy I've
    failed the world all around. 3
Then sing o the holy, holy see
    'The cherry tree carol'
Then steadily shoulder to shoulder
    see 'The old brigade'
Then under full sail see 'America,
    commerce and freedom'
Then up spoke the captain of our
    gallant ship see 'The stormy
    winds do blow'
Then up spoke the chaplain of our
    gallant ship see 'The wrecked
    ship'
Then was a little lady, a little lady
    gay see 'Little lady gay'
Then we'll sing of Lydia Pinkham
    see 'Lydia Pinkham'
'Then you shall be a true lover of
    mine' FL: Choose when you can
    an acre of land. 11
There ain't no more cane on the
    Brazis see 'Ain't no more cane
    on the Brazis'
There ain't no more cane on this
    Brazos see 'No more cane on

see 'Lord Thomas of Winesbur-
ry'; 'Willie o' Winsbury'
There lived a king an' a very great
king see 'Eliza's Bowers'
There lived a knight in the north
see 'Mary Hamilton'
There lived a lad at Rhynie's town
see 'Lang Johnny More'
There lived a lady in merry Scot-
land see 'There was a lady in
merry Scotland'
There lived a lady in Scotland see
'Susie Cleland'
There lived a lady in the north
see 'Yarrow'
There lived a lady in the South see
'The dowie dens o' Yarrow'
There lived a lady in the West see
'The dowie dens o' Yarrow'
There lived a lord in the old coun-
try see 'The two sisters'
There lived a man in Baleno see
'Ally Croaker'
There lived a man in Rhynie's land
see 'Lang Johnnie Moir'
There lived a man in yonder glen
see 'Johnie Blunt'
There lived a wife at Usher's Well
see 'The wife of Usher's Well'
There lived an old lord by the
northern sea see 'The twa
sisters'; 'The two sisters'
There lived an old lord in the north
countree see 'The old lord of
the North Country'
There lived an old woman down by
the seashore, bow down, bow
down see 'The two sisters'
There lived three brothers in fair
Scotland see 'Boldender Martin'
There lived three brothers in merry
Scotland see 'Henry Martin'
'There lived twa sisters' FL: There
lived twa sisters in a bower. 11
There lived a lady in London see
'The cruel mother'
There lives a lady in this place
see 'The dowie dens'
There lives a man in Rynie's land
see 'Lang Johnnie More'
There lives a man on the western
plains see 'The cowboy'
There never was yet a boy or a
man see 'Tinker man'
There once lived an Indian maid
see 'Red Wing'
There once sailed a ship from the
North Amerikee see 'The

Golden Fenadier'
There once was a Balham vicar
see 'The Balham vicar'
There was a bold fisherman who
sailed out from Pimlico see
'Bold fisherman'
There was a braw ball in Edinbro'
see 'Bonnie Lizzie Lindsay'
There once was a country maiden
came to London for a trip see
'And her golden hair was hanging
down her back'
There once was a farmer who took
a young miss see 'Sweet vio-
lets'
There once was a man, a very
tricky man see 'Tol lol sol'
There once was a man who was
boasting the quay see 'The
Golden Vanitee'
There once was a ship she was a-
sailing on the sea see 'The
Golden Willow Tree'
There once was a swagman camped
in a billabong see 'Waltzing
Matilda'
There once was a union maid see
'Union maid'
There once were three brothers
from merry Scotland see 'An-
drew Batann'
There sat two lovers on yon hill
see 'Fair Margaret and Sweet
William'
There she is! There she is! see
'Ain't she sweet'
There she stands, the lovely crea-
ture see 'The lovely creature'
There was a battle in the North
see 'Geordie'
There was a beautiful damsel, from
London she came see 'Pretty
Sally'
'There was a bold captain' FL:
There was a ship sailing in the
North Country. 11
There was a bold soldier, from
Dover he came see 'The bold
soldier'
There was a bold soldier that late-
ly came from sea see 'The poor
soldier'
There was a bonnie shepherd lad
see 'The shepherd lad'
There was a boy and a bonnie boy
see 'The bailie's daughter of
Islington'
There was a desperado from the

wild and woolly West see 'The
desperado'
There was a dirty beggarman see
'The beggarman'
There was a fair lady far crossed
in love see 'The fair maid by
the sea shore'
There was a fair lady, from London
she came see 'Sally the Queen'
There was a fair lady, from London she came see 'Sally the
Queen'
'There was a farmer' FL: There
was a farmer lived in our town.
11
There was a farmer lived in the
east see 'Katherine Jaffrey'
There was a farmer living in town
see 'Worse than men'
There was a farmer's son see
'Blow away the morning dew'
There was a farmer's son keep
sheep all on the hill see 'Blow
away the morning dew'
There was a farmer's son who led
a humble life see 'Blow away
the morning dew'
There was a fine ship started out
on the sea see 'Green Willow
Tree'; 'Turkish Reveille'
There was a frog lived in the
spring see 'The frog in the
spring'
There was a gallant ship and a gal-
lant ship was she see 'The
Goulden vanitee'
There was a gallant soldier see
'The lady and the dragoon'
There was a girl in Denver see
'Love's been good to me'
There was a girl in Westminster
see 'The tinker'
There was a good ship from the
north countrie see 'Low in the
lowlands, low'
There was a gypsy come over the
hill see 'Gypsy Davy'
There was a happy time to me not
many years ago see 'Little
old sod shanty'
There was a jolly beggar, for beg-
gin' he was boun' see 'The
jolly beggar'
'There was a jolly miller' FL:
There was a jolly miller once
lived on the River Dee. 3
There was a jolly miller once lived

by the River Dee see 'The
happy miller'
There was a jolly old farmer man
see 'The farmer who went out
for beer'
There was a jolly shepherd love
see 'Blow away the morning
dew'
There was a jovial beggar see
'The jovial beggar'
There was a knicht an' a lady
bricht see 'Leatherum thee-
thou and a'
There was a knight all clothed in
red see 'Flowers of the valley'
There was a knight and he was
young see 'A song'
There was a knight came from the
Northland see 'The outlandish
knight'
There was a knight, in Scotland
born see 'The fair flower of
Northumberland'
'There was a lady' FL: There was
a lady was she. 11
There was a lady, a lady gay see
'The wife of Usher's Well'
There was a lady, a lady of York
see 'The cruel mother'
There was a lady and a lady gay
see 'Lady gay'; 'The wife of
Usher's Well'
There was a lady and gay was she
see 'The wife of Usher's Well'
There was a lady came from York
see 'The cruel mother'; 'The
greenwood siding'
'There was a lady drest in green'
FL: same. 11
There was a lady dwell in York
see 'The cruel mother'
There was a lady gay see 'The
wife of Usher's Well'
'There was a lady in merry Scot-
land' FL: There lived a lady in
merry Scotland. 11
There was a lady in merry Scot-
land see 'The wife of Usher's
well'
There was a lady in our town see
'The wife of Usher's Well'
'There was a lady in the east' FL:
same. 30
There was a lady in the north see
'The dowie dens of Yarrow'
There was a lady in the north coun-
try see 'Lord Thomas of

Winesbury'; 'A riddle wittily ex-
pounded'
'There was a lady in the West' FL:
same. 11
There was a lady in yonder town
see   'The greenwood side'
There was a lady, lady gay   see
'The three little babes'
There was a lady lived in New York
see   'Fair flowers of Helio'
There was a lady lived in this town
see   'The green wedding'
'There was a lady lived in York'
FL: same. 11
There was a lady lived in York   see
'The cruel mother'; 'Down by the
greenwood side'
There was a lady living in the east
see   'Young Barbour'
There was a lady near the town
see   'The cruel mother'
There was a lady of beauty bright
see   'The three little babes'
There was a lady of beauty rare
see   'The three babes'
There was a lady she was bright
see   'The wife of Usher's Well'
There was a lass in the north coun-
trie   see   'Willie o' Winsbury'
There was a lass near by to this
see   'The gardener lad'
There was a little boat, all fitted
for the sea   see   'Lowlands
lonesome low'
There was a little boy   see   'The
Jew's daughter'
There was a little man and he had
a little can   see   'No more
booze'
There was a little man came from
the west   see   'The daughter of
Peggy O'
There was a little old man that
lived in the west   see   'Dandoo'
There was a little shepherd maid
see   'Earl Richard'
There was a little ship and she
sailed on the sea   see   'The pi-
rate ship'
There was a little ship and she
sailed upon the sea   see   'The
Golden Vanity'; 'The Golden
Willow Tree'; 'The Mary Golden
Tree'; 'The Merry Golden Tree';
'Sinking in the lonesome sea'
There was a little ship in south
Amerikee   see   'The Golden
Vanity'

There was a little ship in the South
Amerikee   see   'The Weeping
Willow Tree'
There was a little ship that sailed
on the sea   see   'The Green
Willow Tree'; 'The Turkish Rebi-
lee'
There was a little ship that sailed
out on the sea   see   'The Mary
Golden Tree'
There was a little ship that sailed upon
the sea   see   'The lonesome sea'
There was a little soldier boy who
lately came from over   see
'Little soldier boy'
There was a little tree in yonders
field   see   'The tree in yonders
field'
There was a little woman   see
'The old woman and the pedlar'
There was a lofty ship   see   'The
Golden Vanity'
There was a lord in Ambertown
see   'Pretty Polly'
There was a lord in London town
see   'Lady Isabel and the elf
knight'
There was the lord lived in the
North country, bow down   see
'The lord of the North Country'
There was a lord lived in this town
see   'The Holland handkerchief'
There was a Lord Mayor in our
town   see   'The two sisters'
There was a maid and she went to
the mill   see   'The maid and the
mill'
There was a man   see   'Bill Grog-
gin's goat'
There was a man a-coming from
the south   see   'The trooper and
the maid'
'There was a man and he was mad'
FL: same. 57
There was a man he had a ship
see   'The Golden Vanity'
There was a man he lived in Lon-
don   see   'A Turkish lady'
There was a man his name was
Burke   see   'The tale of a shirt'
There was a man in ancient times
see   'Lazarus'; 'Lazarus and
Dives'; 'The rich man and Laza-
rus'
There was a man in bondage brought
see   'Lord Bateman and the
Turkish lady'
There was a man in England born

see 'Turkish lady'
'There was a man in the West' FL:
There was a man lived in the
West. 11
There was a man lived in the east
see 'Young M'Tyre'
There was a man lived in the moon
see 'Aiken Drum'
There was a man lived in the west
see 'Ruggleton's daughter of
Iero'; 'There was a man in the
west'; 'The twa sisters'; 'The
wether's skin'
There was a man lived in the west,
bow down, bow down see 'The
two sisters'
There was a man named Dunderbeck
invented a machine see 'Dunder-
beck'
There was a man out in the land
see 'The seven king's daughters'
There was a man that lived in Eng-
land see 'Lord Bateman'
There was a man went up and down
see 'One meat ball'
There was a man when he was first
born see 'The devil and the
farmer's wife'
There was a man who lived in England see 'Lord Batesman'
There was a may and weel far'd
may see 'Katherine Janfarie'
There was a noble English lad see
'The King's daughter fair'
There was a noble lord see 'Lord
Bateman'
There was a pedlar and a pedlar
bold see 'Bold pedlar and
Robin Hood'
There was a poor young man and he
came to New York see 'The
fatal curse of drink'
There was a proper tall young man
see 'Lady Isabel and the elf
knight'
There was a rich farmer in York-
shire did dwell see 'The boy
and the cow'
There was a rich lady, from Eng-
land she came see 'Fair Sally'
There was a rich lady, from Ire-
land she came see 'Pretty Sally'
There was a rich lady from London
she came see 'The brown girl';
'Pretty Sally'; 'A rich lady from
London'
There was a rich lady from Scotland
she came see 'The brown girl'

There was a rich man and he lived
in Jerusalem see 'The rich
man and the poor man'
There was a rich merchant in London did dwell see 'The press
gang'
There was a rich merchant ship
from the northern counteree see
'Golden Vanity'
There was a rich merchant who
lived in Strathdinah see 'Bonnie
Annie'
There was a rich nobleman I've
heard tell see 'The outlandish
knight'
There was a sailor from Dover
from Dover he came see 'Sail-
or from Dover'
'There was a shepherd' Robert
Jones. FL: There was a shepherd that did live. 26
There was a shepherd laddie kept
sheep on yonder hill see 'The
shepherd laddie'
There was a shepherd's daughter
see 'The shepherd's daughter'
There was a shepherd's daughter
was herding on yon hill see
'The knight and the shepherd's
daughter'
There was a shepherd's son see
'Blow the winds I-ho!'; 'Jock
sheep'
There was a ship and a ship of
fame see 'William Glen'
There was a ship a-sailing on the
North Amerikee see 'The Gold-
en Vanity'
There was a ship came from the
north country see 'The Golden
Vanity'
There was a ship from the Northern
country see 'The lowlands low'
There was a ship in the northern
countrie see 'The little cabin
boy'
There was a ship in the south coun-
tree see 'The Golden Willow
Tree'
There was a ship of the North coun-
trie see 'The lowlands low'
There was a ship sailed from the
North Amerikee see 'Sailing
on the lowland low'
There was a ship sailing in the
North country see 'There was a
bold captain'
There was a ship that was sailing

on the sea see 'The lowlands
low'
'There was a silly shepherd' FL:
There was a silly shepherd swain.
11
There was a squire in Edinburgh
town see 'The green wedding'
There was a squire lived in the east
see 'Green wedding'
There was a squire lived in the town
see 'The dowie dens of Yarrow'
There was a squire lived in this
town see 'The Suffolk miracle'
There was a squire of Edinboro
town see 'Katharine Jaffray';
'The squire of Edinboro's town'
'There was a squire of high degree'
FL: same. 11
There was a star in David's land
see 'King Herod and the cock'
There was a tailor had a mouse
see 'The tailor and the mouse'
There was a tall an' handsome man
see 'Lady Isabel and the elf
knight'
There was a tall young man see
'Lady Isabel and the elf knight'
There was a time I was jolly see
'Blue'
There was a tree see 'The green
grass grows all around'
There was a tree grew in the ground
see 'The tree in the wood'
'There was a wealthy farmer' FL:
There was a wealthy farmer who
lived close handly by. 41
There was a wealthy farmer see
'Davie Faa'; 'Yorkshire farmer'
There was a wealthy farmer, in
London he did dwell see 'Old
barn door'
There was a wealthy farmer in the
country thereby see 'Across the
plains of Illinois'
There was a wealthy merchant see
'Lamkin'
'There was a wee cooper that lived
in Fife see 'The wife wrapt in
wether's skin'
There was a wee cooper who lived
in Fife see 'Cooper of Fife'
'There was a widow all forlorn see
'Flowers of the valley'
There was a wild colonial boy see
'The wild colonial boy'
'There was a wily lad' Robert Jones.
FL: same. 26
There was a woman and she was a

widow see 'Flowers of the valley'
There was a woman lived in New
York see 'The cruel mother'
There was a woman lived near the
north see 'The wife of Usher's
well'
There was a young and a lady
bright see 'The wife of Usher's
well'
There was a young lady see
'Pretty Sally of London'
'There was a young lady' FL: same.
11
There was a young lady come a-
trippin' along see 'The gypsy
davy'
There was a young lady from Dub-
lin she came see 'The brown
girl'
There was a young lady from Lon-
don she came see 'The brown
girl'
There was a young lady so fair
see 'The cruel mother'
There was a young lady was walking alone see 'The flower of
Northumberland'
There was a young maiden see
'The brown girl'
There was a young man a very
young man see 'The gypsy
Davy'
There was a young man in old England dwelling see 'Young
Beichan'
There was a young man who lived
out West see 'The youngest
daughter'
'There was a youth' FL: There was
a youth, a loving youth. 11
There was a youth, a cruel youth
see 'The cruel youth'; 'Willow
tree'
There was a youth, a well beloved
youth see 'The bailiff's daughter
of Islington'; 'Lady Isabel and the
elf knight'
There was a youth an' a weel-faurt
youth see 'The bailie's daughter
of Islington'
There was a youth and a comely
youth see 'The bailiff's daughter
of Islington'; 'The comely youth'
There was a youth and a well bred
youth see 'The bailiff's daughter
of Islington'; 'The bellyan's
daughter'

There was an old man who lived in
the West see 'The old man who
lived in the west'; 'The two sisters'
There was an old man who lived
near hell see 'The farmer's
curst wife'
There was an old man who lived
near Hell's gate see 'The devil
and the farmer's wife'
'There was an old man who lived
out west' FL: O there was an old
man who lived out West. 11
There was an old man who lived
under the hill see 'The farmer's
curst wife'; 'The old man that
lived under the hill'
There was an old man who owned a
farm see 'The devil's song'
There was an old man who owned a
small farm see 'The farmer's
curst wife'
There was an old miser in London
did dwell see 'The old miser'
'There was an old soldier' FL: O
there was an old soldier and he
had a wooden leg. 57
'There was an old woman' FL:
There was an old woman who
swallowed a fly. 34
There was an old woman all skin
and bones see 'The scary song'
There was an old woman and in our
town did dwell see 'Singa hipsy
doodle'
'There was an old woman and she had
a little pig' FL: same. 57
There was an old woman and she
had a little pig see 'The old
woman and her pig'
There was an old woman in Northern
'try see 'The two sisters'
There was an old woman in our
town see 'Eggs and marrow
bone'; 'The rich old lady'
There was an old woman in Slab
City see 'Old woman in Slab
City'
There was an old woman lived by
the sea shore see 'The twa
sisters'
There was an old woman lived in
North Countrie see 'The old wo-
man of the North Countrie'
'There was an old woman lived in
the West' FL: same. 11
There was an old woman lived on
the seashore see 'Bow and

balance'; 'The swim swom bonny';
'The two sisters'
'There was an old woman lived
under the hill' FL: There was an
old man and he owned a farm. 11
There was an old woman lived under
the hill see 'The old woman
under the hill'
There was an old woman living on a
hill see 'The farmer's curst wife'
There was an old woman tossed up
in a blanket see 'The old woman tossed up in a blanket'
There was an old woman who lived
by the sea see 'The two sisters'
There was an old woman who swal-
lowed a fly see 'There was an
old woman'
There was blood on the saddle and
blood on the ground see 'Blood
on the saddle'
There was eighty weight of gold
Spanish iron see 'Billy and
Johnny'
There was four and twenty ladies
there see 'Little Musgrave and
Lady Barnard'
There was nine and nine horsemen
see 'Glenlogie'
There was no room found in the inn
see 'Behold that star'
There was some children in fair
Scotland see 'Fair Scotland'
There was such a man as King Wil-
liam there was see 'King Wil-
liam and Lady Margaret'
There was the gallant ship on yon
western counteree see 'The
Golden Victory'
There was three brothers in merry
Scotland see 'Captain Markee'
There was three brothers in old
Scotland see 'Andrew Bardeen'
There was three gypsies come to
the door see 'Wraggle taggle
gypsies'
There was three gypsies in the East
see 'The dark-eyed gypsy O!'
There was three maids a-playing
ball see 'The three maids'
There was three young sisters went
out for a walk see 'The banks
o' Airdrie'
There was two brothers a-going to
school see 'The two brothers'
There was two jolly ships, from old
England they came see 'New
Barbary'

There was two lofty ships, from old
England they set sail see 'High
Barbaree'

There was two ships from old England came see 'The 'Queen of
Russia' and the 'Prince of Wales''

There was two sisters living in the
East see 'Down by the waters
rolling'

'There waur three ladies in a ha''
FL: same. 11

There were a lady, she proved un-
kind see 'The cruel mother'

There were a young lady, from London she came see 'Sally yo'
the queen'

There were bells on the hill see
'Till there was you'

There were four and twenty nobles
stood at the king's ha' see
'Glenlogie'

There were nine ladies o' the east
see 'Little Musgrove and Lady
Barnswell'

There were nine to guard the British
ranks see 'The escape of Old
John Webber'

There were nine to hold the British
ranks see 'Billy and Johnny';
'Billy broke locks'

There were seven bonnie ladies in
yonder ha' see 'Ritchie's lady'

There were seven gypsies all in a
row see 'Seven gypsies'

There were seven ladies in yon ha'
see 'Richie's lady'

There were six and six ladies see
'Bethelnie'; 'Jean o' Bethelnie'

There were six and six nobles see
'Glenlogie'

There were stars in the sky see
'Serenade in the night'

There were three brothers from
merry Scotland see 'Andrew
Batan'

There were three brothers in fair
London town see 'Henry Martyn'

There were three brothers in merry
Scotland see 'Andrew Battam';
'Henry Martin'

There were three brothers in old
Scotland see 'Andrew Bardeen';
'Andrew Briton'; 'The three
Scotch robbers'

There were three brothers, three
brothers in London see 'Henry
Martin'

There were three craws sat upon a

wa' see 'Three craws'

There were three crows in a hickory
tree see 'The three ravens'

There were three crows sat on a
tree see 'Billy Magee Magaw';
'The crow song'; 'Three black
crows'; 'The three ravens'

There were three crows sat on yonder's tree see 'The three ravens'

There were three gypsies a-come
to my door see 'The draggle-
tail gypsies'; 'The wraggle taggle
gypsies'

There were three gypsies all in a
row see 'The gypsie laddie'

There were three gypsies that came
to my door see 'The three
gypsies'

There were three jolly fisherman
see 'Three jolly fishermen'

There were three ladies playing at
the ba see 'Norham, down by
Norham'

There were three little kittens see
'Three little kittens'

There were three maids lived in a
barn see 'Heckey-hi si bernio'

There were three ravens on a tree
see 'The three ravens'

There were three ravens sat on a
tree see 'The three ravens'

There were three sisters fair and
bright see 'The three sisters'

There were three sisters lived in a
bower see 'The banks of Fordie'

There were three sisters picking
flowers see 'The burly, burly
banks of Barbro-o'

There were three sisters playing
at ball see 'Oh Lilly O'

There were twa brotheris at the
schuil see 'The twa brothers'

There were twa pretty pretty boys
went tae the school see 'Twa
brothers'

There were twa sisters in a bower
see 'The bonny bows o' London';
'The Cruel sister'

There were twa sisters lived a ha'
see 'Binorie'

There were twa sisters sat in a
bower see 'Binnorie'; 'The twa
sisters'

There were two brothers in one
school see 'The two brothers'

There were two brothers walked out
one day see 'The two brothers'

There were two crows sat on a
tree see 'The two crows'
There were two gypsies come sing-
ing at the door see 'Wraggle
taggle gypsies O'
There were two lofty ships from old
England came see 'High Barbary'
There were two ships from England
came see 'High Barbary'
There were two ships from England
did sail see 'The coasts of
Barbary'
There were two sisters lived in a
bower see 'Binnorie, O Bin-
norie'
'There will never be another you'
Mack Gordon and Harry Warren.
FL: This is our last dance to-
gether. 70
There wis a auld beggar man see
'The jolly beggar'
There wis an auld carle cam our the
lea see 'The gaberlunzie man'
'There'll be a hot time' Joe Hayden
and Theodore A. Metz. FL:
Come along, get you ready FLC:
When you hear them-a bells go
ding, ling, ling. 1
'There'll be no distinction there'
FL: There'll be no sorrow on
that heavenly shore FLC: There'll
be no distinction there. 57
There'll be no sorrow on that heav-
enly shore see 'There'll be no
distinction there'
There'll be peace and freedom in
this world, I know see 'Good
news'
'There'll be peace in the valley for
me' Thomas A. Dorsey. FL: I
am tired and weary but I must
toil on FLC: There'll be peace in
the valley for me some day. 10
'There'll be some changes made'
Billy Higgins and W. Benton
Overstreet. FL: For there's a
change in the weather FLC: same.
12
There's a baker down the street see
'Cinnamon cake'
There's a bear in yon hill, and he
is a brave fellow see 'Bear in
the hill'
There's a beautiful, beautiful field
see 'Amelia Earhart's last flight'
There's a big day in Dale see
'Stewball'
'There's a big ship sailing' FL:

There's a big ship sailing on the
il-li al-lay. 57
There's a bright golden haze on the
meadow see 'Oh, what a beauti-
ful mornin''
There's a cabaret in this city see
'Sweet and low-down'
There's a charming Irish lady with
a roguish winning way see
'Bedelia'
There's a cheerful little earful see
'Cheerful little earful'
There's a church in the valley by
the wildwood see 'The church
in the wildwood'
There's a collien fair as May see
'The snowy breasted pearl'
There's a dark and troubled side of
life see 'Keep on the sunny
side'
There's a day we fell gay see
'On a Sunday afternoon'
There's a dear little plant that
grows in our Isle see 'The
dear little shamrock'
There's a fair English lady from
London she came see 'Rich
lady from London'
There's a feeling comes a-stealing
and it sets my brain a-reeling
see 'You're a grand old flag'
There's a garden, what a garden
see 'Beer barrel polka'
There's a heavenly home up yonder
see 'When shall I get there'
There's a hole in the bucket, dear
Liza, dear Liza see 'A hole
in the bucket'
'There's a hole in the middle of the
sea' FL: same. 68
There's a little gal a livin' in a
shanty on a claim see 'My gal
on the Rio Grande'
There's a little rosewood casket ly-
ing on a marble stand see
'Rosewood casket'
There's a little side street such as
often you meet see 'The sun-
shine of Paradise Alley'
There's a long green valley on that
old Kentucky shore see 'Nelly
Gray'
There's a long white robe in heaven
I know see 'Good news'
There's a love feast in heaven see
'Love feast in heaven'
There's a low green valley on the
old Kentucky shore see 'Darling

Nelly Gray'
There's a man goin' round takin'
names see 'Man goin' round'
There's a man who leads a life of
danger see 'Secret agent man'
There's a mother there at twilight
see 'Just a baby's prayer at
twilight'
'There's a meeting here tonight'
FL: Camp meeting down in the
wilderness FLC: Get you ready,
there's a meeting here tonight.
38
There's a place for us see 'Somewhere'
There's a place I'd like to be see
'Dear hearts and gentle people'
There's a pretty spot in Ireland
see 'Where the river Shannon
flows'
There's a saying old, says that
love is blind see 'Someone to
watch over me'
'There's a small hotel' Lorenz Hart
and Richard Rodgers. FL: I'd
like to get away, Junior FLC:
There's a small hotel. 42, 59
There's a somebody I'm longing to
see see 'Someone to watch over
me'
'There's a song in the air' Josiah G.
Holland and Karl P. Harrington.
FL: same. 34
'There's a star in the east' FL:
There's a star in the east on
Christmas morn. 13
There's a star in the east on Christmas morn see 'Rise up shepherd, and follow'
There's a story the gypsys know is
true see 'Golden earrings'
There's a tale of two little orphans
who were left in their uncle's
care see 'Two little babes in
the woods'
There's a time in each year that we
always hold dear see 'In the
good old summertime'
There's a tramp sitting on my doorstep see 'Jigsaw puzzle'
There's a tree in my father's garden,
lovely Jimmy, said she see 'The
father in ambush'
There's a valley in Spain called Jarama see 'Jarama Valley'
There's a village hidden deep in
the valley see 'The three bells'
There's a yellow rose in Texas see

'The yellow rose of Texas'
There's battle lines bein' drawn
see 'For what it's worth'
There's comfort in heaven see
'Comfort in heaven'
There's fire in the east and fire in
the west see 'My way's cloudy'
There's gloom around the ranch
house tonight see 'He's gone,
he's gone up the trail'
There's just one fellow for me in
this world see 'I'm just wild
about Harry'
There's more pretty girls than one
see 'More pretty girls than one'
'There's music in the air' Fanny
Crosby and George F. Root.
FL: same. 1
There's no mountain so high see
'Always in my heart'
There's no respect for youth or age
see 'The California stage'
'There's not a swain' Anthony Hen-
ley and Henry Purcell. FL:
There's not a swain on the plain
would be blest. 40
There's not one drop of morning
dew see 'The morning dew'
There's nothing you can do that
can't be done see 'All you
need is love'
There's nought but care on every
han' see 'Green grow the
rushes O'
There's one more river see 'One
more river to cross'
There's one more river to cross
see 'One more river'
There's something happening here
see 'For what it's worth'
There's something on your mind but
you won't tell me see 'I've got
to have a reason'
There's three fair maids went out
to play at ball see 'The cruel
brother'
There's three young gypsies all in
a row see 'The dark-clothed
gypsy'
There's two little brothers going to
school see 'The two brothers'
There've been good times see
'Good times, bad times'
There've been so many girls that
I've known see 'Heart of stone'
'These are my father's children'
FL: And I soon shall be done
with the troubles of the world

FLC: These are my father's children. 38

'These bones goin' to rise again' FL: Lord He thought he'd make a man FLC: I know it, yes, I know it. 57

'These bones gonna rise again' FL: The Lord he thought he'd make a man FLC: These bones gonna rise again. 68

'These boots are made for walkin'' Lee Hazlewood. FL: You keep sayin' you got somethin' for me FLC: These boots are made for walkin' 'n' that's just what they'll do. 45

These cities are burning now see 'The cities are burning'

'These things shall be' John Adding- ton Symonds. FL: These things shall be, a loftier race. 19

'They all laughed' George and Ira Gershwin. FL: The odds were a hundred to one against me FLC: They all laughed at Christopher Columbus. 21

They are taking me to the gallows, mother see 'Allen Bain'

They are talking in the kitchen see 'Mary Hamilton'

They asked me how I knew see 'Smoke gets in your eyes'

They bored a hole through his left shoulder see 'Lord Bateman'

They call her hard hearted Hannah see 'Hard hearted Hannah'

They call me the moonlight gambler see 'Moonlight gambler'

They call, no date see 'I'll walk alone'

'They call the wind Maria' Lerner and Loewe. FL: Away out here they got a name for wind and rain and fire. 6, 42

They call you Lady Luck but there is room for doubt see 'Luck be a lady'

They called her frivolous Sal see 'My gal Sal'

'They can't take that away from me' George and Ira Gershwin. FL: Our romance won't end on a sor- rowful note FLC: The way you wear your hat. 21

They cawn't do it ye know see 'Cawn't do it ye know!'

'They didn't believe me' Herbert Reynolds and Jerome Kern.

FL: And when I told them how beautiful you are. 67

They go to sea with the evening tide see 'Shrimp boats'

They hadn't been there but a very short time see 'The wife of Usher's Well'

They heard the breeze in the trees see 'The birth of the blues'

They lay, they lay, in the bed they lay see 'The keach in the creel'

They left me standing on a platform, a-waiting for a train see 'Sam's waitin' for a train'

They say, dear father, that tonight see 'Blind child's prayer'

They say everything can be re- placed see 'I shall be released'

They say for every boy and girl there's just one love in this old world see 'Young love'

They say I'm crazy, got no sense see 'I don't care'

They say into your early life ro- mance came see 'Sophisticated lady'

They say that freedom is a constant struggle see 'Freedom is a constant struggle'

They say that Richard Cory owns one half of this whole town see 'Richard Cory'

They say there is a stream see 'We're coming Arkansas'

They say there's to be a grand roundup see 'The grand round- up'

They say you've found somebody new see 'Am I that easy to forget'

They started as a thieving line see 'The California stage'

They tell me Joe Turner's come and gone see 'Joe Turner'

They tell me you are going away see 'Live and let live'

They told me last night there were ships in the offing see 'Blow the wind southerly'

They took away my brogues see 'Felix the soldier'

They used to tell me I was building a dream see 'Brother, can you spare a dime?'

They were two little babes in the woods see 'Two little babes in the woods'

They'll never want to see a rake or
plow see 'How 'ya gonna keep
'em down on the farm?'
They're always in the way see
'Father's whiskers'
'They're laying eggs now' FL: We
had some chickens, no eggs would
they lay. 25
'They're moving father's grave' FL:
They're moving father's grave to
build a sewer. 57
'They're moving Granpa's grave' FL:
They're moving Grandpa's grave
to build a sewer. 68
They're taking me to the gallows,
mother see 'Alan Bane'
They're writing songs of love see
'But not for me'
'A thing he had never done before'
C. W. Murphy. FL: The wind it
blowed, the snow it snowed, the
lightning it did light FLC: Twas
a thing he had never done before.
17
'Things about comin' my way' FL:
Ain't got no money, can't buy no
grub FLC: Now after all my hard
travelin'. 57
Things have come to a pretty pass
see 'Let's call the whole thing
off'
The things I used to like I don't like
any more see 'It might as well
be spring'
Things look swell, things look great
see 'Everything's coming up
roses'
'Things we said today' Lennon and
McCartney. FL: You say you
will love me if I have to go. 44
'Think' Mick Jagger and Keith Richard. FL: I'm giving you a piece
of my mind FLC: So think back,
back a little bit. 16
'Think I'll go somewhere' Bill Anderson. FL: I just kissed the
one I love for the last time. 47
'Think of what you've done' FL:
Heart to heart, dear, how I need
you FLC: Is it true I've lost you?
14
'This can't be love' Lorenz Hart and
Richard Rodgers. FL: In Verona
my late cousin Romeo FLC: This
can't be love because I feel so
well. 42
This could be our last goodnight together see 'Please don't tell

me how the story ends'
This dear young girl see 'Dirty
beggarman'
'This guy's in love with you' Hal
David and Burt Bacharach. FL:
You see this guy, this guy's in
love with you. 45, 71
This is a crazy kind of song see
'Hey Lidee'; 'Hey Lollee'
This is a lovely way to spend an
evening see 'A lovely way to
spend an evening'
This is a world full of trouble and
strife see 'What would you give
in exchange for your soul?'
This is my island in the sun see
'Island in the sun'
This is our last dance together
see 'There will never be another
you'
This is the land of milk and honey
see 'Milk and honey'
This is the way we clap our hands
see 'Here we go round the mulberry bush'
This is why we love the Moore
brothers so swell see 'Mr.
Tom Moore'
'This is your birthday' FL: same.
13
This lady was seated in her father's
castle hall see 'Johnny Barbour'
This lass so neat, with smile so
sweet see 'The lass of Rich-
mond Hill'
'This little light of mine' FL: This
little light of mine, I'm gonna let
it shine. 57
This little light of mine see 'Let
my little light shine'
This little maid went up the street
see 'The keach in the creel'
'This love of mine' Frank Sinatra,
Sol Parker and Henry Sanicola.
FL: same. 59
This moment this minute and each
second in it see 'My shining
hour'
'This nearly was mine' Oscar Hammerstein and Richard Rodgers.
FL: One dream in my heart. 24
This night has music, the sweetest
music see 'Yours'
This nine-pound hammer is just a
little bit too heavy see 'Nine-
pound hammer'
This old hammer killed John Henry

see 'Take this hammer'
'This old man' FL: This old man he
played one FLC: Knick knack
patty whack give the dog a bone.
25, 34, 57
'This old time religion' FL: It is
good for the mourner FLC: Oh,
this old time religion. 38
This special time, this special place
see 'May you always'
This story is simple, twas told in a
day see 'A light in the window'
This time we almost made the
pieces fit, didn't we girl? see
'Didn't we'
'This train' FL: This train is bound
for glory, this train. 23, 25,
34, 35, 57
This will be my shining hour see
'My shining hour'
'This world is not my home' FL:
Did Christ o'er sinners weep?
FLC: This world is not my home.
5
This world is not my home see
'I can't feel at home in this world
anymore'
'Tho' Bacchus may boast of his care
killing bowl' FL: same. 3
Tho' oft we meet severe distress
see 'The Rosary'
Tho' we said goodbye when the moon
is high see 'Does your heart
beat for me?'
Tho' you're always waxing senti-
mental see 'You call everybody
darling'
'Thomas o' Winsbury' FL: If ye will
wed my daughter Janet. 11
'Thomas o' Yonderdale' FL: Lady
Maisry lives intill a bower. 11
Those brown eyes I love so well
see 'Brown eyes'
Those Cape Cod girls, they use no
combs heave away see 'Cape
Cod girls'
Those fingers in my hair see
'Witchcraft'
'Those Johnson boys' FL: Those
Johnson boys they never went
places. 23
'Those wedding bells shall not ring
out' Monroe H. Rosenfeld. FL:
A sexton stood one Sabbath eve
within a belfry grand FLC: Those
wedding bells must not ring out.
20
Those who dance and romance while

they dance see 'Dancing with
tears in my eyes'
Thou are great, and Thou art good
see 'Grace'
Thou must buy me my lady a cambrick shirt see 'The tasks'
'Thou poor bird' FL: Thou poor
bird, mournst the tree. 72
'Thou pretty bird' John Danyel. FL:
Thou pretty bird, how do I see.
26
'Thou swell' Lorenz Hart and
Richard Rodgers. FL: Babe, we
are well met. 46
Though age at my elbow has taken
his stand see 'The public spirit
of the women'
Though distant far from Jeffy
charms see 'Her absence will
not alter me'
'Though far from joy' Philip Rosse-
ter. FL: Though far from joy
my sorrows are as far. 26
Though I know that we meet every
night see 'With a song in my
heart'
Though storms may roll the ocean
see 'I'll hang my harp'
Though today is a blue day see
'Maybe'
Thousands of years ago or maybe
more see 'Where did Robinson
Crusoe go with Friday on Saturday night'
'Three babes' FL: Once there was
a fair and a beautiful bride. 11
'The three bells' Bert Reisfeld and
Jean Villard. FL: There's a
village hidden deep in the valley
FLC: All the chapel bells were
ringing. 10
'Three black crows' FL: There were
three crows sat on a tree. 11
'Three black crows' FL: Three old
crows sat on a tree. 11
Three black crows sat on a tree
see 'The three ravens'
'Three blind mice' FL: Three blind
mice, three blind mice. 25, 34,
48, 72
Three bold brothers of Merrie Scotland see 'Andrew Bartin'
'The three brothers' FL: As I walked
on a pleasant green. 11
Three brothers in Scotland, the
story is told see 'Henry Martin'
Three brothers, three brothers in

Scotland did dwell see 'Andrew
Bardee'
'The three butchers' FL: Johnson
was a valiant man. 30
'The three butchers' FL: Tis of a
jolly boasterman. 30
'Three children sliding on the ice'
FL: same. 48
'Three craw' FL: The three craw
sat upon a wa'. 68
'Three craws' FL: There were three
craws sat upon a wa'. 72
'Three drops of poison' FL: Where
are you a-going, my own darling
boy? 11
Three gates in the east see
'Twelve gates of the city'
'The three gypsies' FL: There were
three gypsies that came to my
door. 11
Three gypsies came to oor hall door
see 'The gypsie laddie'
'Three gypsies came to the door'
FL: same. 22
Three gypsy laddies, all in a row
see 'The gypsy laddie'
Three hooded men thru the back-
roads did creep see 'A church
is burning'
Three hundred and ten of bold
Robin Hood's men see 'Robin
Hood's men'
'Three jolly fishermen' FL: There
were three jolly fishermen. 68
Three jolly gypsies all in a row
see 'The gypsy countess';
'Wraggle taggle gypsies O'
'The three knights' FL: There did
three knights come from the West.
11
Three ladies played at cap and ball
see 'The cruel brother'
'The three little babes' FL: A lady,
a lady fair. 11
'Three little babes' FL: A lady lived
in the west country. 11
'Three little babes' FL: Once there
was a poor widow woman. 11
'The three little babes' FL: There
was a lady, lady gay. 11
'The three little babes' FL: There
was a lady of beauty bright. 11
'The three babes' FL: There was a
lady of beauty rare. 11
Three little babies lyin' in bed see
'Short'nin' bread'
Three little forms in the twilight
gray see 'Watching for Pa'

'Three little kittens' FL: There
were three little kittens. 48
'Three little kittens' FL: Three
little kittens, they lost their mit-
tens. 72
Three little lads were seated one
day see 'Her eyes don't shine
like diamonds'
'Three little piggies' FL: Once was
a sow who had three little piggies. 72
'Three little pigs' FL: Oh there
once was a sow who had three
little pigs. 57
'Three little puffins' Eleanor Farje-
on and Marlys Swinger. FL:
same. 13
Three loving brothers from old England came see 'Harry Maltee'
Three loving brothers from old
Scotland see 'Andy Bardean'
Three loving brothers in Scotland
did dwell see 'Andrew Bardeen'
'The three maids' FL: There was
three maids a-playing ball. 11
'Three Moore Brothers' FL: Well
who is that I see come riding'
boy. 28
'Three myopic rodents' FL: same.
68
'Three night spree' FL: The first
night that I came home so drunk
I couldn't see. 11
'Three nights drunk' FL: Well, the
first night that I come home so
drunk I couldn't see. 11
'Three nights experience' FL: The
first night that I came home. 11
'The three nights experience' FL:
I came home the first night drunk
as I could be. 11
Three old crows sat on a tree see
'Three black crows'
Three questions I will give to you
see 'Captain Wedderburn's
courtship'
'The three ravens' FL: There were
three crows in a hickory tree.
11
'The three ravens' FL: There were
three crows sat on a tree. 11
'The three ravens' FL: There were
three crows sat on yonder's tree.
11
'The three ravens' FL: There were
three ravens on a tree. 11
'The three ravens' FL: There were
three ravens sat on a tree. 11,

'Time, cruel time' Samuel Danyel
and John Danyel. FL: Time,
cruel time, canst thou subdue
that brow. 26
'Time for rabbits' Aileen Fisher
and Marlys Swinger. FL: Look,
says the catkin. 13
'A time for us' Larry Kusik, Eddie
Snyder and Nino Rota. FL: A
time for us some day. 71
The time has come to say goodbye
see 'We'll meet again, Sweetheart'
The time is quite near for our Lord
to appear see 'Soon'
The time is swiftly rolling on see
'Hick's farewell'
Time it was and what a time it was
see 'Bookends'
'Time stands still' John Dowland.
FL: Time stands still with gazing
on her face. 26
Time, time, time see what's become of me see 'A hazy shade
of winter'
A time to be reapin' see 'The
green leaves of summer'
'Times a-getting hard, boys' FL:
same. 57
Times have changed see 'Anything
goes'
'Times is mighty hard' FL: Sh-ta-
ra-dah-dey, sh-ta-dey. 19
Timi fol dol di lie do fol lol der
day see 'The Yorkshire boy'
Timmy right, fol de dol de dol de
right see 'The little Yorkshire
boy'
Timothy Kelly who opened a big
store see 'If I knock the 'L'
out of Kelly'
Ting addle, ting addle, ting addle
do-day see 'The old man under
the hill'
'Tinga layo' FL: Me donkey walk,
me donkey talk FLC: Tinga layo!
Come, little donkey, come. 68
'The tinker' FL: Here comes the
farmer's son, with his budget on
his back. 11
'The tinker' FL: There was a girl
in Westminster. 11
'Tinker man' FL: There never was
yet a boy or a man. 7
'Tipperary' FL: Way out in old
South Dakota FLC: His name was
old Tipperary. 43
'Tip-toe thru' the tulips with me'

Al Dubin and Joe Burke. FL:
Shades of night are creeping FLC:
Tip-toe to the window. 46
'Tiranti, my son' FL: Where have
you been to, Tiranti, my son?
11
Tis a gift to be simple see
'Simple gifts'
Tis advertised in Boston, New York
and Buffalo see 'Blow ye
winds'; 'Blow ye winds in the
morning'
Tis done, the edict passed see
'Ode for American independence'
Tis done! the edict passed by heav-
en decreed see 'An ode for the
4th of July'
'Tis Jordan's river' FL: Am I a
soldier of the cross FLC: Tis
Jordan's river and I must go
'cross. 38
Tis money makes the member vote
see 'A Junto song'
Tis of a brave young highwayman
this story I will tell see 'Bren-
nan on the Moor'
Tis of a brisk and country lady!
see 'The brake o' Briars'
Tis of a councillor I write see
'The councillor's daughter, or
the lawyer outwitted'
Tis of a gallant Yankee ship that
flew the stripes and stars see
'The Yankee man-of-war'
Tis of a handsome female as you
may understand see 'Handsome
cabin boy'
Tis of a jolly boasterman see
'The three butchers'
Tis of a pedlar, a pedlar trim see
'Robin Hood and the pedlar'
Tis of a ragged beggar man, came
tripping o'er the plain see 'The
beggar man'
Tis of a rich Irishman's daughter
see 'Lord Thomas of Winesbury'
Tis of a rich merchant who in London did dwell see 'Vilikins and
his Dinah'
Tis of a sea captain down by the
sea side o see 'The undutiful
daughter'
Tis of a shepherd's daughter see
'The knight and the shepherd's
daughter'
Tis of a young squire who lived in
the west see 'The squire who
lived in the West'

Tis the last rose of summer see
'The last rose of summer'

Tis the old ship of Zion see 'The
old ship of Zion'

Tis the old ship of Zion, hallelujah
see 'The old ship of Zion'

'Tis true, my good dear' Henry
Fielding and Mr. Seedo. FL:
same. 40

Tis Washington's health, fill a bumper around see 'A toast'; 'A
toast to Washington'

'Tis women makes us love' FL:
same. 68

'A tisket, a tasket' FL: same. 57

'The Titanic' FL: Oh, they built the
ship Titanic FLC: It was sad, it
was sad. 57

To a New York trader I did belong
see 'The New York trader'

'To all you ladies now on land'
FL: same. 25

To Anacreon in heaven see 'Anacreontic song'

To Batchelors Hall we good fellows
invite see 'Batchelors Hall'

To dream the impossible dream
see 'The impossible dream'

To drive the kine one summer's
morn the tanner took his way
see 'The cow chase'

'To each his own' Jay Livingston
and Ray Evans. FL: Wise men
have shown life is no good alone
FLC: A rose must remain with
the sun and the rain. 47, 59, 70

To ease his heart, and own his
flame see 'The spinning wheel'

To fair Fidele's grassy tomb see
'Dirge'

To follow in your father's footsteps
is a motto for each boy see
'Following in father's footsteps'

To lead a better lie I need my love
to be here see 'Here, there and
everywhere'

To love someone more dearly every
day see 'My task'

To music be the verse addressed
see 'On music'

To my hey rig-a-jig in a low-back
car see 'The bullgine run'

To my muse give attention and deem
it not a mystery see 'Golden
days of good Queen Bess'

To my ri tol looral loralido see
'The crocodile'

To my roll, to my roll, to my

ride-e-o see 'The ox-driving
song'

To my wing wong waddle, to my
jack straw straddle see 'Wing
wong waddle'

'To plead my faith' Earl of Essex
and Daniel Batcheler. FL: To
plead my faith where faith hath
no reward. 26

To Scarborough Fair are you going?
see 'Scarborough Fair'

To show affection see 'My one
and only'

To spend one night with you see
'That's my desire'

'To the commons' FL: The folks on
t'other side of the wave. 55

'To the ladies' FL: Young ladies in
town, and those that live around.
55

To the Lords of Convention twas
Claver'se who spoke see 'The
bonnets of Bonny Dundee'

To the pines to the pines see 'In
the pines'

To the Queen of Hearts goes the
Ace of Sorrow see 'The Queen
of Hearts'

'To the troops in Boston' FL: By
my faith, but I think you're all
makers of bulls. 8

To thee the tuneful anthem soars
see 'America'

To thine almighty arm we owe see
'Victory'

To turn back the Pharaoh's army
see 'Turn back the Pharaoh's
army'

To you good lads that dare oppose
see 'A song made upon the election of new magistrates for this
city'

To you, my heart cries out, Perfidia see 'Perfidia'

'A toast' Francis Hopkinson. FL:
Tis Washington's health, fill a
bumper around. 55, 65

'A toast to Washington' Francis Hopkinson. FL: Tis Washington's
health--fill a bumper around. 49

'Tobacco' Tobias Hume. FL: Tobacco, tobacco, sing sweetly for
tobacco. 26

'Tobacco is an Indian weed' FL:
Tobacco is an Indian weed from
which the Devil did proceed. 7

Tobacco, tobacco, sing sweetly for
tobacco see 'Tobacco'

'Turn back the hands of time' Jimmy
  Eaton, Larry Wagner and Con
  Hammond. FL: So in love and
  all a dream FLC: Turn back the
  hands of time. 67
'Turn back the Pharaoh's army' FL:
  Gwine to write to Massa Jesus
  FLC: To turn back the Pharaoh's
  army. 38
'Turn back, you wanton flier' Thomas
  Campion. FL: same. 26
'Turn the glasses over' FL: I've
  been to Harlem. 57
'The turtle dove' FL: Oh, come
  with me my little love, I will
  take you ten thousand miles. 7
'Turtle dove' FL: Poor little turtle
  dove settin' on a pine. 57, 66
A tutor who tooted the flute see
  'The limerick song'
Tuyo es mi corazón see 'Maria
  Elena'
Twa bonny sisters that lived in a
  bower see 'Binnorie'
'The twa brothers' FL: Can you
  throw a stone. 11
'The twa brothers' FL: There were
  twa brotheris at the schuil. 11
'Twa brothers' FL: There were twa
  pretty pretty boys went tae the
  school. 11
'Twa brothers' FL: Two pretty boys
  were goin' to the school. 11
'The twa brothers' FL: Will you go
  to the footing of the hill. 11
'The twa corbies' FL: As I cam' by
  yon auld house end. 11
'The twa corbies' FL: As I was
  walking all alane. 11
'The twa sisters' FL: It's sister
  dear, sister, wad ye come an
  have a walk? 11
'The twa sisters' FL: There lived
  an old lord by the Northern sea.
  11
'The twa sisters' FL: There was a
  man lived in the West. 11
'The twa sisters' FL: There was an
  old woman lived by the sea shore.
  11
'The twa sisters' FL: There were
  twa sisters sat in a bower. 11
'The twaddle' FL: On sturdy stout
  Dobbin I mounted my saddle. 3
Twas a calm, still night see 'Lilly
  Dale'
Twas a golden, radiant Sabbath morn
  see 'Saved by a child'

Twas a holy day, a high holiday
  see 'Lord Arnold's wife'
Twas a inch by inch I sought the
  Lord see 'Inching along'
Twas a sunny day in June see
  'Dear old girl'
Twas a thing he had never done be-
  fore see 'A thing he had never
  done before'
Twas a very cold night in Decem-
  ber see 'The broke-down brake-
  man'
Twas all in the merry, merry month
  of May see 'Barbara Allen'
Twas an afternoon in springtime
  see 'The schoolhouse fire'
Twas at some western watertank
  see 'The dying hobo'
Twas break of day in 17th, the
  Yankees did surprise us see
  'Bunker Hill'
Twas Christmas Eve and the night
  so dark see 'Al Bowen'
Twas down at Dan McDevitt's at the
  corner of this street see
  'Throw him down M'Closkey'
Twas down at Aunty Jackson's see
  'Walking for that cake'
Twas down by Branigan's corner
  see 'Johnson's motor car'
Twas early, early all in the spring
  see 'Early, early in the spring'
Twas early, early in the spring
  see 'Barbara Allen'; 'Barbara
  Ellen'; 'Barbery Allan'
Twas early in the springtime, all
  in the month of May see 'The
  drownded boy'
Twas Friday morn, when we set
  sail see 'The mermaid'
Twas Friday morn, when we sot
  sail see 'The stormy winds'
Twas Friday night when we set sail
  see 'The mermaid'
Twas in eighteen hundred and fifty-
  three see 'Greenland fisheries'
Twas in the lovely month of May
  see 'Barbara Allen'
Twas in the merry month of May
  see 'Barbara Allen'; 'Get up and
  shut the door'
Twas in the merry month of June
  see 'Barbara Allen'; 'The beggar
  laddie'
Twas in the moon of wintertime
  see 'The Huron Indian carol'
Twas in the pleasant month of May
  see 'Barbara Allen'

Twas in the pleasant month of June
see 'The beggar laddie'; 'The
gaberlunzie laddie'

Twas in the town of Jacksboro see
'Buffalo skinners, or range of the
buffalo'

Twas in the town of Jacksboro in the
spring of '73 see 'The buffalo
skinners'

Twas in the town of Oxford see
'The Oxford girl'

Twas in Trafalgar's Bay see 'The
death of Nelson'

Twas just before Custer's last fierce
charge see 'Custer's last fierce
charge'

Twas late in the night when the captain came home see 'The gypsy
laddie'

Twas midnight on the ocean see
'Midnight on the ocean'

Twas 'n old woman in Tennessee
see 'Ole Dan Tucker'

Twas near a thickets calm retreat
see 'Sternes' Maria'

Twas near St. Giles there dwelled
a lady see 'The bold lieutenant'

Twas nine o'clock by the bells see
'The mermaid'

Twas of a bold tanner in old Devonshire see 'Robin Hood and the
tanner'

Twas of a brisk young farmer see
'The baffled knight'

Twas of a gay young cavalier see
'The three riddles'

Twas of a lady fair, a shepherd's
daughter dear see 'The bloody
gardener'

Twas of a lady in the west counterie
see 'Young Barbour'

Twas of a lady lived in St. Giles
see 'The bold lieutenant'

Twas of a lofty ship, boys, and she
put out to sea see 'The Golden
Vanity'

Twas of a pedlar stout and bold
see 'Robin Hood and the pedlar'

Twas of a rich merchant in London
did dwell see 'The rich merchant's daughter'

Twas of a sea captain came o'er
the salt billow see 'The undutiful daughter'

Twas of a sea captain twas deep in
love see 'The sea captain'

Twas of a shepherd's daughter see
'The shepherd's daughter'

Twas of a shepherd's son see
'Baffled knight'

Twas of a young maiden who lived
all alone see 'The maid on the
shore'; 'The maiden who dwelt by
the shore'

Twas of a youth, and a well bred
youth see 'Lady Isabel and the
elf knight'

Twas of a youth and a well-beloved
youth see 'Six pretty maidens'

Twas old Mr. Johnson that had
troubles of his own see 'The
yaller cat'

Twas on a bright morning in summer see 'The pretty girl milking her cow'

'Twas on a cold and winter's day'
FL: same. 11

Twas on a dark and holiday see
'Sir Hugh'

Twas on a day, a high holiday see
'Little Matha Grove'

Twas on a merry time see 'Cock
Robin and Jenny Wren'

Twas on a Monday morning ring
early in the year see 'Charlie
is my darlin''

Twas on a Thursday morning that
from Cadiz we set sail see
'Barrosa'

Twas on one day and a high holiday
see 'Little Musgrave'; 'Matthy
Groves'

Twas on Thanksgiving Day see
'The storm of Heber Springs,
November 25, 1926'

Twas on the banks of Claudy see
'The banks of Claudy'

Twas on the eighth of January see
'The battle of New Orleans'

Twas on the Horse Shoe in old Arizona see 'I learned about
horses from him'

Twas on the Isle of Capri that I
found her see 'Isle of Capri'

Twas on the Spanish Main that the
Turkish Lavoree see 'Lowlands
low'

Twas once I lived in a scornful
town see 'Barbara Allen'

Twas once in the saddle I used to
go dashing see 'The cowboy's
lament'; 'I once was a carman in
the big mountain con'

Twas past me-ri-dian half past four
see 'Nancy, or the Sailor's jour-
nal'

68
'The two little boys' FL: Oh two
little boys were going to school.
11
Two little boys were going to school
see 'The two brothers'
'Two little children' FL: Two little
children, a boy and a girl. 66
Two little children one morning
see 'You tell me your dream,
I'll tell you mine'
Two little girls in a boat one day
see 'The two sisters'
Two little gypsies live at the East
see 'The gypsy laddie'
'The two little sisters' FL: Johnny
bought the youngest a gay gold
ring. 11
'Two little sisters' FL: Two little
sisters living in the East. 11
'Two little sisters' FL: Two little
sisters walked down the stream.
11
Two little sisters side by side see
'The two sisters'
Two little sisters walking by the
stream see 'The two sisters'
Two lofty ships from old England
sailed see 'High Barbaree'
Two lofty ships of England set sail
see 'The wild Barbaree'
Two lofty ships of war from old
England set sail see 'The
coasts of Barbary'
'The two lovers' FL: I once knew a
little girl and I loved her as my
life and freely. 7
'The two magicians' FL: O she
looked out of the window. 11
'Two maids went a-milking one day'
FL: same. 57
'The two playmates' FL: It rained,
alas! it rained, alas! 11
Two pretty boys were goin' to the
school see 'Twa brothers'
'The two school boys' FL: There is
two school boys in our town. 11
'The two sisters' FL: He gave to
her a beaver hat. 11
'The two sisters' FL: I says to my
dear sister, are ye comin' for
to walk. 11
'The two sisters' FL: Johnny bought
the young one a beaver hat. 11
'The two sisters' FL: Miller, o
miller, there swims a swan. 11
'The two sisters' FL: The miller's
daughter went out one day. 11

'The two sisters' FL: O come, dear
sister, and let's take a walk. 11
'The two sisters' FL: O sister, o
sister, come go with me. 11
'The two sisters' FL: O sister, O
sister, there swims a swan. 11
'The two sisters' FL: Once there
lived two sisters fair. 11
'The two sisters' FL: Peter and I
went down the lane. 11
'The two sisters' FL: Sister, dear
sister, let's walk the seashore.
11
'The two sisters' FL: Sister, O
sister, let's take a walk out. 11
'The two sisters' FL: There lived a
lord in the old country. 11
'The two sisters' FL: There lived
an old lord by the northern sea.
11
'The two sisters' FL: There lived
an old woman down by the seashore, bow down, bow down. 7
'The two sisters' FL: There was a
Lord Mayor in our town. 11
'The two sisters' FL: There was a
man lived in the west, bow down,
bow down. 11
'The two sisters' FL: There was an
old lady lived in the North. 11
'The two sisters' FL: There was an
old man who lived in the West.
11
'The two sisters' FL: There was an
old woman in Northern 'try. 11
'The two sisters' FL: There was an
old woman lived on the seashore.
11
'The two sisters' FL: There was an
old woman who lived by the sea.
11
'The two sisters' FL: Two little
girls in a boat one day. 11
'The two sisters' FL: Two little
sisters side by side. 11
'The two sisters' FL: Two little
sisters walking by the stream.
11
'The two sisters' FL: Two sisters
crossing the river bend. 11
'The two sisters' FL: Two sisters
went down to the river's brim.
11
'The two sisters' FL: Was two
sisters loved one man. 11
'Two sleepy people' Frank Loesser
and Hoagy Carmichael. FL: I
guess we haven't got a sense of

responsibility FLC: Here we are, out of cigarettes. 47, 53

'2000 light years from home' Mick Jagger and Keith Richard. FL: Sun turning 'round with graceful motion. 16

'2000 man' Mick Jagger and Keith Richard. FL: Well, my name is a number. 16

Two were the sisters, one the bride see 'The unquiet grave'

Two wheels around a corner see 'Putting on the style'

'Tyin' a knot in the devil's tail' FL: Way high up in the Sierra peaks. 57

'Tyranty, my son' FL: Oh, where, have you been, Tyranty, my son. 11

- U -

'U.A.W.-C.I.O.' Bess Hawes and Baldwin Hawes. FL: I was standing round a defense town one day FLC: It's the UA double U-CIO. 19

'Uh uh, no' FL: Madam I have come for to court you. 57

'Um-skit-a-rat-tra--si-si do!' Frank Addis Kent. FL: I'll sing of a great musician FLC: Um-skit-a-rat-trap-si-si do. 36

Un panadero fue a misa see 'La cucaracha'

'Un telegrama' Garcia Segura. FL: Antes de que tus labios me confirmaran. 9

Una vez nada má en mi huerto brilló la esperanza see 'You belong to my heart'

'Uncle Fred and Auntie Mabel' FL: same. 57

'Uncle Joe' FL: Did you ever go to meetin' Uncle Joe FLC: Hop up, my ladies, three in a row. 57

'Uncle Johnny sick in bed' FL: Uncle Johnny sick in bed, what shall we send him. 37

'Uncle Sam's managerie' J. William Pope. FL: I'd like to have you all to know that I FLC: Then come with your cash everyone. 36

'Unconstant love' Alfonso Ferrabosco. FL: Unconstant love, why should I make my moan. 26

'Undecided' Sid Robin and Charles Shavers. FL: Now you want to play and then it's no FLC: First you say you do and then you don't. 12, 59

'Under Bethlehem's star' Mary Cochrane, Vojáček, and Vilém Tauský. FL: Under Bethlehem's star so bright. 13

'Under my thumb' Mick Jagger and Keith Richard. FL: Under my thumb's the girl who once had me down. 16

'Under the Anheuser Bush' Harry von Tilzer and Andrew B. Sterling. FL: Talk about the shade of the sheltering palms FL: Come, come come and make eyes with me. 36

'Under the bamboo tree' Bob Cole and J. Rosamond Johnson. FL: Down in the jungle lived a maid FLC: If you lak-a-me, lak I lak-a you. 1, 20

'The under-assistant West Coast promotion man' Mick Jagger and Keith Richard. FL: Well, I'm waiting at the bus stop in downtown L.A. 16

Underneath the gaslight's glitter see 'Won't you buy my pretty flowers?'

'Understand your man' Johnny Cash. FL: Don't call my name out your window. 10

'The undutiful daughter' FL: Tis of a sea captain down by the sea side O. 11

'The undutiful daughter' FL: Twas of a sea captain came o'er the salt billow. 11

'The unfortunate Miss Bailey' FL: A captain bold from Halifax once left his captain quarters FLC: Oh! Miss Bailey, unfortunate Miss Bailey. 23, 57

Unhappy Boston, see thy sons deplore see 'The Boston massacre'

'The unhappy swain' FL: Cease ye fountain, cease to murmer. 3

'Unhappy times' FL: Unhappy times of late we've seen. 8

The union is the place for me see 'On the line'

'Union maid' Woody Guthrie and The Almanac Singers. FL: There once was a union maid FLC: Oh,

you can't scare me, I'm sticking
to the union. 19, 58
'Union man' Albert Morgan. FL: I
think I sing this little song FLC:
Union man! Union man! 19
Union miners, stand together see
'A miner's life'
'Union train' Almanac Singers. FL:
Oh, what is that I see yonder
coming, coming, coming. 19, 57
'United front' Bertolt Brecht and
Hanns Eisler. FL: And just be-
cause he's human. 57
'United Steel Workers are we' M.
T. Montgomery. FL: Oh, we
are the men of the Steelworkers'
Union. 19
'The unquiet grave' FL: Cold blows
the wind to my true love. 57
'The unquiet grave' FL: How pleas-
ant is the wind tonight. 11
'The unquiet grave' FL: O cold is
the wind do blow, sweetheart.
11, 30
'The unquiet grave' FL: O it's fetch
me some water from a dungeon
stone. 11
'The unquiet grave' FL: There been
falling drops of dew, sweetheart.
11
'The unquiet grave' FL: Two were
the sisters, one the bride. 23,
25
'Until it's time for you to go' Buffy
Sainte-Marie. FL: You're not
a dream, you're not an angel.
45
'Until the real thing comes along'
Mann Holiner, Alberta Nichols,
Sammy Cahn, Saul Chaplin and
L. E. Freeman. FL: I'd work
for you, slave for you. 59
Up came the devil to the farmer
one day see 'The farmer's curst
wife'
'Up in a balloon' Leybourne. FL:
One night I went up in a balloon
FLC: Up in a balloon! 36
Up in a dark hollow see 'Little
Sir Hugh'
Up in the mornin' out on the job
see 'That lucky old sun'
'Up on the mountain' FL: Up on the
mountain children call. 57
Up spake the cabin boy of our gal-
lant ship see 'It's three times
around'
Up spoke Lady Oysie's old mother

see 'Donald Macdonald'
Up spoke the boy of our gallant ship
see 'The mermaid'
Up stepped a man of our gallant
ship see 'The mermaid'
Up steps the cabin boy: what will
you give see 'The Green Wil-
low Tree'
Up to the West End, right in the
best end see 'Every little move-
ment'
'Up, up and away' Jim Webb. FL:
Would you like to ride in my
beautiful balloon? 47, 71
'Upidee' FL: The shades of night
were falling fast. 25
Upon Paul's steeple stands a tree
see 'St. Paul's steeple'
Upon the bridge it's raining and
we'll get wet see 'Round dance'
Upon the hill he turned see 'The
soldier's tear'
Upon the Lomons I lay see 'The
Campbells are comin''
Upon the mountain when my Lord
spoke see 'Every time I feel
the spirit'
'Ups and down' Mark Lindsay and
Terry Melcher. FL: Now things
was looking rosy, baby. 47
'Upside down' Howard Paul. FL:
Through eating pickled salmon
before I went to bed. 36
'Uriar, my son' FL: Oh, where
have you been, Uriar, my son?
11
'Used-to-be' FL: You don't love me
anymore, my darlin' FLC: Tomorrow'll be another lonesome
day. 14
'Utah Carol' FL: Kind friends, you
may ask what makes me sad and
still. 43
'Utah Carroll' FL: And now my
friends you ask me what makes
me sad and still. 2
'Utah Carroll' FL: Oh, kind friend,
you may ask me what makes me
sad and still. 57
'The Utah iron horse' FL: The iron
horse draws nigh with his smoke
nostrils high. 57

- V -

'The vacant chair' Henry S. Washburn and George F. Root. FL:

We shall meet, but we shall miss him FLC: same. 63

'The vagabond king waltz' Brian Hooker and Rudolf Friml FL: Hearts may flower for an hour FLC: Never try to bind me. 54

Vamos a la conga ay Dios see 'Say "sí, sí"'

'Vamos a la mar' FL: Vamos a la mar, tum, tum. 51

Vamos a tepa tierra soñada see 'A gay ranchero'

'Vanamburgh's menagerie' W. J. Wetmore. FL: Old Vanamburgh is the man that runs these 'ere shows FLC: The elephant now moves round. 36

'Van Dieman's lands' FL: Come all you gallant poachers FLC: That ramble void of care. 57

A varmer he lived in the West countree see 'The Barkshire tragedy'

'Vaya con Dios' Larry Russell, Inez James and Buddy Pepper. FL: May God be with you my love FLC: Now the hacienda's dark, the town is sleeping. 9, 52

Vdal' hylch prostorakh doroga rulayet see 'Dyevooshkoo chakoi zovoot'

'Vdol' po ulitse' FL: Vdol' po ulitse metelitsa metël. 57

'Venga Jaleo' FL: El diez y ocho día de julio. 57

Venite adoremus, venite adoremus see 'Adeste fideles'

'Venus' Edward H. Marshall. FL: Hey, Venus, oh Venus. 52

The very first blessing that Mary had see 'The seven blessings of Mary'

The very first day I got married see 'The low low lands of Holland'

'A very special day' Oscar Hammerstein and Richard Rodgers. FL: Am I building something up that really isn't there? FLC: I wake up each morning with a feeling in my heart. 24

'The vicar of Bray' FL: In good King Charleses golden time FLC: And this is the law, that I'll maintain. 25, 57

'Vicksburg Blues' FL: I've got the Vicksburg blues and I'm singin' it everywhere I go. 57

'Victory' William Billings. FL: To

thine almighty arm we owe. 65

'La vidalita' FL: Ah so long the day. 23, 25

'Vilikins and his Dinah' John Parry. FL: Tis of a rich merchant who in London did dwell FLC: Singing to la lol la rol lall to ral lal la. 36

'The village church yard' FL: In the dear old village churchyard. 7

'Villikins and his Dinah' FL: It is of a rich merchant I am going for to tell. 17

'Villikins and his Dinah' FL: A wealthy old merchant who in London did dwell FLC: Singing to ral, lal loo ral. 25

'Vine and fig tree' FL: And every man neath his vine and fig tree. 57

'Vigndig and fremd kind' FL: Zolst azoy leon un zayn gezint FLC: Ay-lyu-lyu. 57

Virgil Caine is the name see 'The night they drove old Dixie down'

The Virgin Mary had-a one Son see 'Mary, what you gonna name that pretty little baby'

'A Virgin unspotted' William Billings. FL: A Virgin unspotted, ye prophets foretold FLC: Then let us be merry. 33

'Virginia's bloody soil' FL: Come all you loyal unionists wherever you may be. 57

'Vive la compagnie' FL: Let every good fellow now fill up his glass FLC: Vive la, vivela, vive l'amour. 23, 25

'Vive la quince brigada' FL: same. 57

'Vive l'amour' FL: Let every good fellow now join in a song FLC: Vive l'a-vive l'a, vive l'amour. 68

'Volga boatman' Jerry Silverman. FL: Yo heave ho! Yo heave ho. 25, 57

The volley was fired at sunrise see 'The pardon came too late'

Vor Madrid, im Schützengraben see 'Hans Beimler'

'Vrt' Sa, Dévča' FL: Vrt' Sa, Dévča vrt' sa, dévča okolo mňa. 57

- W -

'The Wabash cannon ball' FL: From

the great Atlantic ocean to the
wide Pacific shore FLC: Hear the
bell and whistle calling.   1, 10,
23, 25, 67
'Wabash cannonball' FL: I stood on
the Atlantic Ocean, on the wide
Pacific shore.   27, 57
'Wade in the water' FL: Jordan's
water is chilly and cold FLC:
Wade in the water.   57
'Wade in the water' FL: See that
host all dressed in white.   7
'Wade in the water' FL: Wade in the
water, wade in the water, children.   4
Waes me that e'er I made your bed
see 'The linkin laddie'
A wage a love a wager, and go
along with me see 'The Broomfield Hill'
A wager, a wager, a wager I will
lay see 'The bonny bushy
broom'
A wager, a wager with you I will
lay see 'The Broomfield wager'
'Wagoner's lad' FL: Oh, hard is the
fortune of all womankind.   56
'The wagoner's lad' FL: Oh, I am a
poor girl, my fortune's been sad.
23, 35
'Waillie' FL: When cockle shells
turn silver bells.   57
'Waillie, waillie' FL: When cockle
shells turn silver bells.   11
'Wait a little while' FL: My heaven-
ly home is bright and fair FLC:
Wait a little while.   38
'Wait for the wagon' R. Bishop
Buckley. FL: Will you come
with me, my Phyllis dear FLC:
Wait for the wagon.   1, 57
'Wait till the sun shines Nellie'
Andrew B. Sterling and Harry
von Tilzer. FL: On a Sunday
morn, sat a maid forlorn FLC:
Wait till the sun shines, Nellie.
1, 20, 31
'Waiting at the church' Fred W.
Leigh and Henry E. Pether. FL:
I'm in a nice bit of trouble, I
confess FLC: There I was, wait-
ing at the church.   17, 20
Waiting for a girl who's got curlers
in her hair see 'Factory girl'
'Wake every breath' William Billings.
FL: Wake ever breath and every
string.   33
'Wake Nicodemus' Henry C. Work.

FL: Nicodemus the slave was of
African birth FLC: The good
time comin', is almost here.   57
'Wake up, children' FL: Old Satan
tho't he had me fast FLC: O
wake up, children, wake up.   5
Wake up every morning see 'The
Midnight Special'
Wake up, wake up, darling Cory
see 'Darling Cory'
Wake up, wake up, you seven sleep-
ers see 'Earl Brand'
Wake you up, wake you up, you
seven sleepers see 'Earl Brand'
'Wakefield on a green' FL: In Wake-
field there lives a jolly Pinder.
11
Waking skies at sunrise see
'Memories of you'
'Walk in Jerusalem' FL: John said
the city was just four-square
FLC: I want to be ready.   57
'Walk Jerusalem, jes' like John'
FL: same.   5
'Walking by a river side' Robert
Jones. FL: same.   26
'Walking John' FL: Walking John
was a big rope FLC: Horse from
over Morongo way.   43
'Walk on by' Kendall Hayes.   FL:
If I see you tomorrow on some
street in town FLC: Just walk on
by.   10
'Walk straight' FL: Well the nigger
like 'lasses and the white man,
too FLC: Wo Lordy, oh my
Lordy, Lord.   28
'Walk through the valley in peace'
FL: Brothers, we'll walk thro'
the valley FLC: We will walk
thro' the valley in peace.   5
Walked up Ellum and I come down
Main see 'Take a whiff on me'
'Walkin' the dog' Shelton Brooks.
FL: Now listen honey, 'bout a
new dance craze FLC: Get way
back and snap your fingers.   31
'Walking for that cake' Ed Harrigan
and Dave Braham. FL: Twas
down at Aunty Jackson's FLC:
So gently on the toe.   1
'Walking the floor over you' Ernest
Tubb.   FL: You left me and you
went away FLC: I'm walking the
floor over you.   10
'Waltz me around again Willie' Will
D. Cobb and Ren Shields. FL:
Willie Fitzgibbons who used to

sell ribbons FLC: Waltz me
around again Willie. 20
'Waltzing Matilda' FL: There once
was a swagman camped in a billabong FLC: Who'll come awaltzing Matilda, my darlin'. 57
'Waly, waly' FL: O Waly, Waly, up
yon bank. 11
'Waly, Waly, old set' FL: O waly,
waly, up yon bank. 11
'Wanderin'' FL: My daddy is an en-
gineer FLC: And it looks like
I'm never gonna cease my wanderin'. 23, 25, 34, 57
Want some sea food mama see
'Hold tight, hold tight'
'Wanting you' Oscar Hammerstein
and Sigmund Romberg. FL: My
heart is aching for someone FLC:
Wanting you, every day I am
wanting you. 24
'A war song' FL: Hark, hark the
sound of war is heard. 49
'War song' FL: Saddled and bridled
and ready for the fray. 50
'Ward, the pirate' FL: Come all you
valiant seamen bold, with courage
beat your drum. 11
'Ward the pirate' FL: Here comes a
ship a sailing. 11
The warden threw a party in the
county jail see 'Jailhouse rock'
Warm as the west wind see 'The
four winds'
'The Warminster song' FL: O, have
you heard of a good little boy?
22
'Wartime blues' FL: What you gonna
do when they send your man to
war. 57
Was an old man in the north country
see 'The old man in the north
country'
Was I reduced to beg my bread see
'Somebody'
Was it in Tahiti? see 'I remember
you'
Was two sisters loved one man see
'The two sisters'
Was you ever in Quebec? see 'Hie-
land laddie'
'The washing day' FL: The sky with
clouds was overcast. 36
'Washington' S. Holyoke. FL: When
Alcides, the son of Olympian Jove.
3
'Washington and Lee swing' Thornton
Allen, C. A. Robbins and

M. W. Sheafe. FL: When Wash-
ington and Lee's men fall in line.
31
Wasn't it a mighty day see
'Mighty day'
'Wasn't that a mighty day!' FL:
same. 33
Wasn't that a pity and a shame?
see 'It was poor little Jesus'
'Waste not, want not' Rollin Howard.
FL: When a child I lived at
Lincoln, with my parents at the
farm FLC: Waste not, want not,
is a maxim I would teach. 63
'Watch what happens' Norman Gim-
bel and Michel Legrand. FL:
Cold, no I can't believe your
heart is cold. 67
'Watching for Pa' Henry C. Work.
FL: Three little forms in the
twilight gray FLC: Watching for
Pa. 63
The water in a river is changed
every day see 'The big black
giant'
Water in the gutter see 'In the
rain'
'The water is wide' FL: Oh, the
water is wide I cannot cross
over. 34, 35
'The water is wide' FL: The water
is wide, I cannot get over. 23,
25, 57
'Water parted from the sea' Pietro
Metastasio and Thomas A. Arne.
FLC: same. 40
'Watermelon man' Gloria Lynne and
Herbie Hancock. FL: Oh! Water-
melon man. 45
'Wat'ry God' FL: The wat'ry God
great Neptune lay. 49
Wave the spear and raise the rifle
see 'Indian war song'
'The waves of Waikiki' Neal Buhler
and Armando Fennevessey. FL:
The waves of Waikiki keep call-
ing, calling me. 67
Way back yonder in Tennessee they
leased the convicts out see
'Buddy, won't you roll down the
line'
Way down in a willow garden see
'Willow garden'
Way down in Alabam' see 'Livery
stable blues'
Way down in Columbus, Georgia
see 'Columbus stockade'; 'Co-
lumbus stockade blues'

Way down south in the yankety yank
    see 'The foolish song'
Way down upon the Swanee River
    see 'Old folks at home!;
    'Swanee River'
Way down upon the Wabash see
    'El-a-noy'
Way down yonder in London town
    see 'Barbara Ellen'
Way down yonder in the graveyard
    walk see 'Free at last'
Way down yonder in the middle of
    the field see 'Let me fly'
Way, haul away, we'll haul away,
    Joe see 'Haul away, Joe'
Way, haul away, we'll haul away
    together see 'Haul away, Joe'
Way high up in the Sierra peaks
    see 'Tyin' a knot in the devil's
    tail'
The way I gained my titles by a
    hobby see 'Champagne Charlie'
A way low down in London town
    see 'Barbara Ellen'
Way out in old South Dakota see
    'Tipperary'
Way out in western Texas, where
    the Clear Fork's waters flow
    see 'The cowboys Christmas ball'
Way over in Egypt land see 'March
    on'
'Way over Jordan' FL: I want to go
    to heaven when I die FLC: Oh,
    way over Jordan. 38
Way up high in the Mogollons among
    the mountain tops see 'High
    chin Bob'
Way up in old Calgary over the line
    see 'Paddy Ryan'
Way up yonder above the moon see
    'Buck-eye Jim'
'The way you look tonight' Dorothy
    Fields and Jerome Kern. FL:
    Some day when I'm awfully low.
    67
The way you wear your hat see
    'They can't take that away from
    me'
'Wayfaring stranger' FL: I am a
    poor wayfaring stranger. 29
'Wayfaring stranger' FL: I'm just a
    poor wayfaring stranger. 4, 50,
    57, 66
'The wayward wind' Herb Newman
    and Stan Lebowsky. FL: Oh, the
    wayward wind is a restless wind.
    67
We all congregate each morning see

'Beans, bacon, and gravy'
'We all go to work but father' Les-
    lie Reed. FL: Oh! we are a
    happy family and I mention it
    with pride FLC: We all go to
    work but father. 17
We all live in a yellow submarine
    see 'Yellow submarine'
'We all went home in a cab' Harry
    Wincott and George Le Brunn.
    FL: Last night I went to a social
    club. 17
We all went on a Christmas Day
    see 'The Shushai'
We are a band of brothers native to
    the soil see 'The bonnie blue
    flag'
We are almost home see 'We're
    almost done'
'We are building a strong union'
    FL: same. 19
We are climbing Jacob's ladder
    see 'Jacob's ladder'
'We are climbing the hills of Zion'
    FL: Oh, brethren, do get ready
    FLC: We are climbing the hills
    of Zion. 38
We are coming from the cotton
    fields see 'Song of the freed-
    man'
We are like some human folks who
    through this world must roam
    see 'The stray'
'We are marching on to victory'
    FL: same. 19
We are off, we are off see 'Off
    to the sea'
We are on the ocean sailing see
    'Move along'
We are seen around New York see
    'All in fun'
'We are soldiers in the army' FL:
    Now if a man has money today.
    57
We are soldiers in the army see
    'Money is king'
We are the peatbog soldiers see
    'The peatbog soldiers'
We ask not that the slave should lie
    see 'The Abolitionist hymn'
'We be three poor mariners' FL:
    same. 25
We came on the sloop John B. see
    'The sloop John B'
'We can work it out' Lennon and
    McCartney. FL: Try to see it
    my way. 44
We come on the sloop John B see

crèche'
'Welcome to my world' Ray Winkler
and John Hathcock. FL: Welcome
to my world. Won't you come in?
10
Well, a ship out on the ocean see
'Amelia Earhart's last flight'
Well, baby, when times are bad
see 'Call on me'
'We'll be together again' Frank
Laine and Carl Fischer. FL: No
tears, no fears. 47
'The well below the valley' FL: A
gentleman was passing by FLC:
At the well below the valley-o.
11
'We'll build a bungalow' Betty Briant
Mayhems and Norris the Trouba-
dour. FL: We'll build a bungalow
big enough for two. 47
Well, come along, boys and listen
to my tale see 'The old Chis-
holm trail'
'We'll die in the field' FL: O what
do you say seekers. 38
Well, every Monday morning see
'John Henry'
We'll have Manhattan, the Bronx,
and Staten Island, too see
'Manhattan'
Well, he gave him his orders at
Monroe, Virginia see 'The
wreck of the old ninety-seven'
Well, here I sit high gettin' ideas
see 'Dang me'
Well I came home the other night
see 'The drunken fool'
Well, I don't mind marryin' see
'Marrying blue yodel'
Well I got a sweet woman, yes,
everybody knows see 'Dangerous
woman'
Well, I got the crane wing, oh my
Lordy see 'I got the crane wing'
Well, I heard the reports of a pistol, whoa man, down the right
away see 'I heard the reports
of a pistol'
Well, I know my God is a man of
war see 'Adam in the garden
pinnin' leaves'
Well, I saw the thing a-comin' out
of the sky see 'The purple
people eater'
Well, I think I'm going out of my
head see 'Goin' out of my head'
Well, I thought the day I met you
see 'I've got a tiger by the tail'

Well, I told friends of mine see
'Surprise, surprise'
Well I was happy here at home see
'Flight 505'
When I was in my sixteenth year
see 'The gardner'
Well I was stung right see 'Stung
right'
Well I went home one night see
'Our goodman'
Well I wish I was in London see
'Handsome Molly'
Well I woke up early this mornin'
see 'On my way to Mexico'
Well, I woke up Sunday mornin'
with no way to hold my head that
didn't hurt see 'Sunday morn-
in' comin' down'
Well, I wonder how the old folks
are at home see 'The home-
stead on the farm'
Well, I wonder what's the matter,
what's the matter with Captain
Mac see 'Ration blues'
Well, if you get the wrong fellow
see 'You can have him'
Well, I'm a rake and a rambling
boy see 'Rake and rambling
boy'
Well, I'm gonna write my Mama
see 'Captain don't feel sorry for
a longtime man'
Well, I'm waiting at the bus stop
in downtown L.A. see 'The
under-assistant West Coast promotion man'
Well, I'm walking down this track
see 'Nine hundred miles'
Well, I'm walkin' the dog and I'm
never blue see 'I'm walking the
dog'
Well, it rained five days and the
sky turned black as night see
'Backwater blues'
Well, it rained forty days and it
rained forty nights see 'Didn't
it rain'
Well it's all, almost done see
'On a Monday'
Well, it's bye, baby bye see
'Goodbye, my lover, goodbye'
Well, it's early in the morning,
when the ding dong ring see
'Early in the morning'
Well, it's good morning, captain
see 'Muleskinner blues'
Well, it's jelly, jelly jelly cause
jam don't shake like that see

see 'Play with fire'
Well-a I'm so glad I can plumb the
line see 'Plumb the line'
Well-a, no more good time, poor
boy in the world for me see
'No more good time in the world
for me'
Went down to the station not many
days ago see 'Jesse James'
Went to Mississippi on a Greyhound
busline see 'Freedom rider'
Went to my doctor yesterday see
'Run that body down'
Went to town the other night see
'Old Dan Tucker'
Went up on the mountain see 'Bile
them cabbage down'
'We're all gonna shine tonight' FL:
We're all gonna shine tonight,
we're all gonna shine. 68
We're all met together here, to sit
and to crack see 'The work of
the weavers'
'We're almost done' FL: Oh, come
along, brothers FLC: We are al-
most home. 38
We're alone, Doney gal, in the rain
and hail see 'Doney gal'
We're brave and gallant miner boys
who work underground see 'The
eight hour day'
'We're coming Arkansas' FL: They
say there is a stream FLC:
We're coming, Arkansas. 57
We're coming, coming, we're com-
ing see 'Away with rum'
We're coming from the nursery see
'Domestic workers' song'
We're coming, we're coming, our
brave little band see 'The song
of the Salvation Army'
We're gonna roll, we're gonna roll
see 'Roll the union on'
Were I laid on Greenland's coast
see 'Over the hills and far away'
We're in the money see 'The gold
digger's song'
We're sailing down the river from
Liverpool see 'Santy Anno'
We're Sergeant Pepper's Lonely
Hearts Club Band see 'Sergeant
Pepper's Lonely Hearts Club Band'
'We're some of the praying people'
FL: And must I be to judgment
brought FLC: We're some of the
praying people. 5
We're tenting tonight on the old camp
ground see 'Tenting tonight'

We're the D-Day Dodgers, way out
in Italy see 'The D-Day Dodgers'
We're the old soldiers of the king
see 'The old soldiers of the
king'
'Were you there?' FL: Were you
there when they crucified my
Lord? 5, 23, 25, 67
'The west countree' FL: There was
an old man lived in the West.
11
The west so they say see 'Forty-
five minutes from Broadway'
'The West Virginia farmer' FL:
Oh, the West Virginia hills. 7
'West Virginia hills' H. E. Engle
and Walter Seacrist. FL: Oh,
those West Virginia hills, so
majestic and so grand FLC:
Over the hills, beautiful hills.
19
'The West Virginny hills' Marvin
Moore and James Leisy. FL: In
the hills of West Virginny lived
a girl named Nancy Brown FLC:
But they came rolling down the
mountain. 35
A western ranch is just a branch
see 'Buttons and bows'
'The wether's skin' FL: There was
a man lived in the West. 11
We've just been introduced see
'Shall we dance?'
We've met again, my love, he said
see 'The house carpenter'
We've met, we've met, my own
true love see 'The daemon
lover'; 'House carpenter'
We've played the game of stay away
see 'I surrender, dear'
We've reached the land of waving
wheat see 'Dakota land'
Whar hae ye been a' day, my boy
Tammy see 'My boy Tammy'
What a beautiful day see 'For me
and my gal'
What a beautiful thought I am think-
ing see 'The great speckled
bird'
'What a court' FL: What a court
hath old England of folly and sin
FLC: Derry down, down, down,
derry down. 8, 65
What a court hath old England, of
folly and sin see 'Fish and
tea'; 'A new song to an old tune'
What a day this has been! see

'Almost like being in love'
'What a difference a day made'
Stanley Adams and Maria Grever.
FL: I dreaded every morning
FLC: What a difference a day
made. 9
'What a diff'rence a day made'
Stanley Adams and Maria Grever.
FL: My yesterdays was blue dear
FLC: What a diff'rence a day
made. 12
'What a difference a day made' Maria
Grever. FL: Recuerda aquel beso
FLC: Cuando vuelva a tu lado. 9
What a dream I had see 'For
Emily, wherever I may find her'
'What a friend we have in Jesus'
Joseph Scriven and C. C. Con-
verse. FL: same. 67
What a happy new year see 'A
happy new year'
What a life, what a life, says the
seafaring man see 'The sea-
faring man'
'What a shame' Mick Jagger and
Keith Richard. FL: What a
shame nothin' seems to be goin'
right. 16
What are we gonna do with the
baby-o see 'Prettiest little
baby in the country-o'
What blood is that all on your shirt?
see 'Edward'
'What blood is this' FL: What blood
is this lies sprinkled on the
ground. 11
'What blood on the point of your
knife?' FL: What blood? What
blood on the p'int of your knife?
11
What can I say to sing my praise of
you see 'Delishious'
What caused this blood on your shirt
sleeve see 'The blood of Fair
Lucy'
'What child is this?' William Chatterton Dix. FL: What child is
this, who, laid to rest. 34
'What did Dewey do to them' R. H.
Brennen and Grant W. Barnett.
FL: Oh when the war with Spain
broke out FLC: What did Dewey
do to them. 36
What did you have for your supper,
Jimmy Randal, my son? see
'Lord Randal'
What did your sweetheart give you
see 'Lord Randal'

What do caterpillars do? see
'Caterpillars'
What do you get when you fall in
love see 'I'll never fall in love
again'
What do you think I made of her
hide? see 'The sow took the
measles'
What do you want for your break-
fast, O, Willie, my dear? see
'The jealous lover'
What does it matter if we're rich
or we're poor see 'Love is
the thing'
What goes up must come down see
'Spinning wheel'
What good is money if your heart
isn't light see 'Love is the
thing'
What good is sitting alone in your
room? see 'Cabaret'
What had you for supper, Durango,
my son? see 'Durango'
What had you for supper, Lord
Ronald my son? see 'Lord
Ronald'
What had you for supper, Orlando,
my son? see 'Lord Randal'
What has came this blood on your
shirt sleeve see 'Edward'
'What have they done to the rain?'
Malvina Reynolds. FL: Just a
little rain falling all around FLC:
Just a little boy standing in the
rain. 4
What have you got in your basket?
see 'The false knight'
What have you got, you pedlar trim?
see 'Bold Robin Hood and the
pedlar'
'What if a day or a month or a
year' Thomas Campion. FL:
same. 26
'What if I sped where I least expected?' Robert Jones. FL:
same. 26
'What is a day' Thomas Campion
and Philip Rosseter. FL: What
is a day, what is a year. 26
'What is beauty but a breath?'
Thomas Greaves. FL: same.
26
What is that blood all on your hand?
see 'The murdered brother'
'What is that on the end of your
sword?' FL: same. 11
What is that on your sword so red?
see 'Edward'

'What is there to say' E. Y. Har-
  burg and Vernon Duke. FL:
  What is there to say and what is
  there to do. 67
What is this that we're living for?
  see 'Applause'
What kind o' fun do yo' fancy mos'
  see 'Louisiana hayride'
'What kind of fool am I?' Leslie
  Bricusse and Anthony Newley.
  FL: same. 42
What kind of shoes is dem you
  wear? see 'Dese dry bones of
  mine'
What loo is that, quoth the brave
  Lor' Heel see 'Prince Charlie'
What made me leave my hooses
  and lan' see 'The gypsy laddie'
'What Marry dat gal?' Harry B.
  Smith and John Stromberg. FL:
  Got a litter jest dis mawnin' FLC:
  What! marry dat gal? 36
What must I tell your father see
  'The two brothers'
What pleasure folks feel, when they
  live out of town see 'Come and
  take tea in the arbour'
'What shall we do with the drunken
  sailor?' FL: same FLC: Hoo-ray
  up she rises. 25, 57
'What shall I give to thee?' FL:
  What shall I give to thee? Dear
  we must part. 7
What ship is that sailing see 'Old
  ship of Zion'
What solemn sounds the ear invade
  see 'Mount Vernon'
What sorrowful sounds do I hear
  see 'Corydon's ghost'
'What the world needs now is love'
  Hal David and Burt Bacharach.
  FL: What the world needs now is
  love, sweet love. 71
'What then is love but mourning'
  Philip Rosseter. FL: same. 26
What think ye, o father dear see
  'Sweet Willie and Fair Annie'
What this country is coming to see
  'The panic is on'
What though America doth pour see
  'The etiquette'
'What to do' Mick Jagger and Keith
  Richard. FL: What to do? Yeah,
  I really don't know. 16
What will ye leave for your brother,
  Lord Ronald, my son? see
  'Lord Ronald'
What wondrous love is this see

'Wondrous love'
What would you do if I sang out of
  tune see 'With a little help
  from my friends'
'What would you give in exchange
  for your soul?' John Hancock
  (Fred Fisher) FL: This is a
  world full of trouble and strife
  FLC: What would you give. 14
'What you goin' to do when the rent
  comes round' Harry von Tilzer
  and Andrew B. Stirling. FL:
  Who's that a-knockin' at the door
  below FLC: Rufus Rastus John-
  son Brown. 57
'What you gonna call yo' pretty
  little baby' FL: Some say it's
  one thing FLC: What you gonna
  call yo' pretty little baby. 33
What you gonna do when they send
  your man to war see 'Wartime
  blues'
What you say, girl? you see what
  is wrong see 'Who's been
  sleeping here?'
What you will to your father Jimmy
  Randolph, my son? see 'Lord
  Randal'
'Whatever will be, will be' Jay
  Livingston and Ray Evans. FL:
  When I was just a little girl
  FLC: Que será, será. 47, 52
'What'll we do with the baby-o' FL:
  Every time the baby cries. 57
What'll you have for dinner, my
  kind old husband see 'Kind old
  husband'
What's it all about Alfie? see
  'Alfie'
'What's new pussycat?' Hal David
  and Burt Bacharach. FL: Pussy
  cat, Pussy cat, I've got flowers
  and lots of hours. 47
What's the matter with my daughter?
  the old man said see 'John
  Barbour'
What's this dull town to me? see
  'Robin Adair'
What's this man's horse a-doing
  here see 'Our Goodman'
Whaur hae ye been a' day, Lord
  Ronald my son? see 'Lord
  Ronald my son'
Whaur hae ye been a the day see
  'The croodin doo'
Whaur hae ye been all the day see
  'Lord Donald'
Wheel about, an' turn about see

trouble Mother Mary comes to
me see 'Let it be'
'When I first came to this land' FL:
same. 57
When I first came to town see
'Katy Cruel'
When I get older, losing my hair
many years from now see 'When
I'm 64'
When I had a beau for a soldier
who'd go see 'Dashing white
sergeant'
When I hear that serenade in blue
see 'Serenade in blue'
When I joined the army a few weeks
ago see 'Tell me boys'
'When I lay down' FL: When I lay
down and die on my old tired
hunkers. 57
When I least expected see 'Out
of nowhere'
When I left old Kentucky see 'I'm
going back to old Kentucky'
When I lost my baby see 'I almost
lost my mind'
When I makes the workers' beer
see 'The man that waters the
workers' beer'
When I play roulette see 'I may
be wrong'
When I set out I was but young see
'Getting ready to die'
'When I take my morning promenade'
A. J. Mills and Bennett Scott.
FL: Since Mother Eve in the
garden long ago FLC: As I take
my morning promenade. 17
'When I take my sugar to tea' Sam-
my Fain, Irving Kahal and Pierre
Norman. FL: I'm just a little
Jack Horner FLC: When I take my
sugar to tea. 53
When I take you out tonight, with
me see 'The surrey with the
fringe on top'
When I think back on all the crap I
learned in high school see
'Kodachrome'
When I think of all the worries that
people seem to find see 'Let's
live for today'
When I think of the last great round-
up see 'The last great round-up'
When I think of Tom I think about a
night see 'Hello young lovers'
When I walk that levee round see
'The bully of the town'
When I want a melody lilting through

the house see 'By Strauss'
When I was a bach'lor I lived all
alone see 'The foggy, foggy
dew'
When I was a bachelor I lived by
myself see 'The foggy, foggy
dew'
When I was a cowboy I learned to
throw the line see 'Sporting
cowboy'
When I was a girl of eighteen years
old see 'The old maid'
When I was a kid about half past
three see 'Taint what you do'
When I was a learner see 'Go tell
it on the mountain'
When I was a little baby, just able
to walk alone see 'The liar's
song'
When I was a little boy I lived by
myself see 'Wing wong waddle'
When I was a little girl I had a rag
doll see 'River deep, mountain
high'
When I was a little lad and so my
mother told me see 'Haul away,
Joe'
When I was a schoolboy aged three
see 'The old bachelor'
When I was a seeker see 'Go tell
it on the mountain'
When I was a student at Cadiz see
'The Spanish guitar'
When I was a young girl I used to
seek pleasure see 'The bad
girl'
When I was a young man and never
been kissed see 'Kisses sweeter than wine'
When I was a young man courting
the girls see 'September song'
When I was a young man in my
prime see 'Round the bay of
Mexico'
When I was a youngster gossips
would say see 'Hey for the life
of a soldier'
When I was apprenticed in London
see 'Blow the candles out'
When I was born into the world see
'I wonder when I'll get to be
called a man'
When I was bound apprentice
in famous Lincolnshire see
'Lincolnshire poacher'; 'The
poacher'
When I was in my sixteenth year
see 'The gardner'

When I was just a little boy see
'Lemon tree'
When I was just a little girl see
'Whatever will be, will be'
When I was just a wee little lad full
of healthy and joy see 'The
marvelous toy'
When I was single see 'Don't I
wish I was a single girl again'
When I was single, go dressed neat
and fine see 'Single girl'
When I was single, I went dressed
fine see 'Don't I wish I was a
single girl again'
When I was single, oh then, oh then
see 'I wish I was single again'
When I was young I used to wait
see 'The blue tail fly'; 'Jim
crack corn'
When I went down to the valley to
pray see 'Rock-a my soul'
When I worked in the mill see 'If
I loved you'
When I'm calling you see 'Indian
love call'
'When I'm 64' Lennon and McCartney.
FL: When I get older, losing my
hair many years from now. 44
When I'm dead and buried see
'Don't you weep after me'
When in death I shall calm recline
see 'Legacy'
When Israel was in Egypt's land
see 'Go down, Moses'
'When it's sleepy time down south'
Leon René, Otis René and Clar-
ence Muse. FL: Soft winds
blowing through the pinewood
trees FLC: Pale moon shining on
the fields below. 12, 59
When Jack, the king's commander
see 'The fate of John Burgoyne'
When January days are here see
'January and February'
'When Jesus wept' William Billings.
FL: When Jesus wept the falling
tear. 33, 65
When John first came out of Egypt
see 'Sabbath has no end'
When John Henry was a little baby
see 'John Henry'
'When Johnny comes marching home'
Patrick S. Gilmore. FL: same.
1, 4, 23, 25, 34, 57
When Johnny Scot saw this big broad
letter see 'Johnie Scot'
When Johnson's ale was new, my
boys see 'Johnson's ale'

When Joseph was a young man see
'The cherry tree carol'
When Joseph was a young man, a
young man was he see 'The
cherry tree'
When Joseph was an old man see
'Cherry tree carol'
When Joseph was old and righteous
was he see 'The cherry tree
carol'
'When Laura smiles' Philip Rosse-
ter. FL: When Laura smiles
her sight revives both night and
day. 26
When Louis came home to the flat
see 'Meet me in St. Louis,
Louis'
When love comes in and takes you
for a spin oo la la la see
'C'est magnifique'
When morning breaks the heaven
high see 'Island in the sun'
'When Moses smote the water' FL:
O children ain't you glad FLC:
When Moses smote the water.
38
'When my baby smiles at me'
Harry von Tilzer, Andrew B.
Sterling, Bill Munro and Ted
Lewis. FL: For when my baby
smiles at me. 59, 67
'When my blue moon turns to gold
again' Wiley Walker and Gene
Sullivan. FL: Memories that
linger in my heart FLC: When
my blue moon turns to gold again.
14
'When my dream boat comes home'
Cliff Friend and Dave Franklin.
FL: Dreams call to me over a
rose-tinted sea FLC: When my
dreamboat comes home. 46
When my fortune does frown see
'The jolly sailor'
'When my sugar walks down the
street' Gene Austin, Jimmy Mc-
Hugh and Irving Mills. FL:
She's so affectionate I'll say this
FLC: When my sugar walks down
the street. 12
When night is creepin' and I should
be sleepin' in bed see 'Daddy
won't you please come home'
When night time comes stealing
see 'Lonesome and sorry'
When old Hannah go to beaming see
'Long hot summer days'
When on a summer morning see

'On a summer morning'
When one's drunk, not a girl but
  looks pretty see 'A blessing on
  brandy and beer'
When Phoebus had melted the ic'les
  of ice see 'Robin Hood and the
  keeper'
When Phoebus had melted the shackles of ice see 'Robin Hood'
When Robin Hood was about twenty
  (eighteen) years old see 'Robin
  Hood and Little John'
When Roger McNally retired from
  the force see 'The beer that
  made Milwaukee famous'
When royal George ruled o'er this
  land see 'The American vicar
  of Bray'
When shadows fall and trees whisper
  see 'Home'
'When shall I get there' FL: There's
  a heavenly home up yonder FLC:
  When shall I get there? 38
When she came to her father's
  house see 'The baffled knight'
When she churns she churns in a
  boot see 'Hobblety bobblety how
  now'
When she's gone, she's gone see
  'Fakin' it'
When summertime is gone see
  'You are my flower'
'When that general roll is called'
  FL: Gwine to see my father, I'll
  be there FLC: I'll be there in the
  morning. 5
When the Alabam's keel was laid
  see 'Roll Alabama, roll'
When the big brass band began to
  play see 'At a Georgia camp
  meeting'
When the breezes blow petticoats of
  Portugal see 'Petticoats of
  Portugal'
When the college bell is ringing see
  'Yodelling song'
When the creel cam' to the top o'
  the lum see 'The keach i' the
  creel'
When the curtains of night are
  pinned back by the stars see
  'I'll remember you love in my
  prayers'
When the dawn flames in the sky
  see 'At dawning'
When the deep purple falls over
  sleepy garden walls see 'Deep
  purple'

When the dream came see 'On the
  way home'
When the little bluebird see 'Let's
  do it'
'When the chariot comes' FL: O
  who will drive the chariot when
  she comes. 5
'When the children are asleep' Os-
  car Hammerstein and Richard
  Rodgers. FL: When we've tucked
  the kids in their downy beds
  FLC: When the children are as-
  leep we'll sit and dream. 24
When the farmer comes to town
  see 'The farmer is the man'
When the green buds show see
  'Sing a song of spring'
When the Hootenanny came to town
  see 'Hootenanny Granny'
'When the lights are soft and low'
  Bert Child and E. Donato. FL:
  Oh, come to me in the evening
  when the sun hides in the West
  FLC: When lights are soft and
  low. 9
When the lime flower white is
  gleaming see 'Song of the is-
  lands'
When the lumberman comes to town
  see 'The lumberman in town'
When the mellow moon begins to
  beam see 'The man I love'
When the moon hits your eye like a
  pizza pie see 'That's amore'
When the night falls silently see
  'Glow worm'
When the night is black and
  the storm clouds crack see
  'Stick close to your bedding
  ground'
When the only sound in the
  empty street see 'Love for
  sale'
'When the saints come marchin' in'
  FL: I have a loving brother FLC:
  Oh when the saints come march-
  in' in. 25
'When the saints come marching in'
  Edward C. Redding. FLC: I am
  just a weary pilgrim FLC: Oh,
  when the saints come marching
  in. 1
'When the saints go marching in'
  FL: And when the saints go
  marching in. 4
'When the saints go marching in'
  FL: I am just a lonely traveler
  FLC: When the saints go marching

in. 23
'When the saints go marching in' FL:
Oh, when the saints go marching
in. 34, 57
When the sky is a bright canary
yellow see 'A cock-eyed opti-
mist'
'When the snow is on the roses'
Larry Kusik, Eddie Snyder and
James Last. FL: Now the golden
sun can see us kiss. 10
When the storm clouds gather see
'God bless America'
When the sun comes back and the
first quail calls see 'Follow
the drinkin' gourd'
When the sun goes down, the tide
goes out see 'Mississippi mud'
When the sun rose this mornin'
see 'Evil-hearted man'
When the swallows see 'Autumn
song'
When the union's inspiration through
workers blood shall run see
'Solidarity forever'
When the water is wet and the air
is dry see 'The swimming
master'
When the wind blows and the rain
feels cold see 'Moonlight mile'
When the wintry winds are blowing
see 'California here I come'
'When the work's all done this fall'
FL: A bunch of jolly cowboys
were discussing plans at ease. 2
'When the works all done this fall'
FL: A group of jolly cowboys
discussing plans one day. 50, 57
When the world goes wrong, as it's
bound to do see 'The sweet-
heart of Sigma Chi'
When there's a shine on your shoes
see 'A shine on your shoes'
When they begin the Beguine see
'Begin the Beguine'
When they played a 'malagueña' it
was more than just a dance see
'Malagueña salerosa'
'When things go wrong with you' Big
Bill Broonzy. FL: I love you,
baby FLC: Cause when things go
wrong. 57
When thirst of gold enslaves the
mind see 'I sold a guiltless
Negro boy'
'When this cruel war is over'
Charles C. Sawyer and Henry
Tucker. FL: Dearest love, do

you remember FLC: Weeping,
sad and lonely. 4
When this old man came in from
his plough see 'The wife wrapt
in wether's skin'
When this warfare'll be ended see
'Children, you'll be called on'
When this world began see 'Some-
body loves me'
'When to her lute Corinna sings'
Thomas Campion. FL: same.
26
When troubles surround us see
'Wings of a dove'
When Washington and Lee's men
fall in line see 'Washington
and Lee swing'
When we got within a mile of the
place see 'Been on the Charlie
so long'
When we older grew and bolder
see 'It's delightful to be mar-
ried'
'When we went out a fishin' J. C.
White and T. Ball. FL: Last
night Tom Snooks says he to me
FLC: With rods and lines and
bait a store. 36
When wild war's deadly black blast
was blawn see 'The sodger's
return'
'When will ye gang, Awa'?' FL:
When will ye gang awa', Jamie.
11
When we've tucked the kids in their
downy beds see 'When the
children are asleep'
'When wilt thou save the people?'
Josiah Booth and Ebenezer Elliott.
FL: same. 19
When ye were sleepin' on your pil-
lows see 'Caller herrin''
'When you and I were young Maggie'
George W. Johnson and James A.
Butterfield. FLC: I wandered
today to the hill, Maggie FLC:
And now we are aged and gray.
1, 25, 63
When you come to the end of a per-
fect day see 'A perfect day'
'When you go a-courtin'' FL: When
you go a-courtin', I'll tell you
where to go. 57
When you go down to yonder town
see 'Rosemary and thyme'
When you hear dem a bells go ding,
ling, ling see 'A hot time in
the old town'

When you hear them-a bells go ding,
ling, ling see 'There'll be a hot
time'
When you held your hand to my
heart see 'Lover'
When you left me all alone see
'Lipstick on your collar'
When you left you broke my heart
see 'Baby, won't you please
come home'
When you look into your mailbox
and you find your questionnaire
see 'Draftee's blues'
When you see a pretty maiden who
has just turned 17 see 'You're
not the only pebble on the beach'
When you wake up in the morning,
hear the ding dong ring see
'Midnight Special'
When you walk through a storm see
'You'll never walk alone'
When you want to see 'You're a
builder upper'
When you watch for feather or fur
see 'Feather or fur'
'When you were sweet 16' James
Thornton. FL: When first I saw
the lovelight in your eye FLC: I
love you as I never loved before.
20, 31, 67
'When your lover has gone' E. A.
Swan. FL: For ages and ages
FLC: When you're alone. 46
When you're in love and you are
wonderin' see 'A sleepin' bee'
'When you're smiling' Mark Fisher,
Joe Goodwin and Larry Shay.
FL: But when you're crying FLC:
When you're smiling. 12
'When you're smiling' Mark Fisher,
Joe Goodwin and Larry Shay.
FL: I saw a blind man FLC:
When you're smiling. 54
When you're weary, feelin' small
see 'Bridge over troubled water'
When you've grown up, my dears
see 'Toyland'
Whence came ye or from what
counterie see 'The old beggar
man'
Whenever I feel afraid see 'I
whistle a happy tune'
Whenever skies are gray see 'Let
a smile be your umbrella'
Whenever we meet you here we say
see 'A little more faith in Jesus'
Where are the boys of the old bri-
gade see 'The old brigade'

'Where are the froggies' FL: Where
are the froggies when the north
winds blow. 13
'Where are the keys of the castle'
FL: I've a fine big castle. 48
Where are you a-going, my own
dealing boy? see 'Three drops
of poison'
'Where are you goin', my good old
man' FL: same. 35
Where are you going? see 'The
false knight upon the road'
Where are you going Billy boy,
Billy boy see 'Billy boy'
Where are you going, Lord Lovel
she said see 'Lord Lovell'
Where are you going? said the
false, false knight see 'The
false knight on the road'
Where are you going? said the
knight in the road see 'The
false knight upon the road'
Where are you going? to Cadrian?
see 'True lover of mine'
'Where are you going to my pretty
maid' FL: same. 25, 48, 68
Where are you going to, my pretty
maid see 'Mowing the barley'
Where dear old Shannon's flowing
see 'Where the River Shannon
flows'
'Where did Robinson Crusoe go with
Friday on Saturday night' Sam
M. Lewis, Joe Young and George
W. Meyer. FL: Thousands of
years ago or maybe more FLC:
And where did Robinson Crusoe
go with Friday on Saturday night?
31
'Where did you borrow that last
sigh?' Sir William Berkeley and
William Lawes. FL: same. 40
'Where did you get that hat?' Jo-
seph J. Sullivan and William
Lorraine. FL: Now how I came
to get this hat tis very strange
and funny FLC: Where did you
get that hat? 20, 36
Where did you stay last night, O
Randal, my son? see 'Lord
Randal'
Where do you think I found my soul
see 'Listen to the angels'
Where ever I'm going and all the
day, long see 'Ballynamony'
Where hae ye been a' day, Lord
Ronald, my son? see 'Lord
Ronald, my son'

Where hae ye been huntin', Lord
Ronald my son see 'Lord Ron-
ald'
Where hae ye been the livelong day
see 'The wee little croodin' doo'
'Where has thou been today?' FL:
same. 11
Where hast thou been since I saw
thee? see 'Ilkley Moor'; 'On
Ilkla moor baht hat'
'Where have all the flowers gone?'
Pete Seeger and Joe Hickson.
FL: same. 4
Where have ye been all the day,
Lord Ronald my son? see
'Lord Ronald'
Where have you been all day Henry
my son? see 'Henry my son'
Where have you been all the day
see 'My boy Tommy O'
Where have you been all the day,
Billy boy, Billy boy see 'Billy
boy'
Where have you been all the day,
Randall my son? see 'Lord
Randall'
Where have you been all this day,
my boy Billy see 'My boy Billy'
Where have you been a-roving,
Jimmy Randal my son see
'Lord Randal'
Where have you been a-roving my
only son? see 'Lord Rendal'
Where have you been Billy Boy?
where have you been, charming
Billy? see 'Billy Boy'
Where have you been courting,
Henry my son? see 'Lord Ren-
del'
Where have you been Henry my son
see 'Henry my son'
Where have you been Johnny Rillus,
my son see 'Johnny Rillus'
Where have you been, Lorendo,
Lorendo, my son? see 'Loren-
do'
Where have you been, my fair pretty
one? see 'Lord Rendel'
Where have you been my sweet, my
love? see 'Mother, make my
bed soon'
Where have you been, Randal, it's
Randal my son see 'Lord Ran-
dal'
Where have you been to all the day,
Henry my son? see 'Lord Ren-
dal'
Where have you been to all this day,

Henry my son see 'Lord Ren-
dal'
Where have you been to Tiranti, my
son? see 'Tiranti, my son'
Where have you been, Willie Ran-
some, Willie Ransome, my son?
see 'Willie Ransome'
Where hev ye been aal the day see
'Billy Boy'
'Where I'm bound' FL: It's a long
and dusty road, it's a hot and
heavy load FLC: But I can't help
but wonder where I'm bound. 14
Where is the home to compare with
mine see 'My adobe hacienda'
Where is little Maggie? see 'Little
Maggie'
Where is the goat see 'Counting
the goats'
Where is the landlord? see 'Lam-
kin'
Where it began, I can't begin to
knowin' see 'Sweet Caroline'
Where, oh, where are you tonight?
see 'Phfft! you were gone!'
'Where, oh where has my little dog
gone?' FL: same. 72
'Where, oh where is dear little
Susie?' FL: same. 57
'Where o where is old Elijah?' FL:
same. 57
Where, oh, where where would I
be! see 'Phfft! You are gone'
(Gospel version)
Where the river is windin' see
'North to Alaska'
'Where the river Shannon flows'
James I. Russell. FL: There's
a pretty spot in Ireland FLC:
Where dear old Shannon's flowing.
20, 31
'Where they were' FL: If you want
to know where the privates are
FLC: I saw them, I saw them.
57
'Where were you all the day, my
own pretty boy?' FL: same. 11
Where were you all day, my own
pretty boy? see 'Lord Randall'
Where were you bred and where
were you born see 'The old
beggarman'
'Where will I get a little wee boy'
FL: same. 11
Where's that boy with the bugle?
see 'If he walked into my life'
Wherever I poke sarcastic joke re-
plete with malice spiteful see

'Nothing whatever to grumble at'
'Whether me do laugh or weep'
Thomas Campion and Philip Ros-
seter. FL: same. 26
'Which side are you on?' Florence
Reece. FL: Come all of you
good workers FLC: Which side
are you on? 19, 58
'The Whig' FL: Would you know what
a Whig is and always was? 49
'While gentle Parthenisa walks' Sir
Richard Steele and Daniel Purcell.
FL: same. 40
While I relate my story, Americans
give ear see 'American taxa-
tion'
While I'm far away from you my
baby see 'Dedicated to the one
I love'
While Mary washed linen see
'Mary washed linen'
While plodding on our way, the toil-
some road of life see 'A boy's
best friend is his mother'
While riding down that green wood
road see 'John of Hazelgreen'
While shepherds kept their watching
see 'Go, tell it on the mountain'
'While shepherds watched' FL: While
shepherds watched their flocks by
night. 33
While strolling along with the city's
vast throng see 'She may have
seen better days'
While strolling down the street one
evening upon mere pleasure bent
see 'Just tell them that you saw
me'
While strolling in the park one day
see 'The fountain in the park'
While strolling thro' Norfolk one day
on a spree see 'Strolling through
Norfolk'
'While strolling through the park' Ed
Haley. FL: While strolling
through the park one day. 1, 25,
57, 67
While the shot and shell were
screaming see 'Break the news
to mother'
While the train rolled onward see
'In the baggage coach ahead'
While tearing off see 'My heart
belongs to Daddy'
'While the dew flies over the green
valley' FL: I married me a wife
and I took her home. 11
While you're away see 'Now is the

hour'
'Whilst through the sharp hawthorn'
Francis Hopkinson. FL: The
traveler benighted and lost. 65
'Whip-poor-will' FL: Whip-poor-will,
whip-poor-will, whip-poor-will.
7
'Whirlwinds of danger' FL: Whirlwinds of danger are ranging
around us FLC: Then forward,
you workers, freedom awaits you.
57
'Whiskey in the jar' FL: As I was
a walkin' round Kilgary Mountain.
35
'Whiskey Johnny' FL: As we sailed
on the water blue. 57
'Whiskey Johnny' FL: In London City
you'll see me here. 41
'Whiskey, you're the devil' FL: Oh
now, brave boys, we'll run for
march FLC: Oh, love, fare thee
well. 57
'Whistle, daughter, whistle' FL:
Mother, I long to get married.
57, 58
'Whistle, daughter, whistle' FL:
Mother, I would marry, yes, I
would be a bride. 35
'The whistling gypsy rover' FL: The
gypsy rover came over the hill
FLC: Ah di du, ah di du da day.
23
'White clouds' Sylvia Beels. FL:
White clouds sailing in the windy
sky. 13
'White coral bells' FL: White coral
bells upon a slender stalk. 13,
34, 57
'White dove' FL: In the deep rolling hills of old Virginia FLC:
White dove will mourn in sorrow.
14
'White house blues' FL: Look here,
you rascal, see what you've done.
14
'White house blues' FL: McKinley
hollered, McKinley squalled. 57
'The white pilgrim' FL: I came to
the place where the White Pilgrim
lay. 7
'The white pilgrim' FL: Oh, I come
to the spot where the white pilgrim lay. 7
'White sand and gray sand' FL:
same. 57
'Whither runneth my sweetheart'
John Bartlet and Robert Jones.

FL: same. 26
'Whittingham Fair' FL: Are you
going to Whittingham Fair. 11
'Who?' Otto Harback, Oscar Hammerstein and Jerome Kern. FL:
When a girl's in love with someone FLC: Who stole my heart
away. 24, 67
'Who can I turn to' Leslie Bricusse
and Anthony Newley. FL: Who
can I turn to when nobody needs
me? 42
'Who cares?' George and Ira Gershwin. FL: Let it rain and thun-
der FLC: Who cares if the sky
cares to fall in the sea? 21
'Who did swallow Jonah?' FL: Who
did, who did, who did. 57
Who do my thoughts loom so large
on me? see 'She smiled sweet-
ly'
Who is at my bedroom window see
'The drowsy sleeper'
'Who killed Cock Robin?' FL: same
FLC: All the birds in the trees
were a-sighin', and a-sobbin'.
72
Who killed Cock Robin? see 'Cock
Robin'
'Who killed Norma Jean?' Norman
Roslew and Pete Seeger. FL:
same. 58
'Who knows why' V. Zakharov and
Jerry Silverman. FL: Every
evening near my home. 57
'Who knows why' V. Zakharov and
M. Isakovsky. FL: Na zakate
khodit paren' vozle doma moevo.
57
Who knows why the sea see 'Can
this be love?'
Who made the mountain see 'Some-
body bigger than you and I'
Who stole my heart away see
'Who?'
'Who threw the overalls in Mistress
Murphy's chowder' George L.
Geifer. FL: Mistress Murphy
gave a party just about a week
ago FLC: Who threw the over-
alls in Mistress Murphy's chow-
der. 20
Who told you you could make it
see 'Go down old Hannah'
Who took the place of De De Dinah?
see 'Patricia, it's Patricia'
Who wants yesterday's papers? see
'Yesterday's papers'

Who will be a witness for my Lord
see 'Witness'
Who will love a little sparrow see
'Sparrow'
Who will shoe your pretty little feet
see 'Lass of Roch Royal'
'Who will shoe your pretty little
foot?' FL: Oh who will shoe
your pretty little foot? 11
'Who wouldn't love you' Bill Carey
and Carl Fischer. FL: same.
59
'Whoa, back, buck' Huddie Ledbet-
ter, John A. Lomax and Alan
Lomax. FL: Tom done buck an'
Bill won' pull FLC: Whoa, back,
Buck, an' gee, by de Lamb. 4
'Whoa buck' FL: Sometimes I plow
old gray horse FLC: Tighten on
the backband. 57
'Whoa, mulie, whoa' FL: I'm the
owner of a mule, the finest mule
in town. 7
Whoa, rattler was a mighty dog see
'Rattler'
Whoa there, mule, I tell you see
'The kickin' mule'
Whoas, dogies, whoa-oh see 'The
cowman's lament'
Who'll buy my caller herrin'? see
'Caller herrin''
Who'll come awaltzing Matilda, my
darlin'? see 'Waltzing Matilda'
Whoop dee-doo-den-doo den-dah
see 'Mary had a William goat'
Whoopee ti yi yo see 'Git along
little dogies'
'Who's been sleeping here?' Mick
Jagger and Keith Richard. FL:
What you say, girl? You see
what is wrong. 16
'Who's dat yondah?' FL: O, little
did I think He was so nigh FLC:
O who's dat yondah. 5
'Who's gonna shoe your pretty little
foot?' FL: same. 23, 35, 57,
58
'Who's in the strawberry patch with
Sally' Irwin Levine and L. Rus-
sell Brown. FL: same. 64
'Who's sorry now?' Bert Kalmar,
Harry Ruby and Ted Snyder.
FL: Right to the end FLC: Who's
sorry now? 12
'Who's that a-callin'' FL: The moon
is shining on the window sill
FLC: Who's that a-callin'? 25
Who's that a-knockin' at the door

below see 'What you goin' to do when the rent comes round'
Who's that gallopin' on the King's Highway see 'Gyps of David'
Who's that yonder dressed in red? see 'Oh, won't you sit down?'
Who's the most important man this country ever knew see 'Barney Google'
Who's there? who's there? see 'Mr. Ghost goes to town'
'Whose corpse is that a-coming this way?' FL: same. 11
Whose horse is that horse where my horse ought to be? see 'Old Wichet'
Whose sheep are those? see 'The false fidee'
'Whoso is tied must needs be bound' Robert Jones. FL: same. 26
'The whummil bore' FL: Seven lang years I have served the king. 11
Why are people gay see 'Love is sweeping the country'
Why are the stars always winkin' and blinkin' above see 'Elmer's tune'
Why brthering, po' me see 'Po' me'
'Why came thou not, as others do' John Danyel. FL: same. 26
Why come ye hither Redcoats? see 'The rifle'; 'Riflemen of Bennington'
Why did I wander? see 'Isn't it a pity?'
Why do birds suddenly appear every time you are near see 'Close to you'
Why do I feel so spry? see 'Looking at the world thru rose-colored glasses'
Why do I just wither and forget all resistence see 'The nearness of you'
'Why do I love you' Oscar Hammerstein and Jerome Kern. FL: I'm walking on the air, dear FLC: Why do I love you? 24, 67
Why do they think up stories that link my name with yours? see 'People will say we're in love'
Why does the sky turn gray every night? see 'Some things just stick in your mind'
'Why don't we do this more often' Charles Newman and Allie Wrubel. FL: same. 59

Why don't we sing the song all together? see 'Sing this all together'
Why don't we stop foolin' ourselves see 'Overs'
'Why don't you do right' Joe McCoy. FL: You had plenty money 1922. 59, 70
'Why don't you write me?' Paul Simon. FL: same. 60
Why, fair maid, have pity on me see 'The heiress of Northumberland'
Why had'st not thou awaked me, my little footboy? see 'The Broomfield Hill'
Why, He's the Lord of Lords see 'He's the Lord of Lords'
Why, Mr. Ghost is goin' to town see 'Mr. Ghost goes to town'
Why need I reward Lampkin? see 'Lampkin'
Why put this sadness inside of me see 'All sold out'
Why should a woman who is healthy and strong see 'Many a new day'
Why should our joys transform to pain? see 'The Indian philosopher'
Why should vain mortals tremble see 'Bunker Hill'
Why should vain mortals tremble at the sight see 'The American hero'
Why should we mourn departing friends see 'China'
'Why shouldn't my goose' FL: Why shouldn't my goose sing as well as thy goose. 34, 57, 72
'Why, soldiers, why' FL: How stands the glass around? 57
Why this feeling? see 'Mr. Wonderful'
'Why was I born?' Oscar Hammerstein and Jerome Kern. FL: Spending these lonesome evenings FLC: Why was I born? 24, 67
Why weep 'eh by the tide, Ladye see 'John of Haselgreen'
Why weep ye by the tide fair maid see 'Jock o' Hazeldean'
Why weep ye by the tide ladye? see 'Jock o Hazeldean'
Why why whack the farrel the farrel la lay see 'The king and the tinker'
'Wi' a hundred pipers' FL: Wi' a

'Wild horses' Mick Jagger and Keith
Richard. FL: Childhood living is
easy to do FLC: Wild horses
couldn't drag me away. 16
'The wilderness lady, or a health to
the king' FL: A lord's house in
London, great merriment held.
30
'Wildwood flower' FL: I will twine
and will mingle my raven black
hair. 1
'Wildwood flower' FL: I will twine
and will mingle my waving black
hair. 27, 35, 56, 57
'Wildwood flower' FL: I will twine
thru my tresses of raven black
hair. 67
'Wildwood flower' FL: I'll entwine
and I'll mingle my raven black
hair. 23, 25
'Wildwood flower' FL: I'll twine 'mid
the ringlets of my raven black
hair. 14
Will I ever find the girl in my mind
see 'My ideal'
Will ye come in into our ha' see
'King Orfeo'
Will ye gang to the Hielands, Leezie
Lindsay see 'Leezie Lindsay'
Will ye gang to the Hielands, my
bonnie love? see 'Gight's ladye'
Will ye go to the Hielan' my bonny
lad see 'Will ye go to the Hie-
lands, Geordie?'
'Will ye go to the Hielans, Geordie?'
FL: Will ye go to the Hielans, my
bonny lad. 11
'Will ye no come back again?' FL:
Bonnie Charlie's now awa' FLC:
Will ye no come back again? 25
'Will you be loving another man?'
Bill Monroe. FL: Now will you
love me, little darlin' FLC:
Will you be lovin' another man.
14
'Will you come to the bower?' FL:
Will you come to the bower I
have shaded for you? 66
Will you come with me, my Phyllis
dear see 'Wait for the wagon'
Will you court me, my pretty little
miss? see 'I'm seventeen come
Sunday'
Will you forsake your house carpen-
ter see 'House carpenter'
'Will you go lassie, go?' FL: Oh
the summertime is coming FLC:
And we'll all go together. 57

Will you go to the footing of the
hill see 'The twa brothers'
Will you go to the highlands my
bonnie love see 'Bog o' Gight'
'Will you love me in December as
you do in May?' J. J. Walker
and Ernest R. Ball. FL: Now in
the summer of life sweetheart
FLC: Will you love me in December as you do in May? 20,
31
Will you please give ear a while
unto me see 'A new English
ballad'
Will you walk into my parlor said
a spider to a fly see 'The
spider and the fly'
Will you wear white, my dear, o
my dear? see 'Jenny Jenkins'
Will you, will you see 'The spider and the fly'
'William and Margaret' FL: As
Miss Margaret was sat in her
bower one day. 11
'William Brown' FL: William Brown
was a clever young man. 41
'William Glen' FL: There was a
ship and a ship of fame. 11
'William Goat' FL: Mary had a
William goat. 72
'William Guiseman' FL: My name
is William Guiseman. 11
'William Taylor' FL: Willie Taylor
was a brisk young sailor. 30,
58
'William Taylor' FL: William Tay-
lor was a brisk young tailor. 57
'William's ghost' FL: There came
a ghost to Margaret's door. 11
Willie bring your little drum see
'Pat-a-pan'
'Willie Doo' FL: O where hae ye
been a' the day. 11
Willie Fitzgibbons who used to sell
ribbons see 'Waltz me around
again, Willie'
'Willie Moore' FL: Willie Moore
was a king. 23, 56, 57
'Willie o' Douglas-dale' FL: Willie
was as brave a lord. 11
'Willie o' Winsbury' FL: As she
was looking over her father's
castle wall. 30
'Willie o' Winsbury' FL: There
lived a girl in a far country. 30
'Willie o Winsbury' FL: There was
a lass in the north countrie. 11
'Willie of Hazel Green' FL: As I

walked out one fine summer's
evening. 11

'Willie of Winsbury' FL: As she
was looking over her father's
castle wall. 11

'Willie of Winsbury' FL: Fair Mary
sat at her father's castle gate.
11

Willie, oh Willie, I love you see
'Beautiful, beautiful brown eyes'

'Willie, Ransome' FL: Where have
you been, Willie Ransome, Willie
Ransome, my son? 11

Willie stands in his stable door see
'Clyde's water'; 'The drowned
lovers'

Willie Taylor was a brisk young
sailor see 'William Taylor'

'Willie the weeper' FL: Did you
ever hear the story 'bout Willie
the Weeper? FLC: Teet tee dee
dee dee. 35, 57

Willie was as brave a lord see
'Willie o' Douglas-dale'

'Willie was drowned in Yarrow'
FL: Her hair it was five quarters long. 11

'Willie's drowned at Gamery' FL:
O Willie's fair and Willie's rare.
11

'Willie's drowned in Gamrie' FL:
On Monday morning at twelve
o'clock. 11

'Willie's drowned in Yarrow' FL:
O Willie's fair and Willie's rare.
11

Willie's fair and Willie's rare
see 'Rare Willie drowned in
Yarrow'

'Willie's fatal visit' FL: Oh, saw ye
my father, or saw ye my mother.
11

'Willie's fate' FL: For Willie's gane
o'er yon high, high hill. 11

'Willie's lady' FL: Willie's taen
him o'er the fame. 11

'Willie's lyke-wake' FL: If my love
loved me, she lets me not know.
11

'Willie's rare' FL: Willie's rare
and Willie's fair. 11

Willie's taen him o'er the fame
see 'Willie's lady'

'Willow garden' FL: Way down in a
willow garden. 35

'The willow song' FL: A poor soul
say sighing by a sycamore tree
FLC: Sing willow, willow, willow,

willow. 57

'Willow tree' FL: There was a
youth, a cruel youth. 25

'Willow willow' FL: The poor soul
sat sighing. 26

'Willows in the snow' William N.
Porter and Erika Hildel. FL:
The willows hanging low. 13

'The willow's lullaby' Z. Topelius.
FL: Sleep, thou little willow
tree. 13

'Willy's rare and Willy's fair' FL:
same. 11

The wind blew high, the wind blew
cold see 'Get up and bar the
door'

The wind blows cold today, sweetheart see 'Cold blows the wind'

The wind blows rain into my face
see 'Child of the moon'

The wind it blowed, the snow it
snowed, the lightning it did light
see 'A thing he had never done
before'

The wind was still and the moon
was clear see 'The mermaid'

'Wind, wind blowing' Paula and
Dehmel and Gottfried Wolters.
FL: same. 13

Winds may blow over the icy sea
see 'A taste of honey'

'Windy Bill' FL: Oh, Windy Bill
was a Texas boy, and he could
rope, you bet. 43

'Windy Bill' FL: Old Windy Bill was
a Texas guy. 2

'Windy Bill' FL: Windy Bill was a
Texas man. 62

'Wing Tee Wee' Hubbard T. Smith.
FL: Wing Tee Wee was a sweet
Chinee. 36

'Wing wong waddle' FL: When I was
a little boy I lived by myself
FLC: To my wing wong waddle,
to my jack straw straddle. 25

'Wings of a dove' Bob Ferguson.
FL: When troubles surround us
FLC: On the wings of a snow
white dove. 10

'Winning the vote' Mrs. A. B.
Smith. FL: I've been down to
Madison to see the folks and
sights FLC: Not from Joe. 57,
58

A winning way, a pleasant smile
see 'Little Annie Rooney'

'The Winnsboro cotton mill blues'
FL: Old man Sargent, sitting at

strike sent out a call see
'Casey Jones'
Working in a weave room fighting
for my life see 'Weave room
blues'
The world is lyrical see 'Dancing
on the ceiling'
'The world over was blue clover
see 'One morning in May'
The world today is mourning see
'Mother Jones'
The world today is mourning the
death of Mother Jones see 'The
death of Mother Jones'
'The world turned upside down' FL:
Goody Bull and her daughter to-
gether fell out. 65
'The world turned upside down' FL:
If buttercups buzzed after the
bee. 8
'World without love' Lennon and
McCartney. FL: Please lock me
away and don't allow the day. 44
'World youth song' L. Oshanin and
M. Wettlin. FL: One great vision
unites us FLC: Everywhere the
youth is singing freedom's song.
57
'The worm song' FL: Did you ever
think as the hearse rolls by. 68
'Worried blues' FL: I've got the
worried blues, Lord. 57
'A worried man' Dave Guard and
Tom Glazer. FL: Got myself a
Cadillac FLC: It takes a worried
man. 10
'Worried man blues' FL: It takes a
worried man to sing a worried
song. 23, 25, 34, 57, 67
'Worse than men' FL: There was a
farmer living in town. 11
'Wotcher 'Ria' Will Herbert and
Bessie Bellwood. FL: I am a
girl what's doing very well in the
vegetable line FLC: Wotcher 'Ria?
'Ria's on the job. 17
'Would God I were the tender apple
blossom' FL: same. 23
Would God I were the tender apple
blossom see 'Londerry air'
Would you deny this heart that I
see 'Amor'
Would you forsake your houses and
home see 'The gypsy laddie'
Would you have freedom from wage
slavery? see 'There is power'
Would you know what a Whig is and
always was? see 'The Whig'

Would you leave your house and
home see 'Gypsy Davy'
Would you like to ride in my beautiful
balloon? see 'Up, up and away'
'Would you like to take a walk'
Mort Dixon, Billy Rose and Harry
Warren. FL: I saw you strolling
by your solitary FLC: Mm mm
mm would you like to take a
walk. 46
'Would you with her you love be
blest' Thomas A. Arne. FL:
same. 40
'Wouldn't it be loverly' Lerner and
Loewe. FL: All I want is a
room somewhere. 64
'Wraggle taggle gipsies' FL: It's of
seven gipsies all of a row. 11
'Wraggle taggle gipsies O!' FL: O
seven jolly gipsies all in a gang.
11
'The wraggle taggle gipsies' FL: O
seven jolly gipsies all in a row. 11
'Wraggle taggle gipsies' FL: There
was three gipsies come to the
door. 11, 57
'The wraggle-taggle gypsies' FL:
There were three gypsies a-come
to my door. 58
'Wraggle taggle gipsies O' FL:
There were two gipsies come
singing at the door. 11
'Wraggle taggle gipsies O' FL:
Three jolly gipsies all in a row.
11
Wrap me up in my black bearskin
see 'The Golden Vanity'
'Wrap me up in my tarpaulin jacket'
FL: same. 25
'The wreck at Maud' FL: One
Christmas Eve, the night was
dark. 37
'The wreck of the F. F. V.' FL:
Along came the F. F. V. 35
'The wreck of the old ninety-seven'
FL: Well, he gave him his orders
at Monroe, Virginia. 14, 27, 57
'A wreck on the C & O' FL: Along
came the F. F. V., the fastest
on the line. 7
'The wrecked ship' FL: Then up
spoke the captain of our gallant
ship. 11
'Wrestling Jacob' FL: Wrestling
Jacob, Jacob, day is a-breaking.
38
'Wunderbar' Cole Porter. FL:
Gazing down on the Jungfrau FLC:

Ye sons of France, awake to glory
see 'La Marseillaise'
'Ye sons of North Britain' FL: Ye
sons of North Britain, you that
used to range. 8
Ye tars of Columbia, give ear to my
story see 'Perry's victory'
Ye Tories all rejoice and sing see
'The Congress'
Ye wrong head, ye strongheads, at-
tend to my strains see 'Song of
the heads'
Ye Yankees who, mole-like still
throw up the earth see 'The
burrowing Yankees'
Yea, ho! the rattlin' bog see 'Bog
in the valley-o'
Yeah, you got satin shoes see
'Can't you hear me knocking'
The years creep slowly by Lorena
see 'Lorena'
The years have changed you some-
how see 'Sophisticated lady'
Years we've been together' see
'Please don't talk about me when
I'm gone'
'Yellow gal' FL: Oh my yella yellow,
yellow, yellow gal. 28
'The yellow rose of Texas' FL:
There's a yellow rose in Texas
FLC: She's the sweetest rose of
color a feller ever knew. 1, 23,
25, 35, 57, 63, 67
'Yellow submarine' Lennon and
McCartney. FL: In the town
where I was born lived a man who
sailed to sea FLC: We all live in
a yellow submarine. 44, 45, 47
'Yeo, yeo, yeo, sir' FL: I am a
brisk and sprightly lad FLC: Yeo,
yeo, yeo, yeo. 25
Yer won't see 'im pullin' the barrer
no more see 'Jeerusalem's
dead!'
'Yerakina' FL: Kinise yerakina FLC:
Druga druga drun drun drun. 57
Yes, He's taken my feet out of the
miry clay see 'Rise, mourners'
Yes, I'll go stepping too, my honey
see 'I'll go stepping too'
Yes, I'm going to study war no
more see 'Going to pull my
war clothes'
'Yes indeed!' Sy Oliver. FL: You
will shout when it hits you. 59
'Yes, let me like a soldier fall' Edward Fitzball and Vincent Wallace.
FL: same. 63

Yes the book of Revolutions to be
bro't forth on that day see
'Mighty day'
Yes, the cat came back, he wouldn't
stay no longer see 'The yaller
cat'
Yes, they'll all come to meet me
see 'Green green grass of home'
Yes, we'll gain this world see
'Down by the river'
Yes, we're all dodging see 'The
dodger song'
Yes, you must have that true reli-
gion see 'You can't cross here'
'Yesterday' Lennon and McCartney.
FL: Yesterday, all my troubles
seemed so far away. 44
'Yesterday I heard the rain' A.
Manzanero. FL: La otra tarde
vi que un ave enamorada FLC:
Esta tarde vi llovar. 9
'Yesterday I heard the rain' Gene
Lees and A. Manzanero. FL:
Out of doorways black umbrellas
came to pursue me FLC: Yester-
day I heard the rain. 9
Yesterday I married a wife see
'The lowlands of Holland'
Yesterday was a high holiday see
'Little Sir Hugh'
Yesterday was a holiday see
'Little Saloo'
Yesterday was a very fine day see
'Little Harry Huston'
'Yesterdays' Otto Harbach and
Jerome Kern. FL: Yesterdays,
yesterdays. 67
'Yesterday's papers' Mick Jagger
and Keith Richard. FL: Who
wants yesterday's papers? 16
Yestre'en the queen had four
Maries see 'Mary Hamilton'
Yey, there's nothing half so sweet
see 'I've never lost my last
train yet'
Yield not to temptation for yielding
is sin see 'The bar-three of a
Sunday night'
Yippie-i-o, yippie-i-ay, bull riders
in the sky see 'Bull riders in
the sky'
Yo heave ho yo heave ho see
'Volga boatman'
Yo ho ho, the wind blows free see
'The Eddystone Light'
Yo soy un hombre sincero see
'Guantanamera'
Yo tengo un castillo see 'Donde

estan las llaves?'
'Yodelling song' FL: When the col-
lege bell is ringing.   25
Yoho, yoho, yoho <u>see</u> 'The snow-
man'
'Yomi, yomi' FL: Yomi, yomi, zing
mir a lidele FLC: Neyn, manenyu,
neyn.   57, 58
'Yon' come Roberta' FL: Yon' come
Roberta, got a hundred all in her
hand.   28
'Yonder' FL: Yonder stand a hand-
some woman.   41
Yonder comes a courteous knight
<u>see</u> 'The over courteous knight'
'Yonder comes the high sheriff' FL:
Yonder comes the high sheriff
ridin' after me.   57
Yonder stand a handsome woman
<u>see</u> 'Yonder'
Yonder stands little Maggie <u>see</u>
'Little Maggie'
'The Yorkshire bite' FL: The boy
took the cow by the horn with his
hand.   11
'The Yorkshire bite' FL: In London
there lived a mason by trade.   11
'Yorkshire bite' FL: The saddle was
riffled and outfit was gold.   11
'The Yorkshire boy' FL: In London
there lived a mason by trade
FLC: Timi fol dol di lie do fol
lol der day.   11
'The Yorkshire farmer' FL: Early
one morning he called for his
man.   11
'Yorkshire farmer' FL: There was a
wealthy farmer.   11
You ain't been blue <u>see</u> 'Mood in-
digo'
You ain't nothin' but a hound dog
<u>see</u> 'Hound dog'
'You and the night and the music'
Howard Dietz and Arthur Schwartz.
FL: Song is in the air FLC: You
and the night and the music.   46
You are always in my heart <u>see</u>
'Always in my heart'
'You are beautiful' Oscar Hammer-
stein and Richard Rodgers.   FL:
Along the Hwang-ho River where
young men walk and dream FLC:
You are beautiful, small and shy.
24
You are gazing now on old Tom
Moore <u>see</u> 'The days of Forty-
nine'
You are leaving me and I will try

to face the world alone <u>see</u>
'Something to remember you by'
'You are love' Oscar Hammerstein
and Jerome Kern.   FL: Once a
wandering ne'er-do-well.   24
'You are my flower' FL: When
summertime is gone FLC: You
are my flower.   14
'You are my sunshine' Jimmie
Davis and Charles Mitchell.   FL:
The other night dear as I lay
sleeping FLC: You are my sun-
shine, my only sunshine.   10
'You are never away' Oscar Ham-
merstein and Richard Rodgers.
FL: You are never away from
your home in my heart.   24
You are the promised kiss of springtime <u>see</u> 'All the things you
are'
You are young and beautiful <u>see</u>
'Don't marry me'
You ask me if I'll forget my baby
<u>see</u> 'Guess things happen that
way'
You ask me to have a discreet
heart <u>see</u> 'I'll follow my secret heart'
You ask what makes this darkie
weep <u>see</u> 'Kitty Wells'
'You belong to me' Pee Wee King
and Redd Stewart and Chilton
Price.   FL: See the pyramids
along the Nile.   52
'You belong to my heart' Agustin
Lara.   FL: Una vez nada má en
mi huerto brilló la esperanza
FLC: Solamente una vez amé en
la vida.   9
'You belong to my heart' Ray Gilbert and Agustin Lara.   FL: We
were gathering stars while a
million guitars played our love
song FLC: You belong to my
heart now and forever.   9
You better watch it, better watch
it <u>see</u> 'Fall tree'
'You call everybody darling' Sam
Martin, Ben Trace and Clem
Watts.   FL: Tho' you're always
waxing sentimental FLC: You
call everybody darling.   70
'You call it madness' Con Conrad,
Gladys Du Bois, Russ Columbo
and Paul Gregory.   FL: I can't
forget the night I met you.   47
You came to me <u>see</u> 'Out of nowhere'

see 'I'm so glad'
'Young Allan' FL: A' the sailors in
merry London FLC: Young Allan
he grat and he wrang his hands.
11
'Young Allan' FL: A' the sailors o'
Miraladen. 11
'Young Allan' FL: As all the skip-
pers o' Scarboro'. 11
'Young Allan' FL: I will wager wi'
you the morn. 11
'Young Allan' FL: The sailors o'
merrily Den. 11
Young Amy was a servant girl see
'Edwin in the lowlands low, or
Young Edward'
'Young and healthy' Al Dubin and
Harry Warren. FL: I know a
bundle of humanity FLC: I'm
young and healthy. 46
'Young Barbour' FL: There was a
lady living in the east. 11
'Young Barbour' FL: Twas of a lady
in the west counterie. 11
'Young Behan' FL: Young Behan
from Glasgow gone. 11
'Young Beichan' FL: A gentleman
from the courts of England. 11
'Young Beichan' FL: I sailed East,
I sailed West. 11
'Young Beichan' FL: I traveled East
and I traveled West. 11
'Young Beichan' FL: In London lived
a worthy man. 11
'Young Beichan' FL: Lord Bacon was
a nobleman. 11
'Young Beichan' FL: Lord Bateman
lived in London town. 61
'Young Beichan' FL: There was a
young man in old England dwelling. 11
'Young Beichan was in London born
see 'Lord Beichan'
'Young Bekie' FL: Young Bekie was
as brave a knight. 11
'Young Benjie' FL: Of a' the maids
o fair Scotland. 11
'Young Charlotte' FL: Young Charlotte lived on the mountain side
in a wild and lonely spot. 7
'Young Collins' FL: Young Collins
out from his fields one day. 7
Young Collins went forth one morning in May see 'Johnnie Collins'
A young cowboy named Billy Joe
grew restless on the farm see
'Don't take your guns to town'

Young Davie he came whistling by
see 'The gypsy laddie'
'Young Essex' FL: O I winna grant
thee thy son back again. 11
Young folks, old folks, everybody
come see 'Bible stories'
'Young girl' Jerry Fuller. FL:
With all the charms of a woman
FLC: Young girl, get out of my
mind. 45
'The young girl was married off'
FL: same FLC: Oh, snow ball
tree. 57, 58
Young Gypsy laddie came merrily
by see 'Gypsy laddie'
Young Hugh he was the best of all
see 'Sir Hugh and the Jew's
daughter'
'Young Hunting' FL: As I walked
out one morning this spring. 11
'Young Hunting' FL: As Lady Margaret was going to bed. 11
'Young Hunting' FL: Come in, come
in, loving Henry, said she. 11
'Young Hunting' FL: Come in, come
in, my old true love. 11
'Young Hunting' FL: Come in, come
in, my own true love. 11
'Young Hunting' FL: Come in, come
in, my pretty little boy. 11
'Young Hunting' FL: Get down, get
down, my Heneree. 11
'Young Hunting' FL: The lady stood
in her bower door. 11
'Young Hunting' FL: Last Friday
night Lady Margaret she lie.
11
'Young Hunting' FL: Last night, last
night, Lady Margaret lay asleep.
11
'Young Hunting' FL: Light, light,
light my little Scotchee. 61
'Young Hunting' FL: Light you down,
light you down, love Henry, she
said. 11
'Young Hunting' FL: O won't you
come in my pretty little bird.
11
'Young Hunting' FL: She sharpened
her knife both sharp and keen.
11
'Young Hunting' FL: You needn't
ride East, you needn't ride West.
11
'Young Hynd Horn' FL: Near Edinbro' was a young child born. 11
A young Irish lady from London she
came see 'The brown girl'

'Young Johnny of Hazelgreen' FL: O,
what is the matter my pretty fair
maid. 11
Young Johnny Steele has an Oldsmobile see 'In my merry Oldsmobile'
'Young Johnie, young Johnie, in the
green woods see 'Johnie Scot'
Young Johnny wrote a broad letter
see 'Johnny Scot'
'Young Johnstone' FL: Bold Johnstone and the young cornel. 11
'Young Johnstone' FL: Oh Johnstone
an' the young cornel. 11
'Young ladies' FL: Come all you
young and gentle ladies, be careful how you court young men. 7
Young ladies in town and those that
live around see 'To the ladies'
'Young Logie' FL: Pretty is the
story I hae to tell. 11
The young lords o' the north coun-
try see 'Lady Maisery'
'Young love' Carole Joyner and Ric
Cartney. FL: They say for
every boy and girl there's just
one love in this old world FLC:
Young love, first love. 10
'Young M'tyre' FL: There was a
man lived in the east. 30
Young man in a roadster see
'Putting on the style'
'The young man who wouldn't hoe
corn' FL: If you will listen well
I'll sing you a song. 7
'The young man who wouldn't hoe
corn' FL: I'll sing you a song
and it's not very long. 4, 23,
25, 57
'Young men, come marry me' FL:
As I roved out one morning in
the lovely month of May. 30
'Young men taken in and done for'
Harry King. FL: As smart a
man as ever lived was I when in
my prime FLC: Young men taken
in and done for. 17
Young men, they say, are bold and
free see 'Beware, oh take care'
'Young Molly, who lived at the foot
of the hill see 'The lass with
the delicate air'
Young Myra is fair as spring's early
flowers see 'The beauties of
friendship'
'Young Peggy' FL: Oh where hae ye
been, Peggy. 11
Young people, listen unto me, a

story I will tell see 'Charlie
Quantrell, oh'
'Young Redin' FL: Young Redin's
till the huntin' gane. 11
'The young sailor cut down in his
prime' FL: One day as I strolled
down by the Royal Albion FLC:
Then beat the drum lowly and
play the fife merrily. 57
'Young Waters' FL: About Zule,
quhen the wind blew cule. 11
Young William he rose early in the
morning see 'Fair Margaret
and Sweet William'
Young Willie stands in his stable
see 'Clyde's Water'
Young Willie was an earl's ae son
see 'The Earl of Douglas and
Dame Oliphant'
Young women they'll run like hare
on the mountains see 'Hares on
the mountains'
'Younger than springtime' Richard
Rodgers and Oscar Hammerstein.
FL: I touch your hand and my
arms grow strong FLC: Younger
than springtime are you. 6, 24,
42
'The youngest daughter' FL: There
was a young man who lived out
West. 11
Your day breaks, your mind aches
see 'For no one'
Your eyes of blue, your kisses too
see 'I can't believe that you're
in love with me'
'Your fair looks inflame my desire'
Thomas Campion. FL: same.
26
'Your love is like a flower' FL: It
was long, long ago in the moonlight FLC: Oh they tell me your
love's like a flower. 14
'Your mother should know' Lennon
and McCartney. FL: Let's all
get up and dance to a song that
was a hit before your mother was
born. 44
Your presence is requested wrote
little Johnny White see 'Don't
bring Lulu'
'Your song' Elton John and Bernie
Taupin. FL: It's a little bit
funny this feeling inside. 45
Your sweet expression see 'It's
easy to remember'
'You're a builder upper' Ira Gershwin, E. Y. Harburg and Harold

Arlen. FL: When you want to FLC: You're a builder upper. 46

'You're a grand old flag' George M. Cohan. FL: There's a feeling comes a-stealing and it sets my brain a-reeling FLC: You're a grand old flag. 12, 20, 31, 67

'You're a million miles from nowhere' Sam M. Lewis, Joe Young and Walter Donaldson. FL: It's the song of Mother's tears FLC: You're a million miles from nowhere. 12

You're an angel from heaven, sent down from above see 'Daddy's little boy'

'You're an old smoothie' B. G. De Sylva, Richard A. Whiting and Herb Brown Nacio. FL: You're the smoothest so and so FLC: You're an old smoothie. 46

You're as pleasant as the morning and refreshing as the rain see 'Scatter-brain'

You're bound to fall for the bugle call see 'Bugle call rag'

You're clear out of this world see 'Out of this world'

'You're driving me crazy!' Walter Donaldson. FL: You--you're driving me crazy. 59

'You're getting to be a habit with me' Al Dubin and Harry Warren. FL: I don't know exactly how it started FLC: Every kiss, every hug. 46

'You're going to lose that girl' Lennon and McCartney. FL: If you don't take her out tonight. 47

'You're in the Army now' FL: same. 1

You're just too marvelous see 'Too marvelous for words'

'You're my everything' Mort Dixon, Joe Young and Harry Warren. FL: I'm so ashamed of my vocabulary FLC: You're my everything. 46

You're my little true lover see 'Auntie'

You're nobody's sweetheart now see 'Nobody's sweetheart'

You're not a dream, you're not an angel see 'Until it's time for you to go'

'You're not the only pebble on the beach' Harry Braisted and Stanley

Carter. FL: When you see a pretty maiden who has just turned 17 FLC: She's not the only pebble on the beach. 20

'You're sixteen' Bob Sherman and Dick Sherman. FL: Ooh, you came out of a dream. 45

You're so delishious see 'Delishious'

You're telling everyone I know see 'I can't believe that you're in love with me'

'You're the flower of my heart, Sweet Adeline' Richard H. Gerhard and Harry Armstrong. FL: In the evening when I set alone a dreaming FLC: Sweet Adeline, my Adeline. 20, 31

You're the kind of girl that men forget see 'Just a girl that men forget'

You're the kind of person you meet at certain dismal dull affairs see '19th nervous breakdown'

You're the smoothest so and so see 'You're an old smoothie'

'You're the top' Cole Porter. FL: At words poetic I'm so pathetic FLC: You're the top! 42, 46

'Yours' Agustin Rodriguez and Gonzalo Roig. FL: Quiéreme mucho dulce amor mío FLC: Cuando se quiere de veras. 9

'Yours' Albert Gamse, Jack Sher and Gonzalo Roig. FL: This night has music, the sweetest music FLC: Yours till the stars lose their glory. 9

'Yours' Albert Gamse, Jack Sher and Gonzala Roig. FL: Yours in the gray of December FLC: Yours till the stars lose their glory. 12

A youth one day in a garden fair see 'The story of the rose'

You've changed, bub, you've changed see 'The man I used to be'

'You've got a long way to go' A. J. Mills and F. W. Carter. FL: One morning in a little tailor's shop I saw FLC: You've got a long way to go. 17

You've got to ac-cent-tchuate the positive see 'Ac-cent-tchu-ate the positive'

'You've got to go down' Woodie Guthrie. FL: You've got to go down and join the union. 19

Part III

INDEX OF COMPOSERS AND LYRICISTS
(with titles)

337

Malagueña
Barab, Seymour
  At the crèche
  "Mary" said St. Joseph
  The season for singing
  Song of the wise men
  Star of Bethelehem
Barberis, B.
  Have you looked into your heart
Barbi, Steve
  Secret agent man
Barcelata, Lorenzo
  Maria Elena
Bare, Bobbie
  Five hundred miles away from home
Baring-Gould, Sabine
  Now the day is over
Barker, George
  The Irish emigrant
Barnby, Joseph
  Now the day is over
  O perfect love
  Sweet and low
Barnes, F. J.
  I've got rings on my fingers
Barnes, Fred J.
  Shall I be an angel, Daddy?
Barnes, Howard
  I really don't want to know
Barnes, R. A.
  My mother-in-law
Barnett, Grant W.
  What did Dewey do to them
Barrett, Richard
  Maybe
Barri, Odoardo
  The old brigade
Barris, Harry
  I surrender, dear
  Mississippi mud
Barron, Bob
  Cindy, oh Cindy
Barroso, Ary
  Brazil
Barry, Jeff
  River deep, mountain high
  Sugar, sugar
Barry, John
  Midnight cowboy
Barth, Klaus
  Off to the sea
Bartholdy, Felix M.
  O for the wings of a dove
Bartholomew, William
  O for the wings of a dove
Bartlet, John
  Whither runneth my sweetheart

Basie, Count
  Sent for you yesterday
Bass, Ralph
  Dedicated to the one I love
Bassman, George
  I'm gettin' sentimental over you
Batcheler, Daniel
  To plead my faith
Bateman, Edgar
  If it wasn't for the 'ouses in between
Bates, Charles
  Hard hearted Hannah
Bates, Katherine Lee
  America, the beautiful
Battishell, Jonathan
  Come here fellow servant
Baxter, Phil
  Piccolo Pete
Bayly, Thomas H.
  Gaily the troubadour
  Long, long ago
  The old bachelor
  She wore a wreath of roses
  The soldier's tear
Beale, William
  Come, let us join the roundelay
Bean, Carl
  Scatter-brain
Beck, Carl
  On, Wisconsin!
Becker, John
  Feather or fur
Beckette, M. T. a'
  He was such a nice man
Beecher, Henry Ward
  Shoo purp don't bodder me
Beels, Sylvia
  White clouds
Beethoven, Ludwig
  Hymn for nations
Behrend, A. H.
  Auntie
Beissel, Johann C.
  God the master of all pagans
Belafonte, Harry
  Island in the sun
Belcher, Supply
  Omega
Belew, Carl
  Am I that easy to forget
Bellwood, Bessie
  Wotcher 'Ria
Ben, Jorge
  The constant rain
  Mas que nada
Benedict, Julius
  The moon has raised her lamp

above
Rock me to sleep
Benham, Asahel
America
Benjamin, Bennie
I don't want to set the world on fire
Benton, Brook
It's just a matter of time
Looking back
Bergantine, Borney
My happiness
Bergman, Marion
It's raining
Berkeley, Sir William
Where did you borrow that last sigh?
Berlin, Irving
God bless America
Bernard, Felix
Winter wonderland
Bernhard, Fred
Cinnamon cake
Bernie, Ben
Sweet Georgia Brown
Berns, Bert
Piece of my heart
Bernstein, Leonard
Maria
One hand, one heart
Somewhere
Tonight
Berrios, Pedro
My shawl
Beuler, J.
Come and take tea in the arbour
Bickerstaffe, Isaac
Cupid, god of soft persuasion
Dear heart, what a terrible life I am led
The echoing horn
If ever I'm catched
My dolly was the fairest thing
My passion in vain
Bicknell, G.
You naughty, naughty men
Bidwell, ----
Friendship
Bigard, Albany
Mood indigo
Bigelow, Bob
Hard hearted Hannah
Billings, William
America
Chester
David's lamentation
Jargon
New Plymouth

Thus saith the high, the lofty one
Victory
A Virgin unspotted
Wake every breath
When Jesus wept
Bingham, G. Clifton
Love's old sweet song
Birch, Harry
Reuben and Rachel
Birchtenbreiter, Maria
Dicky-bird birthday song
Bishop, Henry
My pretty Jane
Home, sweet home
Bito, Irving
Old man atom
Bixio, C. A.
Serenade in the night
Tell me that you love me tonight
Bizet, Georges
Beat out that rhythm on a drum
Dat's love
Black, Johnny
Paper doll
Blackburn, Bryan
Love is blue
Blackwell, Robert
Long tall Sally
Blair, Hal
Please help me I'm falling
Blake, Eubie
I'm just wild about Harry
Memories of you
Blake, James W.
The sidewalks of New York
Blake, William
A new Jerusalem
Blampkin, Charles
Touch the harp gently
Bland, James A.
Carry me back to old Virginny
Blanke, Pat
The suicide song
Blanter, M.
Katiusha
Blasee, ----
The girl that keeps the peanut stand
Blewitt, J.
Tarnation strange
Bliss, Philip P.
Hold the fort
Bloom, Rube
Day in--day out
Fools rush in
Bloomfield, D. F.
O perfect love
Blossom, Henry

Brown, Oscar, Jr.
  Work song
Brown, Sydney
  Maple leaf rag
Browne, Raymond A.
  Only once in a lifetime
Brunies, Henry
  Angry
Brunies, Merritt
  Angry
Bruton, J.
  Anything to make a change
Bryan, Al
  Brown eyes why are you blue?
Bryan, Vincent P.
  Down where the Wurzburger flows
  In my merry Oldsmobile
  Tammany
Bryant, Francis
  Christofo Columbo
Brydges-Willyams, J.
  One and all
Buck, Richard Henry
  Dear old girl
  Kentucky babe
Buckley, Fred
  Kiss me quick and go
Buckley, R. Bishop
  Wait for the wagon
Buhler, Neal
  The waves of Waikiki
Bulla, Clyde R.
  I like winter
Bunn, Alfred
  The dream
Burgess, Lord
  Island in the sun
  Jamaica farewell
Burke, Joe
  Carolina moon
  Dancing with tears in my eyes
  It looks like rain in cherry blos-
    som lane
  Moon over Miami
  Tip-toe thru' the tulips with me
Burke, Johnny
  It could happen to you
  Misty
  Moonlight becomes you
  Scatter-brain
  Swinging on a star
Burke, Sonny
  Somebody bigger than you and I
Burleson, George
  Caterpillars
Burleson, Vonnie
  Spring secret
  The thunder storm

Burns, Robert
  Auld lang syne
  The bonniest lass
  Comin' thro' the rye
  Flow gently, sweet Afton
  A man's a man for a' that
  Scots wha hae
  The sodger's return
Burris, Jim
  Ballin' the jack
Burris, Roy Edward
  Okie from Muskogee
Burton, Val
  Penthouse serenade
Burwell, Cliff
  Sweet Lorraine
Butterfield, James A.
  When you and I were young Mag-
    gie
Butts, Mary Frances
  Winter night
Byles, Dr.
  America

- C -

Cadman, Charles W.
  At dawning
Caesar, Irving
  I want to be happy
  Just a gigolo
  Sometimes I'm happy
  Swanee
  Tea for two
Cahn, Sammy
  Bei mir bist du schön
  I'll walk alone
  It's been a long, long time
  I've heard that song before
  Until the real thing comes along
Calderon, Juan Carlos
  Touch the wind
Calkin, J. Baptiste
  I heard the bells on Christmas
    Day
Calloway, Cab
  Minnie the moocher
Camacho, Johnny
  Cuando vuelas a mí
  Miami Beach rumba
  Si tú pudieras quererme
Campbell, Jimmy
  Good night sweetheart
Campbell, Paul
  Kisses sweeter than wine
Campion, Thomas
  And would you see my mistress'

If I could be with you
Crook, John
Jeerusalem's dead!
Crosby, Bing
I don't stand a ghost of a chance
with you
Crosby, Fanny
Blessed assurance
There's music in the air
Cross, Douglass
I left my heart in San Francisco
Crouch, F. W. N.
Kathleen Mavourneen
Cugat, Xavier
My shawl
Curiel, Gonzalo
Full moon
Curtis, Christine Turner
Sung at harvest time
Curtis, Loyal B.
Drifting and dreaming

- D -

Dacre, Henry
A bicycle built for two
Daisy Bell
Daffan, Ted
Born to lose
Daly, Brian
Jeerusalem's dead!
Dance, George
His lordship winked at the coun-
sel
Daniels, Charles N.
You tell me your dream, I'll tell
you mine
Danks, Hart P.
Silver threads among the gold
Danoff, Bett
Take me home, country roads
Danyel, John
Coy Daphne
Dost thou withdraw thy grace?
Eyes, look no more
I die whenas I do not see her
If I could shut the gate against
my thoughts
Let not Cloris think
Mrs. M. E. her funeral tears
for the death of her husband
Stay, cruel, stay
Thou pretty bird
Time, cruel time
Why canst thou not, as others do
Danyel, Samuel
Time, cruel time

Darion, Joe
The impossible dream
Darling, Captain
Here's to the last to die
Darnley, Herbert
The swimming master
Davenport, John
Fever
David, Hal
Alfie
Baby elephant walk
Close to you
Do you know the way to San Jose
I'll never fall in love again
Promises, promises
Raindrops keep fallin' on my head
This guy's in love with you
What the world needs now is love
What's new pussycat?
You'll never get to heaven
David, Mack
Bibbidi-bobbidi-boo
Cinderella
A dream is a wish your heart
makes
Oh sing sweet nightingale
So this is love
The work song
Davidson, Lenny
I've got to have a reason
Davies, Ivor R.
Jack Frost
Davies, V.
The noble 24th
Davis, Benny
Baby face
Carolina moon
Doin' the Suzi-Q
Lonesome and sorry
Margie
Davis, Gussie L.
In the baggage coach ahead
Davis, Jimmie
Columbus stockade blues
You are my sunshine
Davis, Joe
Cose, cose, cose
Nighty-night
Perhaps, perhaps, perhaps
Davison, Walter
At her fair hands
Dawes, Thomas
Now let rich music sound
Dean, Mary
Half-breed
Deane, Loryn
Mas que nada
Dearmer, Percy

Easter eggs
Dee, Sylvia
  Chickery chick
Dehmel, Paula
  Wind, wind blowing
Dehr, Rich
  Memories are made of this
De Koven, Reginald
  Oh promise me
De Lange, Eddie
  Moonglow
  Solitude
Delettre, Jean
  Hands across the table
Denison, Margaret
  Lippity-lop
Denniker, Paul
  S'posin'
Dennis, Matt
  Let's get away from it all
Densmore, Frances
  The sugar camp
Denver, John
  Follow me
  Leaving on a jet plane
  My sweet lady
  Take me home, country roads
Dermer, Emma
  Eleven cent cotton
De Rose, Peter
  Deep purple
De Sylva, B. G. (Buddy)
  Avalon
  The best things in life are free
  The birth of the blues
  Button up your overcoat
  California here I come
  I'll build a stairway to Paradise
  Look for the silver lining
  Somebody loves me
  When day is done
  You're an old smoothie
Deutsch, Emery
  Play, fiddle, play
  When a gypsy makes his violin
    cry
Dexter, Al
  Pistol packin' Mama
Diamond, Neil
  Holly holy
  Sweet Caroline
Dibdin, Charles
  Dear Heart, what a terrible life
    I am led
  Tom Bowling
Dickinson, John
  In freedom we're born
  The liberty song

Dietz, Howard
  Dancing in the dark
  I guess I'll have to change my
    plan
  Louisiana hayride
  A shine on your shoes
  Something to remember you by
  You and the night and the music
Dillon, William
  I want a girl
Dix, William Chatterton
  What Child is this?
Dixon, Dorsey
  The schoolhouse fire
  Weave room blues
Dixon, Mort
  Bye bye blackbird
  I found a million dollar baby
  I'm looking over a four leaf
    clover
  Nagasaki
  Would you like to take a walk
  You're my everything
Dodd, Dorothy
  Granada
Dodge, Ossian E.
  Ho! westward ho!
Dominguez, Alberto
  Frenesi
  Perfidia
Donald, H. A.
  Hiawatha
Donaldson, Walter
  Carolina in the morning
  How ya gonna keep 'em down on
    the farm?
  Love me or leave me
  Makin' whoopee
  My buddy
  My mammy
  You're a million miles from no-
    where
  You're driving me crazy!
Donato, E.
  When the lights are soft and low
Doplukhanian, A.
  Dyevooshkoo chakoi zovoot
  "Seagull" the maiden is named
Dorsey, Jimmy
  I'm glad there is you
Dorsey, Thomas A.
  There'll be peace in the valley
    for me
Douglas, William
  Annie Laurie
Dowland, John
  Behold a wonder here
  Daphne

Far from triumphing court
I saw my lady weep
In darkness let me dwell
Lachrimae
Lady, is you so spite me
Sorrow, stay!
Time stands still
Drake, Ervin
Tico-tico
Drake, Milton
Mairzy Doats
Dresser, Paul
Just tell them that you saw me
My gal Sal
On the banks of the Wabash, far
away
The pardon came too late
Drummond, M. H.
Pretty Dinah Snow
Dryden, John
Farewell, ungrateful traytor
Dryden, Leo
The miner's dream of home
Dubin, Al
A cup of coffee, a sandwich and
you
Dancing with tears in my eyes
Forty-second Street
The gold diggers' song
I'll string along with you
Just a girl that men forget
Shadow waltz
Tip-toe thru' the tulips with me
Young and healthy
You're getting to be a habit with
me
Du Bois, Gladys
You call it madness
Dufferin, Lady
The Irish emigrant
Duffey, John
The schoolhouse fire
Duke, Vernon
April in Paris
Autumn in New York
I can't get started
What is there to say
Dumont, Frank
The Chinee laundryman
Dunn, Thomas
Ben Bolt
Dunville, T. E.
The fire was burning hot
Dupree, Harry
Lisbon antigua
Durden, Tommy
Heartbreak hotel
Durham, Ed

Sent for you yesterday
I don't want to set the world on
fire
Durrill, John
Dark lady
Durso, Michael
Petticoats of Portugal
Dvorak, Anton
Humoresque
Dwight, N.
Corydon's ghost
Dwight, Timothy
Columbia
Dykes, John Bacchus
Holy, holy, holy
Dylan, Bob
Don't think twice, it's all right
I shall be released
Just like a woman
Lay, lady, lay

- E -

Earle, Fred
Seaweed
Eastwick, Ivy O.
A happy goodmorning
I can't see the wind
On silver sands
Winter walk
Eaton, Jimmy
Turn back the hands of time
Ebb, Fred
Cabaret
Maybe this time
Zorba theme
Eberhart, Nelle R.
At dawning
Eccles, John
A fox may steal your hens, sir
Let's sing of stage coaches
O all ye powers above
A soldier and a sailor
Edwards, ----
Somebody's sweetheart I want to
be
Edwards, Clara
With the wind and the rain in
your hair
Edwards, Gus
I can't tell why I love you, but I
do
In my merry Oldsmobile
School days
Sunbonnet Sue
Tammany
Egan, Raymond B.

Ferrabosco, Alfonso
  Come, my Celia
  Fain I would, but O I dare not
  I am a lover, yet was never loved
  Like hermit poor
  O eyes, O mortal stars
  Shall I seek to ease my grief?
  So, so leave off this last lament-
    ing kiss
  Unconstant love
Fielding, Henry
  O all ye powers above
  Tis true, my good dear
Fields, Dorothy
  Diga diga doo
  I can't give you anything but love
  Lovely to look at
  On the sunny side of the street
  Pick yourself up
  The way you look tonight
  You couldn't be cuter
Fields, G. B.
  Flood of Shawneetown
Fields, Irving
  Miami Beach rumba
Finch, Dick
  Jealous
Fiorito, Ted
  Laugh! Clown! Laugh!
Fischer, Carl
  We'll be together again
  Who wouldn't love you
Fisher, Aileen
  Caterpillars
  Time for rabbits
Fisher, Mark
  When you're smiling
Fitzball, Edward
  My pretty Jane
  Yes, let me like a soldier fall
Fitzgerald, Ella
  A-tisket, a-tasket
Flatt, Lester
  If I should wander back tonight
  Roll in my sweet baby's arms
  We'll meet again, sweetheart
Fletcher, Margaret
  Lippity-lop
Flynn, Allan
  Maybe
Flynn, Joseph
  Down went McGinty
Fogerty, J. C.
  Lodi
  Proud Mary
Foote, Samuel
  Ally croaker
  The tragical history of the life

    and death of Billy Pringle's
    pig
Ford, Walter H.
  The sunshine of Paradise Alley
Forrest, George
  And this is my beloved
  Baubles, bangles, and beads
  Stranger in Paradise
Forrest, Jimmy
  Night train
Fosdick, W. W.
  Aura Lee
Foster, Fred
  Me and Bobby McGee
Foster, Stephen
  Beautiful dreamer
  Camptown races
  Jeanie with the light brown hair
  Massa's in de cold ground
  My old Kentucky home
  Nelly Bly!
  Oh! Susanna
  Old dog Tray
  Old folks at home
  Swanee River
Fowler, Wally
  That's how much I love you
Fox, George D.
  Penny whistler
Fragson, Harry
  The music hall Shakespeare
Frances, John
  The handsome man
Francis, Arthur
  I'll build a stairway to Paradise
  Mischa, Yascha, Toscha, Sascha
Francis, John
  Shall I be an angel, Daddy?
Francois, C.
  My way
Franklin, Dave
  When my dream boat comes home
Frazier, Dallas
  There goes my everything
Freeman, L. E.
  Until the real thing comes along
French, A. W.
  Won't you buy my pretty flowers?
Friedan, Betty
  Liberation now
Friend, Cliff
  When my dream boat comes home
Friml, Rudolf
  Indian love call
  Only a rose
  Rose Marie
  Some day
  Song of the vagabonds

The vagabond king waltz
Fulke, Greville
   Love, the delight of all well-
     thinking minds
Fuller, Jerry
   Young girl
Furber, Douglas
   Lambeth Walk
Fyleman, Rose
   The little tune

- G -

Gabler, Milt
   Danke Schoen
   Wiederseh'n
Gaither, William J.
   He touched me
Galhardo, J.
   Lisbon antigua
Gailliard, John Ernest
   The early horn
   Indian's song
Gallop, Sammy
   Elmer's tune
   Somewhere along the way
Gamble, K.
   Me and Mrs. Jones
Gamse, Albert
   Amapola
   La comparsa
   Miami Beach rumba
   Yours
Gannon, Kim
   Always in my heart
Garcia, Jerome
   Truckin'
Garland, Jim
   I don't want your millions, mister
Garner, Erroll
   Misty
Garnet, Horatio
   Ode for American independence
   An ode for the Fourth of July
Garren, Joe
   Just a girl that men forget
Garrick, David
   Epilogue song
   No ice so cold, so hard, as I
   Ye mortals whom fancies and
     troubles perplex
Gaskill, Clarence
   I can't believe that you're in love
     with me
   Minnie the Moocher
   Prisoner of love
Gasso, Bernard

Guantanamera
Gatty, Alfred Scott
   The burial of the linnet
Gaunt, Percy
   The Bowery
Gay, John
   A fox may steal your hens, sir
   My heart was so free
   Over the hills and far away
Gay, Noel
   Lambeth Walk
Gaze, Heino
   Calcutta
Geibel, Adam
   Kentucky babe
Geifer, George L.
   Who threw the overalls in Mis-
     tress Murphy's chowder
Gelber, Stanley Jay
   Now I know
Geminiani, Francesco
   The tragical history of the life
     and death of Billy Pringle's
     pig
Gensler, Lewis E.
   Love is just around the corner
Geoghegan, J. B.
   Down in a coal mine
George, D.
   A new song for a serenade
George, Daniel
   Ode for American independence
   An ode for the Fourth of July
Gerhard, Richard H.
   You're the flower of my heart,
     sweet Adeline
Gershwin, George
   The Babbitt and the bromide
   The Back Bay polka
   Bess you is my woman now
   Bidin' my time
   Blah-blah-blah
   Blue blue blue
   But not for me
   By Strauss
   Clap yo' hands
   Delishious
   Do-do-do
   Embraceable you
   Fascinating rhythm
   A foggy day
   For you, for me, for evermore
   Funny face
   He loves and she loves
   I got plenty o' nuttin'
   I got rhythm
   I loves you Porgy
   I'll build a stairway to Paradise

Isn't it a pity?
It ain't necessarily so
I've got a crush on you
Let 'em eat cake
Let's call the whole thing off
Liza
Looking for a boy
Lorelei
Love is here to stay
Love is sweeping the country
Love walked in
The man I love
Maybe
Mine
Mischa, Yascha, Toscha, Sascha
My cousin in Milwaukee
My man's gone now
My one and only
Nice work if you can get it
Oh, lady be good
Of thee I sing
The real American folk song
'S Wonderful
Somebody loves me
Someone to watch over me
Soon
Strike up the band
Summertime
Sweet and low-down
That certain feeling
They all laughed
They can't take that away from me
Who cares?
Wintergreen for President
Gershwin, Ira
The Babbitt and the bromide
The Back Bay polka
Bess, you is my woman now
Bidin' my time
Blah-blah-blah
Blue blue blue
But not for me
By Strauss
Cheerful little earful
Clap yo' hands
Delishious
Do-do-do
Embraceable you
Fascinating rhythm
A foggy day
For you, for me for evermore
Funny face
He loves and she loves
I can't get started
I got plenty o' nuttin'
I got rhythm
Isn't it a pity?
It ain't necessarily so

I've got a crush on you
Let 'em eat cake
Let's call the whole thing off
Liza
Long ago and far away
Looking for a boy
Lorelei
Love is here to stay
Love is sweeping the country
Love walked in
The man I love
The man that got away
Maybe
Mine
My cousin in Milwaukee
My one and only
Nice work if you can get it
Oh, lady be good
Of thee I sing
The real American folk song
'S Wonderful
Someone to watch over me
Soon
Strike up the band
Swanee
Sweet and low-down
That certain feeling
They all laughed
They can't take that away from
    me
Who cares?
Wintergreen for President
You're a builder upper
Giardini, Felice de
Cupid, god of soft persuasion
Gibson, Arbie
The honey song
Gilbert, C.
Me and Mrs. Jones
Gilbert, Fred
The man who broke the bank at
    Monte Carlo
Gilbert, L. Wolfe
Green eyes
Marta
The peanut vendor
Gilbert, Ray
Cuanto le gusta
Muskrat ramble
That's a plenty
Without you
You belong to my heart
Gilbert, William S.
The flowers that bloom in the
    spring
Gilkyson, Terry
Memories are made of this
Gill, V. R.

One of the deathless army
Gillespie, Haven
Drifting and dreaming
Honey
That lucky old sun
You go to my head
Gillmore, Patrick S.
When Johnny comes marching
home
Gimbel, Norman
The constant rain
I will wait for you
The Tennessee wig-walk
Watch what happens
Glasser, Dick
Come running back
Glazer, Joe
Automation
The mill was made of marble
Song of the guaranteed wage
Soup song
Too old to work
Glazer, Tom
Today is your birthday
A worried man
Glenn, Artie
Crying in the chapel
Glik, Hirsh
Shtil, di nacht
Zog net keynmol
Glover, Charles W.
The rose of Tralee
Godwin, Will
The miner's dream of home
Goehring, George
Lipstick on your collar
Goetz, E. Ray
For me and my gal
Hawaiian love song
Gold, Jack
Midnight cowboy
Golding, M. E.
Don't go out tonight, dear
Father
Goldstein, Jerry
Come on down to my boat
Gooch, William
Reuben and Rachel
Goodman, Benny
Stompin' at the Savoy
Goodwin, Joe
When you're smiling
Gordon, Mack
Chattanooga choo-choo
The more I see you
Serenade in blue
There will never be another you
You'll never know

Gorney, Jay
Brother, can you spare a dime?
Gorrell, Stuart
Georgia on my mind
Gouldman, Graham
East West
Gove, W. H.
The charming young widow I met
on the train
Graham, R. E.
Cawn't do it ye know!
Grainger, Porter
Tain't nobody's biz-ness if I do
Gram, Hans
Death song of an Indian chief
A shape alone let others prize
Grant, Bert
If I knock the 'L' out of Kelly
My Barney lies over the ocean
Gray, William
She is more to be pitied, than
censured
Grayson, G. B.
Handsome Molly
Train forty-five
Grean, Charles
Hootenanny granny
Sweet violets
Greaves, Thomas
Celestina
Flora
Inconstant Laura
What is beauty but a breath?
Green, Adolph
Just in time
Make someone happy
The party's over
Green, Bud
Sentimental journey
Green, Eddie
A good man is hard to find
Green, Johnny
Body and soul
I cover the waterfront
I wanna be loved
Out of nowhere
Greenaway, Kate
Little wind
Greene, Robert
Ah, were she pitiful
Greenwich, Ellie
River deep, mountain high
Gregory, Paul
You call it madness
Grever, Maria
Magic is the moonlight
What a difference a day made
Grey, Clifford

So far
Some enchanted evening
The song is you
The sound of music
Stouthearted men
Sunday
The surrey with the fringe on top
Ten minutes ago
This nearly was mine
A very special day
Wanting you
When the children are asleep
Who?
Why do I love you?
Why was I born?
You are beautiful
You are love
You are never away
You'll never walk alone
Younger than springtime
Hammond, Con
   Turn back the hands of time
Hanby, Benjamin Russel
   Darling Nelly Gray
Hancock, Herbie
   Watermelon man
Hancock, John (pseud)
   What would you give in exchange
      for your soul?
Handcox, John
   Roll the union on
Handel, G. F.
   Joy to the world
   My dolly was the fairest thing
Handford, George
   Go, sweep, sad soul
Handman, Lou
   Blue
Handy, W. C.
   St. Louis blues
Hanley, James F.
   Zing! went the strings of my
      heart
Hansen, Bill
   Fascination
Harbach, Otto
   The desert song
   Indian love call
   One alone
   The riff song
   Rose Marie
   Smoke gets in your eyes
   Who?
   Yesterdays
Harburg, E. Y.
   April in Paris
   Brother, can you spare a dime?
   How are things in Glocca Morra

It's only a paper moon
Look to the rainbow
What is there to say
You're a builder upper
Hardelot, Guy d'
   Because
Hardin, Tim
   If I were a carpenter
Harling, W. Franke
   Beyond the blue horizon
   Sing you sinners
Harmati, Sandor
   Blue bird of happiness
Harney, Ben
   Mister Johnson, turn me loose
Harnick, Sheldon
   Fiddler on the roof
   If I were a rich man
   Matchmaker
   She loves me
   Sunrise, sunset
Harper, Marjorie
   Negra consentida
Harrigan, Ed
   I never drink behind the bar
   Walking for that cake
Harrigan, Edward
   Maggie Murphy's home
Harrigan, Ned
   I'll never get drunk anymore
   The Mulligan guard
Harrington, Karl P.
   There's a song in the air
Harris, Charles K.
   After the ball
   Break the news to Mother
Harrison, Annie F.
   In the gloaming
Harrison, Charles
   I'm drifting back to dreamland
Harrison, George
   Here comes the sun
   Photograph
   Something
Harry, Albert
   The girl that keeps the peanut
      stand
Hart, Bobby
   If you're thinkin' what I'm
      thinkin'
Hart, Freddie
   Easy loving
Hart, Joe
   Globe trotting Nellie Bly
Hart, Lorenz
   Bewitched
   Dancing on the ceiling
   Have you met Miss Jones?

Kurtz, Manny
  In a sentimental mood
Kusik, Larry
  A time for us
  When the snow is on the roses
Kuskin, Karla
  Rules

- L -

Lacalle, Joseph M.
  Amapola
La Farge, Peter
  The ballad of Ira Hayes
Laine, Frank
  We'll be together again
Lamb, Arthur J.
  Asleep in the deep
  A bird in a gilded cage
  The bird on Nellie's hat
Lamm, Robert
  Saturday in the park
Lane, Burton
  How are things in Glocca Morra
  Look to the rainbow
  On a clear day
Lane, Gerald
  Tatters
Lange, Eddie de
  Heaven can wait
Lange, Johnny
  Somebody bigger than you and I
Lanier, Don
  Here we go again
Lara, Augustin
  Granada
  You belong to my heart
Lara, Maria Teresa
  Be mine tonight
  My rival
Last, James
  Now I know
  When the snow is on the roses
Lauder, Harry
  Nanny
  That's the reason noo I wear a
    kilt
Lavallee, C.
  O Canada
Law, Andrew
  The American hero
  Bunker Hill
Lawes, William
  Where did you borrow that last
    sigh?
Lawlor, Charles B.
  The sidewalks of New York

Lawrence, Jack
  All or nothing at all
  Beyond the sea
  Ciribiribin
  Play, fiddle, play
  Tenderly
  With the wind and the rain in
    your hair
Lawson, Herbert Happy
  Any time
Layton, ----
  After you've gone
Lea, Sir Henry
  Far from triumphing court
Lebowsky, Stan
  The wayward wind
Le Brunn, George
  If it wasn't for the 'ouses in be-
    tween
  I've never lost my last train yet
  We all went home in a cab
Lecuona, Ernesto
  Always in my heart
  The breeze and I
  La comparsa
  The four winds
  Malagueña
  Mi vida
  Noche azul
  Say "sí sí"
Lecuona, Margarita
  Babalu
Ledbetter, Huddie
  Roll on, Columbia
  Whoa, back, Buck
Lee, Alexander
  The soldier's tear
Lee, Alfred
  Champagne Charlie
  Dolly Varden
  The man on the flying trapeze
Lee, Bert
  Heaven will protect an honest
    girl
Lee, Marvin
  Livery stable blues
Lee, Nathaniel
  She walks as she dreams
Leeds, Milton
  Misirlou
  Perfidia
Lees, Gene
  Yesterday I heard the rain
Legrand, Michel
  I will wait for you
  Watch what happens
Leiber, Jerry
  Hound dog

Wouldn't it be loverly
Lesh, Philip
  Truckin'
Leslie, Edgar
  Blue
  For me and my gal
  It looks like rain in cherry blos-
    som lane
  Moon over Miami
  The moon was yellow
  Now she knows how to parle-voo
  Oh! what a pal was Mary
  When grown up ladies act like
    babies
Leveridge, Richard
  Come, fair one, be kind
  Let's have a dance a heath
  My heart was so free
Levin, Ira
  She touched me
Levine, Irwin
  Say, has anybody seen my sweet
    gypsy rose
  Tie a yellow ribbon round the ole
    oak tree
  Who's in the strawberry patch
    with Sally
Levi-Tanai, ----
  Down with darkness
Lewis, Al
  Blueberry Hill
Lewis, Dave
  Mother pin a rose on me
Lewis, Edna
  Lipstick on your collar
Lewis, Sam M.
  Dinah
  Five foot two eyes of blue
  How ya gonna keep 'em down on
    the farm?
  If I knock the 'L' out of Kelly
  I'm sitting on top of the world
  In a little Spanish town
  Just a baby's prayer at twilight
  Laugh! Clown! Laugh!
  My Barney lies over the ocean
  My mammy
  Rock-a-bye your baby with a
    Dixie melody
  Where did Robinson Crusoe go
    with Friday on Saturday night?
  You're a million miles from no-
    where
Lewis, Ted
  When my baby smiles at me
Leybourne, ----
  Up in a balloon
Leybourne, George

Champagne Charlie
  The man on the flying trapeze
Liebling, Howard
  Sunshine, lollipops and rainbows
Lieurance, Thurlow
  By the waters of Minnetonka
Lightfoot, Gordon
  If you could read my mind
Liliukalani, Queen Lydia K.
  Aloha oe
Lilley, Joseph J.
  Jingle jangle jingle
Lincke, Paul
  Glow worm
Lindsay, Mark
  Ups and downs
Lingard, William Horace
  Captain Jinks
Lippman, Sidney
  Chickery chick
Lipton, Leonard
  Puff, the magic dragon
Lisianskii, M.
  Dyevooshkoo chakoi zoovoot
  "Seagull" the maiden is named
Lisle, Rouget de
  La Marseillaise
Little, Jack
  Jealous
Livingston, Jay
  Buttons and bows
  Golden earrings
  Mona Lisa
  To each his own
  Whatever will be, will be
Livingston, Jerry
  Bibbidi-bobbidi-boo
  Cinderella
  A dream is a wish your heart
    makes
  Mairzy doats
  Oh sing sweet nightingale
  So this is love
  The work song
Locklin, Hank
  Send me the pillow you dream
    on
Loeb, John J.
  Boo-hoo
Loesser, Frank
  A bushel and a peck
  Dolores
  Heart and soul
  I don't want to walk without you
  Jingle jangle jingle
  Luck be a lady
  Once in love with Amy
  Praise the Lord and pass the

ammunition!
Small fry
Loewe, Frederich
    Almost like being in love
    Camelot
    I could have danced all night
    I loved you once in silence
    I talk to the trees
    If ever I would leave you
    I've grown accustomed to her
        face
    On the street where you live
    They call the wind Maria
    Wouldn't it be loverly
Lomax, Alan
    Whoa, back, Buck
Lomax, John A.
    Roll on, Columbia
    Whoa, back, Buck
Lombardo, Carmen
    Boo-hoo
    Oooh! Look-a-there, ain't she
        pretty
    Sweethearts on parade
Long, Burt
    Cindy, oh Cindy
Longfellow, Henry Wadsworth
    Excelsior!
    Goodnight, goodnight, beloved
    Hiawatha
    I heard the bells on Christmas
        Day
Loomis, Harvey W.
    In the rain
    Sweet potatoes
Lopez, Ray
    Livery stable blues
Lord, L. C.
    Kiss me, mother, kiss your
        darling
Lorenzo, Ange
    Sleepy time gal
Lorraine, William
    Where did you get that hat?
Loveday, Carroll
    That's my desire
Lowe, Ruth
    I'll never smile again
Luban, Francia
    A gay ranchero
    Say "sí sí"
Lutkin, Peter C.
    The Lord bless and keep you
Lyman, Abe
    Mary Lou
Lynne, Gloria
    Watermelon man

- M -

McAvoy, Dan
    The beer that made Milwaukee
        famous
MacCarteney, Laura Pendleton
    All the birds sing
McCarthy, Harry
    The bonnie blue flag
McCartney, Linda
    Jet
McCartney, Paul
    All my loving
    All you need is love
    And I love her
    Baby you're a rich man
    Back in the USSR
    The ballad of John and Yoko
    Because
    Blackbird
    Can't buy me love
    Carry that weight
    Come together
    Don't let me down
    A day in the life
    Day tripper
    Eight days a week
    Eleanor Rigby
    The fool on the hill
    For no one
    Get back
    Girl
    Give peace a chance
    Golden slumbers
    Good day sunshine
    Got to get you back into my life
    A hard day's night
    Hello goodbye
    Help!
    Here, there and everywhere
    Hey Jude
    Honey pie
    I am the walrus
    I don't want to see you again
    I don't want to spoil the party
    I feel fine
    I want to hold your hand
    If I fell
    I'll follow the sun
    I'm a loser
    In my life
    I've just seen a face
    Lady Madonna
    Let it be
    The long and winding road
    Love me do
    Lucy in the sky with diamonds
    Magical mystery tour

Maxwell's silver hammer
Michelle
Mother Nature's son
Norwegian Wood
Nowhere man
Ob-la-di Ob-la-da
Paperback writer
Penny Lane
Rain
Revolution
Ringo's theme
Rocky raccoon
Sgt. Pepper's Lonely Hearts Club
  band
She came in through the bathroom
  window
She loves you
She's a woman
She's leaving home
Strawberry fields forever
Things we said today
Ticket to ride
We can work it out
When I'm 64
With a little help from my friends
World without love
Yellow submarine
Yesterday
You never give me your money
Your mother should know
You're going to lose that girl
You've got to hide your love away
McClintock, Mac
  The mowing machine
McCoy, Joe
  Why don't you do right
McCurdy, Ed
  Last night I had the strangest
    dream
MacDonald, Ballard
  Clap hands! here comes Charley!
  Somebody loves me
McDonald, Joe
  Janis
McDonald, Ruby
  Song of the guaranteed wage
MacDonough, Glen
  Toyland
McElroy, Jim
  Down in the Tules
McEnery, David
  Amelia Earhart's last flight
McGinley, Phyllis
  Autumn song
McGlennon, Felix
  And her golden hair was hanging
    down her back
  Comrades

I've worked eight hours this day
Oh, what a difference in the
  morning
The ship I love
That is love
Tol lol lol
McHugh, Jimmy
  Diga diga doo
  I can't believe that you're in
    love with me
  I can't give you anything but love
  Lovely to look at
  A lovely way to spend an evening
  On the sunny side of the street
  When my sugar walks down the
    street
Mack, Andrew
  The story of the rose
Mack, Cecil
  Charleston
  Teasing
Mackay, C.
  Cheer, boys, cheer!
Mackey, Charles
  Baby mine
McKuen, Rod
  Jean
  Love's been good to me
Maclagan, T.
  Captain Jinks
McNally, Leonard
  The lass of Richmond Hill
McNally, T.
  Nancy Fat
McPhail, Lindsay
  San
Madden, Frank
  Maybe
Madeira, Paul
  I'm glad there is you
Madriguera, Enric
  Adios
Maeder, J. G.
  Let us all speak our minds
Magidson, Herb
  Enjoy yourself
  I'll buy that dream
  Midnight in Paris
Maker, Frederick Charles
  Dear Lord and Father of man-
    kind
Malie, Tommie
  Jealous
  Looking at the world thru rose-
    colored glasses
Malneck, Matt
  Goody goody
Manazucca, ----

I love life
Mancini, Henry
　Baby elephant walk
　Moon river
Mann, David
　Somebody bad stole de wedding
　　bell
　There! I've said it again
Manners, Gerry
　The man upstairs
Manzanero, A.
　It's impossible
　Yesterday I heard the rain
Marais, Josef
　Blue cheese
Marchetti, F. D.
　Fascination
Marcus, Bob
　Patricia, it's Patricia
Marcus, Sol
　I don't want to set the world on
　　fire
Marion, Dave
　Her eyes don't shine like dia-
　　monds
Markes, Larry
　May you always
Marks, Edward B.
　Mother was a lady
Marks, Walter
　For once in your life
Markush, Fred
　Take me in your arms
Marlow, Rick
　A taste of honey
Marlowe, Christopher
　The passionate shepherd to his
　　love
Marshall, Edward H.
　Venus
Marti, José
　Guantanamera
Martin, C.
　The Connaught Rangers
Martin, R.
　The Connaught Rangers
Martin, Richard
　Change thy mind
Martin, Sam
　You call everybody darling
Martinez, Jesus
　Adios vida mia
Martini, Giovanni
　Plaisir d'amour
Mason, Lowell
　My faith looks up to thee
Massey, Curt
　The honey song

Massey, Louise
　My adobe hacienda
Masters, Frankie
　Scatter-brain
Matson, Vera
　Love me tender
Matusovsky, M.
　Moscow nights
Maxwell, B.
　Razors in the air
Mayhems, Betty Briant
　We'll build a bungalow
Mayhew, Billy
　It's a sin to tell a lie
Meade, Norman
　Cry baby
Means, Alex
　Wondrous love
Mecum, Dudley
　Angry
Meda, Lottie L.
　The tale of a shirt
Meen, George
　O, Fred, tell them to stop!
Melcher, Terry
　Ups and downs
Mendelssohn, Felix
　Hark! the herald angels sing
Mendez, Ricardo Lopez
　Amor
Mendez, Tomas
　Cu-cu-rru-cu-cu, Paloma
Menendez, Nilo
　Green eyes
Mercer, Johnny
　Ac-cent-tchu-ate the positive
　And the angels sing
　Autumn leaves
　Day in--day out
　Dearly beloved
　Fools rush in
　The glow-worm
　Goody goody
　I remember you
　I'm old fashioned
　In the cool, cool, cool of the
　　evening
　Jeepers creepers
　Laura
　Let's take the long way home
　Moon river
　My shining hour
　One for my baby
　Out of this world
　Satin doll
　Tangerine
　That old black magic
　Too marvelous for words

Möller, Edith
Sing a song of spring
Möller, F. W.
On a summer morning
Sing a song of spring
Mogol, ----
Let's live for today
Mohr, Joseph
Silent night
Stille nacht
Moller, Frederick W.
The happy wanderer
Molloy, James L.
Love's old sweet song
Monaco, Jimmie V.
Row, row, row
Monnoye, Bernard de la
Pat-a-pan
Monroe, Bill
Will you be loving another man?
Monroe, Charlie
Red rocking chair
Monroe, Vaughn
Racing with the moon
Montgomery, James
Angels, from the realms of
glory
Montgomery, M. T.
United Steel workers are we
Montross, Percy
Clementine
Moore, Edward
When Damon languished
Moore, G. W.
Dolly Varden
Moore, Marvin
Here we go, baby
The West Virginny hills
Moore, Thomas
Believe me if all those endearing
young charms
The last rose of summer
The minstrel boy
Moran, Jack
Skip a rope
The Moreen
The minstrel boy
Morey, Larry
Little April shower
Morey, Myron L.
Fugitive breakdown
Morgan, Albert
Union man
Morgan, Dorinda
The man upstairs
Morgan, George
Candy kisses
Morgan, Russ

Does your heart beat for me?
Somebody else is taking my
place
Morris, George P.
Woodman, spare that tree
Morris, Lee
Blue velvet
Morse, Theodore F.
Dear old girl
Morton, Richard
La-didily-idily, umti-umti ay!
Morton, Sarah Wentworth
Death song of an Indian chief
Müller, H. v.
At Eastertime
Mundau, Anthony
Beauty sat bathing by a spring
Munro, Bill
When my baby smiles at me
Munson, Eddie
Ida, sweet as apple cider
Murphy, Arthur
Attend, all ye fair
Murphy, C. W.
I live in Trafalgar Square
A thing he had never done before
Murray, Fred
It's alright in the summertime
Muse, Clarence
When it's sleepy time down south

- N -

Nacio, Herb Brown
You're an old smoothie
Nairne, Lady
Caller herrin'
Neale, John M.
Good King Wenceslas
Neil, Fred
Everybody's talkin'
Nelson, Steve
Bouquet of roses
Nelson, Willie
Hello walls
Nemo, ----
Saved by a child
Nemo, Henry
Don't take your love from me
I let a song go out of my heart
Nevin, Ethelbert
Mighty lak' a rose
The Rosary
Newcomb, Bobby
The big sunflower
Newley, Anthony
What kind of fool am I?

Farewell, ungrateful traytor
Paine, Thomas
    Adams and liberty
    Death of General Wolfe
    Rise Columbia!
Palmer, Bee
    Please don't talk about me when
        I'm gone
Palmer, Jack
    Everybody loves my baby
Palmer, John F.
    The band played on
Palmer, Roy
    My faith looks up to thee
Pankow, James
    Feelin' stronger every day
Pardave, Joaquin
    Negra consentida
Parish, Mitchell
    A blues serenade
    Deep purple
    Does your heart beat for me?
    Hands across the table
    Mr. Ghost goes to town
    Moonlight serenade
    One morning in May
    Sentimental gentleman from
        Georgia
    Sophisticated lady
    Star dust
    Stars fell on Alabama
    Sweet Lorraine
    Take me in your arms
Parker, Sir Peter
    A new war song
Parker, Sol
    This love of mine
Parkhurst, Mrs. E. A.
    Father's a drunkard and mother
        is dead
Parnell, Thomas
    My days have been so wondrous
        free
Parrott, Tom
    Pinkville helicopter
Parry, Sir C. Hubert H.
    A new Jerusalem
Parry, John
    Vilikins and his Dinah
Partlow, Vern
    Old man atom
Pasquale, Charles
    Magic is the moonlight
Patton, Gerald
    Men of the soil
Paul, Gene de
    Cow-cow boogie
Paul, Howard

Upside down
Pauling, Lowman
    Dedicated to the one I love
Paxton, Tom
    The marvelous toy
    My ramblin' boy
Payne, John Howard
    Home, sweet home
Peerson, Martin
    Ah, were she pitiful
    At her fair hands
    Now, Robin, laugh and sing
    O precious time
Penn, Don
    A woman left lonely
Penniman, Richard
    Long tall Sally
Penny, Lee
    My adobe hacienda
Pepper, Buddy
    Vaya con Dios
Perkins, Carl Lee
    Blue suede shoes
Perkins, Frank
    Sentimental gentleman from
        Georgia
    Stars fell on Alabama
Perronet, Edward
    Coronation
Perry, Albert
    The huntsman
Persley, G. W.
    Won't you buy my pretty flowers?
Pestalozza, A.
    Ciribiribin
Peterson, Betty
    My happiness
Pether, Henry E.
    Waiting at the church
Petrie, H. W.
    Asleep in the deep
    I don't want to play in your yard
Pettis, Jack
    Bugle call rag
Pfund, Leonore
    Dicky-bird birthday song
Phelge, Nanker
    Play with fire
Phile, Philip
    Hail, Columbia
Phillips, Edward
    The early horn
Phillips, John
    California dreamin'
    Go where you wanna go
    San Francisco
Phillips, Mike
    North to Alaska

Phillips, Walter A.
  A son of the desert am I
Piccolomini, M.
  Saved by a child
Pierpoint, Folliot Sandford
  For the beauty of the earth
Pierpont, John
  Jingle bells
Pigwiggly, Peter the Younger
  Paul Pry
Pike, Cecily
  Jack Frost
Pina, J.
  Misirlou
Pinkard, Maceo
  Sweet Georgia Brown
Pinsuti, Ciro
  Goodnight, goodnight, beloved
Pistilli, Gene
  Sunday will never be the same
Pitts, William S.
  The church in the wildwood
Pockriss, Lee
  Calcutta
Poe, Edgar Allan
  Annabel Lee
Pollack, Lew
  That's a plenty
Poole, Rev. George
  The drownded boy
Poole, J. F.
  No Irish need apply
Pope, J. William
  Uncle Sam's menagerie
Pope, Pauline
  Racing with the moon
Popp, Andre
  L'amour est bleu
  Love is blue
Portela, Raul
  Lisbon antigua
Porter, Cole
  All of you
  Anything goes
  Begin the Beguine
  C'est magnifique
  Friendship
  I get a kick out of you
  I love Paris
  It's d'lovely
  Just one of those things
  Let's do it
  Love for sale
  My heart belongs to Daddy
  Night and day
  So in love
  Wunderbar
  You do something to me

You're the top
Porter, William N.
  Crocuses
  Willows in the snow
Potts, Margaret
  Hurry, hurry, hurry
Poulton, George R.
  Aura Lee
Pounds, Jessie Brown
  Beautiful Isle of somewhere
Prado, Perez
  Patricia, it's Patricia
Presley, Elvis
  Heartbreak hotel
  Love me tender
Prevert, Jacques
  Autumn leaves
Price, Alan
  The house of the rising sun
Price, Chilton
  Slow poke
  You belong to me
Primrose, Joe
  St. James Infirmary
Prince, Hughie
  Beat me, daddy, eight to the bar
Pritzkow, Louis W.
  Take back your gold
Proctor, Adelaide A.
  The lost chord
Purcell, Daniel
  Sabina with an angel's face
  The serenading song
  She walks as she dreams
  The trifle
  While gentle Parthenisa walks
Purcell, Henry
  Dear pretty youth
  Overtures from Richmond
  There's not a swain
Purdy, W. T.
  On, Wisconsin!
Putnam, Curly
  Green green grass of home
  My elusive dreams

- R -

Ragovoy, Jerry
  Piece of my heart
  Try just a little bit harder
Rainger, Ralph
  Blue Hawaii
  June in January
  Love in bloom
  Please
  Thanks for the memory

Raksin, David
  Laura
Raleigh, Sir Walter
  Now what is love
Ramin, Sid
  Music to watch girls by
Ramos, Silvanto R.
  Alla en el rancho grande
  El rancho grande
Randall, James
  Maryland, my Maryland
Randazzo, Teddy
  Goin' out of my head
  Have you looked into your heart
Raskin, Willie
  Wedding bells
Rath, Fred
  Just a girl that men forget
Raven, Carol
  Noche azul
Ray, Maude L.
  My task
Raye, Don
  Beat me, daddy, eight to the bar
  Cow-cow boogie
Razaf, Andy
  Ain't misbehavin'
  Blue turning grey over you
  Keepin' out of mischief now
  Memories of you
  S'posin'
  Stompin' at the Savoy
Read, Daniel
  Holland
Read, Les
  It's not unusual
Reade, Charles A.
  I lose me mine life
Reading, J.
  O come, all ye faithful
Redmond, John
  I let a song go out of my heart
Redner, Lewis H.
  O little town of Bethlehem
Reece, Florence
  Which side are you on?
Reed, Dave
  Nancy Fat
Reed, Leslie
  We all go to work but father
Rehbein, Herbert
  Wiederseh'n
Reinach, Jacquelyn
  Liberation now
Reinagle, Alexander
  America, commerce and freedom
Reisfeld, Bert
  The three bells

Rene, Jo
  Liberation, now
René, Leon
  When it's sleepy time down south
René, Otis
  When it's sleepy time down south
Revaux, J.
  My way
Rexford, Eben E.
  Silver threads among the gold
Reynolds, Herbert
  They didn't believe me
Reynolds, Malvina
  Little boxes
  What have they done to the rain?
Rhodes, Jack
  A satisfied mind
Rice, Seymour
  You tell me your dream, I'll tell
    you mine
Rice, Thomas D.
  Jump Jim Crow
Rice, Tim
  I don't know how to love him
  Superstar
Richard, Keith
  All sold out
  Back street girl
  Bitch
  Blue turns to grey
  Brown sugar
  Can't you hear me knocking
  Child of the moon
  Citadel
  Complicated
  Congratulations
  Connection
  Cool, calm and collected
  Country honk
  Dandelion
  Dead flowers
  Dear doctor
  Don'cha bother me
  Each and every day of the year
  Empty heart
  Factory girl
  Flight 505
  Get off my cloud
  Gimme shelter
  Goin' home
  Gomper
  Good times, bad times
  Gotta get away
  Grown up wrong
  Have you seen your mother, baby,
    standing in the shadow?
  Heart of stone
  High and dry

Honky tonk woman
I am waiting
I got the blues
I'm free
It's not easy
Jigsaw puzzle
Jumpin' Jack Flash
Lady Jane
The lantern
The last time
Let it bleed
Let's spend the night to-
    gether
Live with me
Long long while
Memo from Turner
Midnight rambler
Miss Amanda Jones
Monkey man
Moonlight mile
My obsession
19th nervous breakdown
No expectations
Off the hook
On with the show
One more try
Out of time
Paint it black
Parachute woman
Please go home
Ride on, baby
Ruby Tuesday
Sad day
The salt of the earth
Satisfaction
She smiled sweetly
She's a rainbow
Sing this all together
The singer, not the song
Sister Morphine
Sittin' on a fence
Some things just stick in your
    mind
Something happened to me yester-
    day
The spider and the fly
Stray cat
Street fighting man
Stupid girl
Surprise, surprise
Sway
Sympathy for the Devil
Take it or leave it
Think
Under my thumb
The under-assistant West Coast
    promotion man
We love you

What a shame
What to do
Who's been sleeping here?
Wild horses
Yesterday's papers
You can't always get what you
    want
You got the silver
Richardson, J. P.
  Chantilly lace
Ridding, Edward C.
  When the saints come marching
    in
Ridge, Antonia
  The happy wanderer
  On a summer morning
  Sing a song of spring
Ridley, George
  Cushie Butterfield
Rigual, Carlos
  Love me with all your heart
Rigual, Mario
  Love me with all your heart
Riley, Robert S.
  Just walking in the rain
Robbins, C. A.
  Washington and Lee swing
Robbins, Everett
  Taint' nobody's biz-ness if I do
Robbins, Marty
  Devil woman
  El Paso
Robert, Earl of Essex
  Change thy mind
Roberts, Pete
  The schoolhouse fire
Roberts, Robert S.
  I'm certainly living a ragtime
    life
Robertson, Don
  I don't hurt anymore
  I really don't want to know
  Please help me I'm falling
Robertson, J. Robbie
  The night they drove old Dixie
    down
Robin, Leo
  Beyond the blue horizon
  Blue Hawaii
  For every man there's a woman
  Hallelujah
  Hooray love
  June in January
  Louise
  Love in bloom
  Love is just around the corner
  Moonlight and shadows
  My ideal

The desert song
Lover, come back to me
One alone
The Riff song
Stouthearted men
Wanting you
Root, F. W.
O let me be a blonde, Mother
Root, George F.
Just before the battle, Mother
Kiss me, mother, kiss your
darling
Rosalie, the prairie flower
There's music in the air
Tramp! Tramp! Tramp!
The vacant chair
Rose, Billy
Barney Google
Cheerful little earful
Clap hands! here come Charley
A cup of coffee, a sandwich and
you
Don't bring Lulu
I found a million dollar baby
I wanna be loved
It's only a paper moon
The night is young
Would you like to take a walk
Rose, Ed
Oh Johnny, oh Johnny, oh!
Rose, Fred
Tears on my pillow
Rose, Vincent
Avalon
Blueberry Hill
Pardon me, pretty baby
Rosenberg, G. M.
Streets of Cairo
Rosenfeld, Monroe H.
Take back your gold
Those wedding bells shall not
ring out
Roslev, Norman
Who killed Norma Jean?
Ross, Harold
Mademoiselle from Armentieres
Ross, Jerry
Hernando's hideaway
Hey there
Rosseter, Philip
And would you see my mistress'
face?
Ay me, that love should Nature's
works accuse
If I hope, I pine
If she forsakes me
Kind in unkindness
Shall I come if I swim

Shall then a traitoress kiss?
Though far from joy
What is a day?
What then is love but mourning
When Laura smiles
Whether me do laugh or weep
Rota, Nino
A time for us
Roubanis, N.
Misirlou
Routhier, A.
O Canada
Ruby, Harry
I wanna be loved by you
Mi vida
Who's sorry now?
Ruby, Herman
My honey's lovin' arms
Ruiz, Gabriel
Amor
Cuanto le gusta
Rule, Herbert
Have you paid the rent?
Rumbough, Constance
Potato harvest
Rushing, Jimmy
Sent for you yesterday
Ruskin, Harry
I may be wrong
Russel, Henry
A life on the ocean wave
Woodman, spare that tree
Russell, Bert
Cry baby
Russell, Bob
Full moon
He ain't heavy...he's my brother
Russell, Bobby
Honey
Little green apples
Russell, H.
Cheer, boys, cheer!
Russell, James I.
Where the River Shannon flows
Russell, Larry
Vaya con Dios
Russell, S. K.
Babalu
Brazil
Frenesi
Maria Elena
Misirlou
Ryan, Paddy
The man that waters the workers'
beer

Scarborough Fair/Canticles
7 o'clock news/Silent night
A simple desultory philippic
So long, Frank Lloyd Wright
Somewhere they can't find me
Song for the asking
The sound of silence
Sparrow
We got a groovy thing going
Wednesday morning, 3 A. M.
Why don't you write me?
You don't know where your interest lies
Simons, Moises
Marta
The peanut vendor
Simons, Seymour
Honey
Simpkins, Lewis C.
Night train
Sinatra, Frank
This love of mine
Sinclair, John
Johnny Sands
Singer, Lou
It could be a wonderful world
Sissle, Noble
I'm just wild about Harry
Skelly, Joseph P.
A boy's best friend is his mother
Skylar, Sunny
Amor
Be mine tonight
Besame mucho
Love me with all your heart
Sloan, P. F.
Secret agent man
Smart, Henry
Angels, from the realm of glory
Smith, ----
Attend, all ye fair
Smith, Mrs. A. B.
Winning the vote
Smith, Beasley
That lucky old sun
Smith, Chris
Ballin' the jack
Smith, Dick
When a gypsy makes his violin cry
Winter wonderland
Smith, Edgar
Swim out O'Grady
Smith, Harry B.
Gypsy love song
The sheik of Araby
What! Marry dat gal?
Smith, Hubbard T.

Wing Tee Wee
Smith, J. S.
The star-spangled banner
Smith, Samuel Francis
America
Smith, Seba
The snow storm
Smith, W. D.
Ring the bell softly
Snow, Hank
I'm movin' on
Snyder, Eddie
A time for us
When the snow is on the roses
Snyder, Ted
The sheik of Araby
Who's sorry now?
Soames, Alexander
Rules
Solman, Alfred
The bird on Nellie's hat
Solovyev-Sedoy, V.
Moscow nights
Sondheim, Stephen
Everything's coming up roses
Let me entertain you
Maria
One hand, one heart
Somewhere
Tonight
Sour, Robert
Body and soul
South, Joe
Games people play
Spaulding, Hector
Sweet potatoes
Spector, Phil
River deep, mountain high
Spencer, Frank
Have you seen Sam
Spencer, Mordant
The rose of Tralee
Spencer, Tim
Cigarettes, whusky, and wild, wild women
Spielman, Fred
Paper roses
Spina, Harold
It's so nice to have a man around the house
Spotswood, Robinson W.
Hold tight, hold tight
Sprigato, Sylvester
It isn't fair
Springer, Philip
How little we know
Moonlight gambler
Stafford, Jim

Action
Vernon, Joseph
Epilogue song
Vernor, F. Dudleigh
The sweetheart of Sigma Chi
Villard, Jean
The three bells
Vilona, Tony
Music to watch girls by
Vojáček, ----
Under Bethlehem's star

- W -

Wade, John Francis
O come, all ye faithful
Waggner, George
Mary Lou
Wagner, Larry
Turn back the hands of time
Wakerfield, Samuel
All hail to the morning
Walker, Cindy
Fifteen days
In the misty moonlight
Walker, Jerry J.
Mr. Bojangles
Will you love me in December
as you do in May?
Walker, Wayne
All the time
Walker, Wiley
When my blue moon turns to
gold again
Wallace, Oliver G.
Hindustan
Wallace, Vincent
Yes, let me like a soldier fall
Waller, Jack
Got a date with an angel
Waller, Thomas
Ain't misbehavin'
Blue turning grey over you
Keepin' out of mischief now
Walter, Thomas
Southwel new
Walters, Jane B.
All the birds sing
January and February
Ward, Charles B.
The band played on
Strike up the band
Ward, Samuel Augustus
America, the beautiful
Warfield, Charles
Baby, won't you please come
home

Warren, Harry
Chattanooga choo-choo
Cheerful little earful
Forty-second Street
The gold diggers' song
I found a million dollar baby
I'll string along with you
Jeepers creepers
The more I see you
Nagasaki
Serenade in blue
Shadow waltz
That's amore
There will never be another you
Would you like to take a walk
You must have been a beautiful
baby
You'll never know
Young and healthy
You're getting to be a habit with
me
You're my everything
Warren, Joseph
Free America
A song of liberty
Warshauer, Frank
It isn't fair
Warshawsky, Mark
Oyfm pripetshok
Washburn, Henry S.
The vacant chair
Washington, Ned
High noon
I don't stand a ghost of a chance
with you
I'm gettin' sentimental over you
Love is the thing
The nearness of you
Stella by starlight
Washington, Oscar
Night train
Watson, Johnny
It's a wonderful world
Racing with the moon
Watts, Clem
You call everybody darling
Watts, Isaac
China
Holland
Hush, my Babe
Joy to the world
Thus saith the high, the lofty one
Wayburn, Ned
He ain't no relation of mine
Wayne, Bernie
Blue velvet
Wayne, Mabel
In a little Spanish town

Wayne, Sid
  It's impossible
Weatherly, Fred E.
  Auntie
  Nancy Lee
  The old brigade
Webb, Chick
  Stompin' at the Savoy
Webb, Jimmy
  By the time I get to Phoenix
  Didn't we
  Galveston
  MacArthur Park
  No arms can ever hold you
  Up, up and away
  Wichita lineman
Webber, Andrew Lloyd
  I don't know how to love him
  Superstar
Webster, H. D. L.
  Lorena
Webster, J. P.
  Lorena
Webster, Paul Francis
  The green leaves of summer
Weeks, Harold
  Hindustan
Weill, Kurt
  September song
Weinstein, B.
  Have you looked into your heart
  Goin' out of my head
Weir, R. S.
  O Canada
Weir, Robert
  Truckin'
Weisse, George
  Mr. Wonderful
Wells, Gilbert
  One of the deathless army
Wells, Robert
  The Christmas song
Wendling, Pete
  Hawaiian love song
  Oh! what a pal was Mary
Wesley, Charles
  Hark! the herald angels sing
West, Hedy
  Five hundred miles
  Five hundred miles away from
    home
West, Paul
  I'm on the water wagon now
West, Walter C.
  Only once in a lifetime
Westendorf, Thomas P.
  I'll take you home again, Kathleen
Westmoreland, Paul

Detour
Weston, Harris
  Heaven will protect an honest
    girl
Weston, Paul
  Shrimp boats
Weston, R. P.
  Heaven will protect an honest
    girl
  I've got rings on my fingers
Westmore, W. J.
  Vanamburgh's menagerie
Wettlin, M.
  World youth song
Wharton, Lord Thomas
  Lilliburlero
Wheeler, Billy Edd
  Jackson
Wheeler, Francis
  Let a smile be your umbrella
  The sheik of Araby
Wheeler, G. D.
  Bravo, Dublin Fusiliers
White, J. C.
  When we went out a fishing
Whiting, Richard A.
  Ain't we got fun
  Beyond the blue horizon
  Honey
  Louise
  My ideal
  On the good ship Lollipop
  Sleepy time gal
  Too marvelous for words
  True blue Lou
  You're an old smoothie
Whitley, Ray
  Back in the saddle again
Whittier, John Greenleaf
  Dear Lord and Father of mankind
Whyte-Melville, G. J.
  Goodbye!
Wiggins, Ella Mae
  The mill mother's lament
Wilkins, Ronnie
  Son of a preacher man
Wilkinson, Dudley
  Because of you
Willard, Emma H.
  Rocked in the cradle of the deep
Williams, Charlie
  Five hundred miles away from
    home
Williams, Clarence
  Baby, won't you please come
    home
Williams, Dub
  Release me

Dinah
Five foot two eyes of blue
Hawaiian love song
How ya gonna keep 'em down on
the farm?
If I knock the 'L' out of Kelly
I'm alone because I love you
I'm gonna sit right down and
write myself a letter
I'm sitting on top of the world
In a little Spanish town
Just a baby's prayer at twilight
Laugh! Clown! Laugh!
My Barney lies over the ocean
My mammy
Now she knows how to parle-voo
Rock-a-bye your baby with a
Dixie melody
When grown up ladies act like
babies
Where did Robinson Crusoe go
with Friday on Saturday night?
You're a million miles from no-
where
You're my everything
Young, Kenny
Don't go out into the rain
Young, Neil
On the way home

Young, Victor
Golden earrings
I don't stand a ghost of a chance
with you
Love is the thing
Love letters
Stella by starlight
Yount, Robert
Release me

- Z -

Zakharov, Vladimir
On a raven black horse
Who knows why
Zamencnik, J. S.
Nights of splendor
Zanzig, Augustus D.
Over the meadows
Pat-a-pan
Zaret, Hy
It could be a wonderful world
Zeman, Vasek
Beer barrel polka
Zimmermann, Marianne
The snowman
With a lantern in the hand
Zoeller, Lou
Cinnamon cake